Cases in Public Policy Analysis

Cases in Public Policy Analysis

Third Edition

George M. Guess and Paul G. Farnham

Georgetown University Press
Washington, DC

Georgetown University Press, Washington, D.C.
www.press.georgetown.edu

Library of Congress Cataloging-in-Publication Data
Guess, George M.
Cases in public policy analysis / George M. Guess and Paul G. Farnham. — 3rd ed.
p. cm.
Includes bibliographical references and index.
ISBN 978-1-58901-734-4 (pbk. : alk. paper)
1. Policy sciences—Case studies. I. Farnham, Paul G. II. Title.
H97.G84 2011
361.6'1—dc22
                                        2010037043

∞ This book is printed on acid-free paper meeting the requirements of the American National Standard for Permanence in Paper for Printed Library Materials.

15 14 13 12 11   9 8 7 6 5 4 3 2   First printing
Printed in the United States of America

Contents

✳✳✳

Preface

There are four distinguishing features of the third edition of *Cases in Public Policy Analysis* that may influence its adoption for upper-level or graduate public policy courses. First, because it was written by a political scientist and an economist, both of whom have consulted extensively and worked in various government agencies, the text takes a political economy approach to public policy. This provides an important institutional and political dimension in applying economic methods to policy problems. Second, the text focuses only on the problems and tools applicable generally to the policy analysis process and specifically to decision optimization rather than the entire policymaking cycle. As is known, generic policy processes include policy development, approval, implementation, and evaluation. Third, the book emphasizes that any technical decision tool includes political values. For transparent policy-making, these values must be recognized, weighed, and scored properly.

As William Dunn has noted, researchers and practitioners in the public policy field are still grappling with the issue of how to maximize technocratic guidance without ignoring the values and decision styles that are inherent in policy implementation (Dunn 2008). Many recognize that the field needs analytic methods to ensure balance. However, excessive faith in technocratic policymaking is naïve, whereas excessive emphasis on values and decision styles may result in arbitrary decision making. Policy analysts should provide useful information for decisions, including the results of formal quantitative analyses in order to develop realistic policy options. However, analysts must be aware that decision makers will consider these results in the context of the values of the relevant—and often the most powerful—stakeholders in the policy process.

Fourth, the book uses cases rather than a text/problem approach. We use the case method to educate and train future decision makers for three reasons. First, students will typically achieve and retain a more thorough knowledge through cases than through the text method. Other policy analysis texts share this view. For example, it is clear to those of us who have tested the case method against the exercise method that students gain more understanding of complex decision processes when they apply their knowledge to analyzing and deriving solutions for cases than when they read and memorize text materials (Anthony and Young 1994, 14–15).

Second, cases give students insights into real-world complexity. Textbooks often use hypothetical examples or provide incomplete analyses of messy, complex problems. By contrast, policy cases provide "intellectual tools to aid practitioners in the identification and specification of policy problems and the development of sensible, useful, and politically viable solutions" (deLeon and Steelman 2001, cited in Morse and Struyk 2006, xi). Ultimately, the purpose of using cases is to move students and practitioners from the descriptive to the critical or analytical level of thinking (Morse and Struyk 2006, xii). In the former Soviet Union and in central and eastern Europe, university public policy departments now employ cases as a reaction to the excessively theoretical emphasis of prior pedagogical systems. It is believed that the case approach best prepares professionals with the conceptual and analytical skills for analysis of sectoral and cross-disciplinary public policy issues (Staronova 2007, 6). On the perceived basis of a practical skills gap in public and nonprofit organizations in these regions, the Open Society Institute's Local Government Initiative (LGI) provided grants to universities, nonprofit organizations, and think tanks to develop innovative cases and teaching methods (LGI 2006). The cases are available for classroom use at http://lgi.osi.hu/.

Third, cases show students how important it is to be able to clearly communicate the results of technical analyses. Many policy failures can be traced to technicians' inability to simplify the bases for decision making and communicate the options to the public. For this reason, cases and materials have been developed to improve the writing of policy papers and communication tools used by the public policy community in the policymaking process (Young and Quinn 2002, 1). Cases can demonstrate how decisions are often made under extreme time constraints and with limited or incomplete information.

Some may argue that cases are ambiguous and frustrating because the reader cannot simply apply formal scientific methods to them. However, most nontrivial policy problems cannot be solved solely by applying scientific principles and quantitative techniques. Values are important, data are often incomplete and ambiguous, and time is usually short for obtaining results. Real-world decision makers must work under these constraints or be held accountable for not making decisions under pressure.

The book does not use a case approach exclusively, however. It includes background text material and basic presentations of analytic techniques useful for sorting out relevant facts and reaching conclusions on each issue. It is hoped that this combination of case information and text materials will enable students to learn more about how to apply standard public policy procedures, such as problem definition and cost-benefit analysis, to real policy issues.

To summarize this preface, cases can achieve multiple objectives. Staronova (2007, 11–12) suggests that cases can be used for discussion roles, debate and panel competition, simulation and role-playing, group work, individual research, data gathering and analysis, and presentation and practical skills. These are obviously important results. To attain them, however, instructors need to glean as much as they can from the cases without overwhelming the students. Using as an example a well-known case such as the *Downtown Parking Garage* case (Anthony and Young 1994, 460–63), it is clear that one cannot simply offer the case to the students and hope that they achieve the multiple objectives noted. Based on this rather typical case (i.e., one that includes technical information but incomplete data, and that requires a final decision), a generic analytic approach that might be useful for the cases included in this and other books should, at minimum, require students to:

1. Identify the core issues for decision (here, technical cost and return rates and the interdependency of institutional and demographic variables affecting the larger city as an urban system).

2. Develop a framework for analysis and data collection.

3. Identify the relevant technical concepts and methods that will be used (here, opportunity costs, discount rates, and break-even analysis).

4. Identify relevant policy options and rank by cost-risk.

5. Recommend solutions and identify missing data that, if supplied, could lead to better analysis and better decisions.

Both authors wish to acknowledge the advice and assistance of Don Jacobs, acquisitions editor of Georgetown University Press. They would also like to thank the reviewers, Thomas Birkland and William N. Dunn, for their incisive and helpful comments. George Guess thanks his graduate public policy and administration students at Central European University in Budapest, Hungary; American University in Washington, DC; and the American University public policy program in Haiti for their incisive comments, critical perspectives, and sincere encouragement during his public budgeting and finance courses. He would also like to acknowledge the efforts of his two major public policy teachers, the late Michael D. Reagan and the late Charles R. Adrian of the University of California, Riverside.

Paul Farnham acknowledges his many colleagues at the Centers for Disease Control and Prevention, as well as the public administration students he has taught at Georgia State University, who have forced him to consider how economic evaluation techniques can be applied in real-world policy settings.

The authors alone are responsible for any defects in this book.

REFERENCES

Anthony, Robert, and David Young. 1994. *Management Control in Nonprofit Organizations*. 5th ed. Instructor's Guide. Homewood, IL: Irwin.

deLeon, Peter, and T. A. Steelman. 2001. Making Public Policy Programs Effective and Relevant: The Role of the Policy Sciences. *Journal of Policy Analysis and Management* 20:1.

Dunn, William N. 2008. *Public Policy Analysis: An Introduction*. 4th ed. Englewood Cliffs, NJ: Pearson Prentice Hall.

Local Government Initiative (LGI) of the Open Society Institute. 2006. Developing Innovative Teaching/Training in Public Policy and Administration. http://lgi.osi.hu.

Morse, Kristin, and Raymond J. Struyk. 2006. *Policy Analysis for Effective Development: Strengthening Transition Economies*. Boulder: Lynne Rienner.

Staronova, Katarina, ed. 2007. *Training in Difficult Choices: Five Public Policy Cases from Slovakia*. Bratislava: Institute of Public Policy, Comenius University.

Young, Eoin, and Lisa Quinn. 2002. *Writing Effective Policy Papers: A Guide for Policy Advisers in Central and Eastern Europe*. Budapest: Local Government Initiative of the Open Society Institute.

Chapter 1

The Policymaking Process:
Between Technical Rationality and Politics

Those responsible for decisions about formulating policies, allocating resources for them, maintaining or changing existing policies, and implementing them have faced a bewildering array of challenges in the past decade. These contextual changes reflect larger forces in American policymaking, and it is useful to examine them briefly at the outset as constraints and opportunities. There is widespread agreement that from about 2000 to 2008, under the administration of George W. Bush and Richard Cheney, decision makers worked in an anti-analytical environment. The operating premise of federal government was that the analytic process was largely a waste of time; the goal of any formal policymaking process was to produce decisions consistent with narrow ideological and partisan values. In policy areas such as air quality, immigration, financial regulation, and the war in Iraq, decision makers ran up against the notion that policymaking consisted in engineering political deals and currying partisan and personal favors. Decisions in most cases were overtly political, in the sense of patent exchanges of resources for influence. Many who had worked in developing countries were familiar with this political culture. The process of determining how to maximize net benefits through formal review of alternate means to achieve public ends was either ignored, misunderstood, or distorted. Nor was there a great deal of emphasis on factual rigor during this era. Many who had been educated in public administration and policy schools could be excused for thinking they had learned quaint skills that would become dormant in the newer, simpler world being created.

By contrast, a different cultural climate would favor such tools as the scientific method and such strategies as optimizing resources to achieve the greatest public good. In the United States, presidents Eisenhower, Nixon, Reagan, Clinton, and currently Obama have had pragmatic and open-minded approaches to complex problems. Such presidents surrounded themselves with the best decision makers available and listened to them. They were decisive but also adopted a critical stance toward the information on which they had to act.

This second type of political climate is well illustrated by the textbook rationality reforms of the British National Health Service (NHS) under Tony Blair. Instead of administrative process, prescription, and consultation activities to achieve more efficient outputs, the NHS targeted effectiveness outcomes like decreased waiting times and death rates while increasing the patient cure rates. Structural reforms increased patient choice and competition to control costs. Reintroduction of an internal market provided direct payments to patients and performance transfers (cash incentives for outcome performance) to health care providers. NHS used cost-weighted measures of results and moved beyond targeting and monitoring activities to the levers needed to improve overall health care effectiveness (*The Economist* 2009, 28).

Analysts need to copy the best practices of such reforms and focus critically on the extent to which the apparent successes of these reforms simply reflect increased public spending. There is evidence that about 40% of extra public spending on health has been absorbed by higher pay, meaning that the budget is partly responsible for increasing the cost base of health care (*The Economist* 2009, 29). These are analytic questions, answerable by application of basic tools and methods from our discipline. They are also textbook examples of rational reforms based on empirical analysis; such examples can be found in many policy areas. Examples of successful reform efforts will be noted throughout this book in areas such as primary-secondary education, defense, health care, fiscal management, and urban public transportation. Though improvements in policy results are an uphill battle and often take years, leaders must be professional, bold, and intelligent enough to ensure that their organizational systems generate unbiased information based on technical rationality. Rather obviously, leaders need facts in order to govern properly.

Policy analysts must define problems and generate options for policies, programs, and projects. The normative objective of the analytic process is to make decisions that maximize the net benefits. Facing scarce resources, policymakers need information to produce the best available option to achieve that objective for policies, programs, or projects. Often the three terms are used interchangeably without great damage to understanding. Methods of applied policy analysis are often the same as those used for program analysis (Poister 1978). The general distinction between the analytic levels has to do with the scale, scope, and the degree of capital investment required, as compared to current expenditures. For example, health care *policy* issues of overall cost and coverage can be disaggregated for the Medicare *program* and for municipal hospital *projects*. Governmental efforts to achieve results for these three types of expenditures can be distinguished at three levels: strategic, or policy design; allocational, or the appropriate composition of resources provided to different activities; and operational, or the efficiency of daily management of policy support systems. Whether they are designing programs or policies, decision makers need to review the factors that affect policy design, such as the legal and regulatory framework. Within programs and projects, designers and managers must consider the optimal allocation of resources between activities to achieve results and determine how much to budget for them from each object of expenditure. These are issues of sectoral allocation and cost sharing. Regardless of whether they are considering a policy or program, policy analysts need to examine the salient issues of operational management and systems performance from the perspective of trading off means (resources) and ends (policy objectives). In short, policy analysts need to know where they are and what they are being expected to do within this schematic framework. This will guide their thinking about what tools they need to apply and to adapt.

The analytic process should be less concerned with building pure theory than with producing information that will be useful in political settings for resolving social problems. Policy analysts generate data, forecast options, and develop preferred options for decisions in particular policy areas. The broader subject of *public* policy analysis focuses on the more profound root causes, as well as the immediate individual behavior patterns of social problems, such as crime, that can be affected by the "admittedly limited tools government has at its disposal" (Paris and Reynolds 1983, 34). Akin to an applied public economics or political science discipline, policy analysis uses methods and tools from economics, political science, sociology, and other related fields for problem solving. In the analytic process, tools from social science, engineering, economics, anthropology, and psychology can be applied to produce useful information for decisions in political contexts. Consultants to government, decision makers in government agencies, and staff in nongovernmental organizations all practice applied decision analysis. Preparation for analytic roles often begins with review of appraisals, studies, and reports written by others.

For this reason, analysts need to be critical of the assumptions, premises, calculations, discount rates, definitions, data comprehensiveness, and frameworks used, as well as systems recommended, in such reports. The United States government in the first decade of the twenty-first century is spending a lot of time and resources tracking and eliminating terrorists. While the terrorists have the nimble advantages of small-group flexibility and dynamism, systemic responses have been clumsy, costly, and marginally effective. For instance, the current system for tracking airline passengers uses standard checklists to nominate candidates to "no-fly" lists from "selectee" lists. Department of Homeland Security analysts use formal risk-scoring criteria to enter candidates into such data systems as the Terrorist Identities Datamart

Environment (TIDE) and the Advanced Passenger Information System (APIS). All this sounds impressive until one learns that the systems lacked an automatic feedback loop that would link random reported data on individuals with the list of those with existing US visas. Otherwise, random data on people already entering and leaving the country would be screened out as "noise." This was a basic design flaw in an otherwise complex and expensive system. For this reason, the report to the US Embassy by Umar Abdulmuttalab's father on the curious activities of his son was ignored, allowing the son to enter and nearly explode a bomb on a flight to Detroit (DeYoung and Leahy 2009).

Because of time shortage, threats to existing systems, personal ownership or sunk costs, and ideological commitments, public sector organizations do not always value empirical policy options and recommendations. When empirically based options are developed, the results are often not used. Given tight work schedules and scarce analytic resources, very few decisions in public sector organizations are actually informed by thorough analysis. This is true regardless of the wider political context. In addition, the managers of large organizations often have a perverse tendency to engage in protective persistence in error, despite contrary policy evidence.

Once a questionable objective is established (e.g., sustaining the Diem government in Vietnam through aid policy in the 1950s), the routines of bureaucratic process can subdue intellect and encourage stupidity, which in turn translates into clumsy leadership and management. In such cases, those who were supposed to provide the major source of critical analysis in the first place (e.g., the National Security Council) will tend to ignore contrary advice about objectives and existing policy failures. Ideological commitment to fixed positions can add to bureaucratic inflexibility and prevent organizations from receiving the benefits of critical policy analysis. Decision making under conditions of an overriding ideological objective can promote self-deceit and encourage "working the levers without rational expectations" (Tuchman 1984, 377). To put this another way, "noise" can overwhelm otherwise rational systems and sound database parameters, leading to bad policy or operational level results. This was particularly evident in the decision to go to war in Iraq, in which comparative field advice on what would likely go wrong after invasion was excluded from the planning process (Pfiffner 2010, in Stillman 2010). It might be remembered that even one of the most ideological writers, Ayn Rand, repeatedly exhorted her followers to "check their assumptions and premises." Empirical policy analysts should do the same!

The danger is that persistent action contrary to analytic advice will discourage in-house analysts from producing the forecasts and options, and maintaining the independent databases, needed to change institutional behavior. The problem of unused policy analysis may be due, in part, to the apparent complexity of policy problems and the large variety of policy tools available. Analysis often appears to be an endless process, with myriad variables and overwhelming amounts of data to be considered. Despite our enthusiasm for optimizing resources through formal analysis, the fact is that choices are never fully determined by analytic methods. Policy decisions are rarely rational in a pure sense. Why? The fact is that there is minimal agreement on values, analytic methods, the types of decisions to which they should be applied, and even the quantification of outcomes. This is especially true in health care policy problems such as the determination of quality-adjusted patient lives. Cost-effectiveness tools are applied precisely to get around these problems and achieve the least cost for the most lives saved (in this instance) by ignoring thorny problems of the value of life. Even for more structured problems, such as whether to pave a road or how much toll to charge, decision analysis can take on a life of its own. Strategy meetings, multiple revisions of reports, and maximum participation of staff take up time and resources with no hard decisions reached. In some organizations, analysis may be good public relations and thus may be performed as an end in itself. In addition, even if there are minimal institutional barriers to the utilization of policy analysis, policymakers are often besieged with contrary advice on seemingly sound analytical bases.

Policymakers are answerable to special interests such as lobbies and financial contributors, and not because they are obtuse or venal. Public servants also understand the pull of populist forces and often disregard policy recommendations in final decision making. How else can we explain why Maryland liquor wholesalers and retailers maintain an oligopoly at the expense of consumers and even local wineries? Under current law direct wine shipments are illegal and consumers receiving wine by mail order face felony charges. Because of the power of the liquor lobby, state legislators have been impervious to formal analysis of supply and demand (*Washington Post* 2009). At least the legislators are transparently impervious to analysis. It is cheaper that way, as opposed to paying for expensive consultants to generate unused data and results. For example, the firm of Booz Allen Hamilton conducted a $6 million, twenty-month study of the Washington, DC, police department's structural and management problems that produced many recommendations to improve performance, including the recommendation to move 157 administrative officers to street patrols. As of 1998, none of the Booz Allen recommendations had been implemented (Thompson 1998). It was also found that many of the consultants' conclusions and recommendations were in previous reports already filed at the police department. This suggests the need for policy analysis that balances technical solutions with political feasibility. It also suggests that requests for current policy or program studies should be reconciled with previous studies before funds are authorized.

For such practical reasons, this book seeks to integrate economic analysis with politics. Economic analysis, in our view, needs to take account of institutional and management politics. A political economy approach teaches us that "neither markets nor governments are perfect and that one must accept compromise" (Dixit 1997, 10; Wolf 1993).

This suggests a political context into which the analytic process must fit, lest it run the risk of being ignored. The political context of the larger policy process—public policy formulation and implementation—underscores the need for policymakers to have field experience, as well as a good grasp of the facts, and to possess sound judgment. No collections of policy techniques, such as those found in this book, can replace judgment, the ability to apply wisdom and experience to facts and analysis. Sound judgment is the result of experiences informing one's intellectual frameworks. These frameworks allow the policymaker or the analyst to reject irrelevant facts and include only what is necessary for decision. In the best of worlds, policymakers use data and techniques to narrow their range of uncertainty, but as noted above, data and techniques can rarely provide complete answers or certainty of results. Even the most sound, most thorough analysis can rarely foresee the unintended consequences that occur during policy implementation. More important, policymakers must be able to judge for themselves which facts are important; without judgment, policymakers and managers will remain hopelessly confused and at the mercy of multiple advisors. Bureaucratic survival experts can diffuse responsibility through committees, multiple clearance processes, and the like, but ultimately they have to be accountable for processing policy advice and making a decision.

Policy analysts can help by providing information that serves the short timeframes of public sector decision makers. For example, "windshield surveys" were used in a USAID project in Estonia to assess civil service capacity instead of conducting skills inventories that require much more time and resources (Development Alternatives, Inc. 1997). Such action frameworks are even more commonplace now. In planning new policy areas (such as health care and welfare reform), analysis can take the form of "rolling designs" that permit learning through incremental trial and error, rather than comprehensive methods that recommend linear, multiyear courses of policy action. Through such analytic shortcuts as pilot studies, quick feasibility studies, and action research surveys, marginal sacrifices in analytic accuracy can be made for the benefit of short-term decision making. The analytic process need not lead to abstract reports using heavy mathematics and linear programming; in some cases, the primary value of such approaches may be to scare away opponents of one's recommendations. Finally, policy analysts should anticipate complex social and institutional resistance to proposed policies and provide such alternative processes as public deliberation to resolve tensions between the objectives of efficiency (minimize inputs to achieve a given level of output) and effectiveness (a given level of outcome or improvements in target population for the least cost) (Roberts 1997).

This book attempts to simplify the analytic process and provide useful tools to practitioners who have insufficient time or resources to use the most advanced technical methods available in the discipline of public policy. The overall aim, of course, is to improve the quality of the policy process (Dunn 2008, 56). Our book recognizes the need to learn basic tools for diagnosis of issues, optimization of decisions, and evaluation of policies. As in the second edition of *Cases in Public Policy Analysis*, this edition will attempt to build up those skills by providing cases in messy problem settings to which the tools may be applied.

PUBLIC POLICY AND ITS FORMULATION

Policies derive from legislative statutes and administrative rules. In practice, they are systems of rules and standards that affect the public interest and are established by rulemaking bodies such as parliaments, legislatures, and administrative regulatory agencies. Policies can be formulated for internal institutional governance or for provision of external programs and services. For example, fiscal policies to reform pension systems, reduce subsidies to consumers and producers, revise tax rates, or control budget expenditures are largely internal policies. Internal policies are also reflected in nonservice or nonprogrammatic expenditures, tax expenditures (or tax breaks), and other hidden subsidies to the private sector. These have obvious external effects on public welfare, resource use, and other public programs. For instance, patented mineral claims on federal lands worth thousands of times their market value are regularly sold at deep subsidy prices to private prospectors and mining firms who need only demonstrate the existence of hard-rock minerals in the land. Despite the immense value of these claims to mining firms, the US government receives no royalties. For their part, mining companies in the western United States have polluted more than three thousand miles of streams with hard-rock mining wastes (*The Economist* 1998).

In general, policies are analyzed, monitored, and evaluated in regular cycles (described below and represented in figure 1.1) that involve public inputs, partisan alliances, and coalition strategies formed in an effort to defeat opponents. Analysis of public issues requires formal consideration of costs and consequences, using economic and institutional concepts and methods, in relation to both means and ends. These methods need to measure costs, benefits, and relevant values to determine whether an option is worth the expenditure of public resources. Analysis then refers to formal, critical examination of issues or problems in the context of incomplete facts and figures. To complete the process on time for clients, the analytic process requires application of simplifying theories, frameworks, methods, and factual assumptions. Data are normally missing. The best analysts cannot afford to wait for better data—that will be the task of historical analysis at a later date. The best analysts make clear and transparent assumptions that can be verified or challenged in order to move the process forward and improve policy results.

The analytic process is part of the larger policy or political process. Logically, many question the ability of any government to identify high-return policies or programs and fund them intact through a political process. Analysis is politicized. But the shelf value of sound, objective analysis with clear assumptions remains. For example, many public policies, such as national defense, are formulated through formal and informal interactions between Congress, the executive branch, and the nongovernmental sector (including lobbyists and think tanks). Key power and communications networks form over particular defense issues, involving such actors as the Executive Office of the President, including the National Security Council; the Central Intelligence Agency (CIA); the State Department; and nongovernmental policy actors such as think tanks and universities, relevant defense contractors, and lobbyists. So-called iron triangles form between and among legislative committees or subcommittees, special interests, and parts of the executive bureaucracy with stakes in the outcome of that particular defense issue (Lowi 1979). The same networks affect formulation of other policy areas as well, such as transportation, environment, and education. Contrary to familiar notions of separation of power, the iron triangle mechanism suggests that joint action can overcome opposition. These annual and largely concerted efforts produce policies, the price tag of which is translated into a budget request. At the same time, Congress, under heavy influence from issue networks composed of regional and weapons systems defense experts, and intense lobbying from the defense industry and the Department of Defense itself, reviews and approves the request and translates it into budget authority or appropriations. At best, the triangles stabilize inter-institutional relations and permit enough compromise for a solution. To the extent that political parties and leaders are polarized (from safe districts and extreme hard-line parties), the iron triangles facilitate communication and compromise. At worst, of course, they reify special interests and perpetuate waste and bad policies. Actors ignore their underlying assumptions, and the process becomes dysfunctional, saved occasionally only by bold new leadership on particular issues.

In the literature, iron triangles are considered to be a stabilizing, predictable force in policymaking, but issue networks are considered to be the opposite. These are shared-knowledge groups of experts who have developed an industry on particular policies. The groups keep particular policy issues (such as health care reform) on the agenda and provide substantial influence to each member of the network. At the same time, the activities of issue networks complicate political calculability and decrease predictability (Heclo 1978). For example, the complex issues surrounding deregulation of the electric utility industry have been subject to analyses by issue networks and shifting coalitions of interest and advocacy groups and think tanks. In legislative terms, the complexity perpetuated by the activities of issue networks can slow reform, in the sense that policy approval and implementation are delayed (Hamilton 1997). Information is generated beyond institutional processing capabilities. Research at the local level on issue networks called "stakeholder partnerships" or "advocacy coalitions" confirms the problem of establishing and managing coalitions to achieve optimal results. Leach, Pelkey, and Sabatier (2002) examined forty-four watershed management groups in the states of California and Washington and found that collaborative policymaking took substantial time and resources to achieve evaluation objectives. Consistent with Heclo's 1978 finding that such coalitions often perpetuated high transaction costs and complexity, Leach, Pelkey, and Sabatier (2002) found that the partnerships often aggravated economic problems and efforts to regulate and maintain property rights.

Policies are thus rule systems that can be made by legislatures or administrative agencies. They are the formal rules that compose part of society's institutional framework. Viewed as rules of the game that are implemented by institutional systems and governmental and nongovernmental organizations, the dimensions of political debate and conflict over the meaning of these rules will vary in each case. Politics as the use of resources to exercise influence over a decision is virtually synonymous with lobbying in the case of legislative authorizations and most general fund policy appropriations by Congress or, indeed, by any parliament around the world. For this reason politics is often confused with policy. For operational purposes, we consider politics a means of developing policy rule systems: Political discretion is exercised at least in part on the basis of values, and policy tends to change because political values change.

In the realm of policymaking, political values often boil down to partisan values. Criminal justice policies that advocate increases in recurrent expenditures for police and prisons, for instance, may be more or less valuable to the public than balanced-budget policies. Public values are shaped by cultural influences as much as by the influence of economic policy analysis. Values affect policy outcomes when they form political and analytical biases, and, as noted, values can be expressed collectively through bargaining among the iron triangle and advocacy coalitions. For instance, studies disagree on the effects of minimum wage hikes on unemployment. Answers depend on research design and measurement. In practice, the issue often boils down to choices by employers who, in the face of higher required wage payments, can either continue to fill vacancies (raising employment) or find ways to economize on jobs and maintain output. For the policy analyst, this means weighing and comparing the risks of potential costs in employer profits and consumer prices against the benefits to poorer workers in increased minimum wages (Card and Krueger 1998). This is technical analysis that leads clearly to the point where decisions must be made on explicit values.

In some cases major policy fiascoes can be linked to value distortion in policymaking (Bovens and 't Hart 1996). As will be noted in chapter 2, value differences commonly arise among experts in problem definition, which will affect program design and, later, results on the ground. For example, criminal justice strategies based on the values of deterrence and tough enforcement to change the utility preferences and cost-benefit calculations of criminals are, in principle, appealing (Paris and Reynolds 1983, 35–36). But such strategies have not been very effective in reducing the incidence of major crimes. By contrast, community policing strategies that are based on values of rehabilitation and that address such root causes of crime as poverty and lack of education have been more effective. This latter, more progressive approach to crime control is credited for major drops in urban crime in large US cities, beginning in the late 1990s and persisting now in late 2009.

It could be argued that the US policymaking system has evolved to the point that the ethical public norm is the reduction of undue political influences during policymaking. It was not always this way. Political machines and their party affiliates ran city councils and state legislatures for many years around the turn of the nineteenth century. In the early 1900s, local government activities were often regulated in detail to provide discretionary revenue for city treasuries from the organized, often criminal, machines that controlled and financed "paper" governments. Detailed policy rules and regulations functioned largely as a means of setting prices and negotiating exemptions (Steffens 1931).

On the other hand, attempts to remove all taint of politics from the policy implementation process, or to ignore the benefits of political support for policy successes, often result in prescriptive, puritanical approaches to policymaking. Political will counts for policy success, and since much of this success derives from the knowledge of such local officials as mayors and governors, key groups will support them and cooperate with them. Policy analysis, therefore, needs to include political factors that affect policy implementation; otherwise such analysis risks providing recommendations that are not feasible. In a recent book on welfare policy, for example, Rebecca Blank charged that Aid to Families with Dependent Children (AFDC) suffered from weaknesses in policy design that could have been corrected if only Americans had avoided political rhetoric and paid adequate attention to sound policy research (Blank 1997). The AFDC program was an open-ended matching grant to states to provide assistance to families with children who had one parent absent, unemployed, or incapacitated (Fisher 2007, 593). But according to reviewer Theda Skocpol, in Blank's study "we learn little about who was purveying the rhetoric, and why it resonated so broadly. Because Blank failed to analyze what went wrong politically for welfare in the past, she cannot project feasible strategies for the future" (Skocpol 1997, 119). Skocpol was referring to the AFDC incentive for one parent to avoid work and be absent in order for the family to obtain cash grants. As evidence that the analytic process can inform decisions, AFDC was replaced in 1996 by the Clinton administration's Temporary Assistance for Needy Families (TANF) program, which provides states with lump-sum matching grants to give aid to families, conditioned on the recipients' finding work within two years and on a five-year assistance limit (Fisher 2007, 594).

In policy analysis, a rough consensus exists that political and technical factors have their separate places in the process and that they should not violate each other's territory. In the case of administrative rule systems, it can be seen that politics has a much more circumscribed role. In the United States, the Administrative Procedures Act of 1946 (APA) distinguishes formal from informal rulemaking: formal rulemaking is procedurally identical to formal adjudication (Pierce, Shapiro, and Verkuil 1985, 315). Formal rulemaking effectively means a trial that bogs an agency down in formal testimony and factual issues that can divert attention from important policy considerations. So in administrative law, an agency that intends to adopt a prescriptive standard of action, valid in a number of settings for a variety of parties, cannot realistically proceed by the formal, case-by-case method. Instead, the agency must adopt informal rulemaking, which replaces trial-like activities with opportunities for affected members of the public to comment on proposed rules.

Informal rulemaking is a forum for establishing administrative rules with a minimum of political interference. Such rulemaking implies a negative role for politics beyond a certain threshold, where the public interest is a technical matter. That threshold is the end of the notice-and-comment period for interested or affected parties; at that time the agency publishes a final rule accompanied by a "statement of basis and purpose," which is subject to judicial review. The intent of the threshold is to confine the natural bargaining and lobbying to contacts of record within the structure of the rulemaking process during the notice-and-comment period. Therefore, any unrecorded contact with interested parties during this notice-and-comment period is considered ex parte contact and is assumed to contaminate the rulemaking process with politics, meaning that a resulting rule can be challenged as arbitrary and capricious. Informal rulemaking resembles the process of legislating, with all the implications of politics and lobbying.

The premise of banning ex parte contacts during informal rulemaking is to ensure administrative neutrality. By preventing political lobbying during the diagnostic or notice-and-comment period, the informal rulemaking process attempts to reduce external influences over the selection, weighting, and substantiation of facts (Pierce, Shapiro, and Verkuil 1985, 484). One might question the premise of this bifurcated process, in which administrators can only prejudge broad policy matters but not specific facts. But the process is effective and demonstrates that politics and policy can be institutionally separated to produce policy rules that at least seem not to simply reflect the preferences of powerful lobbyists (Guess 1991, 160).

In the larger policy process, it may be more difficult to isolate political influences from technical processes. From what we have said so far, it would seem that we seek a neutral policy analysis that separates political from technical decision making. But this would be a naïve quest. Much debate still focuses on what we now know to be a false dichotomy. Where discretion in judgment exists, politics intrudes, because support is required for one's viewpoint, technical or not. Discretion exists for practically any technical question—from the alignment of a road, to pavement specifications, to allowable costs and total costs for each alignment option, to who will benefit from each road option.

For example, historically the National Railroad Passenger Corporation (Amtrak) allocated revenues and ridership across its routes on a train-by-train basis, an apparently neutral technical rule. But down at the track-bed level, it was obvious that allocations were "strongly influenced by analytical assumptions" (Congressional Budget Office 1982, 43). How should one allocate split-trip passengers, or those who travel on more than one route? A passenger traveling on the Pioneer from Denver to Seattle must also travel one-third of the way along the Zephyr route from Chicago to Oakland. Before April 1981 the routes were treated as separate operations with identifiable costs, revenues, and mileage; but later, revenues associated with the Zephyr portion were attributed to the Pioneer, and only a portion of Zephyr operating costs were allocated to the Pioneer. The Pioneer's financial performance was thereby enhanced by the "passenger-miles/train-miles" measure, and the Zephyr's performance was correspondingly downgraded (Congressional Budget Office 1982, 44). Why? Technically, the allocation could be explained by the addition of service from Chicago to Seattle in April 1981. Politically, it might be explained by the rise of Senator Bob Packwood (R-OR) to become the chair of the Senate Commerce, Science, and Transportation Committee, since the higher rate of passenger-miles/train-miles for the Pioneer saved the route through his home state of Oregon from discontinuance (Guess 1984, 388).

A FRAMEWORK FOR POLICY ANALYSIS

Having discussed the basics of policy formulation and the role of the analytic process, we should now consider how this decision process fits into the larger cycle of policymaking. The four phases of the policymaking process are well known and covered in most textbooks on governmental and nonprofit organizations. The process of rule promulgation and implementation is similar to the process of policy financing through the budget process or appropriations. For the fields of public budgeting (Axelrod 1995), management control (Anthony and Young 1999), or public policy (Patton and Sawicki 1986), there are typically four phases requiring similar kinds of analytic skills and activities: formulation; decision optimization; implementation; and monitoring, evaluation, and feedback. The main difference in the policy process consists in the institutional responsibilities that require focus on different policy issues—regulation, legislative approval, fiscal impact, grant structure, effects on state-local finances, and so on. Since formal means-ends reviews of both macro and micro problems are required by participants in all phases, analysis is or should be common to the larger policy process. In this book we focus on the more specific analytic process in order to optimize resources. The analytic aim is to maximize net benefits for all issues that pertain to formulation, problem definition, review of costs, and implementation. In order to do this, we need formal tools and methods to apply for each decision topic, together with a formal system to monitor and evaluate results. Since the feedback loop provides data for further analysis to improve policymaking, it is clear that analysis is (or should be) ongoing.

Thus, as indicated in figure 1.1, the first phase focuses on structuring and diagnosing the problem. The second phase concentrates on those tools and techniques that forecast both policy and institutional alternatives. The various policy options will have differing social and fiscal consequences; institutional arrangements will affect the probable effects of each option. To the extent possible, institutional constraints need to be anticipated before policy approval and implementation. Failure to identify institutional constraints at this phase can lead to resource waste and later disincentives to utilize analytic information altogether. In the third phase, we turn our attention to the major analytic techniques for forecasting and comparing policy options, such as simulation-assisted estimation, statistical techniques for linear and nonlinear trends, public pricing, cost effectiveness, and cost-benefit techniques. The third phase consists of providing information for decision making. Decision makers need to know which option maximizes net benefits the most and why. They need to know the costs and risks of selecting recommended options. The fourth phase consists of monitoring and evaluating results and feeding information back into the diagnostic and problem identification phase.

The four phases together constitute the policy process. In all phases, analysts employ frameworks, and these should be explicit and consistent throughout the sequential process of making policy. The term "framework" is commonly used to denote one or more theories or models to describe and explain a policy problem. Typically, specific frameworks are developed for technical policy areas, such as health and transportation. One economist noted that in his view, a major problem faced by policymakers in the United States is that "no single theoretical framework explains all the unexpected changes in the current account"—that is, the sum of the country's trade surplus or deficit, income paid by or received from foreigners, and such net transfers as remittances from migrant workers (*The Economist* 1998, 84).

The term "analysis" is often used interchangeably with "review," "appraisal," and "evaluation." This can lead to confusion over the stage of the policy process. For instance, the distinction is often made between prospective, or ex ante, analysis and post-implementation analysis. Projects are often "appraised," rather than analyzed ex ante. Historical analysis of past policies or ongoing evaluation of new policies is often called "descriptive" policy analysis (Patton and Sawicki 1986, 18). Analysis before implementation consists of predicting or projecting future states from adopting particular policy alternatives. Also called "prospective" policy analysis, this requires identification of problems, comparison of alternative ways to address problems, and generation of useful data for decision making (Patton and Sawicki 1986, 19). Our book focuses on those tools and methods applicable to prospective or pre-

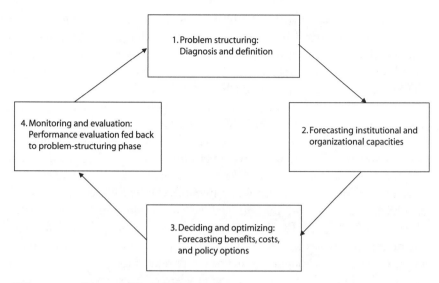

Figure 1.1   Phases of Policy Analysis

implementation decision making. It concentrates on some of the techniques used for systematic evaluation of economic feasibility, political acceptability, and institutional capacity to implement preferred policy options. In short, while covering problem structuring and institutional forecasting, the book focuses on phase three: deciding policies and optimizing net benefits.

ORGANIZATION OF THE BOOK

This book will follow the policy process through the first three phases of figure 1.1, concentrating, as noted, on the third phase: deciding and optimizing. In the initial problem-structuring phase, analysts should define problems, isolate proximate and remote causes, state objectives clearly, and specify target groups. For the first phase, problem definition (chapter 2), we use the case of "Fighting Crime: The Case for Emptier Prisons" to try to illustrate a "messy" or ill-structured policy problem. Typically, in such cases existing policies contribute to new policy problems, budgetary and ideological resources are already heavily committed, and there is a lack of information on policy effectiveness. This case is useful for demonstrating the application of technical methods, as well as for illustrating the need to integrate the competing values or policy premises in policymaking that may have little to do with technical analysis.

For example, faced with the embarrassing task of going through the balanced budget ceiling (the Gramm-Rudman-Hollings law then required sequestration, or reducing all non-exempt spending by a certain percentage, for breach of ceilings to balance planned revenues with expenditures) to pay for the $1.4 billion election-year drug effort, in 1986 the US Senate voted within minutes to breach that ceiling. On the national policy agenda, the drug effort was deemed that important! In 1986 the drug abuse problem in the United States was considered a "national emergency," and the idea of doing nothing was unthinkable (Greenhouse 1986). In fact, trends in illicit drug use had been dropping from a high in 1979 (46% of 18–25 year olds; 25% of 12–17 year olds) to 34% and 17%, respectively, by 1986 (ONDCP, 1998, cited in Rushefsky 2008, 282). Drug use for both age groups continued to drop until 1996 (Rushefsky 2008, 282). By 1998 data seemed to permeate policymaking, and the drug problem was no longer the only emergency in comparison to other major policy issues, although it remained important through its links to other issues such as prison overcrowding, the problem of Mexican drug trafficking across the border, and the impact of drug use on HIV/AIDS programs. Faced with imminent failure of the balanced budget amendment in 1997, Congress had to weigh the luxury of a balanced budget, without counting Social Security trust fund revenues, against the necessity of big cuts in programs such as drug enforcement to make up the difference. Placing Social Security once again off budget (as it was before the unified budget reform in 1968) would have deprived the US Treasury of substantial payroll tax revenues and forced draconian cuts to balance the budget, which most political leaders were unwilling to accept. But leaving Social Security on budget to finance the balanced budget would leave political leaders equally open to the political charge of using a trust fund to pay for general revenues (Novak 1996; Blinder 1997). Studies indicated that the drug problem (measured by illicit use) was probably worse in 2003 than it was in 1986. But demographics (such as the aging population) meant that there was more pressure on elected officials to ward off threats to retirement benefits than to balance the budget or arrest drug pushers. For those who organize strongly and vote with intense preferences for their benefits, the drug problem is less valuable politically than protection of Social Security benefits. In short, it was not analysis of the merits of the drug issue that drove efforts to determine the level of the budget, but political values and tradeoffs.

In chapter 3 we provide guidelines on how to forecast the effects of institutional capacity on policy implementation (phase 2). It is often assumed that executing institutions matter only marginally and that what really counts for effective policymaking and implementation is the amorphous quality of "political will." But institutions such as unions, city councils, government departments, and nongovernmental organizations have a way, for better or worse, of generating momentum themselves. If they persist long enough to develop an organizational climate or culture, they can provide the necessary support to reinforce political will. Political leaders often take greater risks if they have strong stakeholder support through administrative institutions. This often translates into tighter controls over future expenditures. Policies and executing institutions have a symbiotic relationship: The systems created by policies become the institutions that then implement the policies.

The link between policy formulation and execution becomes clearer when one realizes that not all policies are made during the formulation stage. The framework in figure 1.1, which postulates a neat division into four phases, is often contradicted by reality. It will be evident from our review of the influences on financial management systems that neither budgets nor policies should be made during implementation. In addition to the disruption of democratic representation caused by budgeting on the run, time pressures during implementation exclude analysis, and opportunities for error are increased. Unfortunately, key national security policies for provision of Bosnia-style peacekeeping missions are almost necessarily formulated during policy execution. Contingency plans are made and remade each week until a workable strategy can be found (as in Iraq now). Banks and Straussman (1999, 136) suggested that many US national security policies in the post–Korean War period were made without authorization or appropriations and therefore conducted pursuant to unlawful executing mechanisms that permitted spending. The anticipation of potential constraints and opportunities filtered through executing mechanisms is critical for effective policy formulation.

Normally, institutional analysis is considered to be part of the policy implementation phase. But in this book we consider institutional analysis as part of the forecasting and monitoring and evaluation phases. Institutional analysis is necessary for forecasting policy implementation capacity. Sound analysis of the organizational and political variables that will affect implementation depends on data generated and analyzed as part of the regular monitoring and feedback process. The rationale for analyzing institutional contexts is that failure to anticipate problems with the control and delivery systems will diminish the value of the overall policy analysis effort. For example, performance budget systems are frequently installed to improve the link between public expenditures and results. The easiest and most visible method is to develop the budget format without building expensive systems of cost accounting and expenditure reporting. But without these systems, policymakers often rely on hunch or political influence, demoralizing civil servants who observe funds being wasted that should be serving the public interest.

As will be noted in the chapter 3 case, "Washington, DC School Reform," for many years the city has been plagued by dysfunctional school systems and governmental oversight of its performance. The case reviews some of these constraints and the recent efforts of Chancellor Michelle Rhee to turn around the system in face of these phase 2–type constraints. While the chancellor and her team developed a sound long- and short-term strategy and performance evaluation measures for accountability, it is clear that they may have underestimated some of the institutional constraints. At the same time, some of those involved recognized the constraints and believe that they can be reduced or eliminated in order to improve educational results for DC students. Forecasting institutional constraints is an important mapping stage to identify minor and major problems. While financial costs and program benefits need to be analyzed separately, apart from related policies or other extraneous issues, factors that may seriously impede implementation cannot be ignored during the diagnostic phase.

Institutions are the rules of the game for policymakers. Attempts to forecast the effects of these rule systems on policy implementation raise three important questions. First, how will these rule systems work within existing organizational structures, and how will they affect policy implementation? Rule systems may discourage the congruence of goals between layers of the organization. Organizational roles and job descriptions may be so ill defined that, for example, senior managers may waste time on routine billing matters rather than developing programs and ensuring more effective execution of existing work. Second, how do rule systems facilitate effective management? As indicated in the case, staff cutbacks (teachers and school administrators) may be required by both performance criteria and a lack of available funding. The double shock often produces management problems with remaining personnel and parents. With insufficient personnel and resultant morale problems, senior managers (here principals and teachers) are typically unable to deliver the same level and quality of services as before. Third, how effectively can organizational functions be executed within existing rule systems? Very often, internal rules contribute to poor service delivery and policy results. For example, the processes of public certification, licensing, procurement, and payment systems often require many redundant steps that discourage private investment in local communities and create opportunities for bribery, kickbacks, and other forms of corruption to speed the process along.

Not uncommonly, rule systems reviews raise larger structural and functional questions. Structural issues include whether delivery should be through private contractors with public monitoring and regulation, or through public institutions that set central standards and coordinate a variety of providers—private contractors, nongovernmental organizations (e.g., charter and private schools), and public institutions. Structural questions also include management issues. What is the optimal number of layers for effective management? Should the organization be "de-layered" for cost efficiency, and at what cost in management and policy experience and potential effectiveness? How should appropriate spans of control be designed to maximize net resources?

Finally, functional issues must also be examined. For effective policy implementation, institutions must generate, process, and transmit useful information to managers responsible for delivery. Systems of budget allocation and allotment, personnel administration, operations and maintenance planning, program evaluation, cost and managerial accounting, payments to vendors, and cash management must all function as an integrated unit. Accurate and useful information must be available in a timely fashion. As information technology becomes more powerful, earlier problems of data scarcity have been replaced by data glut, drowning policymakers in unprocessed data and information in questionable aggregates. The failure to unclog these systems and have them produce needed information results in the inability to plan and deliver such basic programs as transportation, education, health, law enforcement, and environmental protection.

As indicated in chapter 4 (figure 1.1, phase 3), policy analysis requires projection of present data trends into the future so that policy alternatives can be structured with confidence. This should include analysis of both institutional and policy issues. The case of the Maryland Purple Line examines how a state transit agency develops cost-effective policy options for an urban corridor. Consistent with estimation techniques in other policy areas, such as energy, housing, health, and education, linear and nonlinear statistical and simulation-assisted estimation methods are employed to estimate trips generated by each option. Policy analysts must then develop a high-performance preferred option consistent with Federal Transit Administration criteria for funding. Funders such as FTA know that demographic and economic uncertainties often create havoc with technical projections and render projects that are cost beneficial on paper largely worthless. To counter this problem, FTA and other agencies provide funding solicitors with methods, databases, models, allowable assumptions, and algorithms to generate their options. In this way, all proposals are based on transparent data and consistent methodologies. Making the evaluation framework more rigorous has improved both forecasting and project performance.

In phase 3 forecasting, policy analysts must also employ techniques to measure and compare program costs and benefits. To develop realistic tradeoffs, it is essential that decision makers understand not only the measurement of costs and benefits but also the principles of political economy on which these calculations are based. In chapter 5 we employ economic analysis to examine the issues involved with cigarette taxes. The topic of costs and prices is often erroneously viewed as the exclusive purview of accountants and of the private sector. Here we examine the question of how cigarette taxation affects individual behavior and overall health care policy goals. The chapter considers various empirical approaches used to analyze the effects of taxation and discusses how taxation relates to other public policies designed to reduce smoking behavior.

In chapter 6 we examine the issue of evaluating policy alternatives to attain a given objective, in this case reducing the number of cases of human immunodeficiency virus (HIV) infection. This technique, in which the costs of producing different levels of output to attain an agreed-upon objective are compared, is known as cost-effectiveness analysis (Axelrod 1995). The chapter covers the principles of cost-effectiveness analysis and shows how they have been applied to evaluate alternative HIV screening and treatment policies. Finally, in chapter 7 the strengths and weaknesses of the policy analyst's favorite (though oft misused) tool, cost-benefit analysis, are examined through an application to the case of environmental regulation. The chapter focuses on the US Environmental Protection Agency's policies to reduce the amount of fine particulate matter in the air. The theory and practice of cost-benefit analysis are discussed, with a particular emphasis on valuation of life questions. The chapter also examines the role that various stakeholders have played in this policy arena.

Thus, policy analysis is a sequence of logical steps in which messy data and conflicting information are used to structure alternatives in order to provide a semblance of rational choice. As noted, in this book we restrict ourselves to problem definition in the diagnostic phase and institutional capacity, pricing, cost effectiveness, and cost-benefit analysis in the forecasting phase. It is our view that the analyst who masters these techniques through case analyses will be capable of anticipating problems and resolving them during the actual policy implementation and evaluation phases.

REFERENCES

Anthony, Robert, and David B. Young. 1999. *Management Control in Nonprofit Organizations*. 6th ed. Burr Hill, IL: Irwin/McGraw-Hill.

Axelrod, Donald. 1995. *Budgeting for Modern Government*. 2nd ed. New York: St. Martin's.

Banks, William C., and Jeffrey D. Straussman. 1999. Defense Contingency Budgeting in the Post-Cold-War Period. *Public Administration Review* 59 (March/April): 135–45.

Blank, Rebecca. 1997. *It Takes a Nation: A New Agenda for Fighting Poverty.* Princeton, NJ: Princeton University Press.

Blinder, Alan S. 1997. Constitutional Clutter. *Washington Post*, February 7.

Bovens, Mark, and Paul 't Hart. 1996. *Understanding Policy Fiascoes.* New Brunswick, NJ: Transaction Publishers.

Card, David, and Alan B. Krueger. 1998. Unemployment Chimera. *Washington Post*, March 6.

Congressional Budget Office. 1982. *Federal Subsidies for Rail Passenger Service: An Assessment of Amtrak.* Washington, DC: US Government Printing Office.

Development Alternatives, Inc. 1997. *USAID Public Administration Program in Estonia, Final Report.* Bethesda, MD: Development Alternatives, Inc.

DeYoung, Karen, and Michael Leahy. 2009. Warning on Detroit Suspect Didn't Rise Above the "Noise." *Washington Post*, December 28.

Dixit, Avinash. 1997. Dismal Scientists. *The Economist*, September.

Dunn, William N. 2008. *Public Policy Analysis: An Introduction.* 4th ed. Upper Saddle River, NJ: Pearson Prentice Hall.

The Economist. 1998. Figures to Fret About. July.

———. 2009. After the Gold Rush: Briefing on the National Health Service. December.

Fisher, Ronald C. 2007. *State and Local Public Finance.* 3rd ed. Mason, OH: Thomson Southwestern.

Greenhouse, Linda. 1986. Drug War vs. Budget Deficit: The Senate Blinked. *New York Times*, October 2.

Guess, George M. 1984. Profitability Guardians and Service Advocates: The Evolution of Amtrak Training. *Public Administration Review* 44 (5): 384–93.

———. 1991. The Politics of Administrative Rulemaking. In *Doing Public Administration, Exercises in Public Management,* 3rd ed. ed. Nicholas Henry, 157–71. Dubuque: William C. Brown.

Hamilton, Martha M. 1997. Power Struggle Awaits Utility Deregulation, Competing Interests Could Short-Circuit Quick Passage of Utility Reform. *Washington Post*, April 12.

Heclo, Hugh. 1978. Issue Networks and the Executive Establishment. In *The New Political System*, ed. Anthony King, 87–124. Washington, DC: American Enterprise Institute.

Leach, William D., Neil W. Pelkey, and Paul A. Sabatier. 2002. Stakeholder Partnerships as Collaborative Policymaking: Evaluation Criteria Applied to Watershed Management in California and Washington. *Journal of Policy Analysis and Management* 21 (4): 645–70.

Lowi, Theodore. 1979. *The End of Liberalism.* New York: Norton.

Novak, Robert D. 1996. What Social Security Trust Fund? *Washington Post,* October 5.

Office of National Drug Control Policy (ONDCP). 1998. *National Drug Control Strategy.* Washington, DC: ONDCP.

Paris, David C., and James F. Reynolds. 1983. *The Logic of Policy Inquiry.* New York: Longman.

Patton, Carl V., and David S. Sawicki. 1986. *Basic Methods of Policy Analysis and Planning.* Englewood Cliffs, NJ: Prentice Hall.

Pfiffner, James P. 2010. The Decision to Go to War with Iraq. In *Public Administration: Concepts and Cases,* 9th ed. ed. Richard J. Stillman, 195–207. Boston: Wadsworth Cengage Learning.

Pierce, Richard J., Sidney A. Shapiro, and Paul R. Verkuil. 1985. *Administrative Law and Process.* New York: Foundation Press.

Poister, Theodore H. 1978. *Applied Program Analysis.* University Park, PA: Pennsylvania State University Press.

Rand, Ayn. 1957. *Atlas Shrugged.* New York: Signet, 1999.

Roberts, Nancy. 1997. Public Deliberation: An Alternative Approach to Crafting Policy and Setting Direction. *Public Administration Review* 57 (2): 124–33.

Rushefsky, Mark E. 2008. *Public Policy in the United States at the Dawn of the 21st Century.* 4th ed. Armonk, NY: M. E. Sharpe.

Skocpol, Theda. 1997. The Next Liberalism. *Atlantic Monthly.* April.

Steffens, Lincoln. 1931. *The Autobiography of Lincoln Steffens.* Vol. 2. New York: Harcourt Brace Jovanovich.

Stillman, Richard J. 2010. *Public Administration: Cases and Concepts.* 9th ed. Boston: Wadsworth Cengage Learning.

Thompson, Cheryl W. 1998. Police Using Few Ideas in Report by Consultants. *Washington Post,* October 26.

Tuchman, Barbara W. 1984. *The March of Folly: From Troy to Vietnam.* New York: Ballantine.

The Washington Post. 2009. No Sale: Maryland's Liquor Lobby and the Politics of Obstruction. December 24.

Wolf, Charles. 1993. *Markets or Governments: Choosing between Imperfect Alternatives.* Cambridge: Massachusetts Institute of Technology Press.

Chapter 2

✷✷✷

Problem Identification and Structuring

> After an hour of careful self-counseling and analysis,
> and a thorough survey and methodological setting-
> out of his problems, the jumbled perspectives of his
> life slowly reformed and sanity resumed something
> like its rightful place in the order of things.
>
> —William Boyd, *A Good Man in Africa*

A policy problem is any important issue affecting the public, in relation to which funds may be spent and/or legislation or regulation may be enacted. The problem with this view of a problem is that for some, problems are actually opportunities. In addition, one person's important problem is another person's minor problem. Or one person's problem is another's symptom or underlying problem; for instance, drug trafficking in Mexico might be seen as a symptom of the real problems of weak courts and corrupt police (*The Economist* 2009a). Disagreement is often intense at this phase of policy analysis, and it is hard to get analytic consensus on a workable definition of the problem. Institutional frameworks emphasize "analysis," which often produces options but little consensus on actionable problem definitions—a blueprint for failure.

The first phase of the policy analysis process is, in fact, problem structuring. Clearly, this requires identification and diagnosis of the policy problems. Bardach (1996) and others consider problem definition to be the most important part of policy analysis. Before introducing some basic techniques to structure and define policy problems, it may be useful to indicate why it is critical to have a proper definition of the problem before committing funds to solve it. The answer seems obvious. Given the time lag between policy formulation and the results of implementation, as well as the sunk costs and potential risks of committing large sums of public funds, it is only sensible that funds be targeted to the right problem. Good policy analysis should be able to prevent resource misallocation in the future by focusing on the right problem(s) to be solved.

Obviously, better problem definition cannot reduce the lag time caused by delays in institutional processes in fragmented federal and decentralized systems like those found in the United States.

This chapter's working assumption is that proper problem definition can yield major budgetary savings and improved delivery of services to policy clients. Policy problems are sets of unrealized needs, values, or opportunities for improvement, attainable through public action (Dunn 2008, 3). An important point often lost in discussions of this subject is that policy problems can be either new or ongoing. Failure to define problems properly is like providing incentives to the wrong group to improve program performance (e.g., providing incentives to flight attendants, who really have no control over passenger baggage and flight on-time performance, issues that are basic to solving an airline's profitability problems). More precise definitions of the problems and specification of the levers that can be manipulated to deal with them beforehand can avoid wasting resources and generating public frustration with governmental action. Skillful problem definition can also lead to fiscal savings that, properly reprogrammed, will increase net assistance to the intended beneficiaries of public programs and projects.

CONSTRAINTS TO PROBLEM DIAGNOSIS

It is said that at least four times as much time should be spent on problem definition and diagnosis of policy problems as on analysis of alternative courses of action (Lehan 1984, 73). This is not a reference to the tendency of experts in economics and policy analysis to disagree on conceptual and quantitative assumptions and interpretation of data. Proper definition of macroeconomic problems, such as excessive levels of aggregate demand, will still result in disagreements on the scope and timing of fiscal and monetary policy applications. More precise problem definitions can reduce the scope of later disagreements on how to share the costs and benefits of alternative policy actions. By providing a useful screening methodology, the diagnostic phase can also prevent nonproblems from being defined as policy problems. It is as expensive in both staff time and financial resources to solve the wrong problem (this is known as a Type III error) as it is to elevate nonproblems to the agenda. Both can be avoided by careful diagnosis, structuring, and definition beforehand.

For example, Fumento (1998, 12) argued that the "road rage epidemic" problem is nothing more than old-fashioned aggressive driving hyped by the media. Mistaken creation of a problem by the media, with support from legislators in search of votes, diverted resources away from solutions for real behaviors that caused road accidents and produced deaths and injuries. Although it sounds reasonable to define a problem first before committing resources, in the road rage case, the administrator of the NHTSA said that "we would rather not debate the definition because we have a huge problem staring us in the face and we should focus on solutions" (Davis and Smith 1998, 223). Here is almost a textbook case of how not to proceed with policy formulation. Using appropriate problem-definition techniques that demand empirical evidence could eliminate overbroad classification of existing problems and prevent hyping of non problems. In this chapter we will cover some of the basic problem-structuring techniques. This will allow us to clarify terms and narrow definitional differences before proceeding to the analytic phase. It should be noted that beyond methods and techniques, the failure to rigorously define policy problems is related to three more basic causes.

First, analysts themselves can impede problem analysis by unconsciously imposing definitions that lead them astray. Conceptual straightjackets are often self-imposed. A classic example of this is the "nine-dot problem," which allows the linear imagination to fall into a trap. Suppose a transportation department must link nine cities with only four highways, and because of technical and budgetary reasons, all roads must be straight. No retracing is allowed. If the analyst attempts to solve the problem by trying to stay within its implied boundaries (the implied border formed by nine dots arranged in a square with three rows, as shown in figure 2.1), it cannot be done. A familiar path followed by inveterate number crunchers is to do a quantitative estimate of the distance between the points to demonstrate that the problem is insoluble (Dunn 2008, 94). A recommendation that more roads and funding are needed would then be based on a false formulation of the problem—or solving the wrong problem. The creative solution lies in ignoring the implied boundary of the problem and connecting the dots by going beyond the implied boundaries of the three rows, as indicated in figure 2.1. The point is that the analyst often lacks the critical perspective needed to move beyond a traditional definition of the problem. This may account for the many insoluble problems described by expert analysts in fields ranging from domestic health care to foreign policy.

Second, institutional values and organizational culture may converge in procedures that contribute to the misdefinition of a problem. Given the strength of bureaucratic institutions, this convergence often creates enormous momentum in the wrong direction, which can take years to reverse through legal and budgetary change. For instance, organizations often use decision-making models based on top-down financial control, which tend to screen out or discourage reporting of needed information by subordinates. This can lead

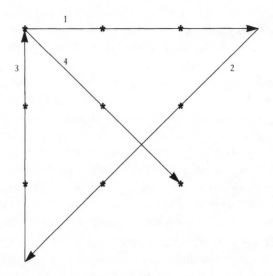

Figure 2.1   Solution for the Nine-Dot Problem

to partial or erroneous definitions of the problem. In regions such as Latin America and Eastern Europe, the well-known statist tendency to centralize decision making weakens policy implementation, because professional managers in such ministries as health and education cannot redistribute personnel or transfer funds to meet contingencies. Instead, the resultant policy failure is defined as a legal problem requiring legislative change (of which there is no chance) or a bureaucratic control problem, leading incorrectly to even tighter restrictions over managers and paradoxically to more wasted funds (Guess and Sitko 2004; Guess 1992).

Cultural style is a well-known institutional problem that is hard to quantify or remedy. This often boils down to lack of leadership. Some organizations seem to reward back-stabbing and internal power games. This perpetuates a culture of distrust and a lack of teamwork and staff loyalty. In public and nonprofit organizations, and especially universities, there is an ample supply of smooth, buck-passing types who carefully defer to their superiors while engaging full-time in palace intrigue. They are not interested in problem solving, but rather in self-promotion and survival. Tribal war prevents improvement and makes it much more difficult to establish teams, discern problems, and find solutions. The preferred remedy is to sack the contaminating figures and hire new management or CEOs.

In the foreign policy area, for instance, where there is a very narrow circle of policymaking responsibility, the sunk costs of even a palpably bad decision are often perceived to be high: better to keep up the flow of support funds than to slow down, reassess, and risk falling into a ditch. In most countries, the making of foreign policy typically produces a rich trove of "policy-based evidence." American institutions seem to specialize in distorted problem formulation and flawed policy execution. Before the 2003 intervention in Iraq, which was based on amateur groupthink screening out critical definitions of the problem (see Pfiffner 2010, 201), the classic example of weak problem diagnosis was US participation in the Vietnam War. Successive definitions by core foreign policy institutions over time (including the State Department, the CIA, the Department of Defense) led to American support of a series of puppet regimes in South Vietnam and increased US military participation to stop Communist-threatened "dominoes" from falling. The mistake was to move ahead in the early 1960s, ignoring such core lessons from the past as the French debacle in Indochina, since many of these lessons were institutionally inconvenient for justification of the expansion option (Tuchman 1984).

One of the lessons of the next chapter is that institutions matter in both policy formulation and implementation. Given this, it can be seen that US military policy actions in Vietnam were analogous to requesting budgets without considering past budgetary bases or their results. Under such irrational conditions, problems are, at best, defined without analytic inputs from the planning and budgeting system. At worst, sensible suggestions for redefinition of policy and reassessment of likely outcomes, as in the case of Iraq, are ignored. The result in that case was a series of bad decisions frozen into policy positions enforced to justify the costs of previous field failures. One can hardly imagine a surer way to waste financial and human resources.

Third, a problem may be misdefined because of ideological or values-based treatment of the clients of existing policies and programs. That ideologies and values affect policy definition is hardly a new insight, but the goal should be to test such values empirically, since ideological influences are almost by definition anti-empirical. Even the absence of hard data to support ideologically based policies will not change minds or lead to the elimination or modification of policies (e.g., abortion, stem cell research, and same-sex marriage). In policy analysis, as anywhere, it is frustrating to argue with true believers. For example, such policymakers as US Representative Tom Coburn (R-OK) are in principle against the practice of needle exchange to slow HIV transmission, because there are empirical arguments that needle exchange can lead to increased drug use (providing needles to people who did not ever exchange them) and to undermine the goal of reducing illicit drug use. But it could also be argued that this position is anti-empirical, since there are hard data indicating that needle exchange is an effective means of slowing HIV transmission (Burr 1997b, 10). In this perspective, the former stance closes off sensible options and prevents public health methods from being applied to the AIDS epidemic.

Similarly, an auto safety initiative by President Clinton to increase seatbelt use from 68 to 85% by 2000 and 90% by 2005 was based on the estimated benefit of 10,000 lives saved per year. But several African American lawmakers and the American Civil Liberties Union (ACLU) opposed the policy initiative, because enforcement of the law would increase police harassment of minorities. In addition, states such as Washington and Colorado also opposed the proposed law because of individualist feelings that "government has no right to tell people what to do in their cars" (Brown 1998). Ideological values were clearly an important element in both drug policy and automobile safety decision making. As in most cases of policy analysis, there has to be a stage in the formulation process in which values can be traded off without degeneration into violence or chaos.

Before turning to this chapter's case, "Fighting Crime: The Case for Emptier Prisons," we need to review the larger constraints to problem definition. These are issues that cannot be dealt with feasibly in the short run, because they deal with institutions and interest-group pressures. Following this review, we will look at basic methods for structuring policy problems and then apply them to the case.

THE CONCEPT OF A POLICY PROBLEM

It will be evident that problems need to be defined not only for macropolicies (or "high" policies), such as foreign aid, health, and transportation, but also for micropolicies, such as municipal animal control and police services. The only difference between these types of policies is the size of the population affected by public rules and procedures. Both macro- and micropolicies require formulation or implementation of public-sector rules and procedures. The distinction also points to overlap between the concepts of "policy," "program," and "service." Since the objects of planned public expenditures are authorized by public laws and serve defined target populations, the analytic distinction between policy, program, and service often breaks down. It should only be noted that program and policy analysis typically involve the same kind of techniques.

Three basic questions should be answered: (1) What is a policy problem? (2) What kinds of policy problems are there? (3) Why is a precise definition important?

First, as noted, a policy problem represents a set of "unrealized values, needs or opportunities, which, however identified, may be attained through public action" (Dunn 2008, 72). A policy problem can also be viewed as a "system of external conditions that produce dissatisfaction among different segments of the community" (Dunn 1981, 99). By this perspective, a policy problem is an event or condition that produces dissatisfaction beyond one or two individuals. People are upset. A single complaint about the slow response of police or fire services does not amount to a policy problem—though, collectively, more complaints would be symptomatic of a policy problem. This helps in the definition. But how do we know whether it is an *actionable* problem, as opposed to something simply annoying? Here it may be useful to define a policy problem by analogy, as in a public question that can be settled by evidence that all rival observers have no choice but to accept (Runciman 1998, 8). Thus congestion, measured by road density and average speed of traffic, and leading to x hours of time wasted and y gallons of fuel consumed, with corresponding increases in measurable levels of nitrogen oxide, can be considered an actionable public policy problem. By contrast, the question of whether President Clinton's new seatbelt initiative was racially based because it could have been used against minorities was not a public policy problem. It was an annoying possibility rather than an actionable condition. At this stage of the policy process, that aspect of the initiative was merely an interesting metaphysical question or an issue of political philosophy, but not a policy problem. Despite the lack of a real problem, action is often taken anyway to kill proposals such as this or to change procedures.

Policy problems should have an empirical basis; the ultimate quest is for evidence-based policy. For example, arguments about the scope of the New York City rat problem turn on the number of reported rat complaints (increasing from 18,045 in 1997 to 32,000 in 2005). But other estimates are anecdotal estimates, such as one rat per New Yorker (*The Economist* 2005, 54; Spurgeon 1997). Some claim that increased complaints were the result of a City Hall hotline that made it easier to complain. This institutional constraint is plausible. In another example, in the early 2000s it was impossible to rationally define the stray dog problem in Bucharest, Romania, despite massive numbers of dogs roaming around town in packs that attacked the public almost randomly, often transmitting rabies. The fragmented, district-based regulatory structures, with their separate dog-catching units, muzzle laws, leash laws, and databases to record numbers of strays and rabies infections, made it impossible to formulate or diagnose the problem properly (Guess 2009, 123).

Similarly, problem truckers caused 13% of the traffic fatalities in 1997, which was up from 9% in 1996. But the National Office of Motor Carrier Safety did not actually keep timely or accurate statistics on problem truckers. How then did one know that this was a policy problem? Here, as in many cases, comparative data from similar jurisdictions can be useful in establishing a norm. The Virginia State Police keep records that reveal that 22% of the trucks inspected have defects so serious that they must be taken off the road. Based on such numbers, Congress called for an investigation of the National Office of Motor Carrier Safety by the US Department of Transportation inspector general and the General Accounting Office (Reid 1998).

What we seek is a practical or actionable statement of a public issue, based on which expenditures can be made, personnel deployed, and procedures developed that reduce or eliminate the undesirable state of affairs without undue harmful consequences for related activities. In principle, policies can be defined and actions taken that do not cause unintended consequences. In practice, unintended consequences need to be anticipated, if possible, through prior analysis of comparative lessons from policy implementation under similar conditions. This should include review of how efficiently administrative mechanisms have deployed resources. Again, this refers to the institutional issue in policy analysis: Management needs the flexibility to change course if a problem has been misdefined.

Policy problems are not conceptual constructs like atoms or cells. Instead, expressed for instance as sulfur dioxide parts per million in the air, they are practical constructs that serve as measures for the design and enforcement of a clean air law or policy. The constructs are the product of thought acting on the environment; they are artificial in the sense that someone subjectively judges these conditions to be problematic. The inherent artificiality of constructs for any policy area makes it easier for policymakers and especially the media to misconstrue the real problem. One way around such misconstrual is to disaggregate the problem. Some argue for a form of rational reductionism of complexity—divide, conquer, simplify, and reduce multifaceted problems into components for action. However, disaggregating policy problems into smaller, more manageable elements runs the risk of providing the right solution to the wrong problem. For example, past concern over what government should do (if anything) about the declining economic international competitiveness of the United States was frequently boiled down to an issue of excessive foreign access to American technology. But Robert Reich (1987, 63) argued that this conclusion misinterpreted the real problem. "The underlying predicament is not that the Japanese are exploiting our discoveries but that we can't turn basic inventions into new products as fast or as well as they can." Defining the problem in this way precludes the policy alternative of holding back basic inventions from foreigners through more regulation and points toward more flexible solutions that give American workers and engineers experience in quickly turning basic inventions into products.

Second, it is important to distinguish among levels of problem complexity. It should be made clear to clients of policy analysis that more complex problems will be harder to solve and take longer. Policymakers often ignore this distinction between simple and complex problems in the rush to gain public approbation. Former House Speaker Newt Gingrich once argued that Clinton's ten-year drug policy strategy was too pessimistic: "The Civil War took just four years to save the union and abolish slavery. Why can't we solve the drug problem, another form of slavery, in just a few years?" Of course, changing the intractable behavioral foundations of policy problems requires time, resources, and continuity of effort. Declines in drug use are gradual everywhere; demanding quick solutions to complex problems to score political points with a populist base can lead to public pressure for more severe penalties, targeting minorities as scapegoats, and, finally, to overall policy fatigue and discouragement (Musto 1998).

For such reasons, policy problems are often divided into "messy" (complex) and "not messy" (simple) categories. The issue is how one should define and distinguish problems for decision making in order to resolve present problems and prevent future policy crises. Coherent, unmessy problems are rare in public-sector work and usually involve routine support matters such as personnel and internal management. Note, however, that routine matters can get out of hand and turn into messy, "high"-policy problems. For example, pine beetle infestations have been occurring for thousands of years and are thought to be cyclical. Foresters have traditionally targeted forests with a range of tools that have been more or less effective at preserving the economic and ecological value of pine forests. When these tools failed, all that was lost were a few forests. Now pine beetles have infested millions of acres of trees in the American West. The once-simple problem has now become complex: Global warming has prevented normal destruction of larvae under the bark, leading to more rotting forests and increased carbon emissions, and jeopardizing policy goals to reduce carbon emissions to 17% of 2005 levels by 2030 (*New York Times* 2009). What had been a simple and local operational problem now affects policies that target messy and complex international problems of how to regulate greenhouse gases and best stimulate alternative sources of energy supplies.

Third, and finally, precise definition of a problem is confounded by the fact that there can be many interpretations of the same information. Different problem definitions derive from the fact that different constituencies or stakeholders are doing the defining. This in turn can lead to policies that dis-proportionately distribute costs and benefits among affected interest groups. For example, "elderly poor" is a census concept. But the distributions of elderly and poor people are often incongruent. This can affect the cost and level of service delivery. There are widely different interpretations of the effects of pro-longed economic expansion in the United States on reducing the poverty problem. The Census Bureau, for example, indicates that the number of very poor Americans increased from 13.5% in 1995 to 13.8% in 1996. This would point to a major policy problem for poverty advocates. But the Census Bureau used a narrow, cash-income definition of poverty, excluding such noncash ben-efits as food stamps and Medicaid. Using a broader income measure leads to the different interpretation that only 10.2% of Americans were below the pov-erty line in 1996, and Latinos, women, and residents of the South were the largest gainers in household income growth from economic expansion (*The Economist* 1997c). Others would note that despite the increase in the poverty income threshold for a family of four from $15,569 to $19,307 (1995–2004), the poverty rate dropped from 13.8% to 12.7% in that period (Rushefsky 2008, 145). Still others might point out that despite the rate decrease, the number of people below the threshold actually increased (from 36.3 million to 36.9 million). This is because the total US population increased, and relative poverty thus declined.

Analysts need problem definitions that recognize geographic and socio-logical differences as a prelude to policy development. Failure to include all constituencies and options that might reasonably be considered in defining policy problems amounts to a major economic and political mistake. That is, a policy that does not deal with all dimensions of the problem at hand will per-mit underlying social conflicts to fester and lead to wasted public expenditures. For this reason, policy development should include safeguards for public notice and comment, active participation, and a transparent appeal process.

As might be expected, the stakeholder with the greatest number of politi-cal resources (technical sophistication, rewards and punishments, charisma, and intense supporters) will have the most influence on problem definition and the ultimate selection of alternatives. For example, suppose that the number of complaints in a community about stray dogs has been increasing annually. Suppose also that the number of impoundments has been decreasing at a sim-ilar rate. This is not in Bucharest, but a typical town in the United States. Based on this limited information, what would be the "animal control prob-lem"? With reference to standard services and fiscal tools available for stray dog problems, the problem can be subdivided into regulatory and investment-related factors. That is, the dog problem might be caused by the absence of regulation and/or by inadequate public investment. In contrast with a regulatory definition of the problem, which focuses on licensing, leashes, fines, and animal contraception (i.e., owner-controlled solutions), a capital investment definition would focus on the need for a larger and more accessible dog pound. Some in the community might take issue with the problem being defined as a lack of capital investment, arguing instead that a new pound would not necessarily eliminate strays (the real objective). That is, a new or larger pound would merely shift to the non-dog-owning public the costs of services required by improper behavior by dog owners. Hence, from this perspective a more appropriate solution would be to require some combination of steeper fines, higher service charges or license fees for dog owners, and animal contraception (a regulatory package) (Lehan 1984, 66–67). Since policy alternatives must ultimately be traded in institutional settings (usually committees), politics will affect the ultimate ranking of a regulatory solution in relation to a capital investment (pound) solution. It should be recognized that strong preferences for capital construction solutions to complex policy problems are often driven by the political pressures of construction firms that donate campaign money and underscore to officeholders the political benefits of creating tangible results for local constituencies.

STRUCTURING A POLICY PROBLEM

Given the difficulty of defining real-world problems objectively and finally, and the necessity of moving quickly toward a policy solution, simplifying techniques must be used. To produce information on the nature of and possible solutions to a problem, one must apply the "policy-analytic procedure of problem structuring," which Dunn calls the "most important but least understood aspect of policy analysis" (1981, 98).

In general, selection of an appropriate technique for problem definition depends first on a preliminary assessment of data trends, causation among variables, and relevant stakeholder positions. New information that can change our assumptions about these subjects will probably emerge during the process of problem structuring. In this event, the definition will change, but the techniques for definition will not. Of initial importance to defining a policy problem is how likely it is, based on the information we have, that the problem can be structured for institutional action in the short or medium term? Dunn (2008, 79–81) suggests that policy problems fall into three classes: well-structured problems, moderately structured problems, and ill-structured problems, based on their degree of complexity and interdependence.

Brewer and deLeon (1983, 51) also recognize that a problem may remain complex, because once the problem is defined by the analyst, it becomes subject to competing individual, organizational, and external environmental (client) preferences.

Well-Structured Problems

William Dunn (2008, 79) defines well-structured problems as those that "involve one or a few decision-makers and a small set of policy alternatives." Low-level agency operational problems, such as the optimal point of replacing agency vehicles, given age, repair, and depreciation costs, are well structured, because all consequences of all policy alternatives can be programmed in advance. Life cycle, maintenance planning and budgeting, and condition assessment systems can provide needed data to make decisions in this relatively simple policy context. For example, the city of Milwaukee uses database systems for condition-based project planning for many of its municipal services, thus enabling officials to anticipate and define problems before they become serious. For surface transportation, the city uses a pavement management system (PMS) to plan more cost-effective paving budgets. This assessment system contains records of more than forty street-condition inventory elements, including type of pavement, age of pavement, and maintenance history. Streets are rated according to the "possible pavement condition index," from very good to very poor, depending on scores received. Milwaukee began using the PMS in 1988, and 20% of its database is updated annually, allowing the city to survey its entire system within five years. For health services, Milwaukee uses three criteria based on condition to determine capital needs: (1) age and condition of facilities, (2) use patterns of facilities, and (3) safety needs of clients (City of Milwaukee 1996, 84).

Throughout the nation, by and large, city garbage problems can be classified as well structured because of the small number of decision makers and policy options. Recycling is becoming more costly because of greater supplies and falling raw materials prices, and this will affect sanitation policy results. With political commitments to recycle at least 50% of garbage, US cities and counties have moved aggressively and cost-effectively and now recycle on average only about 40%. The annual costs per household for moving from 40 to 50% have been calculated and are well known. In Montgomery County, Maryland, which recycles 38% of its garbage, this cost would be $64.66 per year (Day 1997). But the question is whether it is appropriate to charge residents more to reach 50% or, alternatively, to use the money for schools, public safety, recreation, and other recurrent expenditure needs?

The municipal garbage problem might be seen in terms of one or more of the following:

1. The excessive cost of recycling, implying a focus on such means of reducing costs as newly designed garbage trucks that separate paper, glass, and plastic and thus reduce the number of trips required.

2. Excessive quantities of garbage, implying a focus on revised policies, such as refusal to accept lawn clippings or charging by the number of bags of refuse thrown out each week.

3. Overcapacity in the recycling industry, in which too many firms may be competing for recyclables whose prices no longer cover costs, such as newspapers. In other cases, it may now be cheaper to make single-use containers than to recycle. This affects the market price for recyclables and requires higher charges to cities, which must pass these expenses along to households.

4. A problem that may be the result of law, such as the growing number of state laws that mandate minimum thresholds of recycling. Such laws ignore local costs of recycling and constrain the use of policy alternatives such as dumping and incineration (*The Economist* 1997d, 63).

Not infrequently, policy problems can be caused by laws made at another level of government. Practitioners know that these laws often mandate supply without demand and ignore alternative means of achieving the same public purposes. An issue then for managers and the public is how to change the law. In any case, this particular problem is well structured and amenable to standard problem-definition techniques. Whether policymakers and budgetary institutions will use them in policy formulation is a different question.

The New York City rat problem, noted above, is also an example of a well-structured problem. Mayor Rudolph Giuliani declared war on the city's estimated 28 million rats (representing a 4:1 rat-to-resident ratio, double that of Washington, DC) by establishing an interagency Rodent Extermination Task Force with an annual budget of $8 million (Spurgeon 1997). As usual, resolution of the problem required reconciliation of competing problem definitions. As noted, the scope of the problem was estimated first by data on reported rats and rat bites; in other words, rats were and are a public safety issue. But if the problem is defined rather as a health issue, then the solution lies in more competent building inspections and steeper fines for owners and those who leave food for rats to continue breeding and infesting more neighborhoods. The World Health Organization uses the latter definition, noting that rats and their fleas were a major factor in the spread of bubonic plague. By this definition, the problem lies in the behavior of building owners, which can be changed with such disincentives as fines and regulation enforcement. Given the immediacy of the problem, the preferred choice among many groups is one of extermination for public safety: that is, the preference is to poison and kill the existing rats that bite and cause disease. The two definitions of the problem, as in the case of other well-structured problems such as stray dogs, lead in different implementation directions.

Moderately Structured Problems

By contrast, moderately structured problems are "those involving one or a few decision-makers and a relatively limited number of alternatives" (Dunn 2008, 80). The difference is between *a small set* and *a relatively limited* number of available alternatives. The more alternatives available, the more complex is the problem. Unlike the well-structured problem, the outcomes are not calculable within acceptable margins of error or risk. For example, the social insurance problem is commonly described as a "demographic time bomb": Populations in industrial countries are aging quickly, and birth rates are declining. Honoring current commitments means that state pension expenditures will rise steeply, which will mean a sharp rise in taxes for baby boomers, their children, and eventually their grandchildren, who must pay for the elderly. The problem is clear, in that social insurance tax and expenditure forecasts can be reasonably made based on existing demographic data; contingent government liabilities of future budgets can be precisely forecast (*The Economist* 1998b). This part of the problem is well structured in that the need for cash transfers derived from population dynamics and social insurance claims can be forecast within acceptable margins of risk. The Congressional Budget Office (CBO) projects that Social Security outlays will exceed revenues by about $20 billion beginning in 2017 and increasing thereafter. Trust funds will be depleted in 2043, requiring under current law an automatic 17% cut in pension benefits (Committee for a Responsible Federal Budget [CRFB] 2009). Given the enormous increase in forecast spending to cover pension claims, the important problems are how to finance and allocate benefits in the future.

The related but moderately structured problem is that of health care. Current proposals to reorganize the health care system in the United States, which has a very high cost and provides comparatively low value for money, flounder on problem structuring and definition. Health care absorbs 18% of GDP, and Medicare is the fastest growing program liability at the state level. Economists apply the usual concepts of perverse incentives; fragmented rent-seeking institutions; and a free-rider system of payments, with cost-shifting and monopoly pricing, to a sector dominated by lobbies for doctors, insurers, and pharmaceutical companies (Goldhill 2009). Because of the problem's apparent complexity, few agree on the applicability of the various concepts and international models. Even fewer agree on best available solutions. This lack of consensus hinders the development of the mix of market and regulatory solutions needed to control costs and expand coverage. Despite hard facts on the costs of current health care programs (e.g., Medicare and Medicaid), there is less certainty about the cost of expanding benefits to about 40 million people who are not covered by health care insurance. Based on the inability to control costs in the past (Rushefsky 2008, 187–89), major doubt also exists on how to control program costs in the future. The effort to restructure health care involves factors such as the uncertainties of regulation, managed care organizational behavior, and the effects of privatization options on health care costs and service coverage. The outcomes of various solutions to these subproblems are less predictable, making the overall social insurance problem moderately well structured.

Ill-Structured Problems

The more typical and potentially dangerous problems are ill structured, meaning that they involve "many different decision-makers whose utilities (values) are either unknown or impossible to rank in a consistent fashion" (Dunn 2008, 80). Many of the most important policy problems are ill structured. This means that unfortunately for policy analysis, the right tools and methods cannot be taken off the shelf and neatly applied to good data sets. A good example of an ill-structured problem is tobacco smoking. Should it be regulated? How should it be regulated? This is a multidimensional problem involving major health consequences, producer needs, restaurant interests, potential links to more dangerous drugs, and attendant social effects. The problem can also be broken down functionally into overlapping and potentially contradictory organizational responsibilities for each of the component parts of the problem.

Political science, public administration, and other related disciplines teach us that well-structured and moderately structured problems are rarely present in complex governmental settings. One of the main tasks of policy analysis, therefore, is the resolution of ill-structured problems (Dunn 2008, 80). Ill-structured problems are not simply those caused by such difficulties as the inability to forecast the precise demand for program services. Many programs, like hospital care, for example, respond to varying volumes of often uncontrolled demand. This has been a problem with Britain's National Health Service, which provides most medical care at little or no cost. Such a program differs from those with controlled demand, where response is based on programmed resources, such as miles of roads to be maintained (though a harsh winter that destroys roads can change the demand from controlled and forecast to uncontrolled).

Similarly, programs like mass transit face both types of demand. The presence of the sub-problem of excess traffic congestion (measured by average road density and speed of traffic), together with widely varying fuel prices, can generate largely unpredictable demand for transit in some cities. Municipal bus and rail authorities must try to deliver fixed levels of service, at high fixed costs, often with variable fare structures, to passengers whose demand schedules also respond to price changes in comparison to the apparently cheap option of driving (because the price elasticity of demand is high for transit in contrast to other services such as education).

While ill-structured problems create difficulties for budget programming, they are technically no different from known and structured problems. The development and use of accurate forecasting methodologies, as will be explained in chapter 4, can render these problems manageable from the perspective of resource efficiency. An additional variable in dealing with ill-structured problems is that they usually cut across institutional lines. The problems themselves may be technically simple but institutionally messy. Multiple institutional responsibilities for such areas as mine safety can produce different problem definitions that dilute both accountability and responsibility for policy execution, through various forms of shirking behavior. In other areas, regulatory agencies such as the Federal Aviation Agency may have multiple conflicting responsibilities (air traffic promotion versus air safety regulation) that can compromise policy results. In many cases, because of opposing client pressures on responsible institutions, there are major disincentives for these actors to define problems as clearly or as objectively as possible.

For example, the Anti-Drug Abuse Act of 1986 (then-President Reagan's new drug policy) attempted to define and resolve a major ill-structured problem, drug abuse. First, in the drug abuse area there are very few agreed-upon societal values, only those of conflicting individuals and groups. All constituencies (except suppliers) would like to see drug use reduced, but consensus largely ends there. For example, even a shared understanding of addiction is elusive. Do drugs give addicts a habit, or do addicts make a habit of drugs? It may be that addiction is related to a damaging mix of biochemistry and bad social conditions.

Despite the difficulty of neatly structuring the drug abuse problem and the lack of consensus on basic concepts, the bulk of the proposed $1.7 billion drug budget for fiscal year (FY) 1986 (65%, or $1.04 billion) flowed to enforcement, and only 27.5% (or $441 million) was allocated to educational and drug-treatment activities (Brinkley 1986). For comparative purposes, the $17.1 billion FY 1999 request for the overall federal drug control policy allocated $11.1 billion (66%) for enforcement or "supply reduction," and only $6.5 billion (or 34%) for "demand reduction" (Office of National Drug Control Policy 1998, 16). Roughly the same allocation exists in 2009: The Office of National Drug Control Policy (ONDCP) spends 65% of its $12 billion budget on supply-side or enforcement efforts, and only 35% on demand-side prevention and treatment (Maru 2009). While the categories are somewhat confusing ("supply reduction" via the threat of law enforcement also reduces demand), the resultant allocation of funds in both years (which are ten years apart) suggests continuing major differences in both perspective and power resources among actors involved in the formulation of drug policy. Since 1996 the major goal of the national drug control strategy has focused on prevention efforts among youths. Policy analysts advocate rebalancing the national drug budget. Anti-drug war "doves," for example, cite the Rand Corporation study that concluded that treatment is seven times more effective than enforcement in reducing cocaine consumption, and twenty-three times more effective than destroying foreign drug sources (*The Economist* 1999a, 73–74).

Second, in general, policymakers tend to maximize their own values along with key client groups and are not motivated to act on the basis of societal preferences or develop policies to maximize marginal social benefits over costs. Over the past several decades, prospects for substantial antidrug enforcement money quickly turned the chance for a coordinated policy into a gold rush, resulting in predictable turf battles between the US Customs Service and the Coast Guard, both of which then wanted new radar planes from the Senate (Brinkley 1986). Many of these turf battles now continue within the new structure of the Department of Homeland Security (DHS). Thus, any technical difficulties in defining the drug policy problem were overwhelmed by bureaucratic infighting related to available funding. Failure to control the institutional environment through strong policy leadership resulted in misdefinition of the problem, which predictably has led to continued enforcement failures. Institutional inertia ensured that despite evidence of policy failure, this definition remained constant, driving both future drug policies and expenditures. The current climate of revenue scarcity, increasing costs of incarceration, and continued evidence of the failure of supply-side enforcement has produced a new consensus to develop demand-side policies, reduce the harshness of drug laws, and make a rational drug policy (Will 2009).

Third, it follows that commitment of resources to existing policies and programs (based on problem definitions seemingly immune to facts) prevents policymakers from considering new alternatives. This is partly a fixed-cost or sunk-cost budget problem that is exacerbated by an incremental budget process that commits or recycles about 70–80% of the annual base to the next budget year. Most of it is already committed when the formulation process begins. Failure to analyze programs and policies from a "zero" base is part of the problem. Mostly, the uncontrolled, high fixed-cost budget is a problem of scarce time allotted by the budget calendar for analysis and diagnosis. It is also a problem of lack of political will, which derives from intense client pressures to continue programs. For instance, current drug policies are supported by prison construction firms, zero-tolerance groups, and legislators who claim to their constituents that passage of strict laws is equivalent to policy results. This distorted factual context provides real little incentive for analysis of policies that could absorb the remaining 20–30% of funds to use for new initiatives. More powerful stakeholders in the annual budget process are able to lock in expenditure preferences (legally through earmarks, permanent appropriations, or entitlements). These provisions cannot be easily changed because they are permanent law. In Latin American countries and many US states, sectoral expenditure shares are actually mandated by laws and constitutions. This is especially common for health and education services. These are the longer-term policy drivers that work against institutional change and redefinition of policy problems. Try to change them by next fiscal year! The same pattern of expenditure mandates recurs in federal, state, and local government policy processes, removing the bulk of items from policymaker discretion. In this way, the politics of the budget process determines much of the content of public policy.

The problem of perceived political mandates is related to budget mandates. Policymakers make laws and policies (rationally) on the basis of perceived constituent demands, thus driving out policy analysis from the process. As will be discussed further in this chapter's case study, strict enforcement of marijuana laws may paradoxically be driving people to use cocaine and more harmful drugs. Zero-tolerance laws and harsh sentencing for possession of marijuana have increased the risks of cultivation, and this has encouraged growers to produce more potent strains of the drug that bring a higher price with a lower volume of sales (Schlosser 1997, 99). Consistent with basic market economy principles, price increases can lead to gains in producer efficiency. Producers respond to higher prices with investment in more modern equipment for cultivation and transport of drugs, leading to increased competitiveness and greater profitability for the illegal enterprise. Moreover, suppliers prefer cocaine because it is easy to conceal and transport, and its prices are much higher than prices for marijuana, which is bulky and harder to transport. By contrast, enforcers prefer marijuana because its bulk looks impressive before the cameras, and seizure of a few tons increases productivity measures at lower risk than for cocaine. Superficially, program performance measured in tons per seizure for marijuana is higher than for low-bulk but high-enforcement-risk cocaine. Thus, according to law enforcement experts, enforcement of marijuana laws contributes to higher marijuana prices and lower supplies, which drive people to harder drugs (Lindsey 1986). In this context, the 1986 recommendation of Georgia's attorney general to make possession of marijuana a felony instead of a misdemeanor (Hopkins 1986) can be viewed as either the selection of an inappropriate solution contrary to valid and reliable data on policy impact, or simply part of the rush by elected officials racing to "get tough on criminals." Based on available evidence, such a law would increase the use of hard drugs and make enforcement even more difficult. The "get tough" approach exemplified by zero tolerance effectively defines an ill-structured problem as a simple enforcement matter. It also has the effect of criminalizing otherwise law-abiding citizens (including the current president), stimulating gangsterism on a world scale (*The Economist* 2009a), and even driving some children to suicide (Fisher 2009a). By intensifying needless shame and self-doubt, zero-tolerance laws ostracize and isolate many of the best junior and senior high school students unlucky enough to be caught by zealous administrators. Stigmatized as reprobates with no apparent futures, they are often driven to suicide.

These institutional features, together with policymakers' inability to collect enough information on all possible alternatives or predict the range of consequences associated with each alternative, render the ill-structured problem largely immune from conventional definitional techniques. When dealing with the most common types of policy problems, we have to make difficult choices about both methods and facts in order to maintain our credibility as policy analysts. The wrong method or model can select the wrong facts and give us the right solution to the wrong problem (e.g., the crop-eradication or "technical fix" model as a solution to the problem of cultivating cocaine in Bolivia, when definition of the problem should include the dimensions of local power elites and the high demand for cocaine in the United States). Despite these obstacles, let us turn to a "best available" methodology for defining an ill-structured problem.

METHODOLOGIES FOR PROBLEM DEFINITION

"I mentioned to you that a grand vision has certain components. . . . One of them is scale. Don't send me dross. No grapeshot. Not 'Here, Scottie, take this bag of bones and see what your analysts make of it.' Do you follow me?"

"Not quite sir."

"The analysts here are idiots. They don't make connections. They don't see shapes forming in the sky. A man reaps as he sows. Do you understand me? A great intelligencer catches history in the act. We can't expect some nine-to-five fellow on the third floor who's worried about his mortgage to catch history in the act. Can we? It takes a man of vision to catch history in the act. Does it not?"

— *John Le Carré,* The Tailor of Panama

Of the eight universal techniques of problem structuring discussed by Dunn (2008, 95–115), six that can help analysts avoid sending "grapeshot" to their superiors will be examined here. Like other policy analytic procedures, they tend to yield results that are plausible but uncertain. Policy analysts will select from them based typically on the amount of time available for reaching a solution and the analytic capacity for problem definition. These techniques will be useful as the basis for our next step in the process, forecasting policy options (see chapter 4). Let us now review these methods and see how they can be applied to our case in this chapter.

Boundary Analysis

To be certain that one is defining the whole problem, one needs methods to establish boundaries. To define the scope of the problem, the analyst should employ broad survey techniques, review pertinent data, conduct field inspections, and master the special nomenclature associated with that particular policy area. Like a good journalist checking alternative sources to ensure that nothing major has been left out of the story, the policy analyst may employ three procedures.

First, there should be "saturation sampling," which consists of contacting stakeholders by telephone or personal interview and asking them to name additional stakeholders. Stakeholders should include dissident groups of administrators that are often excluded from defining problems. Saturation sampling is continued until no new stakeholders are named. This method also

provides a list of the key influences in policymaking and can be used to estimate their influence in actual problem definition.

Second, analysts can elicit descriptions of the problem from sampled
stakeholders, whose perspectives will vary widely. This technique has been
repeatedly used in an attempt to achieve consensus among stakeholders on a
definition of the forest policy problem in Costa Rica. Earlier efforts in this area
had found that there were major definitional differences among stakeholders.
These included factors such as high rural population growth, the absence of
logging regulation to ensure sustained yields, the lack of a national policy to
protect tropical forest resources, the absence of fiscal incentives to the forest-
based industry, a high US beef import quota that encouraged pasture expansion and burning of forests, and lack of a regulatory framework and lead
enforcement department at the national level (Guess 1979). Problem definition was dominated then as now by the powerful beef-cattle industry, which in
self-serving fashion defined tropical forest elimination as the inevitable effect
of normal expansion of the agricultural frontier. This definition produced a *non-
policy*, or policy vacuum, on several fronts. It perpetuated major loss of tropical
forest resources and associated jobs and income opportunities for the rural poor
of Costa Rica. In eliciting problem representations, the analyst should avoid
"positive hearing," in which "words are put into people's mouths that they
would have said if they'd thought of them at the time" (Le Carré 1996, 277).
Despite the assurance by Le Carré's character that "everybody does it anyway,"
the analyst must guard against the use of positive hearing in interviews (278).

Third, the analyst can estimate boundaries by constructing a frequency
distribution, with cumulative new concepts and problem representations elicited from stakeholders on the vertical axis arrayed against the number of policy
stakeholders on the horizontal axis. When the number of new representations
tapers off, the curve will flatten, indicating the probable boundary of the problem (Dunn 2008, 98).

Classification Analysis

In this technique, the analyst tries to divide up the apparent problem into components to facilitate analysis and the design of remedial actions. Based on
straightforward data classification principles from statistics, analysts break
down problems into logical component parts and classify persons or objects
into larger groups or classes. The rules for both procedures are well known.
There are no absolute guidelines on correct perception of policy problems, but
classifications should be relevant and logically consistent (Dunn 2008, 99).

First, the classification should be relevant. The categories should be designed with action and performance in mind. To this end, in chapter 6 we employ decision analysis to structure a cost-effectiveness problem. Often, analysts engineer major classification efforts that are not relevant to improved decision making. A common problem with many program-budgeting exercises to improve policy results, for example, has been the emphasis on rigid accounting classification of linkages between agency workloads and expected results. The purposes of these exercises are related to accounting and control rather than reprogramming funds to solve policy problems for which the agency was created (e.g., health, education). The emphasis so far has been on research linking levels of expenditure to policy results through yield coefficients or other mathematical relations that are, at best, theoretical in the real world of budget changes. The classifications often yield knowledge for its own sake rather than decisive action. Given the action-oriented and deadline-driven nature of the agency environment, the results of program classification exercises are rarely used in practice, while the exercise itself is often deemed to be a waste of time by practitioners.

Even though classifications need to be relevant, there are no firm guidelines for relevance. One important caution is that the classification should clearly flow from the analyst's views of the causes of the problem. This will allow for transparency of assumptions and avoid narrow definitions of problems. For example, different classifications of poverty problems can be derived from causal assumptions that it is a problem of inadequate income, cultural deprivation, or psychological motivation. Should the analyst focus on only one type of classification, contrary assumptions are ignored, and that can lead to the formulation of flawed policies. Ignoring relevant data may also lead to faulty explanations of poverty rates (e.g., among the elderly and disabled versus families with children) and a corresponding inability to explain groups' differential access to program benefits with cuts in federal Medicaid expenditures (Johnson 1997, 15). Failure to classify data relevantly and to make underlying assumptions explicit can produce erroneous policies.

Second, categories in the classification system should be exhaustive. That is, all subjects should fit into one category or another. If they do not, one must create new categories. They should be mutually exclusive, that is, with subjects assigned to only one category to avoid double counting. Finally, the subjects should be consistent: each category and subcategory should be based on a single classification principle. Otherwise, subclasses will overlap—as in classifying a family according to whether it is above the poverty line or receiving welfare payments (Dunn 2008, 100). Since the same family could be in both categories, the categories are inconsistent. Classification analysis is aided by the use of diagrams and classification schemes to present categories in visual form. Pictures often lead to questions and linkages that can be hidden by language. Diagrams reveal hidden assumptions and facilitate problem definition.

Causal Analysis

The rules guiding causal analysis are the same as those used for classification analysis: relevance, exhaustiveness, mutual exclusiveness, and consistency. The basic purpose here is to identify the controlling variables (Lehan 1984, 74) or those factors that if significantly altered would decisively affect the problem (e.g., jail overcrowding, nutrition status of the elderly, or poverty). From controlling variables it is more feasible to establish objectives and specify performance criteria. Causal or "hierarchy" analysis allows the analyst to distinguish causes from symptoms and to organize data in categories that indicate the differences among the three major kinds of causes, as follows (Dunn 2008, 102–5).

First, *possible* causes are those that are remote but contribute to the occurrence of the problem. Studies linking elite power structures and official conspiracies to the persistence of poverty are satisfying and make riveting tales, but are *actionable* only on the macro-revolutionary level. In most societies this means either a long-term solution—or a very short one! In other cases, the persistent political influence of certain interest groups leads to consistent policy definitions and solutions (e.g., builders and contractors advocate capital expenditure solutions for roaming dogs). Revision of policy and budget formulation processes to include wider public participation is a medium-term solution to deal with more remote or *possible* problems like this.

Second, *plausible* causes are those that are proximate and have been empirically linked. These are the controlling variables that should be actionable in the short run. For example, studies have linked poverty with resistance to work. If the causation is valid, one policy solution would be to use workfare incentive programs with tight monitoring standards and controls; the presumed incentives would be both monetary and nonmonetary (self-esteem). Other studies have found that health coverage for the elderly and access to Medicaid assistance was often provided at the expense of another class of poor people: families with children. A policy solution might be to expand Medicaid coverage to women with children. The results could be improvements in health care equity but at the price of higher program costs (Johnson 1997, 20). In fact, states now have the option to provide in-kind assistance through the flexible Medicaid block grant structure to poor women with children

(Fisher 2007, 600). While equity has improved, Medicaid costs and expenditures have increased as predicted, but not simply because of this limited program expansion.

Similarly, data indicate that the increased incidence of roaming dogs can be linked to both a logistical problem—inefficient impoundment and absence of pound space—and to weak regulatory enforcement, such as the absence of owner incentives to license and control dogs (Lehan 1984, 74). In the health care area, studies have shown that higher fees for hospital and clinic services are associated with reduced demand (a 1% increase in fees reduces demand by 0.3%, which is roughly the same price elasticity of demand as for urban transit) (*The Economist* 1997e, 84). But studies also link higher fees (plausible causes) to higher rates of certain diseases and the possible spread of contagious diseases. This suggests that the problem should be defined to include the plausible impact of fees on both system cost recovery and on poorer groups.

In their quest for plausible causes, analysts have had difficulty distinguishing causality from correlation. To deal with this problem, policy analysts search for an instrumental variable. This variable acts as a proxy for one variable in statistical analysis but is unrelated to the others. For example, in examining the relationship between imprisonment and reduced crime, it is difficult to find much of an effect due to increased incarceration. Increased incarceration could even lead to increased crime through the unintended effect of a convict absorbing collegial training during his or her sentence. But suppose there is another variable related to incarceration that is unrelated to crime rates? Use of an instrumental variable, in this case litigation over prison overcrowding, might clarify the causal relationship between incarceration and crime rates. Using data from 1973 to 1997, researchers found that where litigation is filed and prison populations fall, crime rates increase (*The Economist* 1998d). Finding an instrumental variable in such litigation over prison crowding can strengthen the relationship between the other variables. This technique illustrates the need for the creative use of both empirical analysis and multidisciplinary approaches to problem definition.

Third, *actionable* causes are those that are subject to manipulation by policymakers in the short or medium term. Thus policymakers tend to be interested in both plausible and actionable causes. The purpose of causal analysis is to make decisions based on identification of plausible and actionable causes. Both construction of a dog pound and improved regulations targeting stray dogs are short-term solutions based on actionable causal analysis. Setting alternative fees for health care or bus trips are based on similarly actionable causes to change the behavior of patients or bus riders. The two options for responding to the stray dog problem are favored by different stakeholders, but they also differ politically in that the regulatory approach is a longer-term solution with potential risks of failure, whereas the pound solution is short term and leads to a brand-new building that can provide photo opportunities for leaders. Similarly, with empirical evidence of the effects of health fees on user behavior (based on the price elasticities of demand for different treatments), policies can focus on avoiding harm to sick people who are also poor, thus making hospitals more cost-efficient and pushing doctors to consider costs when prescribing tests and treatments.

Causal analysis also requires consideration of the unintended consequences of otherwise logical policy choices. This is easier said than done—consequences are often unpredictable. Federal prison reforms of 1976 that allowed inmates to write to each other created the structures that later evolved into organized prison gangs (*The Economist* 1998a). Cell phones have now replaced letters as the organizational tool of choice in prison. As an example, suppose again that the policy objective is to reduce the number of stray dogs. Analysis reveals that the option of reducing the number of strays through the construction of a pound could result in more stray or itinerant dogs unless owner behavior is also regulated. That means that regulation and construction should not be viewed as singular and mutually exclusive causes, leading to either-or policies. All relevant policy assumptions and causes need to be reviewed to properly define the problem. Dunn (2008, 104, citing Nagel and Neef 1976) provides the example of pretrial release as a favored policy to reduce jail overcrowding in the United States. Based on a simple causal explanation, the policy overlooks the possible effect of plea bargaining on jail overcrowding. If pretrial release leads to reduced plea bargains, the waiting time for trials may increase, which leads to more overcrowding. Failure to include an additional plausible cause in the matrix leads to a policy with major unintended negative consequences.

Use of Analogies

This tool draws on comparative experience to structure policy problems. Studies repeatedly show that policymakers tend to ignore both past similar problems that could contain lessons for the present and current similar problems experienced by neighboring jurisdictions. Many sound policies are developed through comparative analysis of the experiences of other similar jurisdictions: The Washington, DC, homicide unit used this technique in its recentralization effort, which was linked with later increases in crime-clearance rates; and the United States has looked to California and Massachusetts to determine the impact of universal health insurance and managed care. The United States is still looking for a successful model of health care cost control in a large country! Countries such as Canada and Switzerland are excellent models for expanded coverage but do not control their costs measurably better than the current US system. Tendencies to think that problems are new or must be solved alone ignore the significance of past efforts to grapple with similar issues. For example, over several decades many cities and states have attempted to reform their public budgeting systems, converting them from input to output program measurement tools for management control and policy planning. Many jurisdictions made the same mistakes, overemphasizing technical measurement and fixed definitions of programs and subprograms. In the quest for superficial technical reform, leaders often ignored line management incentives or the authority needed to manage any program. They also ignored legislative interest in object-of-expenditure or line-item formats. Many failures have resulted. The availability of nonthreatening institutional advice from such professional associations as the Government Finance Officers Association and the International City Management Association might have helped penetrate the thicket of isolated policymaking among self-sealing organizations. Demand for comparative reform lessons would have allowed city officials to draw upon the technical experience of their associates in neighboring jurisdictions and to avoid the same costly errors.

Similarly, recent experience with civil service reform policies at the state and local level reveals that they are designed and implemented largely in isolation. Factors such as the unintended negative consequences of downsizing on staff morale, downstream budgetary costs, performance of private contractors, and service delivery quality have been ignored, despite the availability of substantial comparative information on the dimensions of the problem. What this suggests is that in many cases, reforms solve either the wrong problem or one without any basis in practical reality. That these reform efforts fail should not be surprising; that they keep failing again and again in different contexts is consistent with Brown's definition of insanity: repeating the same action and expecting a different result (1983, 68)! When Gulliver visited the Grand Academy of Lagade, which was filled with mad scientists, he found one scientist had spent eight years trying to extract sunbeams from cucumbers. The scientist vowed to succeed in eight more (*The Economist* 2009b)! More recently, journalists and news media have intervened to serve as suppliers of comparative information on such problems as how to cut the size of government, how to privatize, how to stimulate public productivity, and how to measure service delivery effectiveness and develop incentives to improve delivery of certain services.

Finally, many cities have reduced crime rates by restructuring and reorganizing their police departments. In contrast, the Washington, DC, police department ignored most of these lessons for problem structuring. With problems similar to those of Washington, New York City decentralized accountability and authority to its seventy-six precinct commanders and now holds them accountable for results. Boston targets gang crime by including unarmed probation officers on police patrols—this is significant because the officers need no "probable cause" to stop juvenile offenders suspected of violating their terms of probation. And, as part of its community policing program, Chicago's computerized mapping system generates maps of crime to allow police to share information with communities (Harlan 1997).

As suggested by Dunn (2008, 106), policymakers may produce at least four types of analogies to aid in structuring policy problems. First, one can use personal analogies by putting oneself in the position of a stakeholder or client in order to uncover political dimensions. Being in the position of a bus rider who is dependent on public transportation, for example, can reveal the intensity of political opposition to major cuts in bus-rail service and elimination of routes. These were dilemmas faced by policymakers in Miami and Washington, DC. Miami (Metro-Dade County) wanted to eliminate at least ten of its seventy-eight routes and reduce service on fifty-six others, as well as reduce rail service, as part of its FY 1998 budget plan (Vigliucci and Epstein 1997). Despite any technical arguments for fiscal savings, poorer riders were trapped by constraints of distance and time and could not afford cars; therefore, by failing to use personal analogies to reveal the unintended consequence of cutting such bus lines, policymakers risked reducing overall ridership and increasing incentives for car ownership that would further clog already overcrowded roads. In fiscal terms, the short-term savings might lead to longer-term transit system losses, because public funds would then have to be spent for more roads and additional subsidies to cover operating losses of transit systems.

Second, one can use direct analogies by finding similar relationships between two or more problem situations. In structuring problems of drug addiction, for example, analysts may construct direct analogies from experiences with control of contagious diseases (Dunn 2008, 106). Third, policy analysts like to employ symbolic analogies, using such mechanisms as thermostats, electrical circuits, hydraulic systems, ecological systems, and automatic pilots. As indicated in chapter 1, the policy process itself is frequently characterized as an imbalanced ecological system, facing difficult issues in problem formulation, analysis, policy implementation, control, and evaluation. The integrated financial management system described in chapter 3 is also based on a systems analogy. As noted, the systems analogy is flawed in the minds of some, who argue that all components are not equal and that the budgetary allocation in real political systems is the most important function in the system. But use of the analogy allows one to clarify these arguments and narrow the range of disagreement among specialists.

Finally, analysts can use fantasy or fantastic analogies that explore similarities between problem situations and some imaginary state (Dunn 2008, 106). Defense analysts like fantastic analogies. It may be that the problem structuring of the Iraq war and the current analyses of Iran that favor taking out multiple nuclear targets suffer from fantasy, in the sense that probable costs and likely unintended consequences are ignored in favor of fantastic benefits: democracy, stability, etc. To date, no one at the Pentagon has admitted to using fantasy analogies. Sensibly, they would prefer to call the method *direct* analogy.

Brainstorming

This technique is widely used to generate ideas and goals that help identify and conceptualize problems (Dunn 2008, 107). It is one of many types of techniques that attempt to use conflict creatively in structuring policy problems. It is used as much in analysis of film scripts and other artistic endeavors as in the formulation of technical policy solutions. Note that previously discussed techniques rely more on more rational, empirical-technical foundations. This technique focuses on group dynamics and seeks the creative dimensions of problem definition to forge more innovative and effective policies. A similar group approach, such as the Delphi technique, can be used to critique policy solutions, such as alternate revenue forecasts and scenarios, as well as for initial problem definitions. This will be discussed briefly in chapter 4. There are several major guidelines in conducting successful brainstorming. First, groups should be composed of experts from various professions who are knowledgeable about the sources of public dissatisfaction on an issue. Second, it is very important that idea generation, or the free-form phase, and idea evaluation, or the critical phase, should be kept separate (Dunn 2008, 107). This is a common guideline in scriptwriting that is used to avoid eliminating potentially useful insights and sound ideas that more timid analysts might be afraid to express for fear of criticism. It should be used in technical policy analysis to define problems as well. The generation-versus-evaluation structure is designed to avoid premature criticism and debate that can exclude dimensions of policy problems, such as the potential effects of plea bargaining on jail overcrowding.

Assumptional Analysis

Assumptional analysis is a technique that is explicitly designed for ill-structured problems, in which multiple self-contained organizations are involved in sequential policymaking over time and in which the analyst must include other public policies that may affect problem definition. It attempts to synthesize conflicting assumptions about policy problems (Dunn 2008, 111). An example of other policies that might affect problem definition is the mandatory minimum sentencing laws for hard drug abuse that discriminate against African Americans and tend to fill up prisons (*Washington Post* 1997). In such cases, the analyst enters the actual fray needing to learn how assumptions have changed, along with problem definition actors, acronyms, and the real limits that any policy will face no matter how the problem is defined. For this, the policy analyst must have a strong sense of historical connections, be a good storyteller, and perhaps have an absurdist, Kafkaesque sense of humor to guard against being overwhelmed by petty detail.

As with brainstorming, the creative use of conflict can ferret out and challenge assumptions. But unlike previously described techniques, assumptional analysis begins with the policies recommended. The analyst reviews identified stakeholders and works backward from recommended solutions to supporting data and assumptions. When coupled with the data, the assumptions should allow stakeholders to deduce the policies recommended. Explicit specification of problems and assumptions with the same data set allows one to test the reliability of problem definitions and policy recommendations. This technique encourages participants to systematically compare assumptions and counterassumptions (e.g., poverty is caused by lack of income or by psychological deprivation). With synthesis of assumptions either the problem definition is verified in its original form or revised.

Table 2.1 summarizes the methods covered in this chapter for problem definition and provides a brief checklist of factors to consider.

This chapter has focused on structuring policy problems and provided methods for doing that. Identification of a problem and assigning it to policymaking processes and institutions for implementation are separate activities. Stakeholders have to first agree that a problem is in fact a public problem and is worth tackling. Rising global carbon dioxide emissions, for example, is a worthwhile international public problem. But stakeholders also have to agree on how to share remedial costs—meaning an international agreement and actual implementation policies (*The Economist* 2009e, 11). These are difficult methodological and institutional steps! Regardless of whether a problem is well or ill structured, for instance, it may be politically more feasible to unpack

Table 2.1   Problem-Definition Methods

Methods	Factors to Consider
Boundary Analysis	Saturation sampling
	Elicit representations from competing stakeholders
	Construct frequency distribution of new representations
Classification Analysis	Categories relevant to decision making
	Categories exhaustive and mutually exclusive
Causal Analysis	Identify controlling variables
	Distinguish possible (remote) from plausible (proximate) causes
	Focus on actionable causes
	Distinguish short-, medium-, and long-term effects
	Consider unintended consequences of multiple causes
Use of Analogies	Personal impact (e.g., bus service cuts)
	Direct comparison of how related programs treat causes (e.g., contagious diseases)
	Symbolic (e.g., use of systems, circuits for symbols of policy process; triangles for organizational structures)
Brainstorming	Recruit knowledgeable experts on issue
	In group process, separate idea generation from idea evaluation phase
Assumptional Analysis	Start with recommended policies
	Work backward from solutions to stakeholders, data, and supporting assumptions
	For lack of congruence, critically review linkage between policies, data, and assumptions

a problem and solve it incrementally. A major intent of the Kyoto protocol was to provide a decision framework that would solve the carbon problem with a single set of numbers: national caps that would cut all greenhouse gases. This approach is now viewed as a failure in that it tackled the carbon problem holistically when a more incremental or piecemeal method might have produced more results. By contrast, the Montreal protocol of 1987 focused on chlorofluorocarbons (CFCs). It cut all of them in ten years and prevented 189 billion tons of carbon dioxide emissions (compared to only 10 billion tons prevented by Kyoto) (*The Economist* 2009c, 21). In general, since most policy problems are complex and ill structured, a more effective means of solution would be to divide them up or unpack them and solve each one incrementally.

Chapter 2 Case Study

Fighting Crime: The Case for Emptier Prisons

America now imprisons more people than Russia. According to Walmsley (2005, cited in Rushefsky 2008, 260), 714 out of every 100,000 Americans are behind bars. And although blacks comprise only 13% of the population, they account for 40.7% of the country's 2.1 million inmates (Harrison and Beck 2005). That is an increase in incarceration of 130% from 1980 to 1990 and 60% from 1990 to 2004 (Walmsley 2005).

It is true that the United States has more crime than other countries, and that black Americans commit too much of it. But these two factors do not explain everything. Black Americans commit about the same share of violent crime as they did in 1976, and the total crime rate has actually fallen since 1973. Total violent crimes and total victimizations in 2004 were lower than in 1973. The total number of violent crimes in 2004 was only about 45% of the 1973 number. Since the population of the United States increased in the same period, the crime rate has declined even faster (Rushefsky 2008, 260). Nevertheless, over this period, the number of inmates has tripled, and the proportion of black prisoners has increased.

Why, then, do Americans continue to vote for those who vow to lock yet more people away? One reason is that fear of crime does not diminish even when the incidence of crime falls. If one selects different base years, the violent crime rate has increased (14.3% from 1973 to 1981) and increased again (6.7% from 1982 to 1993). But this would be misleading for present policy analysis, in that the overall violent crime rate actually dropped 54% (1973–2004) (Rushefsky 2008, 253, citing US Department of Justice Statistics [BJS] 2005). The rate may have dropped from the deterrent effect of an increase in the rate of arrests compared to total victimizations and reported crimes (Rushefsky 2008, 252). Regardless of the explanation, the overall rate has dropped significantly. Law-abiding people naturally want murderers, rapists, and muggers caged. But this does not explain why the prison population has risen almost ten times faster than the rate of violent crime.

It is not crime that has changed, but punishment. A study of why the prison population has grown attributed about a third of the growth to demographics, the increase in violent crime, more arrests, and longer sentences (cited in *The Economist* 2009a, 71). The other two-thirds came from jailing people for offenses that would not have required prison sentences in the past. In particular, the war on drugs has crammed America's prisons with nonviolent petty criminals. The

US government spends $40 billion a year trying to eliminate the supply of drugs. Each year, all levels of American government together arrest 1.5 million drug offenders, of whom 500,000 are incarcerated. Tougher drug laws are the main reason why one in five black men will spend time in jail (*The Economist* 2009b, 15). In all, the number of people imprisoned for drug offenses tripled between 1986 and 1991, and has continued to grow since; in Washington state, the number of prisoners in for drug crimes has risen almost 1,000% since 1980. California has 170,000 inmates, of whom about 20% are serving time for drug-related crimes (*The Economist* 2009a, 71). One in one hundred Americans is in jail; one in thirty-one is in prison, on parole, or on probation. Michigan spends 22% of its general fund budget on corrections. The program is growing faster than any other except Medicare (which is the fastest growing component of overall state and local spending) (*The Economist* 2009c, 36). Rushefsky asserts that "It would be harder to think of an area of US social policy that has failed more completely than the war on drugs" (2008, 280).

As a result of tough laws incarcerating drug offenders, violent criminals are a decreasing share of the prison population. In 1991, according to the Cato Institute, only one out of five drug offenders in state prisons, and one out of three in federal ones, had a violent history. And the increasing number of drug offenders in prison comes at a time when the use of all illegal drugs is lower than it has been for years, although it remains high in the inner cities.

Black Americans have been disproportionately hit by the war on drugs because they tend to commit the wrong kinds of drug crimes. For example, under federal law the possession of five grams of cocaine powder is a misdemeanor that carries a maximum prison sentence of one year. Possession of five grams of crack cocaine, though, is a felony that carries a mandatory five-year sentence. Blacks are much more likely to smoke crack. In percentage of estimated use, blacks use more than three times the percentage of crack than whites (1.6% to 0.5%) (Rushefsky 2008, 283). The result is a large increase in the number of blacks in prison.

Indeterminate sentencing gives discretion to parole boards, which can reward good behavior and help with overcrowding by reducing inmates' prison time. In 1976, California switched to determinate sentencing. This reflects a philosophy of deterrence and means that prison time is fixed, regardless of good behavior (*The Economist* 2009d, 28). Such determinate or mandatory minimum sentences, at both the federal and the state level, are filling up prisons faster than new ones can be built; more than a dozen states also have three-strikes rules that require long prison stretches for a third felony. The 1995 California law (passed by voter referendum) is the largest and toughest mandatory sentencing law in the United States. Since crime rates were falling before the law was passed, its effect on crime rates is debatable. The law does lengthen the average prison sentence and raise the average age of inmates, costing the state an additional $500 million a year (*The Economist* 2009e, 38). California has passed around one thousand laws mandating tougher sentencing and spends $49,000 per prisoner each year. Mandatory sentences are crude policy tools. In particular, they do not distinguish between levels of seriousness of different types of crime; the federal minimum sentence for possession of a small amount of LSD is ten years, much more than for kidnapping, rape, or attempted murder. California has the worst recidivism rate in the nation (70% compared to the national average of 40%) (*The Economist* 2009d, 28).

The basic aim of the war on drugs has been to remove anyone involved in the drug trade from the street to the cells. Yet demand for drugs remains high in the inner cities, and the history of the trade demonstrates that *supply always meets demand.* Locking up a drug courier does not mean there is one less courier at large: only that an aspiring, often underage, one gets his chance.

Mandatory minimums thus do not inhibit the operations of the drug trade; but they ensure that lots of nonviolent, low-level drug offenders sit in prison for a long time. In 1990, almost 90% of first-time drug offenders in federal courts went to prison, with an average sentence of more than five years. First-time violent offenders went to jail less often and for shorter periods. No wonder the proportion of drug prisoners in federal prisons keeps on rising.

Much of this rampant incarceration is pointless. Drug users do not need to spend five years in jail to know they have offended: Like most petty criminals, most grow out of their bad habits quickly enough. Besides, most give up crime, and hardly anyone starts, after the age of 30. But mandatory sentences mean that more minor villains will stay in prison well past their criminal prime. Spending $40,000 to $50,000 a year for each increasingly creaky inmate is a waste of money that could be better spent on deterring the dangerous young.

The United States is good, and getting better, at locking up the worst and most incorrigible criminals. But it casts too wide a net. The 1995 crime bill, with its proposed $12.2 billion in prison construction and extension of mandatory sentences, was very much in this mold. More recently, 65% of the 2006 Office of National Drug Control Policy budget is allocated to supply-side enforcement, which means increased incarceration rates and more public spending (for often privately operated state prisons) (Maru 2009). There have to be better and more creative ways of dealing with many criminal misfits.

One would be to try to cut the demand for drugs, rather than the supply. The latter has never worked, as the stable or falling street price of drugs makes clear. In 1999, a gram of cocaine cost $142 on the street; in 2006 the price had fallen to only $94 per gram (Maru 2009). Trend analysis of cocaine prices depends often on base years selected and avoidance of interpreting single data spikes. For instance, DEA reports that cocaine prices increased in 2007–08 from $100 to $200 per gram on the street, which may have been due to the Mexican crackdown on drug gangs and consequent interruption of supply (*The Economist* 2009f, 43). Nevertheless, longer-term price trends are downward, and the argument for alternatives to incarceration is empirically strong. A Rand Corporation study found that $1 of drug treatment lowers consumption as much as $7 worth of law enforcement does. Treatment can lower the volume of drugs consumed; the less consumption, the fewer drug-related crimes.

There is also a case for insisting on prison for violent first-time offenders and tougher treatment for violent juveniles. A study by the National Bureau of Economic Research found that the cost of locking up a violent criminal was much less than the cost of the mayhem he would probably have committed.

And there is also a case for developing forms of punishment that stop short of prison. Technical parole or probation violations, such as being caught drinking or in the wrong district, are the most common reasons why people go to prison. That can be an overly harsh—and hugely expensive—punishment for people considered nonthreatening enough to be on the streets.

It is not just criminals who are paying an exaggerated price for America's addiction to incarceration. The criminal minority, in effect, consumes an increasingly disproportionate share of the public purse. From 1986 to 2001, state prison expenditures increased 150%, from $11.7 billion to $29.5 billion (BJS 2005). State spending on prisons has increased more than sixfold in real terms since 1979, using money that could have been spent on education, parks, and hospitals. Getting tough on crime is punishing not just the bad guys, but law-abiding citizens as well.

Questions

What is the crime problem? What is the drug problem?

What tools are useful in reaching your definition?

How do different definitions lead to different policy recommendations?

References for the Case Study

The Economist. 2009a. Virtually Legal. November 14.

————. 2009b. How to Stop the Drug Wars. March 7.

————. 2009c. No More Room, No More Money. May 23.

————. 2009d. Gulags in the Sun. August 15.

————. 2009e. A Voice for the Forsaken. June 13.

————. 2009f. Mixed Signals among the Coca Bushes. June 27.

Harrison, Paige M., and Allen J. Beck. 2005. Prisoners in 2002. Washington, DC: Bureau of Justice Statistics.

Maru, Duncan Smith-Rohrberg. 2009. Wasting Drug War Resources. *Washington Post,* November 24.

Rushefsky, Mark E. 2008. *Public Policy in the United States: At the Dawn of the 21st Century.* 4th ed. Armonk, NY: M. E. Sharpe.

Walmsley, Roy. 2005. *World Prison Population List.* 6th ed. London: International Center for Prison Statistics. www.prisonstudies.org.

ANALYSIS OF CHAPTER 2 CASE STUDY

This provides an excellent opportunity to use many of the problem-definition methods noted earlier in this chapter. For example, first, it appears that past policies seem to have been limited by assumptions introduced by analysts themselves (as in the example of the nine-dot problem). Policymakers often imprison themselves by linear thinking. This should encourage creative thinking and the use of assumptional analysis of past problem definitions in order, for instance, to try to reduce prison populations without increasing crime rates. Second, what are the boundaries of this problem? Have all stakeholders been approached and surveyed? Are current policies based on inadequate boundary analysis? Third, does reclassification of convicts lead to new problem definitions? That is, are current policies based on superficial classification of data? Fourth, what are the causes of jail overcrowding? It was noted that earlier analyses revealed missing causal factors, such as plea bargaining (Nagel and Neef 1976). Fifth, what analogies could be used to contribute to a more comprehensive definition of the problem? Is prison overcrowding analogous to other policy problems? Sixth, would brainstorming help? Here, we can propose ideas for discussion and follow with suggestions for their constructive critique and evaluation.

The Boundary Problem and Linear Thinking

In many states in this country, governors proudly proclaim more annual public expenditure for prison construction to deal with the problem of overcrowded prisons. As noted, state prison construction expenditures increased 150% from 1986 to 2001 (US Department of Justice, Bureau of Justice Statistics [BJS] 2005). In addition to the existing thirty-two prisons holding 170,000 prisoners, California is planning to add six more (*The Economist* 2009d, 71). It is estimated that at least eleven more prisons will be required to keep up with demand. This solution stems from an analysis of the problem that is similar to "the lack of lane space" as a definition of the traffic problem given by highway engineers, leading to policies that must build ahead of demand. It may also remind one of the practice in earlier centuries of locking up debtors until they could pay their debts. Thus, characterized by narrow, self-imposed boundaries, the erroneous definition of the jail problem as somehow separate from the drug control problem highlights flaws in problem definition and the failure or misuse of problem-structuring techniques by policy analysts and decision makers.

One should first approach the issue from the general to the specific. What are some background factors of the political environment that can condition problem structuring? Perhaps as important as the composition of expert teams participating in policy analysis (e.g., are they all prison construction engineers?) is the locus of their activity. For example, is the analysis to be done in a think tank with a political reputation? Is it a study from the state's department of prisons? Will it be a gubernatorial office analytic unit? Will it be a legislative policy analysis unit? The conclusions, for example, from a legislative unit may carry more weight with legislators who ultimately write the laws that guide court decisions or judicial policymaking.

Another general consideration is the question of who participates in the stakeholder analysis. How broad should the definition of who participates be? There are many experts on crime and criminal justice policy in universities and consulting firms, and there are others working out of their converted garage offices. They know about the habits of different types of criminals, what deters them, what could cure them, how demographics affects criminal behavior over time, and so on. As stakeholders, these professional views are essential to forging a comprehensive definition of the problem and a workable and effective public policy. In principle, the ideas of different professionals carry equal weight and stand or fall on their merits. In practice, because of the predominance of the narrower definition of stakeholders, prison officers have become a political force in the land. Their powerful and outspoken support for continued prison construction and three-strikes mandatory sentencing is well recorded (*The Economist* 1997b). Think also of possible links between public works contractor lobbies and the prison construction policy option. Many officials, such as former governor Pete Wilson of California, also supported both approaches to crime control. But it is clear that other stakeholders—including Senator Frank R. Wolf (R-VA) and Richard Riordan, director of Anti-Gang Operations for the City of Los Angeles—rely on technical studies and differing assumptions about current policies and are harshly critical of the hard-line approach (*The Economist* 2008, 24). It is important to maintain a broader definition of stakeholders, including members of the public, employees of correctional facilities, and administrators.

Classification Analysis

The generation and use of data in the crime area is extremely important in that much of policy turns on conflicting interpretations of the data. As in many ill-structured policy areas, the facts often do not speak for themselves. For this reason, the analyst needs to get the facts straight before the interpretation war begins. In the case of prison crowding, there are several significant data trends and data categories that need to be considered to analyze policy, perhaps forcing redefinition of the problem.

First, as indicated in this chapter's case study, since 1980 the prison population has grown ten times faster than the rate of violent crime. While the overall rate of crime has fallen, the rate of violent crime has risen by about 33%. But also since 1980, although the number of inmates has tripled, the proportion of violent criminals in the total prison population has decreased, according to the Cato Institute (2003). The data lead to the obvious question of causation. Some argue that the increased rate of incarceration has led to reduced crime rates. But in New York crime has fallen along with the incarceration rate (*The Economist* 1999b, 30). In general, increasing incarceration can be associated with decreased crime rates. But disaggregated by state and using different time periods, the proportions vary widely—in many states below-average incarceration rates could also be associated with decreases in crime rates. King, Mauer, and Young (2004) estimate that only about 25% of the decrease in crime rates is attributable to increases in incarceration rates (cited in Rushefsky 2008, 262). Thus, causal relationships need to be examined further.

Second, a useful distinction could be made between the categories of prisoners and drug users to get a clearer picture of the problem. What is the profile of incarcerated offenders? One study explains that 67% of the increase in prison population after 1980 is the result of jailing drug offenders (the mandatory sentencing statutes for drug-related sentences did not exist in 1980). Thus, the bulk of prisoners are drug offenders, with nondrug offenders accounting for only about 33% of the prison population increase. The number of people imprisoned for drug offenses tripled from 1986 to 1991. In Washington State the number of prisoners serving time for drug crimes has risen 1,000% since 1980 (Kopel 1994).

To clarify the data further, one might ask: What is the change in reported use of cocaine and other hard drugs since 1986? Use of the moving average technique (which will be explained in chapter 4) results in an expected increase in use of 2.75%. Has it continued to increase? Could actual use be declining, despite an increase in arrests and incarceration of drug offenders? Drug use among the household population (past month, or current use of any illicit drug) is down from its peak of 25,399 (14.1%) to 13,035 (6.1%). Although adolescent drug use increased from 1992 to 1996, it leveled off in 1997 (Office of National Drug Control Policy 2002). Some suggest that law enforcement has caused it to go down. Further, what is the racial composition of offenders and their socioeconomic status? Is there anything distinctive about these data that could point to a need to reexamine problem definitions? In fact, the case suggests that African Americans have been hit disproportionately by the war on drugs. What is the proportion of African Americans in the 67% increase in prison population caused mostly by drug offenders? According to 1998 figures, the incarceration rate for African Americans is eight times that for Caucasians (*The Economist* 1999b, 31), and a large proportion of African Americans are in prison for drug offenses. The case is not clear on this, and a fuller understanding of this issue would be a useful piece of missing information for the analyst.

Finally, is there anything distinctive about the racial component of drug consumption? African Americans consume about 95% of crack cocaine in this country, while Caucasians and Latinos predominate among powder cocaine users (*Washington Post* 1997). Why is the racial component of drug consumption important to a definition of the prison crowding issue? One answer is that under federal law, possession of five grams of cocaine powder is a misdemeanor and carries a maximum sentence of only one year. By contrast, possession of five grams of crack cocaine is a felony and carries a maximum sentence of five years. If the offender is found with more than fifty grams of crack, the mandatory sentence goes to ten years. One difficulty in resolving policy problems is that classification analysis is disrupted by partisan politics and the separation of powers. While many in Congress proposed even greater penalties for cocaine use, the Clinton administration was proposing reduction of the disparity between crack and powder cocaine sentencing.

Causes of Prison Crowding

What kind of problem are we dealing with? As in most public policy issues, this is an ill-structured or messy problem. It is more than a prison problem and therefore requires examination of larger related problems such as drug control. Why is this problem messy or ill structured? One could classify the problem as such because it involves many decision makers (e.g., executive, judicial), and it is the product of many rejected policy alternatives. Messy and ill-structured problems are complex and contain many interdependencies. The statistics point to these interdependencies but do not point to simple solutions—most such solutions would have major unintended consequences.

Despite reduced rates of reported crime for the period 1993–99, the prison population continues to grow. The annual rate of increase in the prison population is now 4.4% (down from 6.2% in 1990), which was still enough to generate a total of 1.8 million inmates in 1999. This amounted to an incarceration rate of 690 inmates per 100,000 inhabitants of the United States, which is five to ten times the incarceration rates of Western European countries (*The Economist* 1999a, 30). By 2004 the total had increased to 2.1 million, or 724 inmates per 100,000 inhabitants (Rushefsky 2008, 261). Between 1980 and 1995, the number of Americans behind bars for drug offenses increased eight times, to a total of 400,000 in 1995. Drug arrests also doubled in this period, reaching a total of 1.1 million in 1995. Despite spending $30 billion at all levels of government for drug control and two-thirds of the federal drug budget for enforcement, drug prices continue to fall. The price of cocaine is now half as much as in 1980, and heroin sells for 40% less than in it did 1989. Purity has also increased—despite enforcement efforts—as supplier efficiency has increased (*The Economist* 1999a, 71).

One reason that the prison crowding issue is complex is that even after the problem is defined, it is subject to competing institutional preferences. For example, in questions of drug control and prison crowding, Congress generally supports interdiction and prison construction. A network of powerful political interests, known as the prison-industrial complex, now supports the boom in prison construction. This multibillion-dollar industry is akin to the military-industrial complex that fuels defense policy (Schlosser 1998, 63). The executive branch of the federal government often supports softer treatment and testing programs, however. But recent legislation such as the Drug Free Communities Act points to a new direction—shifting funds to state and local governments. As in the federal government, the bulk of state and local funds go to enforcement efforts that are perceived to reflect local preferences.

Thus, with a view toward redefinition of the problem and policy reform, it is critical that all forms of causation, including institutional, be examined.

The analyst should begin with remote causes. Remote causes are evident in the drug policy of interdiction and enforcement, which in the process of vice control also creates a strong black market for drug production and sale around the world. This raises the price and encourages new entrants into the market, thus ensuring sustained supplies of crack and powder cocaine, heroin, and related drugs to consumers in the United States. Analysis of remote causes must also include demand as well as supply. Demand for drugs is a function of a number of factors, including the risk of being caught (which is related to the efficacy of enforcement programs). From the supply perspective, the chance is slim that US drug policies can reduce supplies of drugs around the world, making the price so high for drug consumers that they revert to alcohol and cigarettes. In addition, despite political support among several influential circles, the chances of illegal drugs being legalized are slim. In the minds of many legislators and their perceived base of supporters, legalization of drugs would be a defeat for the traditional culture of personal responsibility and self-control; it would be an admission of defeat for crime control advocates who dominate policy debates. These are remote causes and consequences that cannot be changed in the short run.

As noted, more plausible and actionable causes can be found in the relationship between crowding, pretrial release, and plea bargaining. Note that the 1976 study by Nagel and Neef dealt with prison crowding before the advent of new mandatory sentencing statutes. Thus, an additional cause of prison crowding is the effect of antidrug statutes on plea bargaining. If this diminishes plea bargaining and pretrial release, the courts would be even more clogged, leading to an increase in jail overcrowding. Three-strike legislation has resulted in more jury trials in efforts by defendants to avoid prison. While only 3% of the 26,237 Los Angeles Superior Court cases in 1996 were three-strike cases, they accounted for 24% of the jury trials. The three-strike law will require an extra 17,000 jury trials at an expense of $27 million per year (*The Economist* 1997b).

Thus, the major controlling policy variable for prison overcrowding currently seems to be the three-strike type of mandatory sentencing for drug use that is in effect in more than twelve states. It could be that drug policy is working against both sensible prison policy and justice administration. As indicated, a major—perhaps unintended—consequence of the mandatory sentencing laws has been to fill prisons with petty, nonviolent, frequently first-time offenders. Almost 90% of first-time offenders in federal courts went to prison in 1990 with an average sentence of more than five years; first-time violent offenders went to jail less often and for shorter periods. In California, twice as many people have been imprisoned for marijuana offenses as for murder, rape, and kidnapping combined (Schlosser 1997, 92). Under the mandatory sentencing law, a district attorney decides the rank of the crime: misdemeanor or felony. If one is convicted of three felonies, he or she receives the five-year maximum sentence. The third offense may be a misdemeanor (e.g., theft of a piece of pizza) but classed as a felony by the district attorney. If the defendant has committed two violent felonies before, this would be sufficient for imposition of the five-year sentence. Clearly, this is a crude form of legislative action (something like mandating budgetary balance at the federal level) that does not distinguish between levels of seriousness of different kinds of crime. The result is widespread disparities in crime classification and uneven sentencing, which violate the basic legal precept that sanctions should be clear and predictable to avoid violation of due process.

The question is, what can be done about changing the controlling legal variable? Here it is important for the analyst to distinguish and measure the costs of bad effects of drug use and the bad effects of drug abuse control through enforcement (Kleiman 1992, 17). A 1997 California Supreme Court ruling held that presiding judges may exercise their own judgment in deciding whether the third crime or the two committed previously are actually misdemeanors rather than felonies (*The Economist* 1997b). By returning discretion to the judiciary, some of the harsher effects of the laws may be mitigated in the future. This could also replace the confusion caused by the actions of district attorneys with new confusion caused by judges, increasing the overall uncertainty of the sentencing process.

Brainstorming

Here is our opportunity to move out of the nine dots and provide creative policy problem definitions that will lead to solutions. Given the propensity for policy experimentation at the state and local levels of government in the United States, such analysis is useful and often successful in influencing change. Let us propose several ideas that should be constructively assessed, followed by separate criticism and evaluation.

Current drug policy is based largely on an enforcement problem definition: How do we remove anyone involved in the drug trade from the street to the cell? It has been billed as a supply-side drug policy. As noted previously, 66% of the $17.1 billion FY 1999 budget for drug control is for enforcement, and only 34% is for demand reduction through education and treatment programs (Office of National Drug Control Policy 1998, 16). Is this an appropriate definition? Brainstorming can help by providing alternative definitions.

First, one must think counterintuitively. Can one suppose that the overcrowding is functional? Can one suppose that the mandatory sentence laws operate exactly as intended and that the appropriate response now is to construct more prisons and add more juries? This may be similar to the effects of congestion costs on highways, according to economic theorists, in which drivers often react rationally and behave differently in response to major congestion, taking mass transit or driving at different hours. Following this analogy, at least one possible thesis is that fear of prison conditions will cause potential drug offenders to think twice before consuming and ending up in the criminal justice system. In short, suppose that the consequences are not unintentional but exactly as predicted? California officials make this argument in citing the 4.2% drop in violent crime and the 12% drop in the overall crime rate in a six-month period (*The Economist* 1998a). The rate of violent crime in the United States has fallen each year from 1991, dropped 7% in 1996, and is now at its lowest level in ten years (*The Economist* 1997b).

Studies do suggest that existing successes in combating crime reflect a more innovative and aggressive criminal justice system, including its use of community policing. Other studies suggest that the drop is due not to policy but to other factors over which policy has no control: the aging of the population and changes in the crack cocaine market (Thomas 1997). Following this line of thinking, one should consider that existing policy could remove substantial numbers of actors from the drug trade and streets to cells, thereby substantially weakening the drug trade and reducing consumption. Accepting this proposition, the question then is how to minimize the damage to first-time offenders and other nonviolent offenders and focus on the dealers, distributors, and upper-level drug traders? Suggestions here might include, for example, increased judicial discretion in classifying crimes as misdemeanors and increased targeting of hard-core drug traffickers and their allies by more flexible and community-based policing strategies.

Second, suppose that we propose the opposite and recommend legalizing drugs, arguing that the policy problem is one of excess control (analogous to poorly designed internal control systems that attempt to micromanage all expenditures but in fact merely create opportunities for corruption and incentives for mismanagement). Swiss authorities have demonstrated the success of legalizing drugs through a "partial legalization" program that gave one thousand program participants who were dependent on hard drugs injections of pure heroin at nominal prices in exchange for psychological counseling. In recent years, major gains have been achieved among participants in finding permanent jobs, reducing unemployment, reducing drug abusers' involvement in drug and theft crimes, and improving health outcomes. The program is complemented by increased police regulation and enforcement against public use of drugs. Voters in Zurich acknowledged the success of this program by approving it in a referendum in 1996 (Frey 1997). Buoyed by the success of earlier drug programs, in 1998 Swiss voters approved a referendum to legalize the use and sale of marijuana, heroin, and cocaine through the *Drogleg* program (*The Economist* 1998c).

In short, it may be argued that following the comparative example of Switzerland and the analogy of alcohol regulation in the United States, enforcement should be tempered by legalization of drugs and regulation of sales, with strong demand-side enforcement sanctions for misuse by certain classes, such as minors. The following idea could be examined: Since approaches based on prohibition (e.g., enforcement, three-strikes laws) have not stemmed the flow of drugs, policies should be changed to include legalization accompanied by suitable regulations. First, successful legalization could reduce the prison population; reduce capital expenditures for prisons; cut future operations and maintenance commitments from current budgets; and reduce the price of drugs and associated violence among drug lords. (The annual cost per prison inmate in the United States is roughly $21,000 [*The Economist* 1999b]). From this perspective advocating at least partial legalization, the proposed FY 1995 crime bill, with its recommended $12.2 billion in prison construction and extension of mandatory sentences, was largely a waste of money.

Second, legalization would generate revenues for the public sector, similar to the 80% levy for a pack of cigarettes and 60% for whiskey. Third, to legalize narcotics pragmatically and incrementally, the established regulatory regimes for alcohol and tobacco could be replicated with licensed sales outlets and minimum ages for purchase. In many cases, such as with the drug ecstasy, licensing manufacturers could ensure purity and quality (*The Economist* 1997a).

Fourth, we could recommend drug treatment programs as an alternative to prison sentencing. But how effective is this in controlling drug use and abuse? Program evaluation studies have been conducted since the early 1970s, and the success of the Swiss example after two years was cited above. Various forms of treatment programs have been shown to succeed in reducing drug use and forms of antisocial behavior that are outgrowths of drug use. The reduction in costs to society of drug-related crime is much greater than the cost of treatment programs. Drug treatment is cost effective in that it can minimize jail overcrowding in existing prisons and reduce the capital outlays for new ones (Mieczkowski et al. 1992, 347).

Fifth, suppose we recommend enhanced drug testing for prisoners and integrate testing with both prison construction and release programs? In the 1970s President Nixon focused on the demand side of drug use, creating an initiative based on an innovative pilot drug treatment program in Washington, DC. In the 1960s this city, like so many others, was gripped by a heroin epidemic. So it set up a network of clinics offering the synthetic narcotic methadone and other treatments to get addicts off heroin. Impressed by Washington, DC's 5.2% decrease in crime rate (the first decline in years), in 1970 President Nixon created a Narcotics Treatment Administration modeled on the Washington, DC, treatment program. By 1973 the heroin epidemic in that city and the United States as a whole was ebbing, and many attribute its decline to this treatment program (Massing 1998). Subsequent US presidents opted for enforcement, as noted, and now more than two-thirds of federal drug programs are devoted to enforcement or supply-side activities.

Nevertheless, in 1998 President Clinton directed the US attorney general through the Office of Justice Programs to amend guidelines for prison construction grants and require state grantees to establish and maintain a system of reporting on their prison drug abuse problem. The president also instructed the attorney general to draft and submit to Congress legislation allowing states to use federal prison construction funds to provide a full range of drug-testing, sanctions, and treatment programs. Pilot drug-testing programs are now under way in twenty-five of the ninety-four federal judicial districts; their intent is to allow federal judges to determine appropriate release conditions for defendants (*The Economist* 2009a).

Subsequently, as part of brainstorming, critiques of the drug policy prescriptions described above should be presented. First, unreasonably harsh drug policies alone have not produced lower crime rates. (It should also be noted that crime rates nationally have declined irrespective of any state's three-strike laws. There are other factors, too, including the design of enforcement programs themselves, that affect demand.) Second, the social costs of legalization could be higher than at present: It would be harder to stop the spate of available drugs after the country has been flooded with legal drugs than to continue the existing policy. The Swiss failed earlier with their famous "needle park" experiment, which turned Zurich into the drug magnet for Europe. Third, even with the generally positive evaluation of treatment programs, the return to drug use is common. In most programs, better outcomes are associated with such factors as intact marriages, jobs, short histories of drug use, low levels of psychiatric problems, and little or no criminality (Mieczkowski et al. 1992,

347). Both sets of propositions should be developed and critiqued, then synthesized into a concise set of policy recommendations based on a revised definition of the problem.

Problem Analogies

Analogies can also be useful in attacking the problem of overcrowded prisons. Analysts can think of many types of personal and policy-related analogies for dealing with this issue. Two that may be useful are: (1) the regulatory and construction alternatives proposed for the control of stray dogs and other animals in many cities, and (2) disease control and treatment programs that focus on populations similar to those targeted by drug policies.

First, for the stray dog analogy, data are needed to compare the cost benefits of regulatory and construction alternatives. To reach a satisfactory definition of the problem, the analyst needs to correlate the animal control problem (stray dogs) with each alternative. For example, if data support a correlation between licensing and animal owner responsibility, the case can be made that the problem is regulatory. If most nuisances are caused by unlicensed animals, a direct attack on delinquent owners through a census, steep fines, and other such measures might be a worthy alternative to constructing a shelter or increasing staff hours to cope with increasing complaints (Lehan 1984, 76). That is, as in drug use and abuse, if owner motivation can be positively influenced, the animal nuisance situation may be altered at its roots, reducing dog impoundments and eliminating the need for a new pound (analogous to reducing jail overcrowding and eliminating the need for new jail construction) (Lehan 1984, 74). Using the analogy of licensing as a controlling variable for the animal problem, the benefits of modifying drug user behavior through treatment and fines and other penalties for failure to adhere to regulations could be explored.

Second, since addiction is analogous to a disease, one could use the analogy of disease control to explore problem definitions for drug policy. Lessons learned in the area of AIDS control and treatment, for example, may be applicable to drug policy. One significant lesson cited above is that political and ideological constraints impede an appropriate definition of many policy problems. AIDS is a health policy problem but has been treated as a civil rights issue. It is both. The absence of a database of those infected, because of fear of retaliation against those infected, has hindered public health efforts to monitor the spread of the disease (Burr 1997a).

In the case of drug use, the mere mention of drug liberalization or scaling back enforcement seems to cause insanity, not among users but, seemingly, in those who define the drug problem and are charged with development of new policies. During the Reagan administration, a public health approach to drug control was replaced with emphasis on law enforcement. Why? According to Schlosser (1997), drug use was no longer considered an illness; all drug use was deemed immoral, a symbol of the weakness of a liberal and permissive society. It caused the slovenly appearance of youths and accounted for their lack of motivation. Given the current political conservatism of both major parties, drug enforcement has become a bipartisan effort, with nothing to be gained politically by defending drug abusers from excessive punishment (Schlosser 1997, 94). Despite the recent redefinition of drug use as a form of immorality, the analogy of addiction and drug use as an illness is still valid. As already emphasized, the effect of failure to use this analogy is jail overcrowding and administrative stress on the criminal justice system. In short, it is more reasonable to define the drug problem as being in the public health sphere rather than more narrowly as a matter of criminal justice.

Assumptional Analysis

To test our efforts to critique and redefine the problem of prison crowding, the analyst should link existing policies and supporting data with underlying policy assumptions. First, it is recognized that drug and prison policies may be working against each other. Prisons are filling up with low-level, nonviolent drug users, while the perceived availability of drugs seems to remain constant, and violent crime is still a major problem in most cities (despite drops in overall crime rates). The database used to define the problem as one requiring a solution of moving all drug traders and users into cells consisted largely of patterns of drug consumption. But after years of draconian legislation and tough law enforcement, the flow of drugs into the United States seems to be continuing at about the same rate. Data since 1980 indicate that the prison composition has changed and that continuation of existing policies will continue to fill jails without substantially reducing drug use. Based on changed data on prison composition that strongly indicates major unintended consequences of drug policies (supported also by the California Supreme Court ruling taking the discretion to classify the gravity of offenses away from district attorneys and returning it to judges), the assumptions of current definitions of the drug use problem need to be reexamined. What are the assumptions? First, tough law enforcement will stem drug use and reduce supplies. Second, more prison construction will provide space for the new supply of offenders. Given the data and results, the assumptions are questionable, and the analyst should challenge them logically with available data.

Conclusion

This chapter's case study provides the analyst with a good opportunity to employ basic tools to assess the effects of competing definitions of the problem of prison overcrowding. Based on a new definition of the problem, one should now try to compose a goal statement and performance criteria for a new program. For example, the goal statement might be "to reduce the number of repeat drug offenders by 10% in six months" or "to reduce the prison population by 10% in one year by legalizing drugs." Using a target population (drug users going to prison), one could outline performance criteria for a proposed program that might be used for monitoring and post-evaluation of the program later. Included are assumptions, standards, and causal relationships that affect the target population and that will affect the scope and direction of the program. One would also want to develop standards that allow existing policies to work more effectively by precisely hitting intended targets (i.e., hard-core offenders) and using treatment programs for many now sent to jail; or conversely that allow changed policies (i.e., legalization and treatment) to function without generating excessive short-term social costs.

REFERENCES

Bardach, Eugene. 1996. *The 8-Step Path of Policy Analysis. A Handbook for Practice.* Berkeley, CA: Academic Press.

Brewer, Garry D., and Peter deLeon. 1983. *The Foundations of Policy Analysis.* Homewood, IL: Dorsey Press.

Brinkley, Joel. 1986. Drug Law Raises More Than Hope, The Turf Battles Are Likely to Reach New Heights. *New York Times*, November 2.

Brown, Rita Mae. 1983. *Sudden Death.* New York: Bantam Books.

Brown, Warren. 1998. Seat Belt Push Raises Race Issue. *Washington Post*, April 3.

Burr, Chandler. 1997a. The AIDS Exception: Privacy v. Public Health. *Atlantic Monthly*. June.

———. 1997b. Letters. *Atlantic Monthly*. September.

Cato Institute. 2003. *Cato Daily Dispatch*. Available at www.cato.org/dispatch/07-28-030.html. July 28.

City of Milwaukee. 1996. *Capital Improvements Program 1996–2001*. Milwaukee: City of Milwaukee.

Committee for a Responsible Federal Budget. 2009. CBO Releases Social Security Projections. Available at http://crfb.org/document/cbo-releases-social-security-projections.

Davis, Patricia, and Leef Smith. 1998. A Crisis That May Not Exist Is All the Rage. *Washington Post*, November 10.

Day, Katherine. 1997. Recycling: Higher Price, Lower Priority? City Governments Debating Cost Effectiveness of Programs. *Washington Post*, March 30.

Dunn, William N. 1981. *Public Policy Analysis: An Introduction*. Englewood Cliffs, NJ: Prentice Hall.

———. 2008. *Public Policy Analysis: An Introduction*. 4th ed. Upper Saddlewood, NJ: Pearson Prentice Hall.

The Economist. 1997a. Shopping for a Drugs Policy. August 16.

———. 1997b. Three-Strikes Legislation: It Needed a Bit of Tidying Up. April 12.

———. 1997c. Better Off, But Not Much. October 4.

———. 1997d. A Funny Sort of Market. October 18.

———. 1997e. Coughing Up. October 24.

———. 1998a. Out of Jail and Onto the Street. December 5.

———. 1998b. Survey of Health Insurance. October 24.

———. 1998c. On Prescription: Drugs in Switzerland. November 28.

———. 1998d. Journey beyond the Stars. December 19.

———. 1999a. Ending the War on Drugs. January 2.

———. 1999b. Prisoners: More Than Any Other Democracy. March 20.

———. 2005. Rodent News from Gotham: Tails of the City. October 27.

———. 2008. A Balanced Drug Policy (letter). October 18.

———. 2009a. How to Stop the Drug Wars. March 7.

———. 2009b. Why Do Members of the European Parliament Never Learn from Experience? June 13.

———. 2009c. Unpacking the Problem: A Special Report on the Carbon Economy. December 5.

———. 2009d. Virtually Legal. November 14.

———. 2009e. Stopping Climate Change. December 5.

Fisher, Marc. 2009a. Unbending Rules on Drugs in Schools Drive One Teen to the Breaking Point. *Washington Post*, April 5.

Fisher, Ronald C. 2007. *State and Local Public Finance*. 3rd ed. Mason, OH: Thomson Southwestern.

———. 2009b. Zero-Tolerance Policies in Practice. *Washington Post*, April 14.

Frey, Bruno. 1997. Legalizing Drugs. *The Economist*. September 6.

Fumento, Michael. 1998. Road Rage versus Reality. *The Atlantic Monthly*. August.

Goldhill, David. 2009. How American Health Care Killed My Father. *The Atlantic Monthly*. September.

Guess, George M. 1979. Pasture Expansion, Forestry and Development Contradictions: The Case of Costa Rica. *Studies in Comparative International Development* 14 (1): 42–55.

———. 1992. Centralization of Expenditure Control in Latin America. *Public Administration Quarterly* 16 (3): 376–94.

———. 2009. Dog Daze. *The American Interest*. May/June.

Guess, George M., and Stojgniew J. Sitko. 2004. Planning, Budgeting and Health Care Performance in Ukraine. *International Journal of Public Administration* 27 (10): 767–98.

Harlan, Stephen. 1997. We Can Cut Crime. *Washington Post*. April 27.

Hopkins, Sam. 1986. Bowers Suggests Making Possession of Small Amount of Pot a Felony. *Atlanta Constitution*, November 1.

Johnson, Jocelyn M. 1997. The Medicaid Mandates of the 1980s: An Intergovernmental Perspective. *Public Budgeting and Finance* 17 (1): 3–34.

King, Ryan S., Marc Mauer, and Malcolm C. Young. 2004. Incarceration and Crime: A Complex Relationship. Washington, DC: Sentencing Project. http://sentencingproject.org.

Kleiman, Mark. 1992. *Against Excess: Drug Policy for Results*. New York: Basic Books.

Kopel, David B. 1994. Prison Blues: How America's Foolish Sentencing Policies Endanger Public Safety. Cato Policy Analysis no. 208. Washington, DC: Cato Institute.

Le Carré, John. 1996. *The Tailor of Panama*. London: Hodder and Stoughton.

Lehan, Edward. 1984. *Budgetmaking: A Workbook of Public Budgeting Theory and Practice*. New York: St. Martin's.

Lindsey, Robert. 1986. Marijuana Drive Reduces Supplies and Raises Prices. *New York Times*, October 4.

Maru, Duncan Smith-Rohrberg. 2009. Wasting Drug War Resources. *Washington Post*, November 24.

Massing, Michael. 1998. Nixon Had It Right: A 70s Project Showed Drug Treatment Works. *Washington Post*, November 8.

Mieczkowski, Tom, Douglas Anglin, Shirley Coletti, Bruce Johnson, Ethan Nadelmann, and Eric Wish. 1992. Responding to America's Drug Problems: Strategies for the 1980s. *Journal of Urban Areas* 14 (3/4): 337–57.

Musto, David F. 1998. This 10-Year War Can Be Won. *Washington Post*, June 14.

Nagel, Stuart, and Marian G. Neef. 1976. Two Examples from the Legal Process. *Policy Analysis* 2 (2): 356–57.

New York Times. 2009. Hardy Beetles Put Forests, Emission Goals at Risk. August 5.

Office of National Drug Control Policy. 1998. National Drug Control Strategy. Washington, DC: Office of National Drug Control Policy.

————. 2002. Drug Use Trends. Available at http://whitehousedrugpolicy.gov/ publications/factsht/druguse/index.html. Washington, DC: Office of National Drug Control Policy.

Pfiffner, James P. 2010. The Decision to Go to War with Iraq. In *Public Administration: Cases and Concepts*, ed. Richard J. Stillman. 9th ed. Boston: Cengage Wadsworth Learning.

Reich, Robert B. 1987. The Rise of Techno-Nationalism. *Atlantic Monthly*. May.

Reid, Alice. 1998. Majority of Truckers Fail Virginia Inspections. *Washington Post*, October 22.

Rushefsky, Mark E. 2008. *Public Policy in the United States: At the Dawn of the 21st Century*. 4th ed. Armonk, NY: M. E. Sharpe.

Runciman, W. G. 1998. Debatable. *The Economist*. January 10.

Schlosser, Eric. 1997. More Reefer Madness. *Atlantic Monthly*. April.

————. 1998. The Prison-Industrial Complex. *Atlantic Monthly*. December.

Spurgeon, Devon. 1997. Guiliani, New York City Declare War on Rats—All 28 Million of Them. *Washington Post*, October 4.

Thomas, Pierre. 1997. Violent Crime Rate Drops 7% Nationwide. *Washington Post*, June 2.

Tuchman, Barbara W. 1984. *The March of Folly: From Troy to Vietnam*. New York: Ballantine.

US Department of Justice, Bureau of Justice Statistics (BJS). 2005. Prison Construction. http://bjs.ojp.usdoj.gov/index.

Vigliucci, Andres, and Gail Epstein. 1997. Quien Pierde, Quien Gana en Presupuesto de Penelas. *El Nuevo Herald*, September 16.

Washington Post. 1997. Crack and Cocaine Penalties. April 16.

Will, George F. 2009. A Reality Check on Drug Use. *Washington Post*, October 29.

Chapter 3

✹✹✹

Forecasting Institutional Impacts on Public Policy Performance

> The work advanced slowly, impeded by the worsening relationship between the fair's two ruling bodies, the National Commission and the Exposition Company, and by the architect's failure to get their drawings to Chicago on time. All the drawings were late. . . . Moreover, the exposition had entered that precarious early phase common to every great construction project when unexpected obstacles suddenly emerge. . . .
>
> —Erik Larson, *The Devil in the White City*

INTRODUCTION

To the extent that implementation really is the Achilles heel of policy, decision makers should be able to forecast the degree to which the institutional setting is going to be an asset or liability. Douglass North (1990) draws a distinction between the institutional framework of formal and informal rules and systems, on the one hand, and the organizational units that will enforce them, on the other. Implementation of programs, policies, and projects is accomplished with the support of basic institutional systems, such as personnel, payments, and procurement. These systems work within organizational structures, often ministries or departments, to provide timely information, clearances, and notices of required actions. Policies and programs typically cross organizational lines, spanning formal boundaries as functional or sectoral efforts to achieve their objectives. Effective institutional systems facilitate boundary spanning by serving formally or informally as coordinating devices within government and beyond government to NGOs, stakeholders, and civil society organizations. For particular policies to be implemented, analysts need to know how institutions operate within and between public and nongovernmental organizations. This means that for practical purposes, institutions and organizations should function together and support policy.

For instance, based on its assessment of the policy problem, the Obama administration is formulating a health care program that will be implemented across existing organizations (e.g., Medicare, Medicaid, hospitals, clinics, and insurance companies). Institutional systems within these organizations will either serve as assets or liabilities for health improvement. Current decision makers in Congress and the executive branch need to know which systems should be reformed or fixed before the program begins. Similarly, the newly elected Japanese government is faced with a bureaucracy in which "departments often operate in bunker-like isolation. Problems that range across ministries are therefore rarely solved" (*The Economist* 2009b, 31). Governments often forget that they cannot afford to alienate their bureaucratic institutions and organizations, because they need their help to implement policy.

In short, institutional systems are often taken for granted even though they rarely provide full support for any program or policy. If implementation issues are raised during policy formulation and problem definition, they are often raised at the wrong level of analysis. Rather than fix operational level systems by making marginal changes, policy advocates demand structural and organizational changes, despite the fact that this is a medium-term effort with often questionable results. A structural-level response is counterproductive and can actually weaken implementation institutions and policy results further. Decision makers and analysts should have maps of institutional capabilities for particular policies or programs based on objective assessments and criteria. They need to know which institutional systems can be changed (reducing liabilities) and which others may diminish in value (from lack of political or budget support), effectively increasing liabilities and serving as an arbitrary program off-switch that can destabilize systems further for all stakeholders. They also need to know when to resist the temptation to attempt major structural overhauls (i.e., reorganizations) and instead concentrate on management- and operations-level improvements, specifically focusing on energized and well-trained leaders who can manage in the agency or departmental culture (Stier 2009). In the case for this chapter, the comprehensive reform of Washington, DC, schools has been hard enough and faces enormous practical institutional and organizational constraints. But to this toxic mix one must now add the collapse of local revenues caused by the economic recession. This increases implementation constraints and cannot easily be fixed in the short term without the usual reductions in personnel, supplies, and equipment that are vital for the reform program itself.

Through analysis of the Washington, DC, school reform case, this chapter seeks to provide criteria and guidelines for institutional mapping and capacity rating. Our framework for implementation assessment consists of four main variables. First, the legal and regulatory framework affects what program and policy managers do. Managers' discretion and authority will affect program results to the extent that they can hire, fire, and transfer personnel; transfer or reprogram budget funds during the year; and consolidate or eliminate offices of departments. Rules and regulations that govern these actions may flow directly from governmental authorities; they might also indirectly be the result of pressures from civil society organizations such as unions. Second, policy and program results are affected profoundly by the availability of funding, which may be a product of excessive restrictions on approvals (i.e., the legal/regulatory framework) or it could be a product of faulty revenue forecasts derived from real revenue collapse. Funds must be available to use as programmed; they must also be spent and accounted for in a timely and accurate fashion. The strength of budgeting, accounting, and internal control systems must be gauged before programs and projects are approved. Otherwise, spending will be as effective as a grocery store without checkout counters.

For example, dilapidated financial management systems have contributed to more than one policy implementation failure. The absence of road maintenance for capital investment programs is often the product of weak budget management. This permits funds to be reprogrammed into salaries, allows roads to deteriorate prematurely, diminishes the value of public assets, and makes the transportation of goods and passengers more difficult. For these kinds of institutional reasons, road policies in the United States and many other countries have not delivered value for money and waste scarce public resources. The institutional dimension needs to be examined during the phases of problem diagnosis and policy design, not merely during policy implementation, when for all practical purposes it is too late.

Third, organizational boundaries are important for implementation. The functional or program structure through which personnel, financial, and capital resources are spent to achieve stated purposes must be known in advance; coordination arrangements should also be worked out ahead of time. Social transfer programs, for example, in countries such as Peru and Mexico are often implemented across thousands of local organizations that lack the capacity to manage or control the funds transferred to them. The boundaries of implementing organizations are porous, and such organizations are often beyond the reach of higher-level financial controls. This diminishes the otherwise high effectiveness of innovative social transfers and perpetuates the poverty and lack of education that the program was intended to reduce.

Finally, implementing institutions must be sustainable. Where top-level political support for programs or policies is missing or variable, the program could be arbitrarily terminated, leaving clients without intended services or goods. Sustainability in this context also means that leadership should be capable of managing people and systems in the often complex and byzantine cultures of multiple organizations relying on multiple institutional systems. The inability of leadership to effectively serve multiple masters (a required trait in public service) often triggers calls for major reorganization when only leadership and marginal adjustments in existing systems are all that is needed. These four variables constitute our framework, which we will apply later to gauge institutional capabilities and constraints in implementing the DC public school reform program.

Thus, the potential effect of institutions on policy implementation should be reviewed beforehand, based on indirect feedback from stakeholders or direct information from systems that have monitored the performance of this kind of policy. Information for such analysis can be derived from periodic consultant reports or the results of management and performance audits of budget and policy implementation. For new policy initiatives, it is important that institutional analysis be done properly at both the problem-structuring and options-forecasting stages.

INSTITUTIONAL CONTEXT AND PUBLIC POLICY

Overlap exists between policy design and policy administration. Implementing organizations may make rules too (such as administrative regulations), and institutional actions may affect enforcement (such as congressional earmarks in foreign aid policy). In some policy areas (e.g., environmental protection), implementation is charged to several organizations across several levels of government. Multiple organizations make rules and regulations, the combined effect of which is to create an institutional policy network or the kind of "issue network" discussed in chapter 1 (Heclo 1978). Networks within government and between governments and civil society organizations blur the distinction between organizational implementation and institutional policymaking. What this suggests is that forecasting institutional constraints to implementation is itself a messy problem (chapter 2)! If public policy is understood to include any program, project, regulation, or law that costs public money and is intended to provide a potential stream of benefits, then for all public policies we need to know in the diagnostic phase what will constrain results.

More traditional perspectives on public policy reserve this analysis for the implementation phase, on the theory that course corrections will be made based on actions during the evaluation phase. But those actions rarely take place, meaning that the costs and benefits of the institutional delivery arrangements need to be figured into the policy-planning phase. For instance, outsourcing to nongovernmental (often private) organizations means that they are functionally the agents of policy or program implementation. Empirical estimates of the potential savings to be generated by contracting out should be compared to cost estimates of "making" the service in-house rather than "buying" it through private contractors (Michel 2001). Forecasting the results of institutional delivery options can only be as good as comparative policy data allows—it is not hard science! And, unfortunately, policy analysts and their clients need to be aware of weaknesses in the estimates of contracting out services (Boyne 1998). Because of the decentralized nature of program and service delivery in the United States, experiments and pilot programs to improve service efficiency are commonplace. But such innovative programs (e.g., community policing) are often unsupported by deeper changes in policies and administrative systems. Existing programs are often housed in hierarchical bureaucracies featuring command-and-control management systems. New programs rely on existing policies, procedures, and organizational structures that are often defective. These systems may reinforce narrow control purposes rather than supporting a results-driven orientation (Gianakis and Davis 1998). Part of the problem is that administrative and financial management organizations have weak analytic capacities. Exceptions prove the rule.

For example, in Ohio the state contracts and oversees nonprofit health providers for delivery of its health programs. Contracts (and later transfers) are allocated on the basis of reported performance data. Providers report on and are assessed for efficiency (in this instance, unit cost of service levels for diagnosis, counseling, and treatment) and effectiveness (meaning the unit cost of outcome or client improvement attributable to treatment, for such measures as reduction of alcoholism). Efficiency measures unit cost of service (e.g., operating cost per passenger mile of transit service); effectiveness measures how well a service or policy is performed (e.g., length of fire department response times).[1] In Ohio the state negotiates service contracts with providers based on maximum allowable unit costs for each service (Byrnes, Freeman, and Kauffman 1997). This system of transfers from the state budget provides a hard budget constraint on outlays and a set of institutional incentives for efficient and effective service provision. Policy evaluation is fed into the planning phase via the budget process for health program expenditures. (A similar system of performance-based transfers has been used to finance part of urban mass transit operations in the United States.) Thus, policy analysis in such cases includes not only forecasted costs and benefits of eligibility requirements for particular groups, but also the effects of the institutional delivery arrangement itself.

What are the drawbacks of forecasting institutional problems and opportunities? Like all forecasts, they could be wrong. Otherwise sound policies could be delayed by opponents who now can charge that weak implementing institutions will waste even more resources. While this is a danger, one should recognize that weak institutions increase the risk of failure and drive up the costs of most current policies, from defense to health care. To avoid delays caused by false charges, it is important not only to have data on institutions' past performance but also to attempt to specify how this will affect policy implementation. Much of this will have to be done, in fact, during and after implementation (monitoring and evaluation as well as post-audit). But it should also be considered during the diagnostic stage (a kind of institutional pre-audit).

INSTITUTIONAL ASSESSMENT FRAMEWORK

Especially since the 2007 recession sliced into employment, personal incomes, and tax revenues, all levels of government in the United States have been under mandate from voters and political leaders to cut costs and deliver services more efficiently. In this context it is important to try to determine what methods can be used to improve efficiencies without damaging program or policy effectiveness (i.e., allocative efficiency). As will become evident in chapter 4, the institutional and management climate affects not only policy implementation but also the generation of options to cut costs and improve service delivery. For example, a Washington Metropolitan Area Transit Authority (WMATA) rider recently wrote a letter to the editor of the local newspaper to suggest taking low-demand escalators out of service. Any rider of comparable subway systems in New York City or Vienna will find escalators in sleep mode that are activated when demand calls for it (*Washington Post* 2010). To avoid costly breakdowns in the future, it would seem that ideas like this would normally be generated within WMATA and pilot-tested at some of its eighty-six stations. The question is why such an obvious idea must come from the outside? Are there institutional disincentives to generating and applying sound ideas internally? Do inefficiencies persist from internal billing and payment systems that encourage maintenance units to bill for labor performed on existing escalators? Or, worse still, is it simply that no one inside the WMATA thought of it?

Whatever the problem, WMATA should be forced by its governing board to conduct a root-and-branch review (also known as a management review) by major transaction (e.g., maintenance) to unearth the management and systems problems that prevent improved service performance. This may be easier said than done where there is a built-in mismatch between high jurisdictional responsibility for service delivery and weak financial and management resources (Guess 2008, 3). Metropolitan transit organizations such as WMATA face concentrated responsibilities and fragmented authority and financing, all within hypercritical local political environments.

To conduct performance audits and management reviews, governments in this country typically use in-house departments (e.g., the Dade County, Florida, Office of Management and Budget), special teams (e.g., the Organizational Review Team, Dade County), or private consultants (e.g., PricewaterhouseCoopers). There are other alternatives for the public sector. Montgomery County, Maryland, uses a customer service department to determine how well the county delivers social services to the poorest residents, conducts training, and provides public education on county services. The information generated and the authority exercised by such institutions are critical in designing and revising social policies: Rather than simply examining whether regulations are met or paperwork is completed, county workers are held accountable for the outcomes of their efforts toward policy results. Such an innovative approach recognizes that institutions matter as much to public policy planning as to implementation.

Whereas many evaluations focus only on institutional processes, the Montgomery County analysis focuses on its service results and redesigns incentives accordingly. Unfortunately, the political payoffs to elected officials from such insights may be few. Montgomery County has proposed a 5% cut in its current budget, meaning that nine of twenty positions could be cut (Levine and Perez-Rivas 1997). Whatever the political context, the purpose of institutional review should be to determine: (1) whether existing units are effectively carrying out existing functions, and (2) whether the units' resources are being managed economically and efficiently. As noted, the formal name for policy reviews in the United States is a management audit or operations audit. The broader value-for-money purpose of such an audit should be kept in mind: It is not to solve all problems, but only those that can become economically significant.

The economic literature provides one basis for an institutional pre-audit for policy implementation. Institutional economics employs practical concepts such as: complexity leading to high transaction costs; agent accountability and responsibility to principals; asymmetrical information relationships derived from power differences; monopoly service provision; and rent seeking, opportunism, and moral hazard (North 1990). Formal and informal rules (i.e., institutional improvements) are needed to eliminate perverse incentives, reduce complexity, increase policy accountability, and increase informational transparency. Flaws in administrative and institutional systems lead to these economic problems. They need to be remedied by rules that will improve practice and policy results. In short, analysts need to know what kind of implementation capacity they can expect from:

Legal, regulatory, and political systems
Structural design
Functional operations
Financial management systems

Legal, Regulatory, and Political Systems

As indicated in table 3.1, for successful implementation, capacity should be demonstrable in three forms: (1) the provision of adequate legal and regulatory frameworks, (2) the provision of adequate financing, and (3) top-level protection from bureaucratic-political intrusions. First, laws and regulations must be consistent in support of actors that must execute the program or project. If they do not exist, they should be promulgated in advance of implementation. Laws often conflict and may differ between levels of government. Despite the rhetoric of laws, regulations may interfere with implementation by delaying needed administrative and managerial actions. If transit managers are expected to improve performance of bus-rail systems, but lack authority to shift central government fiscal transfers between line items to ensure service, implementation of transportation programs will suffer—and this can be known in advance of legislative approval.

Second and perhaps most critical is demonstration of top-level political support. This can be predicted by the provision of adequate and sustained budget financing. The implementation of decentralization reforms in three Asian countries soon uncovered gaps in the level of budget support to local units. One of the greatest threats to devolution and local government reform is the failure to provide sufficient resources to meet needs and local aspirations (Cochrane 1983, 6). In Pakistan, local governments were in fact given new statutory sources of revenue. In 2005, they actually had the independence to decide on tax rates and fee levies (Guess 2005). Similarly, the Philippine Local Government Code of 1991 assigned local jurisdictions more service responsibility (e.g., infrastructure, hospitals) and provided a transfer based on population, equalization, and land area to pay for them. This led to a decentralization rarity: a centrally funded surplus for local governments (Guess 2005, 220). By contrast, Indonesian organic laws did not assign new revenue powers or borrowing authority to local governments. That jeopardized the link between costs incurred and services demanded by local citizens (Alm, Aten, and Bahl 2001, 7). Despite these gaps, the programs were implemented anyway, and of the three, the Indonesian and Philippine programs were most successful.

Top-level support can also be measured by its longevity and its provision of protection from organizational intruders. Again, in the case of Asian decentralization program implementation, central authorities (regimes) had to demonstrate support for devolution by supervising and overseeing the programs in the face of bureaucratic tendencies to interfere and control. In all three cases, major opposition from central (in the Philippines) or provincial (in Pakistan and Indonesia) authorities had to be overcome. Even after overcoming opposition long enough to promulgate organic laws, transitory leadership with vacillating support threatened the program in the Philippines. The Philippine Department of Health had eight changes of leadership during 1991–2001; the successive leaders held views ranging from recentralization to continuing support for the reform (Razon-Abad 2001, 7–8).

One might ask how any of these three measures (appropriate laws, adequate funding, and protection from major opponents) can be predicted with any certainty? The answer is that these elements should exist in reasonable amounts, or the program is likely to fail. Conflict of laws and regulations is not as important topic in many countries as it is in the United States. In most places there are no organizations charged with elimination of such conflicts. But at least they can be known in advance by program specialists. Note that in the Pakistan case, although funding was insufficient, this was outweighed for a time by higher-level political support, which of course did not last either. The important lesson for diagnosis is that one needs to assess the combined future effects of these measures and to judge whether these elements are so completely absent as to be fatal to the policy, or are found to be sufficiently available to begin policy implementation.

Structural Design

As noted, policy implementation requires an institutional architecture composed of rationalized institutional structures, relevant organizational functions, efficient budget processes, effective personnel systems, and political sustainability. Somehow policy analysts must know which of these over a multiyear period are going to be assets, and whether they can be strengthened, and which are going to be liabilities, and whether they can be eliminated, for the program to succeed. The difficulty of this task pushes the policy system to reward legislative or contract approval and to consider implementation as an afterthought—someone else's responsibility! Despite this discouraging insight, professional policy analysts need to have a broad portfolio of tools to assess institutional and management capacities and to determine if they can properly implement the policy agenda. Most analysts discover that public-sector organizations responsible for policy implementation develop cumbersome structures that impede management authority and make it difficult to achieve program targets. Since multiple public agencies often partner or network with NGOs and other civil society organizations to implement programs, these structures cut across agency and government lines to the point that a public-private distinction is hard to make. Nevertheless, a structure can be defined as an interlocking set of systems, roles, and responsibilities with authority to perform a function. There are four basic structural issues that should be examined within and across organizations during policy diagnosis:

1. Number of management layers
2. Span of task control
3. Reporting systems
4. Scope and method of service delivery

Management Layers

First, in regard to the number of management layers, organizational reform efforts to increase efficiency often focus on such well-known techniques as decentralizing operational authority, consolidating functions, and reducing the number of management layers. Not surprisingly, organizations grow into ill-designed shapes as they expand into new mission areas and occasionally need pruning. For example, organizations may become top-heavy and concentrate excess authority at the upper levels. Organizations may also be heavy around the waistline with too many midlevel officials, thus interfering with performance with too many layers of management between the line officials, or field officials technically responsible for service operations, and the senior staff members.

Accordingly, organizational analysts need to know when to apply the right reform techniques that can tell them with some certainty whether there are too many or too few layers and what to do about it. In some cases, program objectives are straightforward, such as decentralization and the improvement of service response times. For example, after an organizational review to improve the performance of the Washington, DC, police department, Booz Allen Hamilton recommended decentralization of the homicide unit into district stations. This resulted in frustration for detectives that missed important information by being isolated in the districts. So following a study of homicide unit structures in six major US cities by its own detectives, the department moved to recentralize its homicide unit functions (Thompson 1998). In this case, decentralization fragmented authority and responsibility, which reduced response times. This could have been predicted in advance by asking detectives what they need in order to do their job.

Policy analysts need to know when to add layers—to get control of fragmented activities—and when to eliminate them. Elimination of too many midlevel managers, for example, could save response time in the short run but create long-term costs by knocking out vital and often informal communication links between senior staff members, line managers, and people on the shop floor. One theme of modern public-sector reform is to devolve authority to line managers to achieve centrally set performance targets. This can be a delicate balance, since communication links to senior personnel must be maintained without intruding on line manager autonomy. To get some idea of the number of appropriate managers and layers, analysts often employ staffing ratios to compare their operations with, for example, transit agencies, housing authorities, and personnel departments in other jurisdictions. A 1993 analysis of the California state government concluded that it was suffering from an institutional paralysis that had produced a budget deficit of $11 billion. California's "ill-functioning structure of government" was linked to its multiple layers, which served as complicated channels for the buck to be passed among federal, state, and local authorities (*The Economist* 1993, 22). Public sector organizations should regularly review problems of excessive layering and lack of clear lines of authority.

Span of Control

Second, effective task performance during implementation depends on the apportionment of the right amounts of "span of control," which is the authority and capacity of managers to supervise particular types of tasks. Vertical command structures are typical for routinized tasks such as motor vehicle registration and issuing permits and licenses. Narrow spans of control ensure mechanical efficiency and higher productivity. Broader and flatter managerial structures are more typical for complex, non-routine tasks in which professional creativity and discretion should be encouraged. Examples include research, development, and implementation of intergovernmental reform programs in particular sectors like health or education. It happens that organizational designers specify the wrong spans of control by setting up tall, multilayered, hierarchical structures for complex tasks, reducing professional autonomy and hampering results. Professionals such as engineers, architects, and doctors working in government need the freedom and respect to exercise their skills without harassment by multiple layers of management generalists narrowly interpreting detailed regulations.

In principle, organizational structures should permit exploration and innovation, meaning a broader span of control with flat structures and few, if any, layers of management between tasks and staff members. It is important that organizations periodically determine whether they have too many layers or ill-defined spans of controls. Again, they can do this by comparing their structures with the costs and outputs of organizations having similar policy missions in other jurisdictions or levels of government. For this task, the organizations can rely on in-house policy analysis units or outside management consultants. The danger of using outside consultants is that the review and reform experience is not internalized and instead becomes an expensive one-shot deal.

Reporting Systems

Third, policy implementation suffers because organizations often have ill-designed reporting systems. If reporting chains are unclear, employees end up serving several masters at the expense of accountability and performance. This is a common problem in government, where shared authority is the rule and "messy" policy problems cut across jurisdictional and organizational boundaries. An oft used but simplistic solution is to tighten up reporting and control systems—to monitor staff more closely with software programs or closed-circuit television cameras to ensure that they are actually there and producing results. This kind of micromanagement and suspicious paternalism through excessive reporting requirements harms staff morale. Such requirements are often designed to "keep people employed" at more senior levels. Most staff members who do the reporting recognize that they are contributing to excessive data generation and that there is no one to read or analyze it. The inordinate operational time wasted in developing reports might have been more profitably spent in correcting the allocation of resources to improve policy delivery.[2]

Where organizations share reporting responsibility to regulators (e.g., for mine safety), incentives are created to pass the buck and avoid making politically difficult decisions (i.e., repairing or closing the mine). On the fiscal side, excessive layering without clear lines of authority can lead to intergovernmental cannibalism and regulatory failure, with a high probability of major disasters. As noted, the state of California suffered from the information fragmentation problem in 1993, and it is much worse in 2009! Conversely, core fiduciary tasks, such as authorizing checks, reviewing vouchers, and performing internal control operations, require unified command authority with shared information. For such cash-management and control functions, it is important to provide checks and balances through the division of responsibilities and duties. Definitions of reporting roles and responsibilities should be clear. For example, the duties and responsibilities of department heads and supervisory employees should be defined and their relationships set forth in organizational charts and written instructions contained in administrative codes and policy ordinances. If they are not, this can weaken policy implementation.

Service Delivery

Fourth, in considering the scope and method of service delivery, basic structural issues are often critical for effective policy results. Systems may be clogged by internal problems that have major implications for policy results. As will be discussed further, the organization of fiscal management systems can affect the planning and implementation of macroeconomic policies. Weak costing and expenditure planning systems can lead to the underestimation of multiyear investment programs, increasing the instability of policy funding and weakening the fiscal position of government (i.e., greater deficits). Budget systems need to be informed by cost-accounting systems that reveal the full costs of programs to allow for rational cuts and additions to competing programs—for example, primary versus higher education, primary health care versus preventive medicine, or roads versus education. Only through the effective operation of such support systems can policy costs be measured to allow analysis of the relationships between costs and benefits and costs and program effectiveness.

Performing an institutional pre-audit unfortunately requires information for decisions now on the costs and risks of going forward. Improvements in support systems are medium-term propositions and, more importantly, may cost more than they are worth. That is, improvements in cost-accounting, for instance, are not cheap or easy to make, and they take time. For political reasons, it is often easier to ignore these kinds of institutional constraints that might impede the administration of policy and simply paper them over with shiny new computer systems. In the 1990s, the US Internal Revenue Service (IRS) spent more than $4 billion on new computer systems to increase management control over the tax code. The proper approach would have been to perform a root-and-branch review (or institutional pre-audit) to simplify the tax code itself and deal with IRS structural and management problems before automation. Note that, unintentionally, emphasis on the supporting systems in the institutional context distracted focus from problems with the policy rules and procedures themselves. Automation of the IRS can never change the tax code!

In short, an exclusive focus on the institutional and organizational context, without prior change of the policies themselves, can delay reform—or result in implementation of programs that make the problems worse. In other policy areas as well, emphasis on expensive computerization of inefficient and opaque institutional systems may not make much difference. Many government reform efforts are misguided in focusing on automation of bad systems that diminish policy results.

By contrast, where fiscal management systems support sound fiscal policy-making, the results can be both rapid and quite spectacular. From the 1990s up to late 2007, political will at the national level of US government was strong enough to diminish inflation, unemployment, and the growth in fiscal deficits to their lowest levels since the 1960s. In 2000, if one includes revenues from the Social Security trust fund, the federal government budget had a surplus for two years and was projected to continue in the black well into the early part of the twenty-first century. With the banking system bailouts through the Troubled Asset Relief Program (TARP) and other responses to the recession, the fiscal deficit is now at 13.5% of GDP, and unemployment is at 9.7% and growing. The costs of current policies are expected to increase the overall public debt to 300% of GDP by 2080, from only 60% of GDP in 2010 (Committee for a Responsible Federal Budget [CRFB] 2009). In the past, appropriate fiscal policies have created the right environment for economic growth, and they will likely do so in the future as policymakers act on the deficit and debt projections of policy. Effective fiscal policies in the 1980s and 1990s produced "virtuous circles" in which resultant economic growth increased private earnings and public revenues. Assuming some causality, economic growth lowered the fiscal deficit, in turn reducing inflationary pressures on interest rates. Lower interest rates on loans encouraged borrowing and investment, which, as multiplied through the economy, produced further economic growth, and so on (Pearlstein 1997). Improved growth benefits certain policies, such as income and poverty policies, that require less budgetary funding as median household incomes rise. At the same time, policymakers' ability to concentrate public resources on the poor depends largely on knowing fiscal balances and making proper projections on expenditure commitments and available revenues. The current danger is that the virtuous circle could become vicious again, leading to inflation, fiscal instability, and even default.

An important lesson of the current stimulus (around 5.8% of GDP in gross terms) (*The Economist* 2009a) is that more funds and more personnel are often really needed for service and policy performance. Many disagree and imagine that infrastructure and social policies can finance and implement themselves. In the real world, that is dangerous nonsense. That is a lesson that needed relearning after years of downsizing and cutbacks that often achieved worse service, albeit at lower short-run costs. Cuts in the Washington, DC, Public Works Department in the 1990s, for instance, produced declines in street sweeping, paving, and construction. It is also true that such cuts tend to produce marginal reductions in corruption and bloat, which play well to the media and blogs. But what is forgotten is that policy implementation also suffers. Thus, budget increases have improved on-time trash collection, responses to litter complaints, miles of roads resurfaced, and such fleet-management measures as snow-removal vehicle readiness, and decreased time needed to register motor vehicles (Lipton 1998). While the performance falls short of planned improvements, the link between funding and performance is clear.

This is not to say that institutional context can make up for poorly designed policies. Structural factors, specifically definitions of institutional roles and management systems, are important to policy results, but they are not as important as having technically sound policies in the first place. Implementing rules and regulations may not be conducive to good policy results: Organizations may follow these rules with precision but still achieve poor results. For instance, child protection systems that implement social service policies often face this problem. Children are often abused, or even killed, by their caregivers even after social service agencies follow all their rules "to a T"—investigating complaints, tallying reasonable explanations for child injuries, visiting families, and even paying utility bills to keep families together. But in many cases, children are returned to the dangerous, dysfunctional families and continue to be abused by adults. Such situations lead to another round of public complaints and calls for clarification of agency policies and standardization of routines (Jeter and Levine 1997). An important question is whether many policies unrealistically assume that implementing agencies can completely control their environments (e.g., families, dysfunctional adults, confidentiality laws, and laws restricting information sharing with police). The institutions may be administratively weak, they may be legally incapable of controlling all stake-holders outside government, and the policies themselves may be technically deficient and require review.

Two perennial questions pertain to organizational structure: What is the optimal size of the organization implementing policy or delivering the service? And are there cheaper, more effective means of policy implementation than in the public sector?

Optimal Size of Service Delivery Organizations

First, what staff size is needed to deliver a service? A common problem with modern government agencies is mission overload, in which the growth of workloads results in multiple and conflicting activities that are hard to manage and control. The budget of the US Immigration and Naturalization Service (INS) doubled to $3.1 billion in FY 1997 from only four years earlier. After being moved into the Department of Homeland Security (DHS) and becoming the US Citizenship and Immigration Services (USCIS), the agency's budget still increased by 50% from FY 2007 to FY 2009. It is still one of the fastest growing agencies in the federal government, being charged with the conflicting missions of controlling the nation's borders, expelling illegal immigrants, processing citizenship applications, and hiring foreign workers. An earlier proposal recommended the reorganization of INS duties along functional lines. The agency itself would retain border control functions, but citizenship applications and administration of hiring foreign workers would be transferred to the US State and Labor Departments, respectively (Schmitt 1997). As noted, the agency is now the USCIS within DHS.

Under such conditions of growing agency workload and conflicting missions, policy analysis can focus on the results of cost centers. These are the lowest units in which managers are assigned cost responsibility (e.g., school, hospital, or road department). Policy analysis allows management to link costs and results and to measure costs per unit of outputs (either directly or by proxy). Contemporary civil service reforms around the world are concentrating on determining the appropriate size of policy delivery organizations. Such determination is often difficult because the size of organizations may not have been measured correctly. Control over the number of staff positions requires that job descriptions relate clearly to pay and grade scales, and that the latter be linked to the payroll system, eliminating the ghost-worker problem and establishing a base for achieving effective policy results through an optimally sized organization. A common way to determine the optimal size of the civil service by policy area is to use comparative staffing ratios (e.g., staff members per line personnel, employees per capita, teachers to students, and administrators to teachers). Such information assists in the analysis of implementation capacity (e.g., the number and quality of actual professionals assigned to a specific policy).

Improving Implementation Efficiency

Second, should the policy be delivered by a private contractor instead of a public-sector agency? Related to this, should the structure of the lead public-sector agency be modified to exclude particular functions altogether? These are the "what" questions that should be asked early on to streamline policy institutions. Failure to do so can result in the flaws noted above: performing inappropriate tasks more efficiently and computerizing bad systems. To minimize waste in policy implementation, it is critical that management have sufficient authority and responsibility to allocate necessary funds. Since many goods traditionally defined as "public" (nonexcludable and nonrival) have with technology been redefined as "toll goods" (nonrival but excludable) or "common pool goods" (rival but nonexcludable), market and penalty prices as well as subsidies can be applied to achieve policy results (Mikesell 2007, 4). Private firms and NGOs can deliver many of these goods, leaving the public sector to regulate and set appropriate policy norms. Many believe that broadening the policy framework can improve service effectiveness and efficiency. Governments need to provide services and regulate goods; they can deliver them effectively through private and nongovernmental firms. As an incentive to streamline their own operations, governments now attempt to mirror contractor costs and results, and their implementation performance is often compared to them. State and local governments in the United States have been delivering services through outsourcing and privatization in such areas as sanitation, ambulance services, urban transit, airport ownership and operations, prison operation, education, police, fire, hospitals, parking lots, car towing, and tree trimming for many decades. National policies are also implemented through private delivery in areas such as pensions, tax collection, and postal services. Many years of experience with contractor delivery of public services suggests that there are at least five rules that should be followed if privatization is to function properly (Raimondo 1992, 42):

- The goods or services should be precisely defined.
- Selection must be by a truly competitive process.
- Private-contractor performance must be regularly evaluated.

- The public sector must be able to replace inept private contractors.
- Government must be concerned about end results, not the means by which the goods or services are provided.

Functional Operations

When the goal is to improve implementing organizations and policy results, the temptation is to overhaul larger structures. This refers to major recombination of existing organizations and institutional systems across jurisdictional and legal boundaries. Restructuring or reorganization is often large scale, long term, and high visibility (e.g., the "reinventing government" reform efforts and program reviews of the 1980s–90s). New policy frameworks are created. The basis for the large-scale, strategic focus is the notion that the existing organizations operate within structures and perform grouped sets of activities for particular purposes (i.e., functions).

Inadequate functional performance (the "how" questions) can also stymie policy results. These functions are either poorly performed or improperly located and need to be eliminated, fixed, or contracted out. Thus, functional review serves as an aid to rebuilding state structures (UNDP 2001). Functional reviews can also serve as part of the institutional audit to determine policy implementation capacity. Very often, structures are not distinguished from functions, leading to confusion and reform fatigue. Because of this conceptual confusion, very often structural overhaul is called for when all that is needed is new leadership and better management (Stier 2009).

Functional Review and Business Process Analysis

To perform a functional review, the organization should first be subdivided into responsibility centers that relate to core functions. A relatively exhaustive list of core functions would include: policy (e.g., norms as well as forecasting and planning); service delivery (e.g., responsiveness to clients and customers); regulatory (e.g., licensing, certification, inspection, and compliance); supervision and monitoring (e.g., enabling and management of performance progress); and support (e.g., finance management) (UNDP 2001, 39). Related functions should then be combined into single managerial units on the theory that greater results will occur. Over time, organizations face the latest ideas brought in by new chief executive officers and consultants. Repeated reorganizations occur, disrupting the workflow and weakening performance in the process of trying to install new systems based on the latest management fad. Recall the example of the decentralized and recentralized homicide unit of the Washington, DC, police department following two functional reviews that reached different conclusions (Thompson 1998). It is true that functions may be added to strengthen the political influence of an organization as much as to improve its performance. Unrelated functions are often added without improving performance, which later creates management coordination problems. Hence it is wise to periodically determine which functions should be eliminated or consolidated, and this should be done by an institutionalized review process using a tested methodology (UNDP 2001). If no such process exists, it can be done in-house through the management audit process. Outside consultants can serve this function, but ideally an organization should gain the capacity to review its own operations.

Examples abound of misplaced or redundant functions. For example, in many countries the business-licensing (regulatory) function is spread vertically through several levels of government, and horizontally across several departments, within a city administration. This weakens licensing by diffusing inspections and compliance. Revenue surveys may determine what constraints exist to the collection of projected fee and tax yields; these constraints may be caused by faulty revenue functions that impede payments and collections. In such cases, it may be useful to consolidate licensing and revenue functions in one tax office serving a particular area and then review the efficiency of operations. Failure to do this may impede economic growth and service efficiency. In Ukraine, for instance, establishing a business requires contending with forty sets of rules, licenses, and tax requirements administered by several agencies. This is obviously more than an institutional efficiency issue—the very existence of the rules serves as a roadblock to entrepreneurs and benefits crony capitalism (*The Economist* 1997b, 45). Functional reviews serve to identify weak and misplaced functions and focus attention on them as potential constraints to policy implementation.

Comparative analysis of other governments can suggest which functions should be included in an organization and how they should perform. For example, most finance departments in state and local governments in this country include tax, budget, accounting, payroll, and debt management, with purchasing often a separate department and function. Similarly, functional processes may reveal major inefficiencies. Managers may have immersed themselves in the details of a system and fail to reexamine the process systematically with an eye toward elimination of unnecessary steps. The unnecessary steps may also be bribery points and serve the function of a supplementary pay system in poor countries. Since this is the abuse of public position for private gain, it is called corruption. As an example, federally funded municipal road construction and repair projects in Washington, DC, required approvals from twenty-seven different city officials. This complicated approval process delayed road projects and increased costs (through inflated contractor bids to cover for time lost and through payments to officials to move paperwork along). Following a review of process workflows in 1996, the approval process now takes only twelve officials—this should cut the time required for contract approval by up to six months (*Washington Post* 1996).

Financial Management Systems

In our view, financial management systems are the most important of the four variables affecting policy implementation. Following the money to determine what is happening is as important in public policy as in any other field. Structural problems and redefinition of management roles and lines of authority are medium-term matters that take longer than plugging fiscal management holes and straightening out the accounts. Fiscal management problems can be dealt with quickly in many cases. Policy outcomes are affected by the institutional arrangements of financial management, which are traditionally broken down into functional components. To the extent that planning, policymaking, and budgeting are linked by good financial management, policy results are likely to be improved. Government failures are due less to how an agency is organized, and more to the poor performance of senior leadership and their inability to manage people in the culture of that agency (Stier 2009). This problem in the level of analysis being undertaken frequently results in recommendations for major policy changes, when the actual problem is at the level of internal fiscal management. The first formal audit of the Medicare program revealed annual losses of up to $23 billion in overpayments to hospitals, doctors, and other health care providers (*The Economist* 1997a, 25). This suggests that improvements in internal controls and financial management systems may be as much of a cause of high health care expenditures as poor health care policy design. In short, there may be high payoffs in improved policy results from strengthened fiscal management systems. The financing of President Obama's 2009 health care reform proposal to increase coverage to 29 million more citizens is predicated on major cost savings in Medicare. Given more expected savings from Medicare rationalization and the perverse cost incentives created by current regulations (Goldhill 2009), program funding could materialize and achieve deficit neutrality.

Multiple Functions of Public Financial Management Systems

Public financial management (PFM) refers to a series of functions, including budgeting, accounting and reporting, cash management, debt management, payroll, procurement, treasury disbursement, and internal control and audit systems (Coe 1989). In this sense, PFM is an institutional system. The problem for policymaking and policy implementation is that these functions are rarely integrated into an effective system. They tend to perform well or badly in isolation. Under these circumstances, fixing one function normally makes little difference to overall policy implementation, which can leave the erroneous impression that fiscal management makes little difference for policy results.

Governments in the United States federal system and overseas need to strengthen each function and to integrate them into financial management systems. This by itself will not solve all organizational and institutional problems and magically lead to perfect policy implementation. On the other hand, efforts to integrate financial management functions often unearth major problems in both policy design and organizational performance that need to be fixed. The very process of installing an integrated financial management system (IFMS) is itself a form of policy and institutional analysis. In essence, an IFMS means that all financial and physical transactions are recorded in one main account and shared across financial functions and organizational levels for policymaking. This is considered "all-of-government" or "whole-government" accounting. The purpose of an IFMS is to set central standards that allow information to be aggregated and compared across operational units, but not to control these units directly. The IFMS concept presupposes that implementation authority to combine resources and achieve these standards will be delegated to lower operational units. Rigorous fiscal management through the IFMS is combined with operational freedom to manage services without intrusive central controls. The IFMS, then, is an effort to strengthen policy implementation. The system decentralizes fiscal management within a framework of central norms. This strengthens fiscal discipline over sectoral expenditures, such as health and education.

Integrating PFM Systems

Unlike many management information systems (MIS) reforms, IFMS does not presume that more information is better or that all fiscal data is of equal value to decision makers. IFMS reform efforts recognize that different levels of institutional decision making require different levels of information aggregation. This systems-design issue directly affects policy performance. The correct level of data aggregation must be available at each managerial level for different responsibility centers. IFMS design should encompass both responsibility or cost centers (central versus local) and organizational levels (strategic planning versus daily task control). For example, central health officials need information to compare program costs and benefits (vaccination versus treatment of childhood diseases). Regional managers need information to compare regional clinic operating costs—they need both physical and fiscal data. Managers at individual clinics need data on line-item expenditures to compare budgeted with actual figures and other data to measure the clinic's effectiveness (Bartel 1996, 7). At the same time, senior managers at regional health centers do not want to be engaged in routine operational issues, such as billing or fee collections, at the expense of their responsibilities for strategic planning and revenue generation. Senior managers also must be confident that the classification and coverage system (typically the economic classification) is sound, so that reported data reflect actual changes in resources consumed for those items.

The fragmentation of fiscal functions within and across policy institutions prevents policymakers from obtaining timely and accurate data for decision making; this represents a major organizational boundary problem. An IFMS is one way to develop a system for sharing information and tracking policy and program costs. It allows all stakeholders to be integrated into one system for purposes of policy implementation. The core functions of the financial management system, as noted, are budgeting, accounting, and cash and debt management. Budgeting lays out the financial plan to achieve organizational objectives and allots funds to agencies for such purposes as expenditure control and program management. Cash management forecasts the supplies of fiscal resources needed to complete the plan. Accounting records the fiscal effects of implementing policies and provides budget- and cash-management functions with feedback on what resources have been received and expended, and what still needs to be secured to fulfill the financial plan. Debt management arranges financing for longer-term investment projects. Information provided by budget, cash management, and accounting allows the debt or public credit function to arrange timely financing that does not exceed the budget's capacity to cover debt service payments in a sustainable way (Bartel 1996, 13). Ancillary functions that may be added later to the system include asset management, procurement, and personnel management. It is not easy to foresee policy problems if information from these functions is not available and is not used for policy management. For example, failure to link payroll disbursements to the personnel roster can result in over-budgeting for personnel costs. Fixed personnel costs for particular policies become inflated, resulting in superficially high-cost policies that could then be discontinued for the wrong reasons.

If these functions deteriorate, the financial management system can become discredited as a means of planning and allocating resources and implementing policy. Cycles of mutually reinforcing skepticism will diminish incentives for officials to take policy analysis seriously. Under these conditions, in which it is perceived that the existing system has little to do with the fiscal resources needed to attain desired policy results, officials have every incentive to sidestep existing regulations and seek as much "rent" as possible for their ministry, policy area, or even their own pockets.

How can improved financial management systems and institutions lead to better public policy? Suppose, for example, that analysis is needed on the costs and consequences of privatizing water and sewer systems. First, analysts would need to address the question of whether authority should be delegated to private firms. This requires comparative cost and result information on present systems operations. Second, analysts would need information to establish the policy framework, the system of rules in which action should take place (e.g., contracts and implementing regulations should guarantee that concessionaires can cut off service for nonpayment of tariffs by consumers and firms). Third, information is needed on current system problems. In the water and sanitation sector, there are major problems of overstaffed public water authorities, underpricing, leakage or lost water (water that is unaccounted for), and fee collections and billing. All of these contribute to poor service coverage and quality and undermaintained and antiquated systems.

Note that information to perform the analysis is highly specialized and in some cases may not even be available to a government. Yet the required information falls within the purview of several components of the financial management system. The budget should record obligations and outlays to private contractors on water and sanitation concessions; there should be activity statistics in the budget, whether zero-based or performance formats are used; and the statistics should indicate costs per unit and costs per result on a multiyear basis. Budgeted costs and resultant outlays need to be linked by a cost-accounting system that analyzes costs of production. A government unit might not know what it actually costs to deliver sanitation services and, hence, what it should pay in a concession agreement. That is, the government unit knows only what it has been "spending" from the budget and not really "costing" on a procurement basis.

In other cases, if the classification system is overbroad, what is spent may not be clear either. As we will see below, high schools may be spending funds for instruction, which, when broken down, includes payment for many noninstructional personnel. This confuses efforts to link teaching to educational results and to increase the productivity of high per-pupil expenditures. To perform real cost-benefit and cost-effectiveness analysis (see chapters 5–7), public-sector organizations must have either cost-accounting or cost-finding systems that allow costs to be measured and distinguished simply from appropriations expenditures. Organizations without these systems can still rely on analysis from traditional economic budget classifications and improve policy productivity.

The procurement system can contribute to measuring cost of services. The competitive bidding process helps uncover information on fees, performance targets, and qualified operators that governments can use to design fee policies and set performance targets (Haarmeyer and Mody 1997, 37). The revenue system provides information on rates of fee collection, and the accounting system provides information on obligations and outlays. This allows budget officials to monitor expenditure progress and avoid deficit spending. The budget system will provide information on the maintenance needs of existing facilities and operating costs of future capital investments. Together, timely and accurate information from these functions provides policymakers with a composite picture of the fiscal implications of policy decisions.

Thus, each fiscal function needs to be evaluated regularly to guard against breakdown and deterioration. Let us review the relevant components of each function and suggest ways to strengthen them.

Public Budgeting

Budgeting matches needs with resources in a process that results in an approved spending plan. The budget process contains four sequential phases: formulation, approval, implementation, and evaluation.

Budget Formulation and Approval   Budget formulation is critical because it is in this phase that ministries can make their case to the central budget office for new programs and continuation of existing ones. Budget formulation is the translation of government policies and programs into their financial implications. The central budget office—the Office of Management and Budget (OMB) in the United States, or the ministry of finance (MOF) abroad—has the job of reviewing the macroeconomic situation and translating aggregate fiscal balance and debt sustainability limits into budget ceilings for departments. It is important that budget policies be legally and financially transparent, and policies should proceed from representative institutions. In 1981, for example, New York state voters defeated a $500 million bond issue for new prison construction. Governor Cuomo then used the Urban Development

Corporation (a public agency charged with building housing for the poor) to issue revenue bonds. And so state prison policy was decided against voter wishes and used an opaque financing instrument that required higher interest payments than general-obligation, voter-approved bonds (Schlosser 1998, 56). Since interest costs on debt are an opportunity cost for other recurrent programs in the budget, budget policy analysis needs to examine the costs and benefits of such policies as well as the effect on future financial conditions. Naturally, where policies will be decided at higher levels regardless of technical analysis, policy analysts have few incentives to proceed, but it is important to go on record in any case.

Several ingredients are essential in preparing budgets that are transparent to planners and useful to managers. First, budget codes should not contain excessive classifications. Too much detail can hide critical information and overload the system. The basic control classification is economic—salaries, supplies, travel, maintenance, and capital. Within each category—for instance, maintenance—budgeted categories must be linked to precise definitions and ultimately to the chart of accounts. Failure to do this might allow charging minor maintenance to rehabilitation or major maintenance, which is a capital and therefore financed item. This would hide operating expenses. Classification should also cover all sources of revenue and expenditure destinations, including extra-budgetary funds, such as public enterprises and such off-budget items as trust funds. Budget codes and classifications (or structures) should be reorganized periodically to reflect changes in government policies and programs. Otherwise they become outmoded and hinder effective management.

Second, budget ceilings should be communicated in the instructions from the central budget office before submissions by departments. Procedures for budget formulation and expected data for submissions need to be transparent. Failure to make the budget "call" instructions clear severs the link between planning and budgeting, and then real budgeting starts to occur during the execution phase, rather than the expenditure-planning and formulation phase. The result is short-term budgeting, which prevents out forward planning. To encourage proper expenditure planning, ceilings should apply to both current and capital expenditures and be based on a public investment program with inputs from each sector (e.g., health, education).

Third, capital and current budget items should be clearly defined and distinguished to avoid capitalization of operating funds and misallocation of resources. Current budget items should not be normally financed by the capital budget because, as noted, this can hide major operating deficits. At the same time, expenditure planning for both categories should be an integrated annual process. In many countries current and capital budgets are planned separately. This encourages construction of many projects that likely will be undermaintained and prematurely replaced through more debt financing. The resource implications of capital budgets on operating budgets, especially future operating and maintenance requirements, should be displayed clearly for effective policy choice. The relationship between a capital plan and capital budget is illustrated by the following table. This describes a three-project capital budget and six-year capital improvement plan (CIP) that illustrates several points:

- The capital budget is the first year of the capital plan. As the plan changes each year, the first year's portion will be modified (rolled forward) or updated.

- The relation between time and funding requirements is important. Funds must be available at each point or projects will stall. If progress on any one project slips, this affects the viability of the entire CIP. The question then becomes: What methods should be used to allocate funds among unfinished projects of varying urgency?

- Capital expenditures are "lumpy," or unevenly sequenced due to the technical requirements of the construction project. Expenditures occur at different times throughout the calendar year for such necessities as site purchases, architectural and engineering contracts, construction contracts, and furnishings and equipment.

- Inputs from the operating units should enable the central budget office to develop performance measures (physical and fiscal) to assess efficiency and effectiveness. Budgets should be presented in multiyear formats (past, current, planned), with data on both fiscal expenditures and unit costs of activities. Measures should be selected with incentives in mind. For example, use of a cost-per-mile measure for new road paving would encourage managers to skimp on construction quality, thus increasing downstream costs for maintenance in future years. To prevent this kind of gaming with activity statistics, departments could use measures that combine the level and cost of road maintenance.

- Finally, budgets must be realistically finalized. The central budget office must be able to assess whether submitted requests are based on realistic costs. Cost and policy analysts are critical for this. Conversely, the office must be able to appeal arbitrary cuts that ignore analysis and need.

In table 3.1, note that almost 50% of total CIP funds are needed in year 4. This suggests that the financing plan should be evened out. In terms familiar in the United States, municipal bonds should be issued, for example, with maturities so that the annual debt service payments in the operating budget for interest and amortization remain the same over the life of the bond issue. The length of the bond issue should mirror the useful life of the facility to be constructed.

Budget Administration and Expenditure Control Just as figure 1.1 in chapter 1 postulated a neat division between policy formulation or analysis, on the one hand, and implementation, on the other, so also the literature divides budget preparation and budget management, administration or implementation. Budget analysis is performed during preparation, because once the budget is approved there is little time to rethink basics during the pressures of day-to-day operations. Systems that exclude analysis because capacities are lacking or because cynics recognize that revenues will not materialize anyway tend to produce budgets that are relatively meaningless as guides to policy progress. Some policies may be rebudgeted and reviewed during execution; this exercise can improve policy performance. For instance, implementation of the Washington, DC, educational reform policy based on teacher effectiveness may be assisted by a budget process that requires school-level cuts and reallocations to achieve mandated fiscal balance. With almost continuous opposition from the city council and Washington Teachers' Union since the beginning of the reform, the reductions in force required by the budget process offer Chancellor Rhee an opportunity to get rid of underperforming teachers (*Washington Post* 2009), precisely what she has been trying to do without great success in the past.

Since the post–Korean War period in the United States, national security policies have been increasingly made during the execution phase. Lacking authorization or appropriations, operations begin and continue pursuant to such lawful mechanisms as transfers, reprogramming, rescissions, and supplemental funds to finance policies, with either other program funds or budget savings through reestimation of inflation or fluctuations in foreign exchange rates (Banks and Straussman 1999, 136). The war in Iraq was begun and financed during the execution phases of the FY 2003–4 budget years.

Nevertheless, budget administration or implementation is important to public policy, because it is often at this stage that major control problems and opportunities for course corrections arise. Implementation is often called the Achilles heel of public policy and budgeting: During this phase, the central budget office pulls various levers to try to control the budget in action, such as in allotments, pre-audit and internal control, and cash management (Axelrod 1995). (Note: Donald Axelrod considers cash management a budget function, but Margaret Bartel and Charles Coe see it as one of many financial management functions.) Constrictions in budget pipelines are a major cause of

Table 3.1   Example of Capital Budget and Five-Year Program

CIP	Capital Budget ($)		Capital Program ($)			
	2011	2012	2013	2014	2015	2016
Local Hospital	500,000	150,000		3,000,000		500,000
Public Schools	500,000	500,000	500,000	500,000	500,000	
Local Clinic			75,000		2,000,000	
Total	1,000,000	650,000	575,000	3,500,000	2,500,000	500,000

poor service delivery and problems with project implementation, and thus need to be anticipated during policy formulation (via an institutional pre-audit). Ideally, the funds released should match the needs proposed by spending units. To the extent that funding shortfalls occur, line managers need sufficient authority to reprogram funds in order to keep policies on track. In practice, most of government uses a top-down financial control model that is based on distrust and that, in the name of control, largely encourages more distrust. Exceptions to this practice are the Arizona and Oklahoma legislatures, which have broadened the basis of budget execution control from a narrow focus on controlling explanations for specific objects of expenditure like personnel and supplies. The new approach provides broader discretion to managers to shift funds within the budget to achieve program results (Franklin 2002).

Allotment Systems   An allotment system is used to allocate funds to programs and projects on a timely basis. Systemic and procedural bottlenecks delay release of funds; for example, procurement procedures for purchasing may delay the release of funds to departments for needed supplies, materials, and capital equipment. Excessive process can result in losses of discounts and other cost-saving opportunities. The bottlenecks can also generate arrears to suppliers that are carried forward in higher future bids. Both arrears from the system and inflationary bids by suppliers can drive up the costs of policy implementation. Rigid procedures include those covering managers who need flexibility to transfer and reprogram funds to keep services delivered (which also links back to the legal and regulatory framework). When revenues do not materialize and funds are not forthcoming from an OMB, MOF, or central budget office to spending units, the controls discourage management from doing anything other than mindlessly but safely following the expenditure plan made at the beginning of the fiscal year.

At the same time, budget departments must act when revenues collapse or expenditure overruns become evident from monthly reports; they often have to impose cash limits on departmental spending (i.e., emergency measures that convert what was an annual budget into twelve monthly allotments). If such actions are combined with procedures that delay allotments to departments for minor accounting and reporting irregularities, the finance department effectively creates a quarterly or monthly budgeting system. This action increases fiscal uncertainty and planning problems and encourages "repetitive budgeting" (Caiden and Wildavsky 1975). Under "repetitive budgeting" conditions, approved expenditure plans must be constantly remade and will disappear, for all practical purposes, while the ink is still wet on them. They do not guide management or policy decisions. Although they turn off the flow of funds at the source and preserve fiscal balance for macroeconomic reasons, cash limits are very difficult to design so that they do not disrupt policies and programs. They create microeconomic difficulties in exchange for apparent macroeconomic benefits.

As suggested above, flexible controls during budget implementation are needed to encourage managers to allocate resources creatively in order to get the most results from the least funds. Line managers need budget flexibility and the authority to approve transactions. Failure to provide line managers with expenditure approval authority can actually result in transactions being approved by those who have neither the experience nor the authority to do so (Bartel 1996, 22).

Similarly, because most policies face unforeseen difficulties during the year, budget administration needs to be flexible. Flexibility can be hindered in the name of control by: (1) line-item controls over expenditures, (2) narrow limits on transfers and reprogramming during the fiscal year, and (3) pre-audit by internal control accounting personnel. First, controls over line-item expenditures for contracts, personnel positions, and other specific transactions like travel or supplies are usually counterproductive. The controls consume staff time, delay approval requests, restrict managerial flexibility, and discourage optimal approaches to policy implementation (Hayes et al. 1982, 65). Control can be exercised by quarterly allotments processes without the need for line-item control of specific transactions. Such control usually generates a large volume of budget modifications, most of which have little significance for policy or budgeting. Efforts to prevent noncompliance often cost more than they are worth. A more cost-effective approach is typically through ex-post audit (66).

Transfer and Reprogramming Authority   Second, budget transfer authority is not an easy area in which to design controls, and some jurisdictions simply prohibit all budget modification. In the centrally planned economies, such as the former Soviet system, the budget passively executed the plan, and few modifications were necessary for implementing what were conceived of as near-perfect material investment concepts. Rigid controls over modification ensured that managers would not engage in efficient or innovative behavior. In many cases, budget controls resulted in policy failures.

On the other hand, failure to control reprogramming and transfers eliminates the budget as a guideline for expenditures and as an instrument of policy. Funds that were budgeted for the poor, for example, may end up as public-sector salaries. But excessively rigid controls prevent managers from implementing policy—discouraging risk taking and innovative behavior by empowered personnel, which were key concepts in the "reinventing government" movement. Since few policies are self-executing, that invariably meant waste and inefficiency.

A tested option is to exchange discretion for control; in other words, to redesign incentives to get optimal amounts of program management and fiscal control. The Arizona and Oklahoma legislatures have enacted this option to improve policy results. Australian managers have almost complete authority to reprogram funds during the year (including between personnel and nonwage categories) in exchange for significant responsibility for attaining policy targets set by the central finance department. Because this approach combines management incentives for performance with results-oriented budgeting and decentralization of operational responsibilities, the Australian (and New Zealand) models of financial management reform are in vogue around the world. In Australia, the Department of Finance provides "forward estimates" that combine budget ceilings and policy output targets. The "running cost" system provides funding releases in lump sums to departments, whose managers may then transfer between line items and even across fiscal years with Department of Finance approval (Keating and Rosalky 1983). Reprogramming that requires higher-level approval is limited to major line-item shifts (e.g., personnel to nonpersonnel costs). Managers are held accountable for policy performance targets and permitted maximum flexibility in the use of resources to attain them; controls are largely ex-post audit rather than pre-control or pre-audit.

Third, as will be addressed later in this chapter, budget administration can be hampered by excessively rigid internal controls (e.g., procedures for personnel, procurement, and treasury). Rather than verify the sufficiency of funds and the legality of the expenditure consistent with approved appropriations, internal control personnel can be overzealous and begin second-guessing program and policy staff members on technical matters. This is a major problem now with US federal budget contracts for foreign aid.

Excessively rigid and control-oriented behavior is evident in such agencies as the United States Agency for International Development (USAID), in which program officers work for and report to contract officials. Technical officers are agents of contract officials and are called "contracting officers' technical representatives," or COTR (COTR 2009). This means that the contract officials have the last say on what program decisions will be approved in the field. In the context of almost totally unsettled conditions in some foreign countries, USAID contract officials exercise narrow line-item control over minor transfers and second-guess technical program people in the field on questions such as, "Who is a qualified person for the job?" In 1996, a contract official asked the senior author whether a "county" government employee was really a "local" government employee? The request for proposals indicated that local experience would be required, and the USAID contract official decided that county was not local, and therefore the employee was not qualified to work on a USAID local government reform project in Macedonia. As indicated, focusing on internal control transactions in broader batches and employing ex-post control can discourage intrusiveness into program management. These methods can facilitate innovative management and prevent costly delays when decisions have been technically "illegal" (e.g., hiring a county official for a local government position) but probably not an important loss to the government or program. Ex-post control serves as a better deterrent to official malfeasance than costly attempts to prevent noncompliance, which more typically punish initiative and reward sloth.

Monitoring Budget Implementation Monitoring budget implementation results requires a good reporting system—one that records both fiscal and physical program or policy results. It should be well known that line managers need incentives to take time from the uncertainties and frustrations of actual implementation to report ongoing work. It is probably counterproductive to delay funding releases because a report is late or contains errors: This penalizes policy clients and service users and creates further backlogs of budget releases. The result would be to slice up the annual budget into monthly and weekly allotments, which would further impede smooth policy implementation. Excessive reliance on central controls often results in massive reporting requirements that paralyze implementation and weaken policy results. Nevertheless, using real-time computerized reporting systems of IFMSs and financial management information systems (FMISs), managers should be expected to provide timely and accurate feedback to the central budget office on the status of revenues and expenditures. More importantly, if managers can be induced to buy into policy evaluation through incentives, they will report on physical performance as well. Managers in many state and local governments in this country report on unit costs and physical results of current services and capital investment projects. Incentives include actually approving next year's budget or making policy changes consistent with reported performance data; provision of additional personnel; and exemption from controls on budget reprogramming, expenditure approvals, and purchasing.

Traditionally, central budget officials often view delegation of approval authority (for reprogramming funds and reporting uses) as a loss of oversight control. This is a mistaken view, because maintaining authority at the center often results in real loss of budget control in a blizzard of small transactions. The control system intrudes into management discretion but also leads to ineffective policy results. What can be done to delegate authority without giving up oversight control? There are three standard techniques that are widely used in state and local governments in the United States (Bartel 1996, 23). First, budget managers can use "exception reporting." Instead of reviewing all transactions, only those with major planned-versus-actual variances beyond a preset standard are flagged and examined in more detail. Second, managers can review only major financial differences in operating performance between like units (e.g., variations in expenditures for medicine by two clinics). Franklin (2002) noted that two state legislatures take a similar approach, focusing on variations and exceptions in broad batches of line items. Third, managers can decide to review approvals for transactions only above a certain threshold. These three techniques preserve substantive control at higher levels and allow delegation of operating authority to line units. The goal should be to shift expenditure controls to after-the-fact reviews, analogous to post-publication sanctions for libel rather than imposition of prior constraints. Reduction of intrusive pre-controls over expenditures should be part of a package to reform public management in order to improve policy results.

Accounting Systems

Public budgeting can only be as good as its supporting information systems. The two most critical systems are accounting and performance measurement. In particular, accounting systems are considered the "bedrock of budgeting" (Axelrod 1995). To assess an accounting system's capability to implement policy, it is important to know: (1) the fund structure, (2) the rules for measuring revenues and expenditures, and (3) the system's flexibility to relate costs to volume of policy outputs. Note that budgeting refers to public "expenditures," or the cash inputs; a cash accounting system would record these as "expenses" or "costs," that is, the resources consumed in achieving results. But expenditures for resources received occur at different times than expenses for using up or consuming resources. Failure to make this distinction can result in erroneous reporting of fiscal balances (Anthony and Young 1988, 101–2).

Budgetary Expenditures Compared to Costs or Expenses The distinction between costs and expenditures can be seen in the perennial debate on how to strengthen university systems and increase access to higher education. A policy of reducing *expenditures* per student often reduces educational standards, which can be seen in declining faculty-student ratios, classroom overcrowding, uneven quality of teaching and learning, and increases in administrator-faculty ratios. Review of expenditures can prevent reduction of standards where the analysis indicates that most outlays are absorbed by salaries instead of supplies, books, and teaching materials. High per-pupil expenditures, as in Washington, DC, could historically be explained by the high administrator-faculty ratio. Analysis of economic budget categories is useful for predicting implementation success. But the focus on expenditures can only go so far for institutional analysis. The policy objective should be to reduce the *cost* per student through analysis of resource consumption by school organizations and comparison with similar units elsewhere. Cost-accounting systems can provide cost information on the pattern of fixed and variable costs, thus permitting analysis of prices for orders, payments for services, inflationary effects, and so on. A modified accrual system can track commitments and orders before cash payments, leading to improved analysis of costs and thereby to decisions that can improve organizational performance.

By providing data on unit cost of production, the accounting system provides budget and policy analysts with essential information on the cost of attaining policy results. Data on marginal changes in cost per result (e.g., cost per passenger-mile of a transit system) can then be compared with the cost per result of other programs and policies (e.g., cost per graduate of a school system). Examination of such data, along with projected changes in demand for services and the rates of increase or decrease in costs per result, can narrow the basis for allocating resources. Policy analysis, fortified by strong cost accounting, can rationalize budgetary allocations for policies and programs. To the extent that the responsible stakeholders have this cost-analytic capacity, implementation is likely to be more consistent with policy objectives.

To enable analysts to predict the flow and timing of budget resources, governments should account for commitments (that is, obligations for purchase orders or contracts for which funds will be spent later), outlays, and revenues by fund. Funds can be either general or special. General funds cover most transactions of general government, including civil service payments, and intragovernmental revolving funds for support operations within the government (e.g., printing, purchasing, stores, operations). Special funds record dedicated transactions for such specific purposes as service for principal and interest on long-term debt, and enterprise funds for business-type activities like utilities, toll bridges and roads, and trust funds for retirement systems. Cash flows between these funds and particularly general and special funds need to be carefully recorded under "interfund transfers" and monitored to avoid hidden subsidies. For example, budgeting for a state enterprise through the general fund may mask heavy subsidies paid from general revenues to cover its operating losses. This distorted picture can cause policymakers to misallocate resources unknowingly that could have been used for more worthy policy causes. Policy implementation will suffer.

Accounting rules for recording transactions must also be made clear. The purpose of accounting rules is to give policymakers a complete picture of funds available for expenditure. Otherwise, the policymakers can overspend or fail to commit funds that may then revert to the treasury and not be used to benefit program clients. Historically, the US government policy on American Indian trusteeship has been largely a failure, not because of miscalculation of known costs and benefits but because of excluding the costs of defective financial management systems. In particular, the failure by the Bureau of Indian Affairs (BIA) of the Department of the Interior to keep records of income earned on leases inhibited the tracking of collections, investment, and distribution of monies from the Individual Indian Money trust accounting system (*The Economist* 1999, 34–35). Whether a government uses cash accounting or modified accrual accounting, it must be consistent and enforce reporting rules. Otherwise, defects in the existing financial management systems, coupled with frequent indifference to such mundane matters on the part of oversight organizations (here the Interior Department and BIA), will diminish policy results.

Cash versus Modified Accrual Accounting The two major accounting rules in the United States are cash and modified accrual. Cash accounting is based on flow of funds into and out of the budgetary account. Finance directors also need daily information on the organization's cash position—they need to be able to see disbursements, receipts, and statements of operations so they can plan for debt-service obligations and ensure that deficit targets are not exceeded. It is a simple rule, and most budgets are based on estimated cash outlays for the fiscal year. Cash limits, used as a control device by finance departments to deal with revenue shortfalls or unanticipated outlays, are based largely on flow-of-funds analysis. But the cash rule has several problems.

First, the rule can ignore accumulated debt to vendors and result in a floating debt. This complicates cash-management efforts by finance departments and can lead to increases in unfunded liabilities. Second, by estimating budgets on an annual cash basis, multiyear policy benefits tend to be ignored as well, resulting in poor planning. But the use of a modified accrual rule takes account of obligations to pay vendor purchase orders and other contracts. Unlike the cash rule, modified accrual takes account of net liabilities and payables. On the expenditure side, funds are locked up (e.g., by issuance of a purchase order to a vendor) to reveal available balances and to prevent over-expenditure. On the revenue side, revenues are recorded only when available and measurable. If revenues are recorded when due (accrued), budget planners could artificially increase the size of budgets by overestimating future collections. For this reason, the accrual is often modified to record revenues on a cash basis. Whatever rule is used, there is no guarantee that actual costs will be reflected in the accounts.

For policy formulation, policymakers need to know the costs of production and delivery to assess how efficiently services are being delivered. Data on comparative expenditures and expenses (or costs) for similar policies can narrow options for decision making. As is known, the cost of public provision and delivery of many services (paid from the "force account") may differ from the cost of market delivery (contractor outsourcing) of those services. To assess the feasibility of policies that outsource, for instance, education, health, and transportation, individual program costs must be identified and measured. This must include two steps: (1) Expenditures must be converted to expenses by use of cost accounting, and (2) expenses must be allocated to organizational responsibility centers for proper policy management (Kory and Rosenberg 1984, 51). Cost or managerial accounting systems measure fixed, variable, direct, and indirect costs. They also allow development of costs of service and accumulation of data on a job basis (e.g., construction) or process basis (e.g., licensing). In practice, activity costing systems are expensive and rare even in such wealthy countries as the United States. For this reason, some government entities use "cost-finding" systems that rely on existing budget data and simply recast the data periodically to derive the estimates or costs needed (Kory and Rosenberg 1984, 52). The important point is that a jurisdiction should use some reasonable method of ascertaining program costs—almost any method in this area is better than nothing. Many jurisdictions use no method and imply falsely to legislatures and taxpayers that expenditures are the same thing as expenses.

Whether a full-fledged cost-accounting or a partial cost-finding system is used, the accounting system needs to keep the budget people informed so that policies can be developed based on appropriate assessments of costs. One vehicle for this is the cost-accounting report that regularly provides a record of costs incurred against programs and projects (World Bank 1997, 60).

Cash Management

A common institutional problem is that funds become unavailable to finance public policies. As implied here, this is often less a problem of poverty than misallocation and waste due to ill design or poor use of fiscal management system resources. A cash-management system should prevent cash deficits or excesses from occurring over the course of the year. It is more than a system of disbursing funds and should be used to plan and manage the flow of resources to public policies to minimize costs and maximize effectiveness. Whether a cash or accrual accounting system is used, the cash-management function should require preparation of cash flow projections based on the approved budget. Failure to do this can result in a buildup of idle balances. Excess cash on hand should be invested or used to pay down short-term lines of credit. Conversely, approved budgets may suffer from lack of liquidity, resulting in loans from vendors in the form of unpaid bills or arrears. This becomes a cost of ineffective fiscal management policies: Vendors will either increase prices to cover costs tied up in receivables (leading to inflationary pressures) or provide a lower level of service (lowering efficiency) (Bartel 1996, 34).

There are three methods of dealing with cash-management problems: (1) basing budget allotments on solid projections of policy implementation activity, (2) providing flexibility for line managers to transfer and reprogram funds to meet policy targets, and (3) integrating budgeting and cash management. First, the allotments process is one of the major levers that finance departments (the OMB in the United States) exercise in budget control. The finance department allots funds from approved budgets in quarterly payments. But the timing and amounts should be based on inputs from the line agencies. Arbitrarily dividing budgets into twelve equal parts ignores demand and seasonal variations. Policies and programs may either be starved for cash or have excess spending authority at critical points in the service year. Hence, cash flow budgets developed by line agencies as part of the budget-formulation process should reflect cash requirements for the year (or for multiple years if such authority is available). This avoids short-term cash flow problems that lead to repetitive remaking of the budget, which can destroy both agency and client confidence in annual budgets (Caiden and Wildavsky 1975).

Second, budgets should be implemented as planned in order to avoid shifting the actual budgeting stage from formulation to implementation. At the same time, measures need to be built in for unplanned occurrences, such as learning how to do the job better while managing resources. Authority to transfer and reprogram funds during the year should be available and transparent. Overly rigid and time-consuming processes frustrate management, reduce efficiency, and maximize incentives for making end-runs around the system. For this reason, countries such as New Zealand and Australia (and some US states) delegate maximum discretion to line managers for budget implementation within the framework of set fiscal and policy performance targets. This policy maximizes management incentives to learn how to deliver services better and to cut costs. It can also reduce opportunism and the temptation to game the system to make deficits superficially disappear.

For example, faced with political pressure to minimize fiscal deficits and preserve solvency of the Hospital Insurance Trust Fund, in 1996 the Clinton administration transferred $55 billion in home health care expenses from that fund to another Medicare fund (Part B). The trust fund is still financed by payroll taxes and nearly bankrupt, but the Part B fund is covered by US Treasury appropriations. The transfer allowed the administration to avoid asking for an increase in Medicare premiums, resulting in a political benefit. But given the availability of general fund financing, the overall effect of the transfer was to send medical expenditures soaring. As an entitlement, there is no explicit budget constraint, such as the payroll tax base. For this reason, home health care costs during that period rose 10% a year (Chandler 1997). And the transfer simply shifted costs without improving policy effectiveness, thus draining the general budget. Clearly, transfers need to be approved by a quick and transparent process to avoid inefficiencies. But at the same time, the connection between transfers for efficiency reasons and a policy shift that may effectively change approved budget priorities needs to be clarified. Failure to do so allows administrators the discretion to make and change policy during the fiscal year (unacceptable) rather than during budget formulation (acceptable).

Third, budgeting should be linked to cash management to avoid cash flow problems. Cash flow projections should be constantly updated and revised by operating units and passed to the finance department. Properly alerted to the need for cash during the year, the treasury can plan ahead by investing idle balances and protecting the principal from losses. This function (often called treasury management) converts the office from a passive disbursement agency into an active fiscal planner in behalf of budget priorities.

Personnel Administration

Since personnel and staffing resources typically make up the largest item in policy budgets, it is important to plan them out and control them. (Ample evidence exists that they are usually not controlled.) In many developing countries, and occasionally in the United States government, officials have no idea how many people work for the government. For example, USAID's New Management System (NMS) was designed to integrate fiscal and program information systems, including personnel. Previously, there had been eighty databases supporting three different accounting systems. But because of underlying organizational and management deficiencies, the New Management System was not able to reveal USAID staffing levels (Barr 1997). Efforts to streamline government often turn on reducing personnel costs and increasing the productivity of the remaining workers. This depends on the performance of necessary streamlining steps, which include: (1) development of a typical worker salary profile, (2) calculation of gross cost per job abolished (including a comparison of payouts, pensions, and other benefits that must be paid to those severed from employment), and (3) assessment of net benefits (including the flow of new hires and retirees) after one year. To perform these three steps, personnel administrators must have basic data on staffing and wages. Without these data from financial management systems, civil service reform cannot go forward and policies may be more expensive than they should be. Often such data does not exist and cannot easily be obtained for quick decision making.

Planning the salary or wage budget means estimation of workloads, staffing ratios, and necessary overheads. Calculation of time and staffing allows comparison with other jurisdictions but gives no indication about the quality of output or the volume of labor actually needed for a given workload. Analysis of staffing and workloads can flag areas of possible over- or understaffing and raise questions about labor use. For example, in civil service reform efforts it is important to measure whether average total costs (full policy or program costs per number of units) are increasing or decreasing. Since labor represents a major component of total costs, policy analysts need to know whether revenues per employee are increasing faster or slower than costs per employee. Revenues per employee should be converted to hours and tasks per hour to allow an assessment of productivity (output per hour). Using a simple work programming technique, labor-hours can be converted into positions. Multiplying the number of positions by pay grades and scales then gives the total personnel budget (Axelrod 1995). Actual personnel costs include not only fringe benefits, pension, Social Security, and health costs, but also related costs in supplies, travel, and equipment. It is easy to see why personnel costs are the largest item in the budget.

Controlling personnel costs requires more than analysis of and action on workloads. To deal with the tough questions of administrative reform, policymakers have to make unpopular choices that can cost community support and votes. Policy analysis has an obligation to deal with institutional issues if improved results are the goal. In this vein, civil service reforms should focus on the "what" issues before the "how" issues (e.g., whether government should be involved in delivering tourism services at all, before addressing workload efficiency). Reversing the order runs the risk, as noted above, of wasting resources on reforms such as computerizing bad systems that should not be functioning in the first place. Ironically, the most basic "how" issue is to measure the level of staffing in the first place. In many jurisdictions, slippage can occur between the personnel roster, the payroll system, the personnel budget, and the treasury payment system. People become paid no-shows or come to work only to surf the Web. This results in overpayment for no productivity or underpayment of salaries and vendor invoices for those who deserve payment. The problem is linked to weak cash management and lack of internal controls over personnel administration transactions. These kinds of funding leakage problems are the rationale for position controls. The most basic control device is "position control" (Government Finance Officers Association 1978, 88), a system that ensures that people in approved positions (based on job descriptions) are paid at approved standard rates of pay. Making this basic connection prevents personnel fraud and can help ensure that scarce budget funds for public policy implementation are not wasted on unproductive wage payments.

Procurement

A substantial amount of government activity consists of procuring capital goods, equipment, and supplies. The rest of government effectively procures and pays employees. Put another way, much of public policy boils down to civil servants' salaries and items purchased from vendors. When corruption problems exist, they often relate to weak systems of procurement and contracting for goods and services. Given their importance, policymakers should be aware of the capabilities of existing procurement systems. To the extent that purchasing systems are faulty, planned policies will deviate from actual results. Procurement systems should have a number of key elements in place to facilitate efficient purchasing and to prevent fraud and conflict of interest.

First, purchasing should be centralized in a single department rather than allowing each department to purchase independently. This allows for lower-cost bulk purchases and greater financial control, with more timely payment of bills, resulting in vendor discounts for prompt payment.

Second, such core matters as the duties of purchasing agents, threshold amounts for competitive bidding, and how to prequalify bidders and maintain a bid list should be addressed by legislative statutes. These basic purchasing policies should then be spelled out in more detail in administrative procedure manuals for operational personnel.

Third, purchasing agents need to know when and how to standardize materials for bulk purchases of products (e.g., gasoline, office supplies) and facilities (e.g., design specifications for public works construction). Failure to know reasonable prices and how to standardize materials and facilities can drive up the costs of public projects unnecessarily.

Fourth, purchasing commitments must be duly registered by the accounting system and transmitted to the budgetary accounts as an encumbrance (recorded purchase order) to prevent over-expenditure of available appropriations (Coe 1989, 90–100). Purchase orders should be traceable to requisitions and invoices paid for control purposes. When it is part of an IFMS, the procurement function is computerized and linked in real time to commitments and payments, which should reduce many of the problems noted above.

Internal Control and Audit

A lot of what goes wrong with public-sector performance and policy results falls under the categories of corruption and mismanagement. Public policies fail for a variety of reasons, but corruption and leakage of scarce public funds into the wrong hands are among the major reasons. When an official violates public laws, such as by transferring funds into an unauthorized account and spending them to improve policy results, is this corruption? One could argue that such an action is a failure of internal control (perhaps failure of design of internal control procedures) and a violation of law. But it could reasonably be argued that it is not corruption. Some of the best managers and policymakers knowingly violate rules to get the job done, and for this they are often—unjustly, it seems—punished (McAllister 1996).

Corruption and mismanagement often signal a failure of internal control systems, which are organizational procedures and methods to safeguard assets, check reliability of accounting, and promote operational efficiency (Hayes et al. 1982, 82). Internal control systems ensure that procedures are followed for receipt and disbursement of funds. Those who exercise internal control are typically accounting personnel within ministries or departments.

Internal control systems focus on two major themes: (1) procedures for recording receipts and expenditures, and (2) separation of organizational duties to prevent fraud and misappropriation of funds. First, procedures need to be in place for competitive bidding, certification of new civil service hires, authorization of obligations or disbursements, and coverage of obligations by appropriations. Integrated financial management systems (IFMS) are designed to control errors. For example, the computerized accounting system will reject obligations for which unencumbered balances are not available or vouchers for which approved purchase orders or contracts have not been entered (Hayes et al. 1982, 133). Procedures must be enforced by personnel who check source documents (requisitions, purchase orders, external vouchers and invoices) for payroll, contracts, leases, and requests for payment to suppliers.

In principle, internal auditor reviews of internal controls (periodically checking to see if internal controls function properly) should not interfere with substantive program matters and legitimate management discretion. Auditors recognize that accounting control should focus on proper authorization and documentation. But efforts to control procedural compliance can become intrusive. In many government systems, obsession with accounting approvals and line-item controls over budget matters delays action and can drive up the costs of purchases from vendors that suffer from late payments or arrears. The internal controls themselves in such a case contradict the goal of operational efficiency. Known as pre-audit in the United States or pre-control in Latin America, such permissive (or uncontrolled) internal controls lead to unproductive second-guessing of agency decisions, at best (Hayes et al. 1982, 84), and open season for bribery or corruption of internal control officials, at worst.

Procedures need to prevent multistage transactions from being handled by one person. For example, one person should not be able to select vendors and authorize payments to them. Transaction or fiduciary authority should be separated from asset custody (Coe 1989, 30). Failure to divide responsibilities to prevent conflict of interest can derail public policies quickly. In such cases fiscal officials would be like foxes guarding chicken coops. Internal auditors should recommend procedural changes to prevent recurrence of waste or fraud.

Table 3.2   Institutional Assessment Framework

Variable	Measures	Indicators
Legal, regulatory, and political systems	Laws/regulations authorizing key actor discretion to manage personnel and financial resources necessary for purposes of program	Conflicts of laws or regulations
	Sufficient and stable funding	Insufficient or unstable funding
	Protection from intrusions by bureaucratic, political, and civil society organizations; sustained top-level political leadership to cover program at the management and operations levels	Interference from political opponents to delay or derail policy operations
Structural design	Determination of optimal number of management layers	Process for internal management review
	Define appropriate span of management control	Comparison of productivity and structures of similar organizations
	Ensure adequate reporting systems	Progress reports on project/program implementation and research analysis capacity
	Assess scope and method of service delivery	Performance or value-for-money audit unit performs analysis
Functional operations	Define sectoral objectives	Management incentives to specify objectives
	Perform functional analysis classification	Lead organization for functional review selected
	Develop options for future treatment of functions	Methodology selected
	Perform functional output tracking	Monitoring and evaluation (M&E) system
	Develop new organizational structures	Review comparative examples and select based on performance data
Financial management systems	Computerized IFMS	Budget, accounting, procurement, and cash management modules are functioning as designed
	Budgeting	Transparent coverage and classification systems
		Realistic ceilings
		Current capital expenditures distinguished
		Allotment system

Table 3.2 (Continued)

Variable	Measures	Indicators
Financial management systems (continued)	Budgeting (continued)	Transfer/reprogramming authority and incentive system
		M&E system—fiscal and physical results
	Accounting	Fund structure (Government: general, special, capital, debt service; Proprietary: business-like enterprises; Cost-accounting or cost-finding systems
		Clear rules: cash, accrual, modified accrual
	Cash management	Allotments based on implementation of program
		Transfer flexibility
		Integration of budgeting and cash management (i.e., IFMS)
		Treasury investment of idle balances
	Personnel management	Restructuring program (i.e., pay and grading reforms)
		Salary profile/workload data
		Gross cost per job
		Net benefit calculation
		Integration of budget, personnel, accounting, and treasury systems (i.e., IFMS)
	Procurement	Centralized purchasing
		Clear duties of purchasing agents
		Commitments, invoice and inventory control system
		Separation of asset custody and fiduciary authority
	Internal control/audit	Functioning internal controls
		Internal audit independent and reporting outside finance department
		Periodic reassignment of fiscal personnel to prevent conflicts of interest
		Integration of internal control into IFMS

SUMMARY AND CONCLUSION

This chapter has suggested that institutional failures likely to affect policy results relate to four variables: legal, regulatory, and political system support; structural design; functional performance; and fiscal management and budgeting. Analysts performing pre-implementation audits of institutional performance should focus on those rules, procedures, and systems that unreasonably raise transaction costs. Intrusive administrative procedures for receipt of prenatal care, for instance, may discourage treatment by prospective clients and could increase maternal mortality. Because fewer units of service would be provided for the same fixed costs, such procedures would raise unit costs of the program. The analysts focused on the legal and regulatory framework and the cost-accounting system should pick up on such problems. Those data should be transmitted to the finance department. Data on administrative contributions to transaction costs, derived from workflow or service-planning analyses, are often not available to policymakers. This is a failure of several components of the fiscal management system. Other common institutional problems include the following:

- Lack of professional civil service capacity means that decisions have to be made on the basis of weak or nonexistent data.
- Budget administration is constrained by tight pre-audit and complex reprogramming requirements that hamstring management and waste resources.
- Financial functions are handled independently—budget and accounting data are not shared or linked to organizational responsibility centers for management control of operations.
- Budget formulation proceeds without solid accounting data on commitments and outlays from the previous year.
- Studies of physical policy performance are not factored into budget development for the next year.

Let us now turn to a case study of institutional constraints to policymaking and implementation. The study illustrates how the four institutional variables affect an educational policy reform effort in a large American city. It illustrates why structural and management changes necessary for major success may have to be postponed because of political and organizational opposition. The alternative is to postpone the reform itself, which in this case meant more wasted human resources (i.e., students) and perpetuation of poverty and unemployment for substantial portions of the city. The option selected was to tackle the problem incrementally and achieve some progress. As in many cities and at the national level, educational reform is a work in progress.

Chapter 3 Case Study

Washington, DC, School Reform

Roger Query was a teacher in a mid-sized high school in Washington, DC. He had been working for the school system as a teacher for about ten years and hoped to rise someday through the administrative ranks to serve as a principal of his own school. He felt that in order to do so, he should understand more about the position to which he aspired, as well as how the central administrative office of the school system functioned. In an effort to learn more about the policies and operations of the DC public school system (DCPS), he set up informational interviews with key officials. Over the years, Mr. Query had learned firsthand about the constraints imposed on teachers, principals, and support staff by restrictive rules and lack of resources. He also knew about the context of severe poverty in this large, urban school district. If he was going to be a principal someday, it was important that he learn whether and how he could overcome some of these constraints to motivate his students, teach better classes, and improve overall student performance.

Background

Despite Mr. Query's optimism, he knew that the DCPS had serious problems and that students did not learn much in most of its schools. The school system had a high turnover rate among its leadership. Stakeholders such as the mayor's office, board of education, the PTA, teachers' unions, and the city council did not trust each other on matters of school policy or operations. Institutional power games distracted the schools from their main task of facilitating learning for students. Since the bulk of DCPS students regularly performed poorly, many people believed that most students in DC could not learn and that educational reform was nearly impossible.

It was well known that overall DCPS enrollment had been declining for years. While in 1981 the DCPS had over 100,000 students, by 2009 actual enrollment had declined to only 45,000. Despite the 55% drop in enrollment, DCPS still operated and maintained the 143 schools built before 2006. At one point, the number of schools increased to 150. It wasn't that students and their families were leaving Washington, DC. Many of them in fact enrolled in independent charter schools within the city. By 2009, about 64%, or 44,397 of the total 70,044 students, were enrolled in traditional public schools and 36% in charter schools. This was an increase in charter school enrollment of 63.6% in only five years (from 15,500 in 2005).

In 2007 the National Assessment of Educational Progress (NAEP) proficiency scores for DCPS were the lowest of any urban district. Achievement gaps between black and white students measured over 50% in both reading and math. While the $15,000 spending per pupil rate was nearly the highest in the nation, achievement results were almost the lowest. With the exception of a few schools in wealthier DC wards, low student graduation, retention, and promotion rates were almost the norm in DCPS. These figures reflected obvious systemic problems such as spending inefficiency, high overhead costs, and the fact that available funds were not getting to the students.

Mr. Query knew all of this, and many of his former classmates who taught at schools in nearby elite suburban counties (Montgomery County, Maryland, and Fairfax County, Virginia) repeatedly asked him why he stayed on. Yet he persevered and felt that his students needed him there at his school—he felt that his teaching was a "duty" or "service," as he put it. It was enough motivation for him to be told periodically by students and colleagues that he was an effective teacher. A pat on the back now and then was just enough to keep him at his job and focused on his tasks.

As luck would have it, one of Mr. Query's former professors from UC Berkeley, Dr. Horst Ritter, took a leave of absence to study DCPS policymaking and operational results. During Dr. Ritter's stay, in November 2006, Adrian Fenty was elected mayor of DC by a large majority. After only two days in office, he submitted legislation to take over the schools from the board of education. Mayor Fenty then appointed Michelle Rhee as chancellor, with a mandate to improve student achievement as soon as possible. A former elementary teacher in her mid-thirties, Ms. Rhee also enrolled her two children in DC public schools after accepting the position. By abolishing the board of education and appointing Ms. Rhee, Mayor Fenty demonstrated that, for the first time in DC history, there was top-level support for institutional and leadership reforms to improve student achievement and school performance. Ms. Rhee's young, new staff consisted of several former classroom teachers who also had MPP degrees, such as Liz Smith and Margie Krimmel. Roger Query was soon reunited with his professor and introduced to Ms. Krimmel and Ms. Smith.

The Reform Begins

Mr. Query learned from Dr. Ritter that a comprehensive educational reform was about to be implemented. As Mr. Query's fields were biology and mathematics, he wasn't terribly interested in politics and knew little about big policymaking or implementation efforts. The last time he had heard those terms with any regularity was in his Introduction to Political Science class. He had a lot of questions, but for his own edification he wanted to know first the rationale or operating theory behind the reform plans.

Dr. Ritter explained that in theory and in the literature, the planned reform was really nothing new. He referred Mr. Query back to the basic readings on the "new public management" (NPM) reforms of the 1980s and 1990s. Moynihan (2006, 79, citing Allen Schick) summarizes five core NPM concepts: (1) managers have clear goals; (2) managers have the flexibility and discretion to use resources; (3) managers have operational authority; (4) controls focus on outputs and outcomes; and (5) managers are held accountable for resource uses and results. To this list Dr. Ritter added that it is also critical that managers know the availability and limits of operating and capital funds for the year. Figures on available funds should be recognizable and transparent in timely communications from the budget offices. Otherwise, managers could have clear goals, ample discretion, knowledge of needed outputs and outcomes, and still remain unaccountable for performance because of an inability to plan rationally for resource use to achieve goals and objectives. Without funding stability, it is nearly impossible to manage programs or projects.

Dr. Ritter added, finally, that the DCPS reform is probably typical in that reformers never start with a clean slate. "We faced an established bureaucracy," he explained, "and for the first year and a half, most of our efforts were focused on reforming basic practices and systems in both the central administrative offices and the schools. Thus, NPM principles were quite useful as a framework in that we were tackling both public sector governance reforms in general and education reform in particular."

Mr. Query said he knew that these kinds of NPM principles had been applied to health, urban transport, and road maintenance reform programs at the state and local levels as part of the "reinventing government" emphasis of the 1980s and early 1990s. In addition, Query was also familiar with the education policy literature.

"Which principles would apply here and how?" he asked.

Dr. Ritter explained that there is a growing body of empirically based educational policy reform literature: "School systems have applied all or part of the NPM agenda to improve educational achievement in places as diverse as Singapore, Finland, Chile, Edmonton, and the UK; and in this country, Chicago, New York City, Baltimore, Denver, Austin, Newark, Boston, Little Rock, Fairfax County (Virginia), Montgomery County (Maryland), Prince George's County (Maryland), and New Orleans. All have taken slightly different approaches based on their local institutional and cultural environment and other special circumstances. For DCPS, we translated the NPM principles into four operational concepts and designed subprograms around them: (1) choice and competition; (2) decentralization and school autonomy; (3) performance accountability; and (4) financial predictability and sustainability. Let me explain them to you briefly."

"*Choice and competition* are always high on reformer lists," Dr. Ritter explained. "For high achievers, this means making such alternatives as magnet schools available to cover specialized courses. Not every school, even in wealthy districts like Montgomery County next door, can afford to offer specialized courses in every school. For districts like ours with limited means, including most urban areas with large poor populations, choice means that parents can be sure that their children are receiving the best available education—a 'good' education according to accepted norms and achievement criteria. This requires good teachers, facilities, and supplies. Since those cannot always be guaranteed by the public school system, parents and students need an alternative. In many cities including Washington, that is provided by religious (often Catholic) and charter schools. The major alternative to traditional public schools is provided by charter schools. About 1.2 million students attend them in the United States. Another option is giving parents vouchers to allow them to send their children to any school. The theory is that maximizing choice will induce competition and force the worst schools to perform better. As voucher proposals are more radical and long term in their effects, they have been defeated in every ballot referendum. Vouchers are subsidy coupons worth a portion of tuition costs in either private or public schools of parents' choosing. In the DCPS, voucher grants have been set at $7,500, which covers tuition for its 1,700 voucher students (and at least by implication, covers the fixed and variable costs of education per student). Only about 100,000 students receive vouchers in this country. Since Catholic schools are now having resource problems, the major alternative in practice is really charter schools."

"The problem is not just optimizing choice to support some theory. In the DCPS, 27 schools have been classified as 'failing' by multiple criteria. Overall, 90 of 123 schools are under some form of federal notice to meet the standards of the US

No Child Left Behind (NCLB) Act. The law requires that districts adopt one or more 'restructuring' remedies, such as bringing in private firms to manage the schools (privatization); converting them to charters, which are founded and operated by nonprofit organizations; retaining public control over the schools but replacing principals and teachers; allowing the state (or in DC, the US Department of Education) to seize the schools; or devising some other strategy (e.g., lengthening the school day, changing curricula)."

"Schools receive charter status from the Public Charter School Board, which is accountable to the Office of the State Superintendent of Education (OSSE). DCPS does not charter schools. Nevertheless, the administrative and policy arrangement allows relatively efficient establishment and financing of charter schools. With 127 schools and 71,000 students enrolled, Washington, DC, also had 63 charter schools serving about 25,000 students in 2009. DCPS allocates about $370 million a year for charter schools from an annual budget that was about $760 million in 2009. A transfer of $8,500 per student, with facility needs add-ons of between $1,000 and $3,000 per student, is calculated to cover full educational costs. By contrast, the New York City Department of Education, with 1,500 schools and 1.1 million students, has chartered only 78 schools, with enrollment of 24,000 students."

"In short, parents in DC have choice. The other side of the coin is that if parents choose to 'exit' their children, enrollment in public schools will drop. From 146,000 students in 1960, excluding charter students, DCPS now has only about 45,000 students. Not all of the enrollment decline can be attributed to dissatisfaction with public school performance. Some of it is pure demographics—people heading for the suburbs. But a lot of the decline is related to performance. Since 2007, the chancellor has been using choice as a tool of competition—an incentive to improve public school performance. We believe that public school enrollment declines have leveled off and that overall attendance will increase to 47,000 in 2010."

As Query listened to this, it occurred to him that it wasn't as simple as shifting agendas from power to learning through more choice and competition. "I went to a school in a poor neighborhood when I was growing up," he recalled. "Those of us who worked hard to learn and avoid being poor like our parents had to deal with bullies and gangs that waited for us after school. They knew us and where we lived and tended to beat us up regularly."

"Yes, that's a problem here, too," Dr. Ritter agreed. "Some charter schools have to rely on Metro transit police to protect their students after class, because the

DC police believe their job is to protect only regular public schools and not charter schools" (King 2009b).

Both agreed that the formal or informal rule that produced this enforcement inequity needed to be changed since it constrains competition, choice, and learning.

"Another important reform plank is *decentralization and school autonomy*," explained Dr. Ritter. "Here, the premise is that local schools can be more responsive to parents and students than distant central administrative offices can be. The empirical literature indicates that giving principals more discretion over human resources (especially teachers and maintenance staff), budget choices, and students leads to better student achievement. Of course, it is not as simple as that. There is a natural tension between central administration and local schools. Central administrations need to establish common curricula and performance norms, as well as transparent and professional recruitment and promotion criteria; local schools need the autonomy and discretion to shift resources in order to attain performance objectives. In some countries, such as New Zealand, local managers operate on fixed-term, often multiyear, performance-based contracts. To give them maximum discretion to achieve results in areas such as health, education, and urban transport, managers are permitted to hire and fire as they see fit and shift budget resources to attain the required objectives. With this discretion, managers can then be held almost fully accountable for results. We are using the same model, adapted for local practice."

"All reforms are experiments," Dr. Ritter continued, "and this one is no different. It has been repeatedly documented that the main determinant of student success is the teacher: Good teachers lead to more success. Studies link the achievement gap at DCPS largely to underperforming school staff and teachers. Overall, we find a decades-old culture that still accepts mediocrity and chaos at schools and in the classroom. Before we can devolve authority to schools, there must be a professional cadre in place in which we can have confidence. We need be certain that increasing local schools' discretion will serve the students. Until we have that cadre of principals and teachers, we cannot decentralize effectively. Consistent with these basic tenets, the strategy has been to replace underperforming principals and teachers, provide incentive contracts for good teachers to continue, and support better teaching with more supplies and textbooks and better facilities. All strategies must be paid for. The plan is to finance the replacements, incentive contracts, and improved facilities by closing high-cost schools and obtaining additional private financing. So far, twenty-three schools have been closed; more than one hundred central staff and several dozen principals terminated; 150 out of 4,000 teachers have been dismissed; over 11,000 back-logged maintenance requests have been addressed; and a $2.5 billion five-year DCPS capital improvement plan (CIP) has been approved (DCPS 2008)."

"DCPS also developed a two-track incentive system for teachers: The red track would mean status quo with some raises; the green track would mean large bonuses in exchange for forgoing tenure. In general, younger teachers would probably select the green path when the contract with the WTU is approved. Unfortunately, the WTU forced out the 'red-green' plan and strengthened tenure-security provisions for teachers (Turque 2009a). Under a new WTU contract, DCPS principals will have more authority to pick teachers whose positions were cut from schools that have been closed, consolidated, or taken over by an out-side organization; or that have lost enrollment or budget funds. Principals will follow a formula that weights classroom performance highest and seniority low-est (Turque 2009a)."

"Some suggest that, consistent with the local autonomy plank, performance-based budget systems should be installed in order to decentralize authority to schools (and in particular to principals)," Dr. Ritter went on. "The rationale is that this system would allow principals to allocate resources by educational per-formance. It would also allow decisions to be made on the basis of unit cost and cost-effectiveness criteria. I'm sure you're aware of the pros and cons of such budget reform systems. We viewed them as a potentially costly distraction at this stage—a danger that we could end up dealing with two reforms at the same time."

"We found that there are at least two kinds of 'structural' level constraints. One stems from the redundancy of the school itself—time has passed it by and there is no more demand—student enrollment drops and the place is taken over by gangs and dropouts. This happened with Manual High School in Denver a few years ago (Boo 2007). Such places should be declared redundant and students and faculty reassigned to better environments. We already have the perfor-mance and fiscal data to make those choices without changing the allocation system or calendar. The second kind of structural issue is actually a leadership problem. If better principals and teachers are appointed, often the structural constraints disappear! Either way, you cannot manage yourself out of structural problems with tools such as performance budgeting, management by objec-tives, or use of performance-management consultants. Personnel changes and solid leadership are needed."

"We know that Chicago went the management route in order to target resources more precisely on the basis of school performance. They appeared to be trying to manage their way out of a structural problem. In any case, the new budget system, installed with substantial resources of time and money, made little difference to results. What they found after installing their school-based budgeting system was that there was very little variation in allocations between high- and low-performing schools across the main functions of instruction, instructional support, administration, and operations. There were important variations in discretionary spending (Stiefel, Rubenstein, and Schwartz 1999). But this was a low proportion of total expenditures and simply underscored lack of real school autonomy."

"In the DCPS, a professional class of managers, principals, and teachers at the school level is largely missing at this point. We are building the foundation for devolving authority to the schools, but until that cadre exists, resources should be spent on human resources, not on accounting and budgeting systems. We already knew that a big problem was the substantial administrative component of some of the highest expenditures per student in the country, combined with low achievement. In Los Angeles, they estimate that only $0.60 of every $1.00 makes it to the classroom. In DCPS, we knew that an even smaller proportion of total expenditures was making it to the classroom. Analysis of the links between teacher salaries, support, maintenance, capital facilities condition, and student performance can tell us a lot of what we need to know now to proceed. Fiscal and physical performance data and solid methods already exist and we are using them for these purposes. Data are being reported and analyzed from the school level. One of our new incentive programs allows schools with consistent high performance to become autonomous and exempt from many central office regulations."

Dr. Ritter then explained that the third plank, *performance accountability*, was tightly linked to the previous one, decentralization and school autonomy. "Accountability without discretion is meaningless," he noted. "In the decentralization literature, it would be like holding a local mayor accountable for centrally set performance mandates, when mayors typically do not have the discretion to raise local tax bases or rates."

"We found virtually no emphasis on accountability when we arrived," Dr. Ritter recalled. "There was no performance measurement of any kind. It was a culture of low expectations and entitlement to permanent bureaucratic jobs, with their emphasis on the usual inputs of form-filling and frequent meetings. The bureaucracy was bloated and inflexible, and lacked concern for students. A major part of any educational reform is to shift the cultural mindset from inputs to outputs and outcomes. As I've mentioned, budget systems can help, but we already knew what was missing here and went directly for the jugular: regular reporting on performance metrics for students, teachers, and schools. Logically, DCPS would use this data to classify schools, teachers, and students in order to allocate education funds more rationally. DCPS would use this system to raise overall expectations and change the culture. That's what a real reform should do. That's why they still call the DCPS office staff 'change agents!'"

"I've been a teacher here for ten years, and you are right about the lack of interest in performance," Mr. Query agreed. "But sometimes performance becomes a buzzword and efficiency experts take over. Consultants arrive, measure, and take their knowledge with them. They try to measure everything, require more performance reporting. Under increased time pressure, the staff burns out on reporting data that they feel is often pretty useless. What metrics are you using, and how do you know they are the right ones, especially for teachers?"

"DCPS tracks the usual data at the school level—retention, dropout, promotion, and graduation rates for students," Dr. Ritter replied. "With my assistance, we review teacher files to assess their classroom attendance and turnover (transfers to a different district or school, retirement, disciplinary action, dismissal). We also track the condition of facilities and the regular availability of supplies (basics like chalk, books, and computers). We found that data and management systems were extremely bad and were damaging the schools; for example, there were neglected transcripts preventing graduation, weak attendance data on truancy, and delays in processing textbook orders, purchase orders, and monthly teacher salaries. Those have now been fixed with savings of hundreds of thousands of dollars. Empirically based or data-driven decision making allows us to target more funds to the classroom and to the areas of highest need. This has allowed us to target $100 million in capital expenditures in the summer of 2009 to fix up most of the schools, and renovate ten and refurbish twenty fields and playgrounds."

"Teaching evaluations, as you know," continued Dr. Ritter, "are always a contentious issue. Universities rely on students to provide the data used for promotion and tenure. At the primary and secondary levels, the reviews almost all have to come from outside the classroom. Observers come in and observe such indicators as: whether the students are attentive, how much the teacher interacts with the students, how well the teacher is prepared, and whether the teacher either has good classroom supports or uses the blackboard effectively. These are admittedly subjective assessments; their subjectivity seems more extreme because of the fact that primary and secondary evaluators hit only random classes, while university students evaluate a whole course. If these evaluations are announced in advance, the teacher can overprepare; if unannounced, evaluations might take place when primary or secondary teachers are having a bad day in class. Nevertheless, despite these generic methodological limitations, we believe that we have identified a lot of ineffective, poorly performing teachers. Since good teaching is the main determinant of student achievement, we need to have the authority to transfer, dismiss, or sideline and retrain those kinds of teachers. For principals, the evaluation system is designed to weed out ineffectual staff and reward those who are effective. In both cases, the performance assessment is supposed to be linked to student achievement. While this link has been made with teachers, so far it has not been for principals."

"Why not?" asked Mr. Query.

"Reformers believe that school autonomy is not yet sufficient to hold principals accountable," Dr. Ritter explained. "Principals have only minimal staffing authority. If they are dealt a bad hand, they would get the blame. So, the emphasis now is on upgrading data, measuring student performance, and attributing that to teacher performance. At the school level, we have used student achievement data to identify possibilities for institutional synergy. At the outset, the data indicated the need for extreme measures, such as closing twenty-three underperforming high-cost schools. After this brush-clearing effort, we concentrated on innovative resource combinations that could increase achievement. I say 'could'—remember that this is an experiment, like all education reforms. Now in DCPS, special *catalyst* schools act as magnets for particular emphases, such as science. We also have *partnership* schools that allow us to outsource students to charter schools. Since charters are often spectacularly successful in generating student results (such as improving reading and mathematics proficiency scores), this increases market competition for the traditional public schools. Finally, our *collaborative* schools are networks of schools that facilitate transfer of lessons, resources, and skills from higher- to lower-performing schools. They are like mentor relationships. The aim of these new institutional arrangements is to increase student achievement by offering more options and combining resources differently."

"You mentioned that *fiscal predictability and sustainability* are basic to applying NPM reforms to education. What did you mean?" asked Mr. Query.

"The effort to upgrade financial management systems was related to the brush-clearing phase. There were two problems. First, principals found it hard to predict flows of funds for capital and operating purposes. That meant that despite their planned and approved budgets, the actual funds didn't materialize in many cases. There was a major variance between planned and actual expenditures.

Expenditure planning was made more difficult by the existence of twenty-seven different management systems that were not interoperable and did not interface. So principals and budget officers found it hard to consolidate the budgetary base in terms of overall needs. The procurement system was particularly bad. It did not produce cost-effective bids; the goods often didn't arrive; and those that did were often defective or the wrong items. In some cases, the proper goods arrived, were placed in inventory, and later stolen. Thus, schools needed more predictability for both flow of funds and for supplies, equipment, and facilities."

"The second problem was that, lacking performance data and a sound budget system, we could not allocate funds to schools on the basis of targeted needs to produce results. We couldn't distinguish the high from the low performers by school, class, or individual student. As I mentioned before, DCPS is conducting this reform, not a consulting firm. DCPS will gain the knowledge and experience, and its own staff will be able to use it. For this reason, we avoided many of the usual consultant's products, such as performance or program budgeting. We are now in the position of being able to do almost everything such a system is supposed to do in theory—here in practice. We measure and track outputs by school and individual (outputs like improved proficiency in test scores and grad-uation rates are even called 'outcomes' by some); we know the expenditures and have a good feel for the behavior of fixed and variable costs. This allows us to compare unit costs and cost per result, and allocate funds accordingly."

Results

"So, are you pleased with your overall results so far?" asked Mr. Query.

"Let me detail what we've achieved in a little over two years. Most educational reforms take about ten years to mature and be institutionalized. At the structural level, closing twenty-three schools saved substantial funds, and these have been redirected to the classroom through program support, facility maintenance and rehabilitation, and supplies. Savings from closures enabled DCPS to ensure that every student in the system has access to art, music, physical education, and library services. There wasn't enough money to ensure minimum standards for these programs or services before, and we learned that much of the funds that were available were being spent on schools that should have been closed any-way. In addition, twenty-seven more schools have been restructured, consistent with the NCLB Act. At the management level, we have installed new systems for personnel (to track employee status and location); treasury (to facilitate faster preparation of purchase orders and ensure on-time payments); and purchasing (to ensure on-time school openings and timely arrival of textbook orders). At the classroom level, we provided 6,300 new computers and connected 103 schools to high-speed broadband networks; improved security within schools and on student trips to and from them; improved facilities by investing $500 million for capital modernization; completed 20,000 backlogged work orders; and fixed 400 boilers, repaired 2,500 window air conditioners, and overhauled a dozen central cooling systems."

"More importantly," Dr. Ritter went on, "at the school and classroom level, more than 40 principals and 200 teachers have been fired, and 150 more instructors have been placed on 90-day probationary programs. More funds have been allocated to instruction and to school leadership. All these activities at the structural, management, and operational levels have raised the expectations of students, parents, and teachers."

"Let me show you an example of shifted resources at the school level." Dr. Ritter gave Mr. Query a preliminary 2009 budget for Anacostia High School, which showed that 76% of the resources would be spent on instruction, 17% on school leadership, and 7% on instructional support. "This shows our commitment to reducing administrative expenses and targeting more funds to the classroom."

Mr. Query glanced over the budget. "I can't say anything about the totals. But why are classroom supplies and computers considered 'instructional,' rather than 'instructional support'? And, why are the principal and assistant principals part of 'instructional' expenses, when they don't teach? Why would a business manager be classified as 'school leadership,' but not the principal? I only ask these questions because the classification of these kinds of expenses could inflate the percentage of expenditures tagged as instructional. That could be the basis for the budget allocations being claimed as a reform success, when they actually might not be. Am I wrong?"

Mr. Ritter focused on the budget pages for a moment. "No, you are correct. We have to tighten up and rationalize the budget classification system to a greater extent than we have."

"So, how are the schools funded?" Mr. Query went on. "Do they receive foundation grants to cover them on a per pupil basis? Or is it some kind of matching grant?"

Mr. Ritter thanked him for his question. "We use precisely a foundation grant—a lump sum provided to schools that is derived from projected enrollment figures and allocated on the basis of their level and type of school. So, based on a

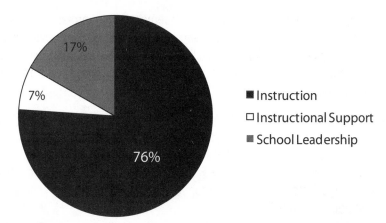

Figure 1 Expenditures of Comprehensive Staffing Model (CSM) Funds by Type

projected enrollment in 2010 of 44,000, our budget is $428.3 million, of which 27.5% will be allocated to grades 9–12. Based on our weighting system, such schools will get $10,173 per pupil, while primary schools will receive only $8,770 per pupil. The weighting is based on average operating costs for those levels. The system is called the Uniform Per Pupil Funding system. As we said, if enrollment doesn't meet our projections, per pupil funding will drop."

"It sounds good," Mr. Query responded. "But lump-sum grants can still be re-allocated within schools and not make it to the classroom. They work best for clients when they are add-ons to per pupil expenditures that are higher than, for example, the $10,173 for grades 9–12. The grant structure encourages fungibil-ity. The other problem might be inability to track funds to the classroom, or leak-age through the core budget codes. Isn't that so?"

"As I said, these are real problems not just here, but in other school systems as well," repeated Dr. Ritter.

"While it is still too early to tell if the reforms are making a difference, from 2007 to 2009, scores on the District of Columbia Comprehensive Assessment System (DC-CAS) tests have increased at the primary level from 38% to 49% in reading and from 29% to 43% in math. At the secondary level, scores have increased from 30% to 42% in reading and from 27% to 39% in math (Turque 2009b). DC-CAS scores revealed that the number of schools with proficiency rates below 20% has been cut from fifty to twenty-nine. Since many of these improving schools are in the poorest neighborhoods, gains can be attributed largely to the efforts of the reform. This means that DCPS students can achieve when teachers, principals, and parents focus on their achievement. When professional leaders remove disincentives to learning and help build a learning environment characterized by solid teaching and good facilities, the students respond quickly. This is why we should not shortchange them any longer with poorly performing educational institutions."

"The only negative," observed Dr. Ritter, "is that enrollment in DCPS continues to drop—by 284 for the 2009–10 year. We hope to turn that around by increasing demand for a better product—supplying the students with more effective public schools. For the first time, DCPS is now operating a student recruitment campaign at selected schools in order to compete with charter schools and other schooling options."

"Positive results in DCPS mirror those of other systems that have adopted the planks of local autonomy, choice, and school responsibility that I mentioned before. Since 2002, New York City schoolteacher salaries have increased 43%, and school funding has gone up 50%. Principals have been given more autonomy in exchange for more accountability. While in 2002, only 50% of fourth graders met state learning standards, today more than 85% meet or exceed math standards and 70% meet or exceed English standards. Graduation rates are also increasing (*The Economist* 2009)."

Institutional Supports and Constraints

"The obvious question, then, is what constraints have you faced along the way?" asked Mr. Query. "Reform is about changing minds, generating top level support, and building institutions that incentivize the right actions to increase achievement. That hasn't been easy in any of the cities you mentioned earlier. What have been the major institutional constraints here?"

"Let's start from the top," said Dr. Ritter. "With the election of a new reformist mayor in 2007, we had the top level support we needed, which had never existed in Washington DC. He knew of the reforms being carried out elsewhere and wanted them to begin here from day one. We got another boost from the election of President Obama in 2008. His selection of Arne Duncan as secretary of education made it clear to DCPS that education reform was a top priority. As the chief of Chicago schools from 2001 to 2009, Duncan pushed ahead with reforms similar to those being implemented by DCPS (focusing on data and outcomes, charter schools, serious teacher evaluations, and incentives for improvement) (Glod 2008)."

"With this broad political cover, DCPS then started to fix its basic systems, most of which were dilapidated. Financial and performance management systems, as I mentioned, were dysfunctional and could not really be used to manage anything. DCPS culture was chaotic and territorial; there was no overall system in place or anyone with enough authority to enforce changes at the structural level. So we began to clear the larger brush away (by closing schools) and then got down to smaller weeds (like books, supplies, facilities). There was some parental resistance to school closure efforts, but not as much as expected—once data were presented on enrollments, costs, and poor past results. It was very much a data-driven exercise."

"There may be further closures, and some schools may be reopened as charter or private schools. But the major stakeholders appear to accept the process of selection and closure—so far. After surplus schools were identified and closures were reasonably underway, we moved on to governance issues. This has been a much more complex problem—one without clear solutions or data categorically indicating that a preferred governance system should be installed, such as decentralized school management and alternative school choice. Thus, governance reforms have been contentious."

"In Washington historically," Dr. Ritter explained, "the central educational bureaucracy has always been perceived as a major part of the problem. With the new mayor came a new education office and dismissal of many of the old guard. The elected board of education was abolished, and its functions were transferred to the mayor. Budget approval and oversight functions now lie with the elected city council. The central administration (DCPS) is no longer perceived as a meddlesome influence, but a positive force for change and improvement. Of course the upbeat demeanor and cool, rational tone of the chancellor, backed by the stern expression of the mayor, has helped greatly in confronting vocal detractors and in generating support among stakeholders."

"Our governance problem boils down to how to energize the roles of teacher and principal. Studies in Tennessee and Dallas showed that if you take students of average ability and put them in classrooms with teachers deemed to be in the top 20% of their profession, the students end up in the top 10% of student performers; if you pair them with teachers in the bottom 20%, they end up at the bottom (*The Economist* 2007)."

"To answer your question, then, reform efforts have faced two major institutional constraints. First, there are the unions, which logically focus on the employment stability of their membership. Legal safeguards for employment have been critically important for US labor, but in times of major reforms, they become a constraint on management. It is here that our proposals have run up against the mighty teaching union (the Washington Teachers' Union, or WTU, an affiliate of the American Federation of Teachers, or AFT) and the effects of vigorous lobbying by older teachers through the city council, which has reconstituted itself as a de facto school board."

"We want the flexibility to fire ineffective teachers," Dr. Ritter explained, "and replace them with the highest paid and most effective ones in the system. If teachers opt for our *green* path, or 'grand bargain,' they give up tenure for one year, and get large incentive bonuses paid for by foundation funds in exchange (e.g., salaries of over $130,000 a year). The foundations will only provide the funds for five years if the chancellor gains authority to: (1) recognize and reward teacher performance (merit pay), (2) identify the most and least effective teachers, and (3) remove poorly performing teachers. So far, the WTU has either refused to vote on the proposal or opposed it. The WTU opposes teacher evaluation on the basis of student scores alone, and wants attendance and other inputs considered for promotion and tenure. The AFT/WTU opposes the abolition of tenure. While the WTU does not oppose the removal of underperforming teachers, it wants it done in 'humane, fair, and fast ways.' This would include training and support before a final dismissal decision is made (Turque 2009c). If talks collapse between Chancellor Rhee and AFT President Randi Weingarten, the decision falls first to the DC Board of Public Employee Relations. If there is still an impasse, the decision goes to a mediator. If that fails, it goes then to binding arbitration. In short, the major constraint is the fear of many teachers and their AFT representatives that they will be replaced unfairly. The fear of the chancellor is that the AFT will slow the momentum we have built to focus on improving teachers. If that stalls, so does our reform. All of us, like you, have been teachers, and we want to reward the best ones, who will bring the most benefit to their students."

"The second constraint is the political structure and incentive system of the city council—any city council. The electoral system based on districts or wards politicizes the schools, making them just another political resource to use to get elected and stay in office. This makes policymaking and financing decisions overtly political and subject more to pressure politics than to technical considerations like student and school performance. Mayor Fenty was right to abolish the board of education. We need to maximize what administrative strength the school district has in order to increase educational performance (Bennett 2009). Failure to do this allows school administrators to play power games at the expense of student achievement—as happened in DC under the school board."

"Improved public-sector governance of educational reform is crucial if the reform is to be successful (Bennett 2009). Top-level support, together with DCPS efforts to narrow the span of administrative control, will strengthen school administration by forcing managers to focus on the mission of educational reform. Chubb and Moe (1990) asserted that outside influences often distract school administrators from their primary task. This has been true here, and DCPS needs structural reform, including changes to the incentive system, to minimize those distractions. For example, politicizing what should be straightforward administrative and policy decisions based on existing empirical data is a waste of time and resources. But this is often what happens. The city council has in many ways replaced the board's functions (more precisely 'dysfunctions') and now serves as a new political constraint on the reforms."

The Sequence of Reform

"I opted for the green path, so I know what you are up against," said Mr. Query. "What about the sequence of the reform? You mentioned that you tried to move from fixing basic failed systems to governance issues. Can you be more specific about the sequence of reform activities?"

Dr. Ritter shifted visibly in his chair. "In fact, we know very little about the optimal sequencing of school reform—or any other policy really. Some have postulated a three-step sequence in the face of challenges to a reform like ours. First, you build top-level support. Then you assess how severe are the constraints imposed by cultural obstacles and longstanding institutional rules. If they are adaptable or changeable, then you move to the third step. Here, you need to come up with a feasible sequence of technical activities to repair and replace broken administrative and policy systems so that reforms are institutionalized (Guess 2005)."

"In our case, we had the top-level support of Mayor Fenty and Chancellor Rhee. We followed the lead of other jurisdictions, such as New York City under Mayor Michael Bloomberg. But despite astonishing increases in student performance, teacher salaries, and school funding there, the state legislature may recentralize control under partisan political leadership (*The Economist* 2009). This would fly in the face of both AFT wishes and a major tenet of federalist fiscal theory—that you assign authority and responsibility to the lowest effective level. So, we can't take our victory for granted. We could lose that top-level support and that would severely impede reform momentum."

"For the second challenge, we had to face a decades-old culture of mediocrity, reinforced by a patronizing school board and make-work unions that knew or cared little about what local students could achieve. So, instead of logically and incrementally moving from step 1 to 2, we started with step 1, and moved to step 3 to repair the systems desiccation at both school and central office levels. This had to include both the teachers and the school systems. Otherwise, the reform would fail and neither the students nor we would have achieved anything. That meant facing off immediately against the union and the council on restructuring, closing schools, and replacing ineffective teachers."

"In short, using the traditional reform sequence as a guide would have suggested spending more time on the second step—changing the culture. Only if the culture (the teachers, the unions, the parents, and the council) bought into the reform would it be safe to go forward to technical sequencing of operational reforms. This is what the textbooks suggested. But unlike, say, a national decentralization reform that really has no time limit, we faced future elections, poorly taught students each day, and enormous stakeholder skepticism at the outset. DCPS had little time, and the students were being penalized everyday. Given these constraints, we were impatient to increase achievement."

"So, we instituted a flurry of pilot programs and policy changes that increased demands on teachers (e.g., Saturday programs to prepare students for DC-CAS tests); a push to integrate special-education students in regular classes; a new accelerated math program; cash rewards for selected middle schools; and new guidelines for bilingual, arts, and health education (Turque 2009d). The chancellor also pledged that teacher job evaluations would now be based not just on standardized test scores, but also on student growth, and teacher pay would be based on what teachers achieved individually and collectively."

"In retrospect," Dr. Ritter concluded, "overwhelming the teachers and the stakeholders with many new proposals and initiatives by trying to fix everything at once created major resistance problems. DCPS ignored the cultural constraint and the institutional rules. Both had to be changed, but DCPS did not spend enough time trying to convince stakeholders that the changes would definitely be an improvement. In 2007–08, teachers learned about restructuring, closing of schools, and proposals for declaring the whole system an emergency (as was done in New Orleans) (Turque 2008). This move would pave the way for privatizing schools and hiring nonunion charter and autonomous schools to run the district, which could leave a lot of existing teachers out of a job. There was more talk and lots of rumors about mysterious donors who would pay $100 million to support teachers who cooperated with the performance-based reform. Foundation funds are not unusual. But this would be the first time that private founda-tions would be paying for teacher compensation (King 2009a). Much of the privatization and emergency talk is off the table now (Turque 2009e). The chan-cellor is now facing the cultural and institutional variables, and learning that if the reform is to persist beyond this regime, mental habits and supporting rules must be changed—perhaps more slowly."

Mr. Query thanked Dr. Ritter for his time and said he would mull over what he had learned and get back to him with more questions. Dr. Ritter suggested that he talk with representatives of the other institutional actors first, such as WTU and PTAs.

Aftermath

Since Mr. Query's interviews, three events have occurred. First, 2009 DCPS enrollment was reported as only 37,000 (despite assertions that it would reach 45,000 and possibly 47,000 by 2010). Since the announcement in August 2009, enrollment has crept up to 39,000, and when the numbers are audited the figure could reach 44,000 after all. The latest figures are 44,681 planned and 44,397 actual (Turque 2009f). Much of the decline in enrollment so far can be attributed to a reporting lag in the data systems. Second, the WTU forced Chancellor Rhee to modify and water down some of her boldest reform proposals—the fast-track incentive for pay in exchange for tenure, and principal autonomy to hire and fire teachers. This all speaks to the power of institutions to negatively affect formula-tion and implementation of successful, empirically based policies. Third, the unanticipated shortfall of $43.9 million in budgeted funds for DC government in 2009–10 forced the DCPS to propose $40 million in cuts, first in nonpersonnel categories, then in personnel such as new teachers (Turque 2009f). On October 2, 2009, in response to the citywide belt-tightening because of declining tax rev-enue, Chancellor Rhee terminated 266 teachers and other personnel (Turque 2009g). Both the WTU and city council have reacted strongly, charging her with everything from age discrimination on the cuts (eliminated teachers tended to be older and more senior) to illegal reprogramming of budget funds (she can trans-fer funds without approval because less money was spent than budgeted, not more). The institutional constraints to reform mount! Raise your hands if you want to do the chancellor's job!

Questions

Design a decision framework containing a generic sequence for institutional and policy reform. Would the framework necessarily be different for education than for other policy areas, such as health or urban transportation?

The case mentions other instances of school reform. Selecting some of them for review, are there comparative lessons that could be applied to the Washington school reform case?

What are the lessons of the Washington school reform case for anticipating and responding to the challenges of institutional constraints? Are there lessons that can be built into the design and appraisal stage of policymaking that would facilitate later implementation? What course corrections, if any, would you recommend to the chancellor now to improve the odds of reform success?

Would you change any of the four operating principles or planks of the Washington reform? Would you sequence them differently after reading the case?

How should reformers change cultures and institutional rules when, for electoral or financial reasons, they don't have a lot of time?

References for the Case Study

Bennett, Lamar. 2009. Administrative Strength, Reform and School District Performance. PhD dissertation, American University, School of Public Affairs.

Boo, Katherine. 2007. Expectations. *The New Yorker*, January 15.

Chubb, John E., and Terry M. Moe. 1990. *Politics, Markets, and America's Schools.* Washington, DC: Brookings Institution.

District of Columbia Public Schools (DCPS). 2008. District of Columbia Public Schools Progress Report: 2007–2008 School Year. Washington, DC: DCPS.

The Economist. 2007. How to Be Top. October 20.

———. 2009. Political Prisoners: Mayoral Control of Schools in New York. June 20.

Glod, Maria. 2008. Chicago School Reform Could Be a U.S. Model. *Washington Post*, December 30.

Guess, George M. 2005. Comparative Decentralization Lessons from Pakistan, Indonesia and the Philippines. *Public Administration Review* 65 (2): 217–31.

King, Colbert I. 2009a. The Federal Lab Rat. *Washington Post*, January 17.

———. 2009b. Trouble Awaits after Class Is Dismissed. *Washington Post*, October 3.

Moynihan, Donald. 2006. Managing for Results in State Governments: Evaluating a Decade of Reform. *Public Administration Review* 66 (1): 77–89.

Stiefel, Leanna, Ross Rubenstein, and Amy Ellen Schwartz. 1999. Using Adjusted Performance Measures for Evaluating Resource Use. *Public Budgeting and Finance* 19 (3): 67–85.

Turque, Bill. 2008. Fenty, Rhee Look for Ways around Union. *Washington Post*, February 20.

———. 2009a. Rhee, Union May Be Close to Deal. *Washington Post*, September 11.

———. 2009b. Two Years of Hard Lessons for D.C. Schools' Agents of Change. *Washington Post*, June 14.

———. 2009c. Education Heavyweights Prepare for D.C. Contract Fight. *Washington Post*, February 1.

———. 2009d. Rhee Says Fixes Likely Too Much Too Soon. *Washington Post*, March 14.

———. 2009e. Takeover Idea Out of Consideration, Rhee Says. *Washington Post*, February 20.

———. 2009f. D.C. Schools Face Bigger Classes, Layoffs Due to $40m Gap. *Washington Post*, September 17.

———. 2009g. D.C. Council, Rhee Tensions Grow over Budget Cuts. *Washington Post*, October 30.

Note

This case was prepared by George M. Guess, scholar in residence in public administration and policy at American University, Washington, DC. The author wishes to thank Margery Yeager in the Office of the Chancellor at DCPS for her invaluable guidance in preparing the case. The conclusions are the authors and any data errors or inconsistencies are the author's fault.

ANALYSIS OF CHAPTER 3 CASE STUDY

Institutions are the formal and informal rules that, as noted, combine to affect implementation of policy through networks of organizations. These regulations and procedural systems are often driven by objectives that conflict with those of the policy to be implemented. It is useful to know in advance that the agendas of civil society institutions such as lobbies and unions may derail the most rational and coherent objectives. Policy rationalists, analyzing the costs and benefits of such policies as health care, education, transportation, and energy, for example, employ many of the tools presented in this book. Their aims are to focus on policy problems comprehensively, instead of in isolated pieces, and to apply the tools of rational analysis. The progressives of the late nineteenth century and early twentieth century, as well as presidents such as Carter, Clinton, and Obama, presumed that governance could be improved through application of formal social science methods. This approach has been marked by "striking policy failures" (Broder 2009). Instead, policy is made through the messiness of a representative democratic process. Ironically, even the system that administers voting and elections is not the product of rational organization. The very system for producing democratic representation and legitimacy is itself the product of about thirty thousand local governments organized into fifty different state systems. The highly variable standards and practices, as well as the questionable results, have been termed "dysfunctional decentralization" (International Institute for Democracy and Electoral Assistance [IDEA] 2006). For elections as well as most policies, the Constitution apportions power among many different policy players, each with jurisdiction and control of only small pieces of the puzzle. In most cases, these players in legislatures, city councils, and in Congress are more concerned with their own agendas than with systematic policy coherence (Broder 2009).

One means of circumventing this dilemma is to channel the political impulses into economically efficient ends to serve policy. A successful policy mechanism for doing this to achieve such ends as poverty reduction is conditional performance transfers. Perhaps the best-known example is the Brazilian *Bolsa Família* program, which gives 12 million families small but lifesaving amounts of cash in return for having their children vaccinated and keeping them in school. By boosting domestic demand, these policies also contribute to economic growth. Through conditional performance transfers, institutional incentives can be modified for mutual benefit of many intended policy beneficiaries. In education policy, quid pro quo deals and bargains can be made to shift the parochial agendas of such actors as teaching unions and lobbyists. President Obama included $4.35 billion in the economic stimulus bill, for example, to provide competitive grants to states for improvement of elementary and secondary education. Eligibility requirements for these "Race to the Top" funds stipulate that states must lift restrictions on the number of charter schools and eliminate laws or regulations that prohibit linking teacher pay to student performance. So far, seven states have revoked limits on charter schools, and about $450 million has been appropriated for increased pay for those teachers and principals responsible for improving student performance in high-poverty areas (Marcus 2009). In short, the powerful effects of carefully targeted fiscal incentives are already overwhelming the parochial institutional agendas that have constrained educational reform in the past. Transfers that provide incentives to change institutional behavior have also worked in other areas of policy implementation, such as urban public transport (for improved cost and passenger mile performance of local transit systems) and health care (hospitals in the United Kingdom). These are important lessons for policy design and forecasting of institutional constraints to implementation.

In the case of Washington school reform, it should be clear that a series of evidence-based activities within an overall educational policy reform is running up against institutional constraints. Evidence indicates that institutional arrangements make a difference to student learning; organizations and intermediate factors have important impacts on school operations; accountability for performance is increased where budget authority for nonpayroll items is delegated to schools; autonomy must be accompanied by standardized exams to compare school performance over time (Savedoff 1998, 12–15).

Issues

The first step is to identify the major issues affecting implementation. From the case one should be able to spot issues such as the following. First, the major institutional actors need to be identified and assessed as to their roles as assets or liabilities for implementation, through an institutional map or rapid "stakeholder analysis." This need not be elaborate, as those familiar with the issue intuitively know who the actors are and how they are likely to behave. A thorough stakeholder analysis may require substantial personnel resources and amounts of time. While its purpose is to "indicate whose interests should be taken into account when making a decision" (Crosby 1991), our purpose is predictive—to predict with some certainty the institutional and organizational obstacles and supports available for policy implementation. In the case of Washington school reform, as with most educational policy implementations, the relevant actors include the city council, the education department (DCPS), charter schools, parents, teachers, teaching unions (WTU), principals, police, and the mayor's office. On the supporting side will be DCPS, the mayor's office, most principals, some teachers, some parents, charter schools, police, and principals. Probable opponents will be the WTU and most of the city council. As indicated in table 3.3, the roles, incentives, and measures to reduce opposition or gain support will vary by actor. The second and related structural issue is the role of the city council. As noted, educational policy responsibility was shifted from the city council to DCPS; currently the council wants to get this authority back from DCPS technocrats.

Third, the functional performance of schools is an important determinant of student learning and performance. The teaching function is most critical and it is clear that this has been performed badly. Incentives to change teacher performance are needed. These tools are well known in the education industry and revolve around pay for performance; increased pay incentives in exchange for more school control over hiring and firing of teachers based on performance. This includes shifting from permanent positions to long-term contracts with performance standards (exchange of tenure for more pay).

Table 3.3   Educational Reform Stakeholder Analysis

Actor/Stakeholder	Incentive/Action	Means Necessary to Increase Support or Reduce Opposition
Mayor's Office	Initiated reform	Need reelection
DCPS	Responsible for implementation	Chancellor needs continued top-level support
Parents	Some fear change and school closures in neighborhoods	DCPS needs to provide more outreach and persuasion
Principals	Now responsible for school achievement and gain more fiscal and personnel authority; most are supportive	Need more personnel and fiscal authority
WTU	Opposed to most ideas of reform	Contract negotiation with teachers will be hard part to maintain momentum
Teachers	Older ones fear dismissal; many poor performers opposed; younger teachers supportive	DCPS needs to keep performance measurement going and institutionalize reward and punishment system
Students	Support varies by school and performance	Need more school support and protection after class
Police	Supportive, but inequity in charter security enforcement	Mayor needs to change enforcement rules for charter protection
City Council	Mostly opposed to reform	Voters need to give opponents a message
Charter Schools	Strong supporters; need more funds	Need more funding and police protection

Other related functions critical to learning include school supplies and the condition of facilities. Administrators have to perform these functions well at the school level in support of teaching and learning. As is evident from the case, these were not initially performed well but have been since the reform.

Fourth, there are legal and regulatory constraints over the establishment and support of charter schools in many places, including Washington. These rules and procedures do not benefit student learning, either for students in public schools (which without resources condemn students to poor education) or for students in charter schools (since there are still not enough of them to meet demand). Those students who enroll in nearby suburban county schools (in Virginia and Maryland) and those who enroll in charter schools have repeatedly demonstrated that poorly performing students from poor backgrounds can, in fact, learn quickly. The results are clear: The school environment matters greatly to achievement and learning, and teaching and support of teaching are central to this impact. Despite this, the rules remain as constraints.

Fifth, school spending patterns indicate that higher per-pupil expenditures do not result in better student performance. The fiscal management system may not be providing data from which to allocate resources properly; spending patterns reflect a base that has not been analyzed comprehensively and that recycles similar allocation patterns each year. The reform has changed that by attempting to link performance to funding.

Analytic Framework

Once the issues have been identified, the next step is to develop the appropriate analytic toolkit. Most toolkits in public policy analysis combine formal quantitative analysis with more heuristic methods, such as broad-based consultations and judgment (Ghosh, Ostry, and Tamirisa 2009, 36). The institutional assessment framework (IAF) presented here is mostly heuristic. Applying the framework will identify threshold points for vulnerability, threat, or support. That is, scales should be developed for each parameter or variable. With this information, however, predictive power will be mostly judgmental and experiential. It is a general framework intended to organize data collection and analysis. Pre-implementation assessment should not be research or full analysis. Time is of the essence, and analysts should select which variables and measures they judge important.

Using the IAF, it is clear that implementation faces hurdles and support from all four parameters. It is up to educational policy planners to decide whether taken together, the reform is worth the costs. Here, reformers forged ahead in 2006 probably knowing what most of the information in the IAF would be.

Legal, Regulatory, and Political Systems

Several items are important here from table 3.1. It is apparent that top-level supports did exist at the political and fiscal level, but are now under threat of deterioration. Revenue collapse from the recession forced budget cutbacks that affect teachers, administrators, and ultimately students. Chancellor Rhee is attempting to turn this constraint into an opportunity by using it to dismiss poorly performing teachers first. But this has run into WTU opposition. The NCLB Act forces action on failing schools and one action has been to create more charter schools. In Washington DC, there are more schools per student than in neighboring counties and in larger cities such as New York. But more are needed to increase competition with public schools and improve performance of the latter. Other than the apparent inequity in police failure to enforce protection of charter students off-campus after school (which, if an operating rule, needs to be changed), legal restrictions on charters are not a major constraint in Washington, DC, at this point. The trend here, as in other reform cities, is to reduce the traditional distinction between public and private schools. In Chile, for instance, nongovernmental schools compete successfully with public schools; many private schools are publicly funded and students in them achieve higher test scores (Savedoff 1998, 17).

School governance changed in 2006 as the elected school board was abolished, and DCPS and the mayor's office absorbed its policy functions. The fear now is that the council is attempting to acquire this authority in the name of democratic representation. In fact, this clearly means responsiveness to the union and populist community demands for continuance of the status quo. In practice, that means opposition to provisions in the teacher's contract with DCPS that weaken tenure security, increase principal authority over personnel decisions, and increase teacher and principal performance accountability. These facts suggest a hazardous environment in which to attempt policy reform. But top-level political support was broadened in 2008 by the arrival of a president focused on education with a new secretary of education who favors charter schools and teacher accountability (Marcus 2009), precisely the kinds of reforms being attempted in Washington. This should permit political and financial stability (because of the conditional performance stimulus grants) to execute the reforms here and in other cities at least until the next election in 2012.

Structural Design

The starting place for structural analysis is usually the size of the government itself in relation to the tasks to be performed. A common technique used in civil service reforms around the world is work programming, which includes development of staffing ratios. Civil service reforms or state modernization efforts involve review of structures and functions of government, as well as the roles and responsibilities of departments and their managers, to produce cost-effective and accountable program delivery. This is a big order that is often subsumed under "reinventing government" to "empower" employees through "reinvention laboratories," and other buzz words. Merely downsizing aggregate numbers to reduce payroll will of course lower expenditures, reduce fiscal deficits, and appear to satisfy fiscal rectitude criteria. A 2009 Brazilian civil service reform allowed workers to be laid off when payroll costs exceeded 60% of total revenues (*The Economist* 2009c, 12). But often this merely hides needed expenditures for services, operations and maintenance, and construction needs that will cost more later.

Work programming or analysis of staffing needs is a critical element in building the personal services budgets (which can represent up to 60% of total costs in some jurisdictions). To do this, analysts might:

1. Estimate workload (e.g., by student enrollment, number of tax returns, number of bus passenger miles, or number of unemployment claims). Demand analysis should also link incoming workload to resource allocation—for instance, deployment of police in response to call patterns or demand for business licenses and reallocation of department personnel to accommodate the demand (Ammons 1991, 22).

2. Estimate unit time and costs (e.g., number of tax examiners per hundred thousand returns, student-faculty ratios by discipline, administrative overhead rule of thumb based on past experience [8–10%]).

Developing time-output and staffing ratios runs into problems with professional groups that oppose measurement on the grounds that this development ignores quality and task complexity, is based on statistical averages, becomes a straitjacket, and ends up displacing the goal itself. That is, the measurement of work becomes the goal, rather than delivering quality services that require judgment and flexibility. Nevertheless, if used as a rough guide, work programming can limit budget damage and enable agencies to rid themselves of redundant personnel and to redeploy labor for particular tasks (Axelrod 1995). In the case of Washington, DC, it should be noted that although the city has had one of the highest personnel-to-citizen ratios in the world, the public works department is still understaffed for the construction management and maintenance tasks that it must accomplish: Staffing ratios indicate that the bureau is only half as large as those of cities of similar size (Reid 1996).

Functional Operations

Often school reform is framed as a debate between centralization and decentralization. This characterization is often a distraction, in that the real issues are what functions are performed best by whom (Savedoff 1998, 7) and what incentives should be provided to achieve the best results. The performance question often boils down to differences in how efficiently functions are divided among different levels of government (usually subnational). The case indicates that the reform is driven by incentives to maximize teacher performance. This implies that teaching will be supported by adequate recurrent supplies and capital facilities. Since 2006 strong emphasis has been placed on strengthening performance reporting systems, measuring school performance , and ensuring that school operations and management are monitored and evaluated regularly. DCPS regularly publishes performance reports on each of its schools both online and in hard copy. It is also clear that for DCPS reformers, assignment of budget authority to the school level and selection of teachers on the basis of performance are top priorities. Additionally, rational behavior to increase performance is not assumed: Funds are provided as incentives in performance-based transfers (paralleling those efforts from the US Department of Education).

DCPS did not perform a formal functional review to arrive at its objectives. As noted, the objectives were derived from successful reforms elsewhere and from the tenets of "the new public management," or NPM. NPM refers to distinctive reforms of public bureaucracies to improve performance, such as operational decentralization, service outsourcing, flexible hiring contracts, and incentive-based pay (Barzelay 2001). A formal functional review of the type described in table 3.1 is more useful in areas where there is less experience with successful reform. As those areas diminish, policy-specific methods will become more plentiful.

Financial Management Systems

Historically, Washington has been infamous for its public financial management problems. But the Financial Control Board and new leadership in its financial institutions have made all the difference. Washington has maintained AAA bond ratings and, at least until the recent financial crisis, adequate reserves in its rainy day fund.

Nevertheless, basic fiscal functions such as personnel, procurement, contracting, and internal audit are still weak. These are interrelated functions, as noted. But cuts and reforms often treat them as if they were separate. First, staffing cuts expose remaining employees to requirements that delay needed work. While the public works department has lost hundreds of its staff members in the past, it still had to answer to a layered city bureaucracy that delays projects by up to six months (Reid 1996). Staffing cuts that save budget funds in the short run are often squandered by bureaucratic constraints, driving up transaction costs for remaining personnel.

Second, despite having an IFMS, institutional boundaries and cultures preserve fragmented information systems that weaken budget planning and control. There are still islands of information that permit transactions to fall through the cracks, such as paying employees without budgeted slots before it becomes clear that a department has exceeded its personnel costs (Flaherty 1995). Evidence of failures to link payroll with personnel rosters and budgets still exists, despite efforts to integrate the two databases. The city uses an employee identification numbering system to safeguard against fraud, but audits found 1,734 people on the payrolls without numbers who were paid anyway. Nearly two hundred people shared numbers, and personnel numbers existed for eight dead people. Individuals appeared on the payroll file but were not listed on personnel and budget files, meaning that although they were paid there was no audit trail in the files to document their existence (Horwitz and Strauss 1997). Integration of fiscal and personnel data helps. But an internal audit unit is needed to oversee these transactions on a periodic basis. Budget administration is weakened by a system that allows deficits to be financed by staff withholding accounting entries that remain undetected by internal controls or auditors. The major fiscal scandal of 2007, in which a wide network of DC officials absconded with $40 million in property tax refunds over a five-year period, indicated that the internal audit was passive and that the network of corruption was wide enough to pay off anyone that would be likely to disclose it. The fraud was discovered by a manager at a commercial bank— someone who was not regularly associated with the others (Nakamura and Harris 2008).

While these problems persist in DC government at large, fiscal management problems have so far not been significant obstacles to educational reform progress. The major problem identified in the case was that of incomplete coverage and classification of expenditures. Failure to classify expenditures precisely can diminish the value of data reported in broad or incorrect categories and thereby weaken policy analysis. Budget analysts cannot properly recommend where funds should be allocated because they do not have a clear idea of where they are being spent. As noted in the Anacostia High School budget, expenditures for instruction, support, and leadership are mixed up. Schools are rewarded for efficiency and effectiveness of instruction. To classify administrators as instructional personnel exaggerates the school emphasis on instruction and could lead to unjust rewards.

NOTES

1. The efficiency-effectiveness distinction in public administration is often confusing to economists, who define both as subcategories of efficiency. "Technical efficiency" refers to least cost and maximization of output per unit of input; "allocative efficiency" refers to client access and service quality, which satisfies consumer preferences (World Bank 1995, 30).

2. A common problem in policy analysis today is the simplistic assumption that information can always improve the quality of decisions. Based on this premise, considerable sums are expended on information-reporting systems, the implicit assumption being that some manager will use the data for some purpose. But more timely and accurate fiscal and economic data flows may not produce valuable information for better decision making. Many management and policy problems derive from issues of organizational structure. Having more data available does not necessarily help policymakers to articulate the questions that need attention in order to solve problems. A fundamental presumption of information technology is that more and better information increases public-sector control over costs and service performance. Public management theorists and practitioners presume that the more and better the information on project cost, schedule, and quality in computer systems, the greater the project control and the less the actual performance variances.

   In an empirical study of management control systems for ninety-nine defense contracts, E. Sam Overman and Donna Loraine (1994, 195) found that the "quality, detail, timeliness and cost of information do not have a positive effect on project control." Despite these findings, "most managers still believed that collecting and reporting information led to project control." In short, data are collected and processed into information largely to "support the illusion of control" or for "symbolic value." Given this disturbing finding, there should likely be an upper limit or hard budget constraint on generation of information as a management tool for most organizations. Rather, organizations should likely emphasize incentives that help management to engage in critical policy thinking and to turn the most important data into useful information for decisions. Information, it seems, can guide better policymaking. But it cannot prevent problems caused by the modern tendency to demand all data and the failure to seek more precise data around defined questions and problems.

Much of the advice to policymakers from frameworks such as ours tends to be "Delphic." That is, engage in tricky maneuvers to sanction poor teachers without penalizing good ones; make efficiency cuts without damaging student motivation to learn, etc. The tools are intended as decision frameworks to be used by experts in particular policies (here education). They are not intended as learning devices for outsiders and those who merely want to study the problems further. Consider them action tools for which only the most pertinent variables and measures should be employed by policy experts to make decisions and to communicate their rationale to political leaders. Like all of the tools examined in this book, they are means, not ends in themselves.

REFERENCES

Alm, James, Robert H. Aten, and Roy Bahl. 2001. *Can Indonesia Decentralize Successfully? Plans, Problems, and Prospects.* Jakarta, Indonesia: US Agency for International Development.

Ammons, David N. 1991. *Administrative Analysis for Local Governments.* Athens: University of Georgia, Carl Vinson Institute of Government.

Anthony, Robert N., and David W. Young. 1988. *Management Control in Nonprofit Organizations.* Homewood, IL: Irwin.

Axelrod, Donald. 1995. *Budgeting for Modern Government.* 2nd ed. New York: St. Martin's.

Banks, William C., and Jeffrey D. Straussman. 1999. Defense Contingency Budgeting in the Post-Cold-War Period. *Public Administration Review* 59 (March/April): 135–45.

Barr, Stephen. 1997. AID's $71 Million Global Computer Link Sidelined by Software, Design Problems. *Washington Post*, May 5.

Bartel, Margaret. 1996. *Integrated Financial Management Systems: A Guide Based on the Experience in Latin America* (draft). Washington, DC: World Bank.Barzelay, Michael. 2001.

Barzelay, Michael. 2001. *The New Public Management: Improving Research and Policy Dialogue.* Berkeley: University of California Press.

Boyne, George A. 1998. Bureaucratic Theory Meets Reality: Public Choice and Service Contracting in U.S. Local Government. *Public Administration Review* 58 (6): 474–84.

Broder, David S. 2009. Mr. Policy Hits a Wall. *Washington Post*, September 24.

Byrnes, Patricia, Mark Freeman, and Dean Kauffman. 1997. Performance Measurement and Financial Incentives for Community Behavioral Health Service Provision. *International Journal of Public Administration* 20 (8/9): 1555–78.

Caiden, Naomi, and Aaron Wildavsky. 1975. *Planning and Budgeting in Poor Countries.* New York: John Wiley.

Chandler, Clay. 1997. Medicare Accounting Dispute Could Threaten Early Budget Accord. *Washington Post,* January 10.

Cochrane, Glynn. 1983. *Policies for Strengthening Local Government in Developing Countries.* Staff Working Paper No. 582. Washington, DC: World Bank.

Coe, Charles K. 1989. *Public Financial Management.* Englewood Cliffs, NJ: Prentice Hall.

Committee for a Responsible Federal Budget (CRFB). 2009. *The Cost of "Current Policy."* Washington, DC: Committee for a Responsible Federal Budget.

COTR/AOTR Continuing Education. 2009. Washington, DC: USAID.

Crosby, Benjamin L. 1991. *Stakeholder Analysis: A Vital Tool for Strategic Managers.* Washington, DC: Management Science International/USAID.

The Economist. 1993. Government in California: Buckling under the Strain. February 13.

———. 1997a. Just What the Doctors Ordered? July 26.

———. 1997b. Fraudulent Behavior. July 26.

———. 1999. Government in Disgrace: Bilking the Tribes. March 13.

———. 2009a. Big Government Fights Back. January 31.

———. 2009b. Japan's Election: Lost in Translation. September 5.

———. 2009c. Getting It Together at Last. November 14.

Flaherty, Mary Pat. 1995. Failure to Compute Adds to D.C.'s Bills. *Washington Post,* May 5.

Franklin, Aimee L. 2002. An Examination of the Impact of Budget Reform on Arizona and Oklahoma Appropriations. *Public Budgeting and Finance* 22:25–45.

Ghosh, Atish R., Jonathan D. Ostry, and Natalia Tamirisa. 2009. Anticipating the Next Crisis. *Finance and Development* 46 (3): 35–37.

Gianakis, Gerasimos A., and John G. Davis. 1998. Reinventing or Replacing Public Services? The Case of Community-Oriented Policing. *Public Administration Review* 58 (6): 43–51.

Goldhill, David. 2009. How American Health Care Killed My Father. *The Atlantic Monthly,* September.

Government Finance Officers Association. 1978. *An Operating Budget Handbook for Small Cities and Other Governmental Units.* Chicago: Government Finance Officers Association.

Guess, George M. 2005. Comparative Decentralization Lessons from Pakistan, Indonesia, and the Philippines. *Public Administration Review* 65 (2): 217–31.

———, ed. 2008. *Managing and Financing Urban Public Transport Systems, An International Perspective.* Budapest: Local Government and Public Service Reform Initiative of the Open Society Institute.

Haarmeyer, David, and Ashoka Mody. 1997. Private Capital in Water and Sanitation. *Finance and Development* 34 (1): 34–37.

Hayes, Frederick O., David A. Grossman, Jerry E. Mechling, John S. Thomas, and Steven J. Rosenbloom. 1982. *Linkages: Improving Financial Management in Local Government*. Washington, DC: Urban Institute.

Heclo, Hugh. 1978. Issue Networks and the Executive Establishment. In *The New Political System*, ed. Anthony King, 87–124. Washington, DC: American Enterprise Institute.

Horwitz, Sari, and Valerie Strauss. 1997. A Well-Financed Failure: System Protects Jobs While Shortchanging Classrooms. *Washington Post*, February 16.

International Institute for Democracy and Electoral Assistance (IDEA). 2006. *Electoral Management Design: The International IDEA Handbook*. Stockholm: IDEA.

Jeter, Jon, and Susan Levine. 1997. Montgomery Agency Handled Boy's Case Correctly, Officials Say (But Child Protection System Has Problems, Task Force Finds). *Washington Post*, May 2.

Keating, Michael, and David Rosalky. 1983. Rolling Expenditure Plans: Australian Experience and Prognosis. In *Government Budgeting and Expenditure Controls, Theory and Practice*, ed. A. Premchand, 72–97. Washington, DC: International Monetary Fund.

Kory, Ross C., and Philip Rosenberg. 1984. Costing Municipal Services. In *Practical Financial Management*, ed. John Matzer, 50–60. Washington, DC: International City Management Association.

Larson, Erik. 2003. *The Devil in the White City*. New York: Vintage.

Levine, Susan, and Manuel Perez-Rivas. 1997. Montgomery Targets Services Watchdog, Accountability Office Is in Line for 50% Budget Cut. *Washington Post*, May 14.

Lipton, Eric. 1998. A Cleanup Job Left Unfinished. *Washington Post*, December 9.

Marcus, Ruth. 2009. Obama's Quiet Success on Schools. *Washington Post*, September 23.

McAllister, Bill. 1996. Bottom Line or By-the-Book: Postal Services Public-Private Identity Crisis. *Washington Post*, December 25.

Michel, R. Gregory. 2001. *Decision Tools for Budgetary Analysis*. Chicago: Government Finance Officers Association.

Mikesell, John L. 2007. *Fiscal Administration: Analysis and Applications for the Public Sector*. Boston: Thomson Wadsworth.

Nakamura, David, and Hamil R. Harris. 2008. Report on Embezzlement Blames "Culture of Apathy and Silence." *Washington Post*, December 16.

North, Douglass C. 1990. *Institutions, Institutional Change and Economic Performance*. Cambridge: Cambridge University Press.

Overman, E. Sam, and Donna T. Loraine. 1994. Information for Control: Another Management Proverb? *Public Administration Review* 54 (2): 193–96.

Pearlstein, Steven. 1997. The Thriving Economy That Keeps on Surprising. *Washington Post*, May 3.

Raimondo, Henry J. 1978. *The Economics of State and Local Government*. New York: Praeger.

Razon-Abad, Henedina. 2001. *A Decade of Taking Root: Synopsis Report and Action Plan*. Manila, Philippines: US Agency for International Development/ Accelerating Growth, Investment and Liberalization with Equity.

Reid, Alice. 1996. Public Works Positions Cut But Management Layers Remain. *Washington Post*, March 27.

Savedoff, William D., ed. 1998. *Organization Matters: Agency Problems in Health and Education in Latin America*. Washington, DC: Inter-American Development Bank.

Schlosser, Eric. 1998. The Prison-Industrial Complex. *Atlantic Monthly*, December.

Schmitt, Eric. 1997. Panel Urges Abolishing Immigration Agency. *International Herald Tribune*, August 6.

Stier, Max. 2009. The Flow-Chart Fallacy. *Washington Post*, June 8.

Thompson, Cheryl W. 1998. Homicide Unit to Return Officers to Headquarters: Study of Other Cities' Departments Prompts Police Officials to Abandon Decentralization Effort. *Washington Post*, January 21.

United Nations Development Program (UNDP). 2001. *Rebuilding State Structures: Methods and Approaches*. New York: UNDP.

Washington Post. 1996. D.C., U.S. Streamline Road-Project Approval Process. June 7.

———. 2009. Ms. Rhee's Belt-Tightening: How D.C.'s Budget Cuts Can Eliminate Ineffective Teachers. September 29.

———. 2010. Out of Order: Should Metro's Escalators Be Taken Out of Service When Demand Is Low? January 1.

World Bank. 1995. *Better Urban Services: Finding the Right Incentives*. Washington, DC: International Bank for Reconstruction and Development.

———. 1997. *The Public Expenditure Management Handbook*. Washington, DC: World Bank.

Chapter 4

Forecasting Policy Options

Experts are narrowly focused persons who need to "tunnel." When [the prediction experts] were right, they attributed it to their own depth of understanding and expertise; when wrong, it was either the situation that was to blame, since it was unusual, or, worse, they did not recognize they were wrong and spun stories around it. They found it difficult to accept that their grasp was a little short.

—Nassim Nicholas Taleb, *The Black Swan*

As indicated in chapter 2, in the process of acquiring data, the analyst decides whether an actionable policy problem exists; in other words, the analyst has to determine whether direct or indirect public action can reduce the effects of the problem. Through assessment of data trends, the analyst structures the policy problem, reviewing its degree of complexity and stakeholder involvement as well as its potential solubility in the short or medium term. At this stage, evidence mounts to show whether a problem is simple and well structured or messy and ill structured. As the foundation of evidence-based policy, the evidence should indicate whether a problem exists at all, and, if it does, just how actionable it is. The conclusion that a problem does or does not exist is the product of the first part of the diagnostic phase of policy analysis.

The second part of the policy analysis process seeks to uncover the future behavior or persistence of variables used to define the problem. Clearly the two phases are related, because additional diagnosis might not be warranted if preliminary data indicate that the problem will solve itself in the near future. As a lurid example to emphasize this point, marine experts in the 1997 film *The Beast* recommended a do-nothing option to the police, arguing that the giant squid eating local fishermen was simply passing through, and that any police actions could anger the monster and encourage it to retaliate against the entire town. That is, let the problem solve itself. Similarly, in the Alpine Swiss village of the senior author's sister-in-law, a mountain dog had been attacking hikers and locals for several years until he decided to go for more challenging prey—automobiles. Villagers feared police intervention might harm tight interfamily bonds of trust and simply tolerated the attacks. The problem solved itself when the dog was run over by a tractor. Unfortunately, most public problems do not solve themselves. Policy analysts need to know two things at this stage. First, they need data and methods to forecast the future behavior of variables related to the problem. Second, they need to know the costs and benefits of proposed policy solutions, or those options identified as solutions. Neither task is easy or straightforward.

In this chapter we focus on efforts to forecast the future behavior of policy problems and to decide on a preferred solution. The development of reliable data forecasts gives us a baseline from which to develop policy options and solutions. As we learned in chapter 2, failure to define a problem properly often leads to costly and inefficient omnibus approaches like throwing dollars at the problem. The difficulty of definition increases with the number of decision makers and options. Chapter 2 described how, as decision values become harder to measure and rank, and the impact of options becomes harder to predict, the problem transforms from simple and well structured (i.e., few decision, few options—e.g., municipal recycling), to moderately structured (i.e., few decisions but imprecise outcomes—e.g., pensions), and finally, to really ill structured (many hard-to-rank decisions, multidimensional problems—e.g., urban transport corridor planning). Most real policy problems are of the latter types.

Failure to establish how problem variables will behave in the future results in public expenditures that could actually worsen the problem by failing to control for unanticipated consequences. If, for example, drug abuse is a problem understood on the basis of past trends, then setting out viable policy alternatives will depend on accurate forecasts of sub-problem component behavior in the future. Whether the problem is viewed as well structured or ill structured, it will require generation of data trends that can be converted into useful decision information. Being able to project trends accurately depends on experience (judgment), the accuracy of past data (time-series), and a thorough understanding of such drug abuse determinants as hunger and homelessness (causal model). Similarly, it is clear that current arguments over health care reform turn on assessments of past treatment and cost trends, as well as the need for agreement on a preferred set of policy options. To date, there is little agreement on either the trends, the level of problem severity, or overall solutions.

Finally, once data trends have been developed and policy options identi-fied, policymakers need an institutional framework with a mechanism to rank the options objectively and decide on a preferred solution. In federal systems or states such as the United States, policy problems span vertical and horizontal jurisdictional boundaries. They are the responsibility of multiple jurisdictions serving multiple constituencies. There is also the institutional secrecy problem; namely, that despite all the checks and balances and multiple jurisdictions in competition, major policy decisions can be made on weak or fraudulent data and implemented. It has been argued that for the Iraq war decision, in making fantastical claims about Saddam Hussein's imminent acquisition of nuclear weapons that were not vetted by the CIA or the National Security Council, Vice President Cheney created "policy-based evidence," rather than evidence-based policy (*The Economist* 2009a). As indicated in chapter 3, the decision process must include relevant stakeholders or policy implementation will fail. In this chapter, we will use a case of transportation corridor policy planning in two counties of suburban Maryland outside Washington, DC. The case may resemble a more typical ill-structured problem in that there is intense conflict over options and data trends, which has to be resolved through a lengthy mul-tistage, multilevel decision process. Planning for the Purple Line (light-rail transit line) between Montgomery County and Prince George's County, for instance, has been characterized as a confrontational standoff between multi-ple interests. It is said of the stakeholders that they are "all right—so right and so committed to their path as the one true way that their positions have hard-ened and the very notion of compromise strikes them as abhorrent" (M. Fisher 2008). Can improved or different kinds of policy analysis break the deadlock? If all stakeholders are correct, how can a rational public choice be made to resolve a messy problem such as this?

Based on the needs of decision makers who are often faced with multiple options and solutions to ill-structured or messy policy problems, this chapter will discuss: (1) the general purposes of forecasting, (2) the kinds of forecasts commonly developed, (3) useful techniques for forecasting problem data trends, and (4) techniques to structure decisions and select options or solutions for both well- and ill-structured problems. This framework will then be applied to the case study of the Purple Line.

PREDICTING THE FUTURE, CAUTIOUSLY

Before examining the range of techniques needed to predict the future, we need to know the objectives of forecasting. Public-sector stakeholders, such as a municipal credit-rating agency, need specifics on future financial conditions, such as the level of operating expenses for maintenance of capital investment projects five years from now, or expected levels of sales tax revenue collections in that city for the year 2015. To forecast gasoline tax revenues for 2015, stakeholders would want to know the expected level of gas consumption in that year. Regulators and other stakeholder institutions regularly want to know the current and future fiscal condition of revenue-generating units in the public sector—from state and local enterprises (e.g., city water authorities and state transit agencies such as the Metropolitan Atlanta Rapid Transit Authority, or MARTA) to national railroads (e.g., Amtrak). Just as importantly, public agency managers themselves need to know revenue and expenditure trends so that they can manage their budgets for the year and deliver services effectively. They cannot do so without accurate forecasts based on sound methodologies, supplemented by good monitoring of the budget to determine when they should alter expenditure plans in response to new forecasts. Nonfinancial forecasts are also critical for policy decisions. Federal land managers (including the Bureau of Land Management and the US Forest Service), for example, need to know the behavior of forest fires to prevent loss of firefighter life and property damage. For this purpose, researchers at the Los Alamos National Laboratory have been developing "crisis forecasting" techniques based on predictive computer simulations (Lane 1998).

Typically, the policy analyst will begin work by developing "projections" (or a range of forecasts based on extrapolations of current and historical claims into the future) to avoid being pinned down on one figure (or forecast). "Forecasts" are single projections chosen from a series of possibilities based on currently plausible assumptions. Policy analysts tend to avoid the term *prediction* (or forecasts based on explicit theoretical assumptions) because it implies "a statement of certainty about future events that obscures the conditional basis on which each of the projections, including the forecast, are based" (Klay 1983, 289). William Klay notes, for example, that the US Bureau of the Census publishes several series of projections based on different assumptions about fertility, mortality, and migration, "but it resists identifying any one of these projections as an official forecast" (289). At the same time, revenue policy analysts use the term "best available prediction," selected from baseline "forecasts." They know that the predictions are never certain (Mikesell 2007, 514), but still must serve as the foundation of fiscal discipline.

Before learning more about statistical forecasting techniques, one might reasonably ask how accurate they are. For instance, many have noted the surprising inability of most economists to predict the most spectacular economic and financial crisis in decades, which started in 2007. According to the IMF, the elegant mathematical models developed by the organization's economists underappreciated systemic risks coming from financial sector feedbacks into the real economy (Samuelson 2009). Innovative financial instruments were traded on overvalued underlying mortgage loans, ultimately turning the entire market into a pyramid scheme (i.e., claims of previous investors are paid off with newer investors' cash). Few used the appropriate data to predict what would ultimately happen—financial sector collapse.

William Dunn (1994, 192) notes, for example, that for the period 1971–83, the larger econometric firms had an average forecasting error, as a proportion of actual changes in gross national product, of 50%. He suggests that the accuracy of predictions based on complex theoretical models has been no greater than the accuracy of projections and conjectures made on the basis of simple extrapolative models and informed judgments. Consistent with this statement, we noted in the previous edition of this book (Guess and Farnham 2000, 205) that even the best data and most sophisticated methods still cannot predict "cyclical timing" and tend to presume that the future will look like the past. So the answer to the question of how accurate the forecasting techniques are is that the techniques are accurate if the data is accurate. Since one cannot obtain discontinuous data trends in advance, the methods should be used with caution and circumspection—not with the intellectual hubris of mathematical economics applied to finance or any other policy area!

By contrast, shorter-term forecasts of US budget deficits have been more accurate, even when obvious political incentives exist to vary the final figures. Between 1993 and 1996, the difference between the fourteen fiscal deficit forecasts of the US Office of Management and Budget (OMB) and the Congressional Budget Office (CBO) was only $13 billion. More surprisingly, both OMB and CBO projected higher deficits than actually came to pass (Congressional Budget Office 1997, 58). Several months after publishing its forecasts, CBO discovered with new revenue data that they were actually off by $45 billion per year, or $225 billion for their five-year forecast (Chandler 1997). Instead of continued fiscal deficits, the budget would actually be in surplus. CBO projected budget surpluses to rise from 1.4% of gross domestic product (GDP) in 2000 to 2.8% of GDP in 2009 (*The Economist* 1999a, 42). Despite missing the revenue forecast by only 9% in 1991–92 (Axelrod 1995, 78), OMB was vilified by outside observers for inaccuracy. The trouble is that all other forecasters, including CBO and commercial banks, came up with roughly the same forecasts. Of course, the deficit and debt projections are radically different in 2010. The Peterson-Pew Commission currently forecasts budget deficits to increase from 10% to 16% of GDP by 2038; debt held by the public is projected to rise from 40% to 200% of GDP in the same period, due to retirements, health care costs, and interest on the debt itself (Committee for a Responsible Federal Budget [CRFB] 2009). In short, often the problem is not with the forecasters, but with the "inherent impossibility of predicting even a few months in advance the performance of a volatile $3 trillion economy" (which is now a $20 trillion GDP in 2010) (Humbert 1984, 2).

The fiscal deficit forecasting problem of the late 1990s was likely a combination of overreliance on technical models, normal bureaucratic caution, and CBO interest in jacking up the size of the deficit to make the Clinton administration look bad. Despite the complexity of forecasting what is now a $12 billion annual deficit, the rules, the systems for gaming the rules, and the data sources are well known by all actors. So ultimately, barring a discontinuous event such as the current financial crisis, the deficit should be marginally different from the previous year. In our policy terminology, it is a moderately well-structured problem. By requiring forecasts from both the CBO and the OMB, the Congressional Budget Impoundment and Control Act of 1974 institutionalized competitive forecasting and increased the overall accuracy of results. This suggests that greater forecasting accuracy lies in balancing the technical assumptions of any method against political and historical contextual factors. In this case, policy changes enacted after both CBO and OMB had issued their forecasts had the net effect of reducing the deficit (a statistical phenomenon known as "endogeneity"). Failure to develop proper forecasts leaves the policymaker in the position of running and trying to hit a moving target. Good forecasting and wise use of techniques pay dividends if it is recognized that use of high-powered forecasting techniques requires valid data based on adequate sample sizes. It is often the case that projections of revenue receipts are based on small sample sizes that can compromise the power of statistical tests (Nelson and Cornia 1997, 42).

How important are revenue forecasts for budget policy and national politics? One might do worse than to ask former French president Jacques Chirac. To qualify for the European single currency, the euro, the Maastricht Treaty required that the French 1998 budget deficit (and those of other applicants) be no larger than 3.0% of GDP. But President Chirac's treasury forecast a budget deficit of 3.7% in 1997 and 4.5% in 1998. Based on this forecast, he questioned even trying for adoption of the single currency. He then called an election ten months early in which his Gaullist Party supporters suffered major losses. For the subsequent government of Socialist Prime Minister Lionel Jospin, the treasury forecasted deficits of 3.1% in 1997 and 3.0% in 1998, based largely on higher economic growth (3.0%) and major cuts in defense spending (*The Economist* 1997b). In short, policy forecasters can actually make or break governments. Much can turn on the single number forecast by competent professionals, if it is deemed by other experts and the public to be "evidence-based policy" and not the reverse!

Forecasts can sometimes literally mean life or death for governments and individuals, especially in the case of providing the public with flood warnings. Unlike earthquake predictions, which remain in the realm of discontinuous phenomena, storms and flood patterns are regular—and they and their effects on surrounding populations can be discerned with appropriate forecasting methods. A good example of this was the Northern California floods of 1996. California's fourteen hundred dams and reservoirs are operated by a network of federal, state, and local agencies, plus power companies, irrigation districts, and water agencies. At its river forecast centers, the National Weather Service uses an orographic-hydrological model fed by information from the US Geological Survey (USGS) and the California Department of Water Resources at more than two hundred hydrometeorological measuring stations in rivers and streams.

The model still forecasts precipitation produced by air lifted over mountains. Predictions of wind, temperature, and humidity up to 20,000 feet are combined with land elevation data at three-mile intervals to pinpoint precipitation amounts and locations in the mountains. Data from satellite pictures and Doppler radar are collected and used to track storms for flood management decision making. (Flood management consists of juggling inflows and releases from reservoirs and dams to control the level of runoff.) While much of the guesswork in the models has been eliminated, "flood forecasting remains an inexact science" (Kiester 1997, 36). In December 1996, based on observations and predictions from an orographic model and a good bit of experience, a major storm was forecast. Even though the timing of rainfall occasionally eluded forecasters, the total amount forecast for the three storms was exceptionally close to what actually fell (44). The hydrologists came up with mostly accurate predictions of not only amounts but locations as well. Although the floods swept out several critical USGS stations, the management of flood control space by the US Army Corps of Engineers saved countless dollars in flood damage.

Similarly, as part of their annual budget preparation exercises in late summer and early fall, state and local governments in the United States need to budget for next year's snow removal based on forecasts of snowfall for the season. This puts part of subnational government finances at the mercy of nature and the selection of forecasting methods. The unwritten rule is to "budget accordingly." This works well for northern states such as Michigan, which receives between one hundred and two hundred inches of snow per year. The lake effect causes tons of snow to fall until the lake freezes over in January and the snowfall pattern becomes more regular and predictable (Halsey 2009). Snow rarely closes streets, even when sixty-four inches fell in December 2009. The annual snow removal budget in Petoskey, Michigan is $11,055 per mile. But in areas such as Washington, where it may snow three inches in one year (2001–2) and forty inches the very next year (2002–3), how can we connect the dots to form a predictable pattern for financing? The problem is not just the annual pattern but single storms that absorb most of the budgets. The snowstorm of December 2009 used $4 million of a $6.2 million snow removal budget (65%) in Washington, DC (Halsey 2009). Maryland spent $20 million out of a $26 million budget (77%) and had to spend $8 million more in funds transferred from other state agencies. In contrast with Petoskey, Michigan, based on its forecasts, Maryland spends only $1,529 per mile per year on snow removal. If global warming continues, this may save funds for snow removal. But to avoid political backlash from angry drivers and parents of schoolchildren, the key is predictable snowfall!

PURPOSES OF POLICY FORECASTING

The purposes of policy forecasting vary according to the goals and objectives of policy and definitions of the problem. William Dunn (2008, 136–37) distinguishes between forecasts of existing and new policies and the potential support behavior of stakeholders. Clients need to know the effect of present macroeconomic policies without changes and new policies on stakeholder groups.

Macropolicy Impacts

Policy forecasts may have macropolicy objectives, such as an energy policy that reduces the balance of payments deficit and reduces the inflationary costs of oil imports). Forecasts of new policy trends, in which new government actions are taken in response to market forces, tend to allow a wide range of assumptions and conclusions. For example, oil-pricing forecasts often seek the point at which drilling becomes profitable. Based on a price of $15 to $20 for a barrel of oil (the price was $71 a barrel in September 2009, down from $94 in September 2008, or a 33% drop), US oil production declined by 2% in 1985–86 while imports increased by 8% in the same period. If these trends had continued until a stable $22 a barrel price was reached, that would have been the profitability point for drilling in the United States (Daniels 1986). Macroeconomists employ theory-based policy forecasts at the macro level: They try to forecast aggregate demand in the economy and project how large the inflation or output gap will be. Using an income-determination model of aggregate demand, or the likely amount of expenditures by government, investors, and consumers from their respective incomes, economic policy analysts try to predict how much inflation or unemployment will occur from this level of predicted demand; that is, aggregate demand or (D) = consumption (C) + investment (I) + government spending (G). From this they recommend appropriate fiscal and monetary policies. As noted, macroeconomists tend to ignore financial economic impacts on the nonfinancial or real sector in developing their forecasts. This creates more problems for forecasters of new policies!

Existing Policy Impacts

Forecasts may take existing policies as a given. The US budget process begins with expenditure forecasts based on no changes in existing policy. "Current services estimates" of expenditures are inflation-adjusted changes in expenditures with modifications only for changes in agency workloads. The budget baseline or current services estimate is an estimate of the receipts, outlays, and deficits that current law would produce; it should be a "policy-neutral benchmark" against which proposals and options can be compared without interference from the economy (Mikesell 2007, 85). Forecasts of existing revenue trends, where no new government actions are taken to change tax or fee structures, typically seek one predictive figure (e.g., a 4% increase in revenues for the next three fiscal years).

The Atlanta rail-bus transit agency (MARTA, a state enterprise) annually requires by law exact knowledge of sales tax revenues for at least the following four years. The agency must have these data to avoid budget deficits or surpluses that would rouse the enmity of various stakeholders. These include public-sector unions, bondholders, the appointed MARTA board, riders who would face a fare increase or service cuts, and such bond-rating agencies as Standard and Poor's. To illustrate the seriousness of revenue forecasts in the determination of policy, in FY 1987 the sales tax forecast of $155.8 million overestimated revenue collections by $8.8 million. The resultant budget deficit had to be financed by a fare increase in June 1987 (Roughton 1987). Fare increases are always dangerous because, if patronage falls, farebox revenues deteriorate and create greater deficits in the future. Transit demand, unlike that for other local services, is price-elastic, or very sensitive to price changes. Since price-elastic transit fare increases would increase the relative price of service compared to reasonable options (i.e., autos) in most US cities while increasing the purchasing power of riders, they are very likely to exit the service and not return. In the late 1980s an entire fleet of new buses in Birmingham, Alabama, was warehoused because of exactly such a downward spiral in ridership caused by fare increases. Fare increases were followed by more fare increases to make up the previous shortfall, thus causing further ridership reductions, and so on. This is similar to raising tax rates on small tax bases and expecting revenues to increase. In most cases, taxpayers evade or avoid excessively high tax rates or leave altogether so that total collections decrease (as the Laffer curve would predict).

In addition to developing revenue and expenditure trends for the service, then, decision makers need detailed knowledge of price and income elasticities of demand to make accurate revenue forecasts for alternate pricing structures. Price elasticities for large transit systems are about 1.30 (meaning that for every $1 fare increase, demand decreases by about 33%). For smaller transit systems, price elasticities are larger, from 2.00 to 4.00 (Litman 2004), meaning that Birmingham-type results are probable for even minor fare increases. The concept of elasticity is discussed in detail in chapter 5.

Impacts on Stakeholders

Forecasts must also be made about the contents of new policies and the behavior of policy stakeholders. As noted in chapter 3, it is extremely difficult to forecast the behavior of institutions during implementation. Thus, the bases of these forecasts are "judgmental," despite the fact that the forecasts often have a heavy quantitative foundation (ironically, the more quantitative the forecast, the more judgmental it is!). Two examples should suffice here, one from a political and the other from an economic policy perspective. First, "high" policy analysis increasingly attempts to forecast the political stability of nations as a service to investors and other interested patrons. This involves forecasting the relationship between economic and political stability, based on past patterns and the quality of the current government. Political risk analysis is an effort to forecast the behavior of policy stakeholders by using such techniques as "political feasibility assessment" (*New York Times* 1986; Coplin and O'Leary 1976). In this technique, data are examined from multiple sources covering a variety of structural and policy questions, and the country is given a rating from a panel of experts. The rating is converted into an index or multiplier for forecasting existing trends into the future. Foreign investors then have an indicator of the political, as well as economic and financial, risk of success or failure.

Second, in some cases, economists try to forecast the effects of existing policies for both investors and policymakers. For example, an important current question for both groups is whether the current public-sector stimulus programs will lead to economic stabilization, and if so, at what costs in debt and inflation? It is even hard to compare the magnitude of stimulus programs, given the variation in budget classifications and treatment of expenditures as grants or loans. Thus, the US stimulus in gross terms is about 5.8% of GDP, China's is 15.0%, while Brazil's is only 0.2% of GDP. The Chinese stimulus is largely infrastructure, tax cuts, and nonbank bailouts (real sector). The US stimulus employs every conceivable tool, from loan guarantees, nationalizations, asset purchases, capital injections, and liquidity provisions to infrastructure spending and tax cuts (*The Economist* 2009b). Much of the forecast turns on whether the programs are viewed as temporary or permanent. The US program is already being dismantled as loans are repaid and the stimulus expires in 2010. The Brazilian program has been small because the crisis was minor. The health of the Brazilian financial and banking sectors, together with tight public finance discipline and low deficits, have allowed "policy space" to invest in infrastructure and social services to stimulate growth and improve quality of life. The Chinese program is more likely to be permanent and could cause inflation and major debt problems for the future. Infrastructure spending will likely increase the efficiency of capital allocation and productivity. But medium-term forecasts based on the effects of currently low inflation, tax cuts, and excess liquidity (lending grew by 34% in 2009, or four times the rate of nominal GDP) predict sustained asset-price inflation. This could lead to another asset bubble and higher inflation (*The Economist* 2009c). Forecast accuracy depends almost on daily behavior of borrowers and investors in each country in response to these incentives. Using data on the past behavior of core variables in comparative cases, analysts can provide warning signals to policy-makers and guidance on when to tighten stimulus-driven fiscal and monetary policies.

KINDS OF POLICY FORECASTS

A major purpose of this book is to provide a working knowledge of policy techniques and their bases. In this section we critically examine four commonly used forecasting techniques. It should be stressed that theoretical elegance and technical sophistication are less important than providing a reasonably accurate forecast in the least possible time with a minimum of resources. The four major approaches are:

- *Judgmental*, which means an intuitive or qualitative approach that leads to conjectures from analysis of hard data.

- *Trend extrapolation,* which uses time-series data to develop projections.

- *Causal or econometric modeling,* which uses statistical analyses of data, including simulations, to clarify economic issues (R. Fisher 2007, 84) and to develop predictions.

- *Decision structuring and communications,* which is suited for multidimensional, ill-structured problems, to integrate options, preferred solutions, and public notice and comment.

Whereas there are important similarities and differences between these approaches, it should be stressed that in practice most policy analysts use some combination of all four. Choice of method or methods often turns on the quality of the available data and time allotted for the task. Interval data allow for more sophisticated techniques than nominal- or ordinal-level data. That is, nominal categories are nonnumerical scales such as zip codes and race. They cannot be ranked. Ordinal-level categories are more sophisticated and can be ranked from low to high, such as opinion scales to measure political attitudes. Such measures can be ranked, but the distance between ordinal categories is not precisely known. Interval data categories can be ranked and the distance between them precisely defined (Healey 2005, 11–14). Analysts often have to decide whether interval data are actually "interval enough" to justify interval methods. It is often the case that analysts use interval statistical methods with ordinal data, which can bias results (Hedderson 1991, 92–93). So choice of method often boils down to a combination of data quality and the analyst's judgment. Nevertheless, it is prudent to compare forecast results obtained from the use of each method, if possible. As noted above, in the second edition of this book, we illustrated this point with the MARTA tax-forecasting case. Use of the causal or econometric modeling technique was only slightly more accurate than use of the judgmental technique. As noted then, professional forecasters such as the Economic Forecasting Center of Georgia State University in Atlanta employ multivariate recursive and nonrecursive (causal) models, linear and nonlinear extrapolative techniques, and judgment to overcome weaknesses in the data and uncertainties about policymaker behavior. Policy analysts should recognize that forecasting policy options, such as revenue policy, involves more than mathematics and technique. Frequently, more depends on the administration of numbers and institutional issues of accounting by the client. In the final analysis, forecasting policy options is really an exercise in explaining how people behave in institutions, a subject eminently suited for economic and public administration analysis.

Judgmental Forecasting

The wise practitioner uses judgment to some extent in all forecasting. All forecasts involve some judgment, but judgment should not produce all forecasts. The *intuitive*, *qualitative*, and *subjective* methods are applied where "theory and/or empirical data are unavailable or inadequate" (Dunn 2008, 138–39) or where one finds "the failure to use the data in systematic, mathematical projections" (Toulmin and Wright 1983, 221). Informed judgments—which can be the product of deductive; observational and inductive; and experiential influences—are the basis of judgmental forecasts. This is often called "retroductive logic" in that it begins with claims about the future, then works backward to the information and assumptions to support these claims (Dunn 2008, 139). The danger of this method is that estimation based on similar past events may create the cognitive illusion that these events will happen again. That is, the decision maker may overestimate the probability of recurrence (from a flood one hundred years ago compared to one three years ago) or ignore the probability of the future event altogether (Michel 2001, 94).

Judgmental Forecasts

The first type of judgmental forecast is based on deductive logic, which involves reasoning from general statements or laws to specific (sets of) information. This can be deceptive for policy analysis. In his *Devil's Dictionary* (1911, 196), Ambrose Bierce gives a nice absurdist example of deductive logic for working out labor productivity. "Major premise: 60 people can do a piece of work 60 times as fast as one person; Minor premise: one person can dig a post hole in 60 seconds; Conclusion: therefore 60 people can dig a post hole in 1 second." US Defense Department policy forecasts, for example, based on kill ratios and nuclear deterrence often seem to have absurd conclusions following from sound major premises that have been lost somewhere in the chain of reasoning.

More to the point, economic forecasts are typically based on a model's theoretical assumptions and thus deductive. A deductive theory or model is tested with empirical data. If data trends support the theory, then the theory may—if data and sample size are acceptable—be confirmed. For instance, if one assumes that maximization of the general welfare is possible through majority voting, then the median voter's preference becomes the norm. Aggregate community service spending preferences lower than this norm will lead to dissatisfaction and reduced welfare. If one assumes that the median voter also has the median income, where his or her preferences for spending are exceeded by community by combinations of richer and poorer voters (outside the range of middle voters or the median), then he or she is likely to be incentivized to move or find a cheaper house. Such movements will increase local service costs and reduce local revenue and possibly services supplied. Data supporting such behavior are available; this lends qualified support to the deductive theory of decentralized local government service markets. An important theoretical assumption is that each person seeks to maximize personal utility and that the collective of such decisions maximizes social welfare. In short, deductive-based forecasts can either confirm or reject the majority vote rule/median voter theorem as the means to maximize welfare in particular circumstances (R. Fisher 2007, 62).

Observational and Inductive Forecasts

In contrast to deductive forecasts, observational and inductive forecasts are based on trend extrapolation from inductive logic. Inductive logic involves reasoning about particular observations (such as time-series data) and reaching general conclusions from extrapolated trends. For example, a major continuing policy issue in California has been how to accurately forecast public-service burdens, particularly in education, caused by massive international immigration to that state. Answers require trend extrapolation from time-series data on immigration, school enrollments, and public expenditures. The CBO's current attempt to forecast the ten-year costs of rebuilding the US health insurance system is at the forefront of policy debate over health care reform. The projected costs of expanding coverage vary with assumptions on how businesses and people will react to a bewildering array of new economic incentives. In addition, most predictive models are based on experience. Here there are only the Massachusetts case and international cases, which may not be directly comparable to the national reform effort in the United States. Despite its best efforts, CBO suggests that its latest cost estimate of $1.04 trillion has a range of uncertainty of up to 20% (Montgomery 2009).

Experiential Forecasts

"Retroductive" logic is used where theory and data are unavailable and the policymaker has to work backward to the information and assumptions necessary to support claims. When data patterns are irregular, discontinuous, noncyclical, and characterized by sudden shifts, analysts are in the unenviable position of trying to forecast abrupt changes or catastrophes, such as military surrenders, weather events, or stock market collapses (Dunn 1994, 213). Economists' failure to forecast the recent meltdown of the financial and banking sector appears to stem from a reliance on elegant models that, on the one hand, downplayed systemic risk, and on the other hand, blithely accepted superficial data trends from the mortgage and financial sectors. Economists tended to assume systemic stability and ignored the financial sector (Samuelson 2009). In short, to make proper experiential forecasts, one needs to include the experience of all relevant institutions that can affect results!

In the real world, to develop improved responses to earthquakes—provision of advance public notice and after-event response—better earthquake prediction methods are needed. Despite almost daily radio forecasts from experts in California (using, say, such techniques as surveys of animal behavior), the current state of earthquake forecasting is mostly conjectural, and the field is populated with quacks who alarm both the public and government. Clearly, a breakthrough is needed for new forecasting techniques based on experience with discontinuous natural science and economic events.

Constraints to Accurate Judgmental Forecasting

The problem for policy forecasting in the real world is that life and history are not linear. We expect events to progress in a foreseeable way, like water slowly and predictably coming to a boil. In fact, many events are more analogous to critical masses triggering radical change. The temperature of pure water can be lowered to below the freezing point, and the water will still remain a liquid. But touch the water and it suddenly will turn to ice. In public policy small changes feed on themselves, causing people and institutions to behave differently. At a certain tipping point, elements suddenly crystallize into huge shifts that are hard to predict (Samuelson 1998). Judgmental forecasting of budget behavior provides good examples of the "tipping point" problem.

Unanticipated Agency Actions   As one would expect, judgmental policy projections are used to a greater extent on the expenditure rather than the revenue side of the budget. The difficulty in projecting fiscal deficits has already been noted. Expenditures depend on some combination of unanticipated institutional actions (to purchase goods or employ personnel) and individual decisions (e.g., to claim retirement, unemployment, welfare, or medical benefits) that are based on laws and administrative regulations (e.g., creating trust funds for future expenditures and providing entitlements). Expenditures for policies derived from messy problems are often affected by more frequent institutional interventions and changes in laws. By contrast, revenue decisions are fixed by laws or authority board decisions that remain in force for longer periods. Revenue decisions persist long enough to generate linear data patterns, while expenditure levels can change almost daily. In general, revenue estimation allows analysts to examine the individual sources of revenue collections and expenditure outlays and commitments from the past year, probable patterns in the current year, and estimations for the next budget year. More importantly, analysts can focus on rather common causes of variance that will affect revenue yields, such as changes in tax base (e.g., types of buildings subject to property tax assessment) or economic conditions that could affect sales tax receipts (McMaster 1991, 99). Expenditure variances are harder to predict.

Administrative Accounting Procedures Forecasts are also affected by data quality and technical capacity. For instance, despite its seasonal regularity, data on revenue receipts may be flawed, preventing calculation of formal statistics. Part of the problem may be small sample size. A more basic issue is that it is difficult to sort out measurement noise produced by administrative and accounting procedures on time-series and trend data. Methods to forecast the variable effects of institutional and financial management practices on public policy were reviewed in chapter 3. "Because of late filing and incorrect accounting procedures, monthly receipts may not occur independent of each other. For example, untimely closing of the books during one month may induce an arbitrary assignment of revenue in subsequent months. Such an instance may cause one month of unexpectedly large receipts followed by several months of lesser revenue" (Nelson and Cornia 1997, 47). In short, one must pay particular attention to the source and quality of time-series data before applying forecasting techniques.

Related to the issue of data quality is that of technical forecast capacity. The agency may not know how to make predictions based on obvious data trends. The Australian national treasury made an "embarrassing blunder" in 1997, underestimating corporate income tax collections by $1.6 billion over two years. According to the secretary of the treasury, the "department clearly did not look carefully enough in analyzing trends in company tax collections." There had been a surge in 1995 tax collections ahead of an increase in company tax rates, followed by a sharp decline in collections for 1997 (Cleary 1997).

Further, receipts may be affected by collection efficiency for such basic services as water, sanitation, public transit, parking, electricity, urban markets, and telephone. For this reason, policy analysts should periodically examine the relationship between the collection efficiency of and the charges for such services.

Billing may not match collections because of pipe leaks and underbilling. For other services, such as recreation, demand (and thus revenues) may be constrained by inefficient agency workload patterns. Agency personnel may not be matched to demand patterns for service, thus constraining potential demand and potential revenues. In this case, analysts can forecast increased revenues from changes in staffing patterns and workload routines of agencies (Ammons 1991). Again, institutional constraints can affect both policy forecasts and results. Policy forecasts need to take the operations of institutions into account in forecasting revenues as well as improving collection efficiency.

In practice, attempts to forecast results and to explain variations in program performance, whether physical or purely fiscal, involve a lot of judgment. To simplify these tasks in government budgeting offices, expenditure forecasters normally employ different rules of thumb for each line item. For example, salaries and benefits can be estimated by payroll but must include the flow of retirements, new hires, and official retrenchments to be accurate. Operations and maintenance expenditures (e.g., for roads) require estimation of vehicle demand, varying road conditions from inventory or maintenance information systems, and allocation of workloads to road crews and their vehicles. Each line item carries its own forecasting and evaluation methodology. Aggregating line items plus workload and inflation can provide a reasonable estimate of planned expenditures for the year. Unfortunately, forecasts are often limited to one year and ignore downstream recurrent costs or savings of future investment projects. Rarely are multiyear estimates made of how new investments will generate new operation expenditures or save maintenance costs (McMaster 1991, 108).

Variations within Years   It is even harder to predict expenditure variations within a year for particular programs. Prediction problems might be hard to believe, given the enormous amount of expenditure data available. But because of intervening political and legal factors, public expenditure time-series data are often nonlinear (Dunn 1994, 212). There may be oscillations within persistent patterns, such as the regular variation of education budgets from seasonal factors. Or variation in expenditures may reflect departures from annual linearity, but may reveal regularity when compared with quarter-on-quarter expenditures between years. The patterns may reflect agency workloads, such as bus and rail ridership or snow removal service within an urban area. Without careful understanding of these background factors, such expenditure patterns could create havoc for analysts relying solely upon their linear, nonlinear, and causal forecasting models.

Oscillations and cycles are hard to predict for such social phenomena as homelessness. For example, a city's policymakers may want to forecast the number of shelter users in order to calculate operating subsidies to the shelters. The number of homeless people who will take advantage of shelter programs might be a function of the following:

- Personal needs (it may be more feasible to use a nearby shelter than to live in an apartment)
- The economy, usually meaning the level of unemployment and consumer expenditures for housing and food (based on other "above-ground," or empirical, and "underground," or emotional, forecasts) (Silk 1986)
- Other factors, such as the local real estate market (affecting the construction and maintenance of single-room-occupancy hotels)

This may be an excessively muddy or complex picture for forecasters. Actual or aggregate demand for homeless services may be less difficult to forecast than potential demand covered by existing programs. Demand for existing program services varies widely by migration, weather, and demographic influences on daily and monthly usage. "The more uncertain the future chain of events, the more likely that judgmental forecasting will be the only basis for making expenditure projections" (Toulmin and Wright 1983, 221). Put another way, it would be difficult to forecast potential homeless demand, or the number of eligible homeless people, without a modicum of program experience (expert judgment). Still, even the inexperienced analyst with solid grounding in methodology should be able to arrive at reasonably sound judgments on shelter demand for the year based on past patterns of demand. The best policy analysts use their experience to judge the results of quantitative techniques. In the words of Dunn (1994, 203): "They know their technical assumptions but do not strictly or rigidly rely upon them. Over-reliance on method alone could produce numbers that, as one consultant put it, 'get us all fired!'"

In most public-sector organizations, forecasts often boil down to expert judgments because of the simple reality that practitioners are often the only ones who know their business. They also know better than most the limits of their own professions in terms of measurement and prediction. For instance, who is in a better position to describe present and future maintenance needs for a rail transit system than the crews in the maintenance department? Would the average budget or program analyst be likely to know the point at which the operating efficiency of tunnel fans would decline from absence of regular maintenance? Maintenance people can provide the best judgmental forecasts of such phenomena, and with improved databases they could probably provide both extrapolative and causal forecasts as well. The question is: What incentives do they have to avoid inflating requests? How can generalists know if the forecasts are inflated or otherwise flawed? Maintenance personnel may know how to accurately forecast maintenance costs, but if the budget process is punitive, they may quite reasonably inflate the costs to avoid being caught short later. A big scandal in which those in technical positions exploit their technical knowledge to inflate budget requests naturally generates suspicion of experts. As in the recent case of private banking and financial market experts, disasters can result in elaborate attempts to control, or at least counter, experts' judgmental claims through the use of detailed regulations or panels of other experts. On the other hand, public-sector experts in front of the media often end up scaring or outraging the public with their overly technical and arrogant explanations of accidents, problems, and other events. Politically sensitive policy analysts with sound technical credentials should have bright futures in any public agency. The process of managing expert judgments can either produce better forecasts or, through intrusive micromanagement, make everything harder to manage.

Intervening Variables   If good data exist, there is still the uncertainty problem of intervening variables that demand explicit use of judgment. Very few public problems lend themselves to mechanical, off-the-shelf forecasting methods. For example, in developing budget requests for county budget offices, department heads must use their judgment to forecast even the next year's costs of salary and fringe benefits. This will be based on their more intimate knowledge, for instance, of who is leaving in midyear and whether a new employee has decided to join the pension plan. Department staff members often know the short-term effects of inflationary changes on particular line items, such as purchases of supplies and equipment for health and education services. These are easier because they are often based on past actual changes in expenditures. But they may know less about how to predict medium-term price changes in these items. Estimates from the budget personnel are often challenged by other officials, such as an assistant county manager or members of a county commission (who will usually compare the estimates with private-sector forecasts).

What about intervention by management in policy decisions? Suppose managers alter budgets because planned receipts do not materialize, through accounting and processing errors such as premature closing of the books, as noted above (Nelson and Cornia 1997, 38). Suppose, alternatively, that managers take corrective action based on midyear price increases that lead to inflated expenditures? Under the first set of internal conditions, managers should probably not take corrective action: If they do, it will likely contaminate the very accuracy of their revenue and expenditure forecasts. In the latter case of external influences, such as reduced purchases leading to lower sales tax collections, corrective action would be justified. The problem, of course, is sorting out the effect of combined influences on budget execution for later forecasts.

In some cases public expenditure patterns are affected by more iffy intervening variables, such as powerful weather cycles. Peruvian budget policy forecasters, for example, typically have to include the likely effects of El Niño. This welling up of warm water drives away the anchovies and, with them, much of the industrial employment activity of the next few years, which is based on anchovy harvests. El Niño is also known to cause droughts and floods: Peruvians know that it can cost them 10% of GDP, cut farm output by 8.5%, and fisheries output by 40%, as was the case in 1982–83. So, based on this experience, forecasters included funds for infrastructure and higher current expenditures in FY 1998 to cover unemployment caused by this intervening variable. The expenditure effects of climatology still require lots of judgment (*The Economist* 1997a). To cover these kinds of uncertainties in policy forecasting, technical methods should be supplemented by "expert group consensus" methods (Toulmin and Wright 1983, 223). These include approaches such as the "Delphi technique," which is based on "informed multiple advocacy, structured conflict and selective anonymity" (Dunn 2008, 181–82), or a "bargaining approach" to generate a constructive clash of projections that can lead to agreement on a realistic forecast.

The policy consensus approach to forecasting is similar to political risk analysis, in which experts generate conflicting data projections on the future behavior of such variables as groups in conflict (e.g., unions, political parties), different economic trade policies, and long-term debt repayment scenarios, and then merge them into one forecast. This kind of forecasting produces a "workable" (second-best) science, rather than an exact one; but the flaws need not be fatal. As was noted, in the policy-forecasting business even the most sophisticated methods and tools do not ensure precision. Method alone does not ensure that assumptions are made explicit, meaning that subjectivity levels are high, and that "facts" are actually often "values" (Dunn 1981, 210). Further, expert judgmental forecasts for new programs or countries in volatile states of political conflict presume that "the positions of stakeholders are independent and that they occur at the same point in time. These assumptions are unrealistic, since they ignore processes of coalition formation over time and the fact that one stakeholder's position is frequently determined by changes in the position of another" (Dunn 1981, 210). But with little else to rely on to forecast the future of policy expenditures, the analyst has little choice but to apply expert group consensus to existing data sources.

Ongoing public policies are driven by the budget cycle that makes forecasts at the margin potentially more rigorous and successful. Existing programs often seem immune to the major political and economic vicissitudes that affect new programs, and they permit more systematic and quantitative treatment of data (meaning proportionately less judgment mixed into the final forecast). The fact that most governments budget their future annual resources incrementally from the previous year's base—under pressure from staff budgetary guardians who want to cut their requests and to allow spenders to achieve no more than their fair shares—means that to a large extent the following year's appropriations will be around 5–15% of the previous year's for most line items (Wildavsky 1984). This conservative feature of the budget policymaking process helps expenditure forecasters.

Finally, it almost goes without saying that judgmental forecasts require hard data. The "accounting identity-based" technique (Toulmin and Wright 1983, 224) or "deterministic" approach (Schroeder 1984, 272) forecasts revenues or expenditures by developing a multiplier (usually a ratio) to be attached to last year's base—for example, the price of a gallon of gasoline (rate) times the number of gallons of gasoline sold (base) should provide a multiplier from which to accurately forecast the next year's tax receipts (if the price of gasoline behaves as estimated). The product of the base and this rate then equals the forecast for the required period. For revenues, development of the rate often presumes knowledge of the determinants of future revenue-producing behavior for each revenue source (e.g., sales, property, and income taxes), such as consumer spending, population migration, and inflation. Unless one employs trend or causal forecasting techniques to find the unknown at this point, use of a mathematical percentage for the rate then cloaks the essentially judgmental process in scientific aura. For this reason, the deterministic approach is included under judgmental approaches to forecasting, rather than as a separate topic. The question begged by the deterministic approach remains: How do you reliably estimate the rate that is to be added to the base?

The deterministic approach is more commonly used for expenditure forecasting. Schroeder suggests that "nearly all cities . . . use basically a deterministic method to forecast spending" (1984, 272). Again, the purpose is to develop a per capita cost multiplier for the base in order to relate inputs to planned outputs or expenditures (average cost of providing given levels of service). For example, "in San Antonio, while the price assumptions are made centrally, departments are requested to produce documented projections of how many units of the several types of inputs will be required to produce services over the forecast period" (272).

In practice, this means beginning at a micro level of analysis within a cost center. For example, with a bus-maintenance cost center in a transit agency, it can be calculated that below a certain level of inputs (maintenance pay hours), the ratio of bus miles to mechanical breakdowns decreases, which jeopardizes ridership. Decreasing farebox coverage ratios will decrease agency fiscal integrity and perhaps future bond ratings. Thus, using the deterministic method, the percentage increase in pay hours required to maintain service levels (the per capita cost multiplier) could be added to the prior year's base to determine the forecast for the future. This method combines empirical data from past expenditures with judgments on the relationship between service outputs and required new expenditures. Again, these are expert opinions, derived from experience and refined through group bargaining on their validity. These data, which are primarily useful for the purposes of expenditure reporting and control of budget implementation, may also be very valuable for analysis of policy cost effectiveness and cost benefits (this will be discussed further in chapters 5 and 6). But the problem is that such quality data are not often available for these kinds of analyses.

Trend Extrapolation

> There's a strange rhythm to the Ripper murders. There are cyclical rhythms which control other things. There are rhythms which control the sun spots. Every seventeen years a particular kind of locust swarms and flies. Every fourteen years the price of nutmeg peaks then drops again. But in the Ripper murders, it is always 126 days between the first and second murder, but only 63 days between the second and last.
>
> "Isn't it weird? I've heard of these rhythms. What causes them?"
>
> "Ah, that is one of the mysteries of the universe!"
>
> —"Yours Truly, Jack the Ripper"
> episode of Boris Karloff's Thriller series

In contrast to judgmental forecasting, which is based largely on post hoc rationalizations of claims about the future based on limited data, trend forecasting is based on inductive logic, or reasoning from particular observations such as time-series data. Trend forecasting usually begins with some form of time-series analysis, or numbers collected at multiple and chronological points in time. According to Dunn (1994, 203), the purpose of time-series analysis is "to provide summary measures (averages) of the amount and rate of change in past and future years."

Trend or extrapolative forecasting can be accurate only where three assumptions hold: (1) Past observed patterns will persist into the future, (2) past variations will recur regularly in the future, and (3) trends are measured validly and reliably. According to Larry Schroeder (1984, 272): "Trend techniques extrapolate revenues or expenditures based purely on recent history. Most commonly, linear trends or linear growth rates are used as the underlying 'model.' Again, while relatively low-cost in terms of its data and computational costs, the approach is incapable of forecasting downturns if the past is characterized by continuous growth." As noted earlier, tipping points, at which, for example, multiple factors combine to produce a plunge in crime rates from what had been a small but steady drop, are hard to predict (Samuelson 1998). But, as we shall see, this weakness also applies to nonlinear trend forecasting and causal models. The only difference is that in the latter case, we have more confidence in the techniques because they can ostensibly take account of a more dynamic reality.

Computer Software Applications for Forecasting

Public policy tool kits have been compared with the equipment needed for plumbing jobs. One selects tools until the leaking pipes are isolated and fixed. Much has been made of this analogy: Analysts bring the wrong tools, or use them improperly, or do not know when to try less mechanical approaches, such as actually finding out what the needs are beforehand. The use of analytic tools might also be compared with housing construction. It may be faster to ignore such topics as wall construction and methods of customizing external appearance. After all, modular construction techniques have advanced to the point that builders can construct homes from prefabricated parts. But when things go wrong, such as when parts or materials are not available, it is useful to know the topic from the ground up.

In trend forecasting, much of the statistical grunt work has been eliminated by the widespread availability of user-friendly software packages. For example, the 2008 version of Microsoft Excel provides many full-service options for analysis of statistical data: F-tests, t-tests, correlation analysis, and an exponential smoothing tool to predict values based on forecasts of the prior period, adjusted for error in that prior period (Finkler 2009, 116–19). Other software packages combine statistical, fiscal, and demographic analyses for use by governments. For example, the FISCALS program (developed by Tischer and Associates, Bethesda, MD) calculates the fiscal impact of changing public service demands on municipal budgets, revenue rates, and bonding capacities, based on land use and demographic changes in the community. The program also generates budget summaries to show tax rates required to balance total revenues. Like Lotus 1-2-3, Excel, and SPSS packages (see Hedderson 1991), it allows exploration of "what-if" scenarios by varying underlying revenue and expenditure assumptions. Computer tools for statistical analysis are available free online, and there are many textbooks that clearly explain time-series analysis, proportionate change, regression analysis, and causal forecasting from single- or multiple-equation regression models. For a basic discussion of these tools here, turn to appendix 4A.

CAUSAL MODELING AND SIMULATIONS

Our case study for this chapter requires making a choice among policy options based on different data estimates for each option. The simulation tool allows use of forecasted data to estimate the effects of various choices. Once acceptable forecasts have been made using standard statistical techniques, and other data obtained to assist in estimating results, expected impacts can be narrowed down by "simulating" or comparing mathematical estimates of existing figures. To put it another way, there are two approaches to forecasting. First, time-series data can be projected into the future using appropriate statistical methods. As indicated in appendix 4A, the accuracy of statistical forecasts for such common uses as revenue depend on the behavior of the relevant economic variables, such as state income and employment. Nevertheless, the data needs and methodological requirements are well known. Second, policymakers can use formula-driven simulations. As noted in chapter 3, institutions affect policy implementation. Policy results also depend on levels of expenditure and the mechanisms through which funds are spent. For most US public policies, expenditures are made through grant or transfer mechanisms. Policymakers need to know the differential impact of a proposed health, education, poverty, or transportation policy that will be implemented through the grants system. This means that the level of state expenditure for national policy purposes, such as quality health care for the poor, or equalization of educational opportunity, will be affected by the type of grant used.

There are two main types of grants, and most programs are some combination of these two together with additional conditions. The first type, lump-sum grants to states, stimulate per capita expenditures but also allow grantee fungibility that could end up wasting funds or achieving unintended purposes.

Conditions and controls on the grants, such as targets and level of expenditure-effort requirements, can focus lump-sum grants and tighten the match between purposes and outcomes. Flexibility can also be built in and linked to targets by using lump-sum block grants. This is the approach used, for example, by the Temporary Assistance for Needy Families (TANF) program. The second type of mechanism is called matching grants. These encourage state expenditures by lowering the relative tax price or local cost of making the expenditure. The grantor provides local incentives to spend for intended policy purposes by lowering the local match requirement. For example, a 90/10 match means that for spending only 10%, the grantee receives 90% of the funds. In this way, matching grants increase purchasing power and typically stimulate more targeted expenditures than lump-sum mechanisms do.

By 2003, Medicaid expenditures for the poor were the largest and fastest-growing US social welfare program, at $275 billion a year. Medicaid remains one of the largest (21%) and the fastest-growing component of state budgets (R. Fisher 2007, 592). Its funds are allocated via matching in-kind or noncash transfers to service providers on behalf of clients. It is important to forecast the likely impact of policies that are functionally difficult to separate from their financing mechanisms. Depending on state per capita income, the US government provides matching funds in the range of 50–83%. Wealthier states pick up more of the tab (e.g., Maryland pays 50%) than poorer ones do (Mississippi pays only 23%). Given the complexity of sorting out policies from financing mechanisms, it is difficult to define outcomes more profoundly than numbers of clients paid or benefits received (that is, in common public policy parlance, expenditures and allocations are considered only inputs) (2002–3 Social Security Bulletin, cited in R. Fisher 2007, 598–99). Efforts to link TANF and Medicaid expenditures to effects on per capita income and changes in income distribution very much depend on grant structure. Policymakers would want to know the probable effects of their grant program on local spending and taxing decisions.

A simple example should suffice. Suppose a policy seeks equalization of educational opportunity through state and local district financing. An important historical policy problem in the United States has been that wealthier districts have the better schools, which impedes access by many urban poor students to educational opportunities. According to Ronald Fisher (2007, 505–12), from whom this example is taken, educational equalization policy since the 1970s has been implemented through two main types of grants. First, there are lump-sum grants that attempt to provide a minimum per pupil expenditure. The lump-sum grant to a school district requires spending up to a certain limit based on standard costs of providing elementary and secondary education. Like most grants, the lump sum is based on a formula that is inversely related to local wealth, measured as per pupil tax base. The grantee does nothing to receive the grant via the formula. Nevertheless, it can increase the grant amount by raising its own tax rate or increasing its tax effort. Increasing the tax rate or tax base increases the tax revenue as a fraction of income. The same would be true if property tax rates were increased as a fraction of income (R. Fisher 2007, 212). Tax efforts lead to greater grant revenue under the formula. Thus, the school district is incentivized to maximize a low tax base by raising its rate; it can do this and spend the extra funds on other needs while satisfying the expenditure minimum of the formula (e.g., $500 per student). The foundation grant sets a minimum per pupil expenditure level and provides the district the funding to attain that level. That is, the lump-sum foundation grant changes the income of the school district.

Second, there are matching grants that seek to equalize the basis of wealth, measured by the per pupil property tax base (e.g., $200,000). The matching grant mechanism attempts to make the educational system wealth-neutral on the basis of property value per student. The matching or "power-equalizing" grant artificially attempts to set an equal per pupil tax base for all districts. By providing for expenditure based on a minimum tax base, matching grants decouple local educational expenditures from district wealth. If a district has less tax wealth per pupil than the guaranteed base, it receives a grant to make up the difference. The matching grant lowers the local cost of funding (tax price) and increases local purchasing power, thus providing a strong incentive for the district to maximize its tax base through educational spending.

The lump-sum grant, by contrast, relies on an income effect. It adds income to the local district, which it can use to meet the minimum spending requirement (e.g., $500 per pupil), or if it planned to exceed that amount anyway, it can reprogram the extra funds to other uses or even lower tax rates. In theory, the matching grant should have greater expenditure impact. By decreasing the price of added expenditure (or marginal cost), the lump sum is more effective than increasing local income through a lump-sum grant. As a fungible resource, the increased income may be spent on other purposes than that intended by the grant. In practice, then, the effects of these grants depend on data and assumptions about price and income elasticity of demand (local services are largely price and income inelastic, or largely insensitive to price or income changes; e.g., education has a price elasticity of demand [PED] of 0.5; income elasticity of demand [IED] of 1.0). The policy questions have to do with how much a particular formula grant will induce local educational expenditures, and what effect they will have on local property taxes. Assuming family income of 50% of property value, the elasticities of demand given above, a lump-sum grant of $500 for districts with less than $200,000 property tax base, and a goal of $200,000 guaranteed base, what do the figures and formula predict for four different types of school districts?

Suppose that state X proposes an education grant program to equalize school district spending per pupil. The state wants to guarantee a minimum $200,000 tax base, allowing districts to apply property tax rates to finance education. Districts with a tax base greater than $200,000 would receive nothing; those with lower bases receive grants inversely proportional to per pupil wealth. So, the state proposes a grant determination formula of:

Grant Per Pupil = $500 + ($200,000 − V) R

> $500 = Foundation lump-sum grant (for per pupil value less than minimum tax-base wealth + local educational cost factor)
>
> V = Per pupil district tax-base value
>
> R = Per pupil district tax-rate value

The policy question is: What effect will this grant program formula have on educational spending and property taxes in each district? The appropriate forecasting method is simulation of the formula effects. Empirically based assumptions and multipliers must be used to translate data into useful information. In this case, current figures are available and largely accepted from existing data sources. Given the above formula and assumptions (e.g., spending equals financial and program results), forecasting proceeds by the use of simple mathematics. District spending per pupil is largely constant—it was forecasted several years earlier and the assumption now is that it is valid for purposes of further analysis. The taxable value per pupil is also known. Recent nationwide decreases in property values will cause some overestimation of the tax base and therefore the level of current educational expenditure. To be more accurate, the simulation should be run every quarter to compare with reality, which is easily done once the new numbers are known.

Table 4.1 Education Grant Simulation

	A	B	C	D
V =	$100,000	$130,000	$200,000	$225,000
R =	$55.00	$53.85	$45.00	$60.00
E =	$5,500	$7,000	$9,000	$13,500

V= Per pupil tax base; R = Per pupil district tax rate; E = Per pupil expenditure
Source: Fisher 2007, 508.

In this example, as a low-tax, low-spending, relatively poor district, district A will receive both the basic lump-sum grant of $500 and the maximum matching grant. The $500 amounts to 1% more income ($500/$50,000 × 100%), which should increase spending per pupil by $55, based on the IED of 1.0; that is, $(0.1)(5500)(1.0)$. The matching component of the program has other incentives. It reduces the price of spending on schools by 50% ($100,000 existing base/$200,000 guaranteed base). District A can increase its expenditures by $1 per pupil by raising tax rates only $0.50. Since the local tax price because of the grant is $0.50, at a PED of 0.5, district A will increase its spending per pupil by 25% (half of the 50% reduction in tax price), or $1,375, for a total of $6,875. Since A receives both a lump sum and a matching grant, the incentive effects are greater and spending should equalize more in this district than, for example, in district C, which only receives the matching grant (it does not receive the lump sum because its tax base is $200,000) (R. Fisher 2007, 511). Thus, use of the simulation technique allows us to forecast tax and expenditure options based on existing data and transparent, testable assumptions about grantee behavior in education.

Notice that for the simulation, most of the data were given (e.g., PED, per pupil tax base, and guaranteed tax base). For other policy areas, variables, coefficients, and model-generated data are provided. The task of the policy analyst is to work through the formula, applying the data and coefficients to develop the data required. In the case of public transit, for instance, the needed estimate is daily transit trips generated. This allows assessment of the cost-effectiveness both of the existing system and of new project proposals. Two commonly used decision tools to organize the data on estimations of alternate policy options are expected value tables and weighted score tables.

Expected Value Tables

This tool allows the analyst to estimate expected values by weighting the results. For example, weighting the cost of fixing a water pump by the probability that it will break (Michel 2001, 13) allows one to decide between two purchase options by price and quality. Suppose the US Army Corps of Engineers wanted to build a dike around New Orleans in 1995. By examining weighted data for two options (high and low dike levels under normal and flood conditions), they could make an optimal choice. Either they did not use this decision tool properly or picked the wrong option before the arrival of Hurricane Katrina in 2005! The expected value table requires good scenario probabilities and cost data. Cost data are easier to provide than scenario data;

Table 4.2 Expected Value Table

Options	Scenarios	Scenario Probabilities (%)	Outcome	Weighted Outcome	Expected Value of Each Option
Low Dike	Normal Rainfall	90	−$1.5 million	−$1.35 million (.90 × 1.5)	−$1.90 million (1.35 + 0.55)
	Major Flood	5	−$11.0 million	−$0.55 million	
High Dike	Normal Rainfall	95	−$3.5 million	−$3.33 million	−$3.46 million
	Major Flood	5	−$2.5 million	−$0.13 million	

Note: Table structure source: Michel 2001, 14.

the latter are typically available from industry specialists in such areas as water-sewerage, urban transit, road construction and maintenance, and airport construction. Some call this a serious weakness (Michel 2001, 15); others find that industry specialists know their trade and can estimate probabilities well. The table for two dike options would appear as above.

The table is useful for transparently organizing data to compare options on price and quality. The accuracy of the expected or weighted outcome forecasts depends on the reliability of the probability data (Michel 2001, 15). A timely current application could be to evaluate forecasted options to minimize budget shortfalls in the face of revenue scarcity. In the recessionary climate of 2009–10, urban transit authorities want to raise fares and cut service to reduce projected deficits. WMATA (Washington Metropolitan Area Transit Authority), for example, projects a $40 million deficit for 2010 from a $1.37 billion operating budget, due in part to a 4% drop in ridership beginning late 2009. Analysts came up with four options to produce about $4 million in savings. They are: (1) lengthening the time between trains on weekends, late evenings, and midday ($2 million savings); (2) increasing wait times by two minutes for trains from 6:00 to 6:30 a.m. on weekdays ($114,000); (3) eliminating eight-car trains during peak hours ($672,000); and (4) closing ten stations at 8 p.m. on weekends and five stations on weekdays ($200,000) (Tyson 2010). The question for analysts should be the net effect of these options on ridership, and hence revenues. Given the elasticity of demand for transit in relation to prices of gas and carpooling, the preferred option should minimize cost disincentives for use of transit.

Table 4.3   Expected Value of Transit Deficit Reduction Options

Option	Probability of Decrease in Ridership, –1 (low) to –10 (high)	Projected Savings	Net Savings or Net Benefit	Weighted Outcome or Expected Benefit
Eliminate eight-car trains during peak hours	0.90	$672,000	$604,800	$302,400 (50% of projected cost savings × 0.90 weight for ridership loss)

As indicated in table 4.2, the expected value table would be useful here. Columns should organize data by: (1) the four options/scenarios; (2) the probability of decrease in ridership, from –1 (low) to –10 (high); (3) projected savings; (4) net savings or net benefit; and (5) weighted outcome or expected benefit. Focusing on option 3, eight-car trains were originally added to reduce station congestion and waiting times. One should question the actual savings likely if these were reduced back to six-car trains. Why would the maintenance and electricity costs of three eight-car trains be more than four six-car trains (= twenty-four car trips)? Beyond the opaque cost savings, eliminating eight-car trains during peak hours would have the severest impact on ridership of the four options. Thus, following the table format: Option 3 has a –0.90 weight based on PED, with projected savings of $672,000, which amounts to a net savings of $604,800 (–0.90 × 672000), for a total weighted outcome or expected benefit of $302,400 ($672,000 less recalculated cost savings weighted by revenue loss from reduced ridership, e.g., $336,000 × –0.90 = $302,400).

Weighted Score Tables

This variant of the expected value tool allows analysts to evaluate alternatives according to multiple criteria of different importance. The tool is commonly used in planning for capital improvements to weight, score, and rank projects in order to develop a capital plan. That plan is then matched with available revenue to determine the capital budget. Participants in the analytic process for policies and projects include stakeholders from government and community groups. Criteria for evaluation are both hard (quantitative measures such as benefit-cost ratios, cost, reliability, speed), and soft (e.g., resident satisfaction, consistency with city goals, and political acceptance).

There are four steps to using this tool. First, officials and other stakeholders must agree on strategic criteria (whether soft or hard). Second, participants in the process must weight the importance of each criterion. Not all criteria for

Table 4.4 Weighted Score

Criteria	Alternatives Weights	Rail Car A Score	Rail Car A Weighted Score	Rail Car B Score	Rail Car B Weighted Score	Rail Car C Score	Rail Car C Weighted Score
Cost	.60	4	2.4	6	3.6	7	4.2
Reliability	.90	6	5.4	2	1.8	2	1.8
Speed	.40	5	2.0	4	1.6	8	3.2
Total Weighted Score			9.8		7.0		9.2

Note: Table structure source: Michel 2001, 16.

a policy decision are of equal importance, and the tool allows quantification of these preferences (i.e., a range from 0.0 to 1.0). Third, each project is scored (1 to 10) according to the degree to which participants believe the project is consistent with the strategic criteria. Fourth, multiplying the weighted criteria by the project score provides the weighted score. The weighted project scores are then ranked. This is the most contentious part of any policy process, and the tool is a mechanism for structuring the conflict by narrowing the range of options through a transparent process. The tool provides a data trail to which analysts and external stakeholders can refer to justify rankings. It is limited ostensibly by its subjectivity, potential for manipulation, and the difficulty of assigning numerical scores to nonquantitative criteria such as resident satisfaction (Michel 2001, 15–16). Despite these limits, the results of the tool can be perfected through repeated plays of the game until participants in the process achieve high degrees of acceptability and political trust.

Decision Structuring and Policy Communication

Once the estimation of an option is developed and compared with other options, the results need to be translated to wider publics for actual decision making. Consensus is difficult to achieve in decentralized democracies such as the United States, because it involves the intense interplay of technical advocates and special interest guardians who are typically generalists. Technical specialists have the habit of assuming that everyone understands their numbers, assumptions, and formulae, and that if more information is provided, eventually everyone will agree and the right decision will be made. Worse still, professional public servants may become defensive or arrogant, using their technical knowledge as a weapon against public criticism. This is generally a bad idea! Officials dealing with the public (such as representatives of NGOs, government organizations, and universities) need to recognize that much is lost in translation, and arriving at the right decision often requires many steps in long, iterative processes. Technical policy information is meshed with financing alternatives and public input from multiple directions.

Under these normal conditions, what is the policy analyst to do? How can the analyst best communicate objective information that contains many assumptions and scenarios to audiences that often consist of groups focused intensely on single issues? The confident policy professional knows the work that went into the case and is likely satisfied that these are the best available figures and calculations. The professional is also likely to support the preferred option that is being presented. A more serious problem is that professionals may be opposed by people who want to: (1) have them sacked, (2) destroy their career, (3) inflict bodily injury during or after the proceedings, and/or (4) impugn their technical credibility. The professional faced with problems (1) or (2) can get even, which is much more effective than getting mad. The professional facing problem (3) should either delegate authority quickly or hire a security guard. The professional faced with problem (4) is lucky, since that situation merely requires proper translation, communication, and presentation of the technical materials in a cogent and persuasive manner.

Much has been written on the issue of how to engage in effective policy communications. Most writers agree that it is probably the most crucial stage of the policy process. Yet not much attention is paid to this phase in practice. American voters and citizens are deeply suspicious of and cynical about officials and bureaucrats. In the "monopoly agenda-control" model (R. Fisher 2007, 66; Niskanen 1971), officials and bureaucrats have better information and use it to persuade the public that they should go along with their policy agenda. Such officials maximize their budgets to stay in power and set policy agendas about which diffuse publics are less informed. A less nefarious interpretation is that persuasion is a normal "policy instrument" and that the "shaping of information is an inevitable part of communication and an integral part of strategic behavior" (Stone 1988, 284). Stone argues that information is not neutral, people are not primarily rational, and that indoctrination (i.e., manipulation, destruction or withholding of information) therefore occurs even in liberal democracies (284). She is not talking about formal censorship or evil officials manipulating for their own ends. Rather, most cases are simply efforts to control the agenda, in order to promote what professionals, based on their analysis, believe to be the best policy options. Agenda control is often a defensive reaction. Knowing that they face intense and often quite irrational opposition from people who distort facts via blogs and twitters on a daily basis, officials understandably withdraw to their facts and figures. In the media contest, this appears secretive, when it is simply sensible behavior given what officials must actually endure! Decades ago, the problem was a passive citizenry that was often asked to make decisions for which they lacked information (Wildavsky 1979, 260). Currently, the problem is how to control a hyperactive citizenry that is armed with bits and pieces of information from multiple sources, often Web based. Policymakers must confront these "citizen analysts" and persuade them (252). That is the tough task of policy communications today.

Three examples should suffice. First, the Centers for Disease Control and Prevention (CDC) is currently coordinating the US pandemic-preparedness plan. The US government responded to the swine flu (H1N1) epidemic of 2009 with the largest vaccination program since the antipolio campaign in the 1950s (Brownlee and Lenzer 2009, 44). Swine flu is already a known threat, having killed thousands worldwide. It is also considered different from the seasonal flu variety. Despite the apparent uncertainty of attacking seasonal influenza or flu-like illnesses—including over two hundred known viruses and other pathogens—with a single vaccine, vaccination is the preferred policy option. Each year the viruses quickly mutate into different genetic versions of the previous flu season's infection. To forecast vaccine options, the CDC and the World Health Organization (WHO) collect data from the previous year on circulated viruses, then make an educated guess about which viruses are likely to circulate the coming fall. Based on this information, the US Food and Drug Administration (FDA) issues orders to drug manufacturers in February for a vaccine that includes the three most likely strains (Brownlee and Lenzer 2009, 46). Communication of these policies to the public is considered routine, and there is little opposition.

Given advance warning on swine flu (thousands dead worldwide and medical knowledge that it targets the very young), policymakers in the United States had ample opportunity to observe the strengths and weaknesses of responses in other countries (e.g., Mexico and several European nations). The US media and diverse publics also were alarmed and afraid of the epidemic—there was little doubt that it was real and would hit here. This made the public more receptive to inoculations encouraged by the CDC and state and local health authorities. Effective policy communications by CDC medical professionals have soothed public fears and made it easier to implement the vaccination program.

Stone (1988, 199) cited the example of patient choice in the face of uncertainty over the effectiveness of two competing vaccines (one conventional and one experimental). This common situation makes it hard to communicate preferred options—the most effective vaccine may be experimental, and therefore information may be insufficient to make or recommend a completely rational choice. In that case, how the issue is rhetorically framed and how alternatives are structured can make all the difference to public receptivity and policy effectiveness. In 2009, there was only one vaccine; it was in short supply and demand far exceeded availability. The Department of Homeland Security stated that the fact that 120 million doses of swine flu vaccine were ordered, but by November only 28 million were actually available, was "not a situation that is cause for panic" (Stein 2009). In short, there was little fear of the vaccine out there; the major fear was that it would not be available! The only communications issue was how to explain why the vaccine was in short supply. Explanations circulating in the public included: normal routines of science, company conspiracies, hoarding, and government withholding of information. This meant that even under relatively structured and simple problem conditions, the media and the public could distort the context and make it difficult to make sensible official decisions.

Second, as noted in chapter 3, students from Washington, DC, schools have historically performed very poorly on national and state tests. At the same time, per pupil spending is the highest of any school system. Productivity and value for money have been extremely poor, and after election in 2006, Mayor Adrian Fenty's administration vowed to do something about it. In less than three years, the mayor's appointee, Chancellor Michelle Rhee, has done just that: first reversing declining test scores and then increasing them (*Washington Post* 2009), providing curriculum options, rehabilitating school facilities, improving purchasing, increasing efficiencies through IT systems, and so on. More significantly, since the reforms depend on better teachers, she has replaced poorly performing teachers and principals and instituted a rigorous monitoring system for school performance. All this would sound like textbook public administration reform and routine activities consistent with national reforms in the same direction, such as President Obama's "Race to the Top" stimulus funds for schools and the "No Child Left Behind Act" that focuses on school accountability, performance, and alternative delivery systems. The problem has been the strong local vested interests that have resisted these changes and would like to see the chancellor disappear from policy control over the school system. A core technical problem with wider policy implications is that despite Chancellor Rhee's efforts to include teacher input in the design of a new performance-assessment system, the teachers think it is designed to remove them, not to help them improve (Turque 2009). The friction between the teaching union and the city council increased when she dismissed 229 teachers after the school year began. Unlike teachers dismissed for performance reasons in 2008, these teachers were laid off for budgetary reasons (Bradley, Harreld, and Hill 2009), because of revenue collapse related to the recession. Opponents have combined the two kinds of actions into vehement opposition to her blunt style and fierce advocacy for students.

Chancellor Rhee was going through the most turbulent and polarizing period of a 28-month tenure marked by broad upheaval over personnel and policy decisions. She is reported to have asked, "What can I do to regain the trust of my teachers?" In her words: "We need to do a better job of making sure we (are) communicating effectively with our educators. There are a lot of distractions and we have to remain focused on the task at hand" (Turque 2009). Quite clearly, Chancellor Rhee and District of Columbia Public Schools (DCPS) had a policy communications problem in that they were perceived as zealots for school accountability and performance results. Much of the public and the city council believed she was moving too fast and should act consistently with local cultural mores. It would seem that if her successful reform efforts have a chance of being sustained after the 2010 election, she will need to broaden out her strategy. Since Mayor Fenty did lose and one of her council opponents won, Chancellor Rhee resigned and her deputy was appointed interim chancellor. Kaya Henderson has now been appointed chancellor. To successfully continue Ms. Rhee's reforms, Ms. Henderson could shift from precise technical emphasis on performance, accountability, test scores, and achievements to more ambiguous use of symbols. As noted by Stone (1988, 123), while ambiguity is anathema in science, since politics is more like art, ambiguity is central. Use of ambiguity and symbols would permit aggregation of support from different quarters for the single educational policy reform. This can provide space for opponents—who now appear united on behalf of teachers and principals, regardless of performance—to shift allegiances. It can increase the maneuvering room of some leaders who may want better schools but disagree with some of the chancellor's blunt methods. The strategy can provide more decision space for DCPS and facilitate negotiation and compromise with the Washington Teachers' Union on a new teachers' contract. At present, reformers and opponents are focused on narrow technical matters, which inhibits chances for any compromise on how the reform should proceed. One means of doing this under present conditions would be to showcase good or improving teachers as much as students. This would provide a new symbol that human resources are the key ingredients in students' education.

Third, as will be noted in the case below, the Purple Line urban transit proposal linking Montgomery County and Prince George's County in Maryland has been debated for years among advocates and opponents. Planning for the Purple Line has been characterized as a frozen standoff between multiple interests. For this reason, capital projects like this require formal appraisal using economic planning methods and systems. These include both hard (quantitative) and soft (consensus-building) methods. So far, groups have been largely deadlocked, and the question is whether and how public proponents of this project can overcome the standoff? More troubling is the fact that most stakeholders believe they are correct. If all the stakeholders on this project proposal are correct, how can a rational public choice be made?

What should be apparent from the above discussion is that more technical methods and data may not persuade anyone. Each stakeholder believes they have the data and information they need, and their minds are unlikely to be changed. For example, the hiker-biker proponents will not accommodate a light-rail line parallel to their trails, as it would destroy serenity. Light-rail transit (LRT) consists of multi-car electric trains, mostly at street level, which are called "trams" in Europe. LRT can include streetcar service (without dedicated lanes) and dedicated-lane rail service. Hiker-biker and nature groups oppose the Purple Line despite evidence from other systems in the United States (Portland, Oregon, and St. Louis, Missouri), Canada (Montreal), Europe (Le Mans, France, and Freiburg, Germany), and Australia (Port Melbourne) that the two land uses are complementary and can easily coexist (Maryland Transit Administration [MTA] 2008). Trees will be removed but others will grow larger, as happens all over the Washington area for new projects. Some wildlife will be temporarily displaced, but there is no shortage of natural homes for them in this area!

Thus, some opponents need to be convinced through consistent messages that LRT is environmentally friendly and serves broader green purposes (fuel savings, less street congestion, air quality improvements). As noted by Young and Quinn (2002, 17), this can be accomplished through dissemination of policy ideas in public meetings and through the media. The communications should appeal to multiple audiences and be written in simple, jargon-free language. Consistent with this advice, MTA has taken its message to the public and media through multiple means—at least eight community focus-group presentations, more than three hundred presentations to civic associations and community groups, dozens of roundtable discussions, more than 150 open house meetings, and many personal briefings. These efforts have targeted NGOs and political leaders. Presentations feature slides and explanations in simple language of such topics as: project specifics, cost and results comparison of alternatives, how the line will accommodate travel patterns and commuting needs, probable funding sources, and required steps in the planning process (MTA 2009). Over three thousand comments have been received so far from twenty-seven hundred individuals and organizations. The result is that by

2009, systems planning and alternatives analyses have been completed with broad public inputs, and the governor of Maryland has chosen the preferred alternative selected by the MTA—medium-cost LRT—over the seven other options. As a result of MTA skill in policy communications, and a long, iterative planning process, many of the hardliners have compromised and provided substantial local support for the policy or project option preferred by the MTA.

What is common to the three examples is the fact that the knowledge and skills needed to conduct policy analysis are different from those needed to develop policy-related documents and to communicate forecasts, analyses, options, and preferred options to the public and media (Dunn 2008, 423). The ideal policy analyst is one with significant technical knowledge, cool patience, and genuine social skills. That policy person is usually not a salesman or narrow specialist. He or she often finds it difficult to perform the thankless task of convincing the public that often long-range forecasts are solid, despite assumptions that could change next week. Opponents have a way of chewing these types and their policy forecasts into small pieces.

Transit Options for Metro's Purple Line

Bob Melvin, MPP '05, has worked for two years as a policy analyst at the Maryland Transit Authority (MTA). His boss, Richard Gregor, has been in charge of project planning for the Purple Line corridor and transit project for almost five years. During this time, as is normal for a large public capital project, substantial amounts of public and private debate have taken place; piles of analytical and evaluative reports have been developed in response to state and federal requirements; enormous amounts of primary and secondary data have been generated and released to the public; some interest groups have mobilized and are hysterically opposed, while other groups are quite indifferent; and gas prices have crept up to record highs, increasing transit ridership for the Washington metropolitan area. At the same time the economic recession has cost the city many jobs, which have cut into ridership figures. The good news is that the economic recovery package from the US government has produced capital funds for capital investment projects such as this, which are intended to produce income and employment benefits (local economic development).

In this situation, Bob wants to do well. His boss has assigned him the tasks of (1) analyzing the costs and benefits of each option for the project, consistent with local criteria and Federal Transit Administration (FTA) "New Starts" criteria; (2) forecasting the impacts of each option; and (3) justifying a preferred alternative among others that have been rejected. Since much of the work has already been done by other analysts and private consultants, his task is mainly to review their findings and confirm or reject them.

Background

To get him started, Mr. Gregor called Bob Melvin into his office at MTA to provide a review of the current situation for him. Mr. Gregor began:

"A lot of this you already know, but I will go over some basics for you anyway. First, after the Washington Metropolitan Area Transit Authority (WMATA) metrorail system functioned for about twenty years or so, it was clear that major economic activity was occurring around stations, especially the Red Line. High ridership stimulated economic activity around stations and created the very congestion they were designed to reduce! Income and employment came in these areas, which generated more housing opportunities and residential development. Now the larger problem was how to get between these suburban centers when the Red Line (all lines, really) was shaped like a loop from the suburbs to the center of the city. Circumferential travel patterns were creating major problems in congestion, time lost, and air pollution. You might say our rail-transit success created this problem—in predictable fashion, as all solutions create new problems!"

"So, in 2003 we commissioned the first real study of the corridor using the term 'Purple Line,' called 'Capital Beltway and Purple Line Study' (MTA 2004). This was a forecast of current demographic trends in the corridor, which, not surprisingly, confirmed what we knew already—development was generating congestion and commuter trips were increasingly long. Thousands of gallons of fuel were being wasted annually, which translated into delays averaging almost seventy hours per peak traveler per year in this corridor (Schrank and Lomax 2005). That's almost two weeks of work per year wasted in traffic! Such congestion will eventually inhibit development in particular areas and also push the congestion around the broad study corridor—a classic urban spatial externality (i.e., a market failure with negative spillovers). Something needed to be done. The purpose of our project would be to provide more direct, reliable east-west transit service in this corridor, which would connect the four major activity centers (MTA 2008e, ES-2)."

"After many internal and external meetings and discussions, participants came up with a rough project description that, with some variations in alignment, holds true today. A Purple Line transit system would be built along the sixteen-mile corridor spanning two counties—Montgomery and Prince George's. Connecting the Red, Green, and Orange WMATA rail lines, it would also connect with Amtrak, several MARC (Maryland Area Regional Commuter) rail lines, and many local bus services (WMATA Metrobus and Montgomery County Ride-On). It would connect the four major activity centers in the corridor: Bethesda, Silver Spring, College Park/University of Maryland, and New Carrollton. There would be twenty-one stations along the route, and the line is expected to remove about 20,000 auto trips per day from the roads in this area, which would contribute to improved air quality. That's a general overview of the project and its major expected benefits."

"Now, I'll briefly go over the alternatives selected and the forecasted benefits and costs for our preferred option. You need to know how we got those forecasts. The process requires analysis by MTA to determine if one of the options will be selected for implementation. The process of estimating, forecasting, and comparing benefits and costs is what is done normally to plan and develop any capital project. FTA calls it 'alternatives analysis,' and it is required under the

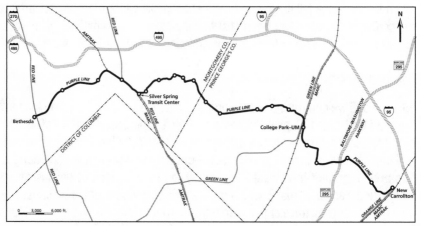

Figure 1 Map of Purple Line Corridor, Project Location, and Alternative Alignments

Section 5309 New Starts program if we want to qualify for capital assistance from them. Of course, we do! In fact, it may be that none of the options are cost effective, in which case the process really ends. Cost-effectiveness determines the unit cost of particular benefits, like the cost per life saved; the cost per garbage can collected, and here, the cost per user benefit. The advantage of cost-effectiveness analysis for urban transport projects, I'm sure you know, is that one needs only to specify the primary benefit and compare it to monetary cost (Michel 2001, 78). So what we did was to compare each of the alternatives using the same evaluation measures to determine which one produces the greatest benefit for the least cost (see chapter 6). In FTA terms, these are called 'transportation system user benefits,' or TSUB; the most cost-effective option produces the maximum forecasted time-savings for users for the least amount of capital and operating funds. If the resultant option is consistent with our objectives and local stakeholder input, we then go forward in applying for funding to FTA and other sources. Since the main source for large capital projects like this is FTA, we'll discuss the FTA evaluation system and what we are up against to see this project through. First, we came up with eight alternatives. OK?"

Bob said, "OK, I'm ready!"

Mr. Gregor went on: "The process really focused on three main options: (1) build nothing, and rely on marginal improvements of existing systems, (2) bus rapid transit, and (3) light rail transit. Suboptions within each bring the total to eight possibilities. The no-build or do-nothing alternative is the baseline. It means that traffic volumes, forecasted demographics, and transit-service levels move forward in the corridor area at projected levels until 2030. As mentioned, someone is bound to notice that serious problems are occurring before 2030! The second suboption is called Transportation System Management (TSM). This is the baseline for FTA New Starts funding, in that it indicates the results of efforts to maximize local services without a new transitway. This option includes improved traffic signalization, expanded use of articulated and express buses, highway upgrades and minor widening, and shortened bus headways (MTA 2008d)."

"We then evaluated six build options. The first is called low-investment bus rapid transit (BRT). These operate in places like Phoenix and Los Angeles, as well as South American cities like Quito and Guayaquil, Ecuador, and Santiago, Chile. They consist of express buses operating between designated stations, either on existing streets or with grade separation. The major difference between low- and medium-investment BRT options is that the latter utilizes more dedicated lanes. The high-investment BRT option would include vertical grade separation and horizontal traffic separation. Tunnels and aerial structures are included to reduce delays and improve travel time."

"The next three options were based on light-rail transit (LRT). Light-rail systems use streetcars that can travel on dedicated lines (quickly) or in traffic, with little traffic or grade separation (more slowly). Some LRT systems, as in San Francisco and San Diego, feature this change of status on the same lines. LRT cars may travel 70 mph between some stations and 5 mph between others. Given that most are in cities, the quicker they are, the more costly they become."

"Were the cost calculations for these options pretty straightforward?" asked Bob. "How were opportunity costs and discount rates calculated? How many years' operations and maintenance (O&M) costs were included in the project costs?"

"Good questions, Bob. Let's start with the totals. As indicated in table 1, capital costs increase incrementally by option from TSM and low- to high-investment BRT, and from low- to high-investment LRT, in almost straight-line fashion. So, TSM is $82 million, low BRT is $386 million, high BRT is $1.08 billion. Low LRT is $1.20 billion, and high LRT is $1.63 billion (MTA 2008a). FTA mandates a discount rate (7%) to take account of the time value of money. The discount rate reflects the government's cost of borrowing or a community preference for present versus future consumption. A low discount rate suggests preference for investing in the future. The discount rate is like an exchange rate that converts dollars in the future into dollars today. So, the Purple Line has future costs and benefits and these need to be converted into present value for purposes of comparison and rational decision making (Michel 2001, 50)."

"Did you use multiple discount rates to see how sensitive the project was to changes in timing of benefits or costs, or changes in the economic climate?" Bob asked.

"We didn't do that," Mr. Gregor responded, "because FTA uses a cost-effectiveness test rather than rate of return or break-even analysis. Capital budgeting normally uses multiple discount rates, so you are right to ask the question. To answer your question on O&M costs, they were included in the FTA methodology for cost effectiveness. The formula requires that the capital, O&M costs, non-federal funding, and user benefits be converted to present value and expressed in annual terms (MTA 2008a, 4–5). For O&M costs, we used the resource build-up approach, as required by the FTA New Starts methodology. Costs are computed by estimating labor and materials needed to provide a given level of service, and then multiplying this by the unit cost of the labor and materials. The method involves disaggregating O&M costs from recent years into categories that will vary with service levels (e.g., fuel costs are variable costs since they vary by mile). The FTA methodology is called the "resource productivity approach." MTA used bus and rail models, multiplying units of service (number of passenger miles and hours) by capital assets (number of vehicles) by financial operating statistics (costs of labor and materials) for recent years by mode. The results were then validated, and it was found that the bus model varied by only 6% (actual versus predicted values), while the rail model was less accurate: 52% variance in 2003! (MTA 2008b, 3–11)."

"One problem has been the recent increases in the costs of fuel, energy, and lubricants, which have increased more than 100% since 2000. Employee fringe benefits for health care have increased more than 150% since 2000 for both bus and light rail. In short, we have to be careful on annual O&M costs, and they may be less predictable than capital costs. Nevertheless, the range of O&M costs for the seven alternatives (TSM through high-investment LRT) is only $8.2 million (from $14.6 million to $22.8 million) (table 1). O&M costs for the BRT options are not significantly higher than for the TSM option ($14.6 million for TSM versus $15.8 million for high BRT). LRT requires considerably more O&M costs than the other options (e.g., $15.8 million for high BRT and $26.4 million for low LRT—a difference of almost $11 million per year) (MTA 2009, 5)."

"Before I get lost in all the data," Bob asked, "could we go through the FTA cost-effectiveness evaluation criteria? I'd like to know how these data were used to forecast the options and our preferred option."

"Of course, let's do that tomorrow!"

Table 1 Comparison of Alternatives for Purple Line Corridor

Alternative	Capital Cost, in Millions (2007 $)	Annualized Capital Cost, in Millions (2007 $)	Annual O&M Cost, in Millions (2007 $)	End-to-End Travel Time (in minutes)	Annual User Benefit (in millions of hours)	Average Weekday Ridership (unlinked trips)	Annualized Cost per Hour of User Benefit (cost effectiveness)
TSM	82	7.0	14.6	108	1.9m	16,900	—
Low BRT	386	31.2	17.3	96	3.4m	40,000	18.24
Med BRT	580	46.9	17.3	73	5.0m	51,800	14.01
High BRT	1,088	87.0	15.8	60	6.1m	58,900	19.34
Low LRT	1,206	96.4	26.4	62	5.7m	59,300	26.51
Med LRT	1,220	97.6	25.0	59	6.3m	62,600	22.82
High LRT	1,635	125.8	22.8	50	7.2m	68,100	23.71

Source: MTA 2008.

Bob Melvin went home and thought for a long time about this project. Some of the variables were easily forecast, like passenger boardings and ridership. If the models were wrong, calibration studies would show that, and the model would be changed. So that was relatively easy. But how can we forecast environmental or economic development effects and work them into cost-effectiveness in a robust way?

Bob knew there were some technical issues with transit-systems forecasting, like using unlinked versus linked trips to count passengers. So far, presentations to the public and media used unlinked trips as the measure. Since actual people cannot be counted using passes, joint tickets, and transfers, systems collect and report only boardings or unlinked trip data. While the vast number of people take only two trips per day (to and from their destination), about 10–30% must transfer to a second and third vehicle (e.g., bus to rail and back to bus). Linked trips measure passenger trips from origin to destination (MTA 2008c, 2–11). Even with several transfers, the trip is counted as a single trip. This means that using multiple *boardings* or unlinked trips as the measure typically overestimates actual trips by about 45% (a large amount of double-counting) (USDOT 2005). For example, the Purple Line low BRT average weekly ridership figure is presented as 40,000. If this figure is a 45% overestimation of actual trips, the linked trips would then be 22,000. In MTA's technical report, the linked figure is in fact 22,300, which is consistent with the measurement problem mentioned (MTA 2008c, 2–12). Bob also knew that some transit project appraisals had attempted to use unlinked trips as the forecast of actual ridership, when linked trips were more accurate. He was a bit concerned that MTA used unlinked trips, since this measure inflated ridership to the public and could backfire later—even though its technical reports presented linked trips!

While it was clear to Bob that passenger forecasts had been inaccurate in past rail projects, such as the Miami Metrorail, he knew that they were no longer central to FTA New Start evaluations. He would learn more about this tomorrow. Nevertheless, several things bothered him about the MTA passenger forecasts from a methodological perspective. He had learned in his MPP classes that analysts should engage in "specification analysis," or a review of the reasonableness of assumptions (Finkler 2005, 122). So, presenting a twenty-one-year forecast (2009–30) seemed to presume a longer-term linear progression, which might not be true. It also seemed to presume a constant variation that would end positively. But data points may not uniformly scatter around the estimation line, due to changes in demographics and the economy. Certainly the analysts had subjected estimates to sensitivity analysis. But twenty-one years is a long time! Most importantly, he questioned the naïve causality that time caused trips. That might be true for an existing line, such as the Red Line. But here, there is only a planning corridor consisting of all kinds of modal trips—from walking and bicycles to buses. MTA identified 169,000 daily transit trips in the corridor now and found that 134,000 of them were associated with the major activity centers (e.g., Silver Spring). But only 9,000 of them were from one center to another (MTA 2008c, 2–11). The question then is whether the new LRT line would actually generate the projected trips within and between the centers? The tone of the report was certainty—there were no obvious doubts about methods or conclusions!

It was late, but Bob decided to do some forecasting of his own. He had WMATA data for ten years and could forecast the next several years easily. He used an ordinary least-squares method, as explained in appendix figure A4.2 and the Microsoft Excel instructions, available at: www.musc.edu/hap/costaccounting/exercise/chapter7/Information/linearregression.htm.

First, he noticed again, as with MTA, that the performance measures were opaque and really misleading unless the audience knew exactly what was being measured. But here he was forecasting "annual passenger trips," which he assumed would be linked, or one origin-to-destination trip, regardless of the number of intermediate boardings and departures. In fact, FTA requires measurement of annual ridership in "linked trips" to develop "incremental cost/incremental passenger" baselines (see http://www.americandreamcoalition.org/transit/ftanewrider.html).

The trouble was that "annual unlinked trips" should then be around 45% more than linked trips (USDOT 2005). But here, each year (1999–2008) they were about 30% less than linked trips for rail and 20% less for bus. That caused some head-scratching. Bob felt that conclusions based on this contradictory measure could be problematic, in that most uniform transit-system operating statistics are based on the notion of passenger trips. If the measure could be wildly different for different kinds of trips, but these were all called "annual passenger trips," then any conclusions drawn from these measures would be off.

Bob knew that operating expenses per passenger trip is a measure of how effectively a system spends funds to carry each passenger. It can also be viewed as the operating efficiency of providing one ride. Use of this measure allows analysts to compare the efficiency and effectiveness of similar transit systems. Additionally, passenger trips per vehicle revenue mile is a measure of how efficiently a transit system provides service. It reflects ridership trends, and the two indicators are related—a positive trend would reflect increases in ridership. If more vehicle miles are provided than passenger trips, this indicates a lack of efficiency and productivity (i.e., there are empty buses driving around) (DLS 2008, 2).

Table 2 Washington Area Transit Authority Passenger Data

Fiscal Year	Annual Vehicle Revenue Miles	Annual Vehicle Revenue Hours	Annual Unlinked Trips	Annual Passenger Trips
1999				
Metrobus	33,168,939	2,979,136	143,240,114	474,556,961
Metrorail	46,166,860	2,165,262	212,620,976	1,044,703,469
Metro Access	2,528,931	173,872	210,078	2,018,976
2000				
Metrobus	34,192,726	3,095,946	129,524,241	452,855,175
Metrorail	48,243,553	2,260,586	218,273,257	1,190,448,841
Metro Access	3,643,119	238,648	246,071	2,493,629
2001				
Metrobus	36,447,570	3,247,015	142,647,640	457,028,244
Metrorail	51,553,445	2,316,049	235,731,726	1,352,866,338
Metro Access	5,569,594	357,000	556,932	5,419,598
2002				
Metrobus	37,934,187	3,349,152	147,771,191	450,768,806
Metrorail	52,192,185	2,269,529	242,794,078	1,438,333,161
Metro Access	8,021,812	505,105	738,284	8,021,812
2003				
Metrobus	38,897,499	3,433,521	147,831,547	447,551,132
Metrorail	56,470,216	2,241,771	243,188,066	1,451,856,563
Metro Access	9,788,253	631,341	872,426	9,785,050
2004				
Metrobus	38,901,318	3,458,658	146,010,344	438,436,653
Metrorail	58,206,385	2,312,490	250,659,990	1,507,072,920
Metro Access	11,030,419	698,401	1,112,358	12,263,306
2005				
Metrobus	38,458,955	3,422,983	153,392,000	453,291,328
Metrorail	62,152,938	2,400,432	259,430,066	1,401,106,158
Metro Access	12,179,777	765,719	1,253,948	13,688,293
2006				
Metrobus	38,889,844	3,657,092	132,880,812	423,501,766
Metrorail	63,577,383	2,513,934	274,767,272	1,577,789,264
Metro Access	12,135,331	1,015,815	1,340,201	14,318,204
2007				
Metrobus	38,939,524	3,500,518	133,695,295	418,055,395
Metrorail	66,988,010	2,635,021	207,907,332	1,588,657,621
Metro Access	12,469,267	1,123,848	1,276,870	17,442,601
2008*				
Metrobus	38,036,841	3,659,962	132,848,806	445,952,733
Metrorail	68,455,275	2,916,819	288,039,725	1,639,628,551
Metro Access	15,000,435	1,303,915	1,712,537	20,036,683

*Preliminary Data
Source: National Transit Database.

Despite these misgivings, Bob proceeded with his forecast for WMATA Metrorail passengers. Using Excel, he found a straightforward upward trend, from 271.9 million annual unlinked trips in 2008 to 292.7 million in 2012. Metrobus passenger trips, by contrast, were forecast to drop from 137.7 million in 2008 to 135.3 million in 2012 (See appendix A4.2). Furthermore, given the assumptions he questioned on the MTA study and the fact that now we were forecasting ridership on a nonexistent system (the Purple Line) for twenty-one years, how confident could one be in the figures?

That night Bob dreamed he had been given a new job standing in front of metro stations asking people if they were *boardings* or merely *passengers*? With great difficulty, he emerged from his apartment the next morning and went back to work. He went directly to Richard Gregor's office to continue his briefing. Before Bob could ask his first question, Mr. Gregor began with, "So, Bob, I bet you're wondering if our forecasts will be accurate."

"The thought had occurred to me," Bob admitted.

"Let me say that each one of the options we reviewed has different risks and benefits. We quantified them in physical and sometimes monetary terms consistent with the methods used in the urban transport industry and required by FTA. We think they are largely accurate and will be validated by history after the project is built. They may end up inflated or, if gas prices increase, they could be on the low end. Either way, demographics and spatial externalities in the corridor are not going to disappear or reverse themselves. Beyond the accuracy question, the technical calculation requirements are relatively straightforward for all transit systems. We need to come up with an acceptable numerator (annualized capital and operating costs) over a denominator (benefit calculation, expressed in hours) to demonstrate the cost-effectiveness of our preferred option. The denominator is based on our regional travel model using best available data sources."

"You probably also noticed from the forecast study that ridership will increase. Fortunately for us, ridership is not the major determinant of our build alternative. Based on FTA criteria, we think we make our strongest case on effectiveness grounds: environmental (air quality), traffic (congestion reduction), and cost-benefit analysis (cost per hour of user benefit)."

"This is a problem, and we have a major opportunity here for some rational planning. Portland, Oregon, was once a giant riverside dump—look at it now! Most of its spectacular success was because of forward transportation planning, stressing LRT! There were many skeptics there too—most of whom ride the Tri-Met system now."

"I just want to be ready for criticism when it comes," said Bob.

"Let's move on to the figures," continued Mr. Gregor, "so you can better understand how and why we generated the data that we did. This should clarify how it all points to our preferred alternative (i.e., medium-investment LRT), on which the governor just signed off. So, we reviewed the eight transit options. Now let's examine the six evaluation criteria that, if we agree on an alternative here and need funding, we must meet according to Section 5309 of the FTA New Starts Process."

"Most of the issues in cost-versus-benefits and cost-effectiveness involve the benefits measures, not the costs. The costs are fairly straightforward, since there are ample precedents for most capital projects. Cost estimates are often based on measures and models used by similar systems in particular industries—here, urban public transport. As indicated in table 1 above, the capital and operating costs increase from TSM to high-investment LRT. The exception to the linear trend is that O&M costs for the high LRT are lower than for the medium LRT option; and O&M costs for both medium and high LRT are lower than for the low LRT option. For both capital and operating costs, predictive models are used based on known service characteristics. For LRT, the service characteristics are peak number of vehicles in service, track miles, passenger car revenue hours (multi-car trains), and revenue miles. In each case, an industry cost factor or multiplier is applied to the expected number, based on service to be provided. For example, to generate O&M costs for annual passenger-car revenue miles, the cost multiplier is: $108.85. This is a given and can only be confirmed by validation."

"How does that happen?" Bob asked.

"Each model is validated by comparing the data predicted with what actually occurs, and then working back to the assumptions. The LRT model was based on a typical year of service. By contrast, the WMATA bus model used three years of data and predicted actual costs within 6% (MTA 2008b, 3–4). As one would expect, the LRT model was not very accurate, meaning its forecasts are subject to even minor changes in service patterns. Similarly, the capital costs are based on industry models and FTA guidelines for estimating capital costs. Data for unit cost multipliers is obtained directly from databases of other US transit systems that compare bids with completed projects (MTA 2008a, 3–11). Data are also used from the Maryland Department of Transportation and the US Bureau of Labor Statistics and adjusted for local conditions. So there is not much controversy surrounding the cost estimates for any of the options."

"To a large extent, all the projected benefits from all eight options depend upon two factors: (1) the number of new transit trips to be generated, and (2) the amount of time saved per user. The idea is to maximize demand from users who prefer time savings with a newly supplied public transit option (i.e., new trips or new ridership). We used six different criteria (five technical and one for financial feasibility) and all depend on the figures generated for these two variables."

"But aren't the LRT and BRT modes different from each other and from making minor changes in systems management (TSM)?" asked Bob.

"For purposes of differentiating between modes, some of them are. Headway, number of seats per train versus bus, and overall ridership will vary by mode. The big difference is in user time saved. For example, impact on local economic development will be a function of transit-oriented development (TOD) occurring around stations. Clearly there are economic cycle factors, such as low property investment in a recession. But the number of developers and buyers around stations will be a function of estimated new trips per mode and time saved per mode. The more trips offered and time saved by new users, the greater likelihood of TOD."

"But what about the project's environmental impact?" Bob wondered. "All the proposed alignments are about the same and will require residential displacements and running trains or buses near the trails. The number of riders or trips matters less than the fact that the trams or buses are running through the forests and near the trails."

"That's correct," Mr. Gregor replied. "The environmentalists have been most implacable and immune to rational arguments. Any loss of trees, open spaces, animals, and trail solitude along the way is viewed as a major threat, not subject to compromise. The threat to golfers at the Bethesda Country Club (the lines will cut through some of the fairways and greens) is considered a major cost of the project. This is peculiar to us, given the compatibility of rail-trail uses in other cities such as Seattle, Portland, Toronto, and so on. Even more perplexing is the fact that the proposed design will improve trails and plant more trees—so much so that we probably underestimated the damage they will cause to either the tram or bus system when in operation!"

"So," Bob observed, "the strength of the Purple Line case comes down to new trips supplied and user time saved—greater operating efficiency and more cost effectiveness."

"That's right. Remember that we need to show least cost per user benefit per mode. Notice that the optimizing public investment criteria include the cost-effectiveness measure of cost per user-benefit hour. This composite *primary benefit* measure is a product of the number of daily minutes saved (from the mobility and access criteria) and the number of new riders generated compared to the no-build option (from the operating efficiencies criteria). Using this criterion, as indicated in table 1, the medium-investment LRT comes out the most cost effective, at $22.82."

"But using the FTA range," Bob noted, "the cost-effectiveness ratio of the preferred option is not very high, is it?"

"Not on the FTA scale. But few large project proposals rank high or even medium-high. According to the FTA benchmarks: a cost-effectiveness ratio greater than $12.00 is considered very highly cost effective (i.e., the primary benefits of time savings could be obtained from an investment of only $12.00). Cost-effectiveness ratios from $12.00 to $15.49 are considered medium-high."

"The medium BRT ranked medium-high in cost-effectiveness, at $14.01," Bob inquired. "Why was it not the preferred option?"

"Because the two jurisdictions, Montgomery and Prince George's Counties, both voted for LRT over BRT. They also argued that LRT is permanent and will induce greater TOD, as investors rightly see a sunk cost in rails that is not there with bus lanes. So, the locally preferred option (medium BRT) has a medium cost-effectiveness, at $22.82 (within the FTA range of $15.50–$23.99) (MTA 2008e, ES-26)."

"So if these figures are derived from industry unit-cost indices and multipliers, and the models used to predict them have been validated, all I need to do is replicate the benefit numbers to ensure that the cost-effectiveness forecasts are accurate."

"That's right," Mr. Gregor agreed. "MTA developed a common travel-demand forecasting model for several corridors in the Washington, DC, regional area. Using the no-build option as the baseline for future forecasts, the plan was to use that forecasting model for the Purple Line. But this model was not validated. So MTA used an enhanced version of the Council of Governments (COG) model for the Purple Line corridor forecasts of trips and time-saved benefits. This model estimated 169,000 current daily transit trips associated with the Purple Line corridor, or around 10% of all transit trips in the Washington region. About 135,000 of the trips are associated with the major activity centers, such as Silver Spring and College Park (MTA 2008c, 2–11). The COG model is a classic four-step model with six static iterations of feedback through trip generation, distribution, mode choice, and assignment. However, even this model was not validated for comprehensive transit analysis. For this, a *post processor* was developed to predict person trip types and modes (MTA 2008c, 1-1), and that was the model used to develop benefits estimates for the eight options. The model estimates that transit trips associated with the corridor will grow 38% by 2030, to 234,000 trips, and within the corridor to 62,000, or an increase of 43% (MTA 2008c, 2–14)."

"You are concerned with predictive accuracy," Mr. Gregor went on. "We can't just present figures in FTA forms—we have to present our worksheets, like in an exam. FTA will recalculate much of what we present to ensure validity and reliability."

"I'm still curious about how accurately we can predict trips generated and user benefits for twenty-one years using data from other models, industry assumptions, and new trip patterns for a system that does not now exist," Bob commented. "How valid can they be?"

"In theory, there are methodological problems, such as using a few years to predict linear patterns for twenty-one years from now, assuming demographic and economic changes in that period that qualify some of the projections, and so on. This is judgmental forecasting. But don't forget that even large-scale econometric models are dependent on judgment (Dunn 2008, 180). The 'street' method used by transit experts is to develop the quantitative models, forecast the data, then step back and compare it with reality and see what we think of the data and trends."

"A kind of Delphi or panel-of-experts approach?" Bob asked.

"Except that here we have the data and ask experts what they think of it," Mr. Gregor responded. "Now that we have gone through the options and evaluation criteria, I'd like you to become familiar with one of our pre-appraisal techniques. We use these as threshold models to determine whether we should go forward with more sophisticated techniques. Called 'pivot-point' models, they are logit models that generate time elasticity of demand for transit line projects. They are something like the threshold technique called 'payback analysis' to compare benefits and costs without discounting. They provide ballpark figures."

"Do you mean the sensitivity of demand to a proposed transit line?"

"That's right. This is a simple model that assumes no changes in demographics or other variables. Everything is controlled except for the transit project; the only change going forward is the transit project. This provides us a preliminary forecast of what the demand would likely be in the forecast year for that project. If there are multiple options, as here, we can use this technique to forecast demand sensitivity to any or all of them."

"Would this be a reliable technique for the Purple Line?" Bob asked.

"No. The market here is not mature yet. The proposed line crosses multiple activity centers served by many forms of transportation. Trip changes and resultant demand are not subject to simple linear forecasts. So, for instance, projects like the proposed extension of the commuter rail line to Wilmington, Delaware (MARC), or the Red Line extension in Baltimore are amenable to pivot-point modeling, because it can be accurately assumed that none of the other variables will change much—only the impact of the planned transit line. We use simple threshold models like this because they assume that going forward from the existing market, the only change will be the transit line. The model helps us focus on the modal choices among alternate transit proposals—as is the case with the Purple Line and its eight options for one corridor."

"What I would like you to do for me," Mr. Gregor continued, "is a simple transit-demand estimation exercise. You know how to apply *linear forecasting* techniques to time-series data (e.g., WMATA). Here, we are *simulating* the behavior of aggregate trip-mode data across a geographic region. This is particularly relevant for projects like the Purple Line that cross urban areas. For example, as we discussed, MTA projects a 38% increase in daily transit trips in the corridor attributable to the project (from 169,000 to 234,000) by 2030. FTA will ask us how we got that figure. Cost-effectiveness means the lowest numerator (cost) for the highest denominator (value maximized, here transit trips or user benefits). For purposes of estimating the denominator or trips, as indicated below, we use a five-mode multinomial modal choice logit model (USDOT 2003). Here is how it works: Using the data provided, I would like you to estimate the utilities, data probabilities, and number of trips for all modes. Here are your instructions and data," Mr. Gregor concluded, handing Bob the following exercise.

Transit-Demand Estimation Exercise

The work-trip mode choice model is a five-mode logit model consisting of the transit mode and four auto-occupancy modes: drive alone, two-person carpool, three-person carpool, and four-or-more–person carpool. The general form of the model is:

$$P_i = \frac{e^{u_i}}{\displaystyle\sum_{i=1}^{n} e^{u_i}}$$

Where:

P_i = probability of taking mode i (share)

U_i = utility of mode i

e = base of natural logarithms.

The variables in the model, used to compute (U_i) are:

OVT (out-of-vehicle time): for auto travel, the time spent walking to and from the car; for transit, the time spent walking to and from bus stops, and waiting for the bus.

IVT (in-vehicle time): for auto and transit, the time spent riding in the vehicle.

COST (out-of-pocket cost): for auto, operating cost, tolls, and parking costs; for transit, fare.

The general form of the utility function is:

$$U_i = a_i - 0.05 \; OVT_i - 0.025 \; IVT_i - 0.0024 \; COST_i$$

where a_i is a mode-specific constant for mode i.

Data

The model will be applied to the interchange between Zone 5 and Zone 1 in Utown. Table 3 provides the data for this application.

You will first calculate the mode probabilities for the trip interchanges between Zone 5 and Zone 1. Use the tables on the next page.

In Part A, you will calculate the modal utilities based on the values of the mode-specific constants and the three variables used in the model (i.e., OVT, IVT, and COST).

Table 3 Level of Service Data

Mode		OVT	IVT	COST
		(min.)	(min.)	(cents)
1 person	5	17	200.0	
2-person carpool	5	21	100.0	
3-person carpool	5	23	66.6	
4+-person carpool	5	25	50.0	
Transit		7	33	160.0

Part A: Calculate the utilities for transit as follows:

(1) First, insert in the table the appropriate values for OVT, IVT, and COST.
(2) Second, calculate the utility relative to each variable by multiplying the variable by the coefficient that is shown in parentheses at the top of the column.
(3) Finally, sum the utilities (including the mode-specific constant), and note the total in the last column.

Part B: Calculate the mode probabilities as follows:

(1) Insert the utility for transit in the first column.
(2) Calculate e^{u_i} for each mode.
(3) Sum the e^{u_i} for all modes and note in the "Total" line.
(4) Calculate the probabilities by mode, using the formula:

$$P_i = \frac{e^{u_i}}{\sum\limits_{i=1}^{n} e^{u_i}}$$

Table for Part A:

Table 4 Utilities

Mode*		Mode-Specific Constant	OVT (−0.050)	IVT (−0.025)	COST (−0.0024)	TOTAL Ui
Solo driver:	Variable		5	17	200	
	Utility	0.0	−0.25	−0.425	−0.48	−1.155
2-person carpool:	Variable		5	21	100	
	Utility	−0.25	−0.25	−0.525	−0.24	−1.265
3-person carpool:	Variable		5	23	66.6	
	Utility	−0.30	−0.25	−0.575	−0.16	−1.285
4+-person carpool:	Variable		5	25	50.0	
	Utility	−0.35	−0.25	−0.625	−0.12	−1.345
Transit:	Variable					
	Utility	−0.30				

*Coefficients for variables in capital letters at the top of each column are from the Level of Service Data (Chapter 4 Case, Table 3).

Table for Part B:

Table 5

Mode	Utility	e^{ui}	Data Probability
Solo driver	−1.155	0.31506	0.244
2-person carpool	−1.265	0.28224	0.219
3-person carpool	−1.285	0.27665	0.214
4+-person carpool	−1.345	0.26054	0.202
Transit:			
Total			

From trip distribution, the number of trips from Zone 5 to Zone 1 was 14,891. Calculate the number of trips by mode from Zone 5 to Zone 1, using the probabilities calculated.

Table 6

Mode	Trips (Zone 5 to Zone 1)
Solo driver	
2-person carpool	
3-person carpool	
4+-person carpool	
Transit	
TOTAL	14,891

Questions for Discussion

Using the provided data (1999–2008), forecast annual unlinked trips and annual passenger trips for WMATA for the years 2009–12, using any of the statistical techniques presented in this chapter.

Using the logit trip choice model and data provided, calculate the number of transit trips expected from Zone 5 to Zone 1.

What are the assumptions for the coefficients used in this model? How were the weights derived? What questions would you ask as a policy analyst?

Using the data and any of the methods provided, what would your forecast be for Purple Line benefits? Will it be cost effective by FTA measures? Would you use other measures?

References for the Case Study

Department of Legislative Services (DLS). 2008. Fiscal and Policy Note: MTA—Public Transit Services—Efficiency and Performance Standards. Annapolis: Maryland General Assembly.

Dunn, William N. 2008. *Public Policy Analysis: An Introduction.* 4th ed. Englewood Cliffs, NJ: Pearson Prentice Hall.

Finkler, Steven A. 2005. *Financial Management for Public, Health, and Not-for-Profit Organizations.* 2nd ed. Englewood Cliffs, NJ: Pearson.

Maryland Transit Administration (MTA). 2004. Bi-County Transitway Scoping Process Report. Baltimore: MTA.

———. 2008a. Capital Cost Estimating Methodology: Technical Report. Baltimore: MTA.

———. 2008b. Operating and Maintenance Cost Estimate: Technical Report. Baltimore: MTA.

———. 2008c. Travel Demand Forecasting Technical Report. Baltimore: MTA.

———. 2008d. Public Outreach and Coordination: Technical Report. Baltimore: MTA.

———. 2008e. Purple Line Alternatives Analysis and Draft EIS: Executive Summary. Baltimore: MTA.

———. 2009. Re-Connecting Washington's Streetcar Suburbs. Baltimore: MTA.

Michel, R. Gregory. 2001. *Decision Tools for Budgetary Analysis*. Chicago: Government Finance Officers Association.

Schrank, David, and Tim Lomax. 2005. *The Urban Mobility Problem*. College Station, TX: Texas Transportation Institute/Texas A&M University. http://mobility.tamu.html.

US Department of Transportation, Federal Highway Administration. 2003. Introduction to Urban Travel Demand Forecasting. National Highway Institute Course 152054.

US Department of Transportation, Research and Innovative Technology Administration (RITA). 2005. Unlinked Passenger Trips vs. Number of Passengers. Washington, DC: USDOT.

Note

This case was prepared by George M. Guess. The author wishes to thank Michael Madden, project manager at the Office of Planning, Maryland Transit Administration in Baltimore; Greg Benz of Parsons, Brinckerhoff, Tudor in Baltimore; and Christine Romans of the MTA finance department, also in Baltimore, for their invaluable guidance in preparing this case. The characters are fictitious, the conclusions are the authors, and any data errors or inconsistencies are completely the author's fault.

ANALYSIS OF CHAPTER 4 CASE STUDY

Analysts need to use appropriate methods to forecast or estimate data points that by definition do not exist. In most cases, analysts know why they are forecasting; that is, the exercise is not simply a case of pure research to improve forecasting methods. They are forecasting options, for example, to avoid application of the 35% policy rule that requires service or staff cutbacks (MARTA). They are forecasting to avoid depleting the snow removal budget for the year, which would threaten overall city finances and credit ratings. In our case, they are forecasting to meet Federal Transit Administration (FTA) cost-effectiveness criteria in order to obtain billions of dollars in federal capital financing (Purple Line).

Problems such as policy responses to snowfall, flooding, and demand for urban mobility and access are relatively well structured. This is an advantage for application of techniques to forecast relevant policy options. For transit forecasting, the demand for and supply of urban space, as well as costs of current traffic and transit flows (in time, fuel, and air quality), are measurable and predictable. Because urban planners, traffic and transit engineers, and economists analyze and update patterns regularly, databases for forecasting are considered excellent. For these reasons, decision criteria for expected value tables and weighted score tables can be calculated, weighted, and scored with high probabilities of success. In the case, costs are calculated according to given methodologies (FTA), and benefits must be calculated according to approved regional planning models with transparent assumptions. More importantly, FTA provides the analytic framework (cost-effectiveness), measures, indicators, and evaluation standards for proposed projects. Proposed lines must achieve a cost-effectiveness ratio between $12 and $30. Those projects with a ratio of $12 or higher are considered very low cost and high benefit and have the best chance of being accepted and funded. Those in the $12.00–$15.49 range are considered to have a very high chance of being accepted; $15.50–$23.99, a medium chance; $24.00–$30.00, a medium to low chance; and higher than $30.00, a low or poor chance of being accepted or funded. Given these transparent parameters, the preferred option will be the one with the least cost per user benefit. The FTA will compare the preferred options for particular systems (here, WMATA/MTA) against all other systems soliciting project funding for their options. Within this system-wide cost-effectiveness framework, approvals and funding decisions are transparent and typically accepted by most losers in the annual competition. Urban transport is not a unique policy area. Similar frameworks, methods, and measures are provided

by funders for projects in health, energy, education, roads, and municipal services such as water-sewerage and water purification systems.

There are two general approaches to forecasting: (1) regression estimation
and (2) simulation-assisted estimation. First, decisions can be informed by
regressions of normal time-series data. Analysts need to know how many units
of the target variable Y are associated with a one-unit change in the independent variable or variables X, which is indicated by the slope of the line, or the
regression coefficient (B). The fit of the line (or curve) should be the sum of
the squared differences between the actual data points and those on the trend
line. The goal of the linear regression process is to estimate a line that is close
as possible to the given data points (Finkler 2009, 119). If the fit is right and
residual variation minimized (indicated by the coefficient of determination),
enough of the variation in Y should be explained to produce an accurate forecast (Nachmias 1979, 118). So, if the future is like the past, the line should
forecast the results for several units (e.g., years) ahead. This is what Bob Melvin did with the WMATA data points that produced valid but unreliable
results—unreliable because of the shocks of the economic recession of 2008–9
on transit ridership. Like ridership forecasts, revenue forecasts for taxes and
fees are based on regressions using time-series data and multiple explanatory
variables to predict future collections.

It follows that where good time-series data exist (e.g., revenues and ridership for transit), forecasts should be more accurate. Transit revenue and
ridership-demand data are available over many decades. Techniques such as
proportionate change, averaging, and ordinary least-squares (OLS) regression can be easily applied to develop forecasts. In the case, Bob Melvin forecast WMATA unlinked trips (boardings) for both Metrobus and Metrorail
using the OLS method. He used Excel to input data and calculate the inter-
cepts (b) and slopes (x-coefficients) from 1999–2008 data to forecast ridership
for the next four years. As is evident from appendix 4B, the results were as follows: annual unlinked Metrorail trips 2008–12 will increase by 7.6%, while
Metrobus trips will decrease by 9.7%. Fluctuations in ridership over the 1999–
2008 period make projections forward to 2012 more risky. Nevertheless,
annual passenger trips (linked) for both rail and bus are forecasted to change in
about the same proportion over that period.

Despite what has been said about the predictability of revenue and
demand, techniques overlay data patterns with linear or curvilinear predictive
frameworks. That means that they cannot account for sudden transforma-
tional shifts or events, such as recessions. Thus, the trend up to 2008 of
increasing demand suddenly dropped dramatically in 2009. Because of the
recession, there were fewer riders because of lost jobs, and those who rode were

taking shorter trips. This reduced expected farebox revenues by $35 million. Actual 2009 Metrorail ridership fell 6% and Metrorail fell 10% compared to 2008 (Weir 2009). Diminished ridership and system revenue in 2009 has affected the operations of all US transit systems to some extent. Unfortunately, there is no tool or method to compensate for this problem; instabilities generated by large, discontinuous events such as economic and institutional shocks transmit through state and local governments and affect services. Predictions become totally speculative. As Boris Karloff might say, the rhythms are clearly discernable to a careful observer. But if Jack the Ripper's past rhythms suddenly change, that becomes a mystery of the universe!

Second, analysts can derive estimates of the target variable Y (e.g., demand) by formulae using simulations, weights, coefficients, and probabilities (for the effects of commuter-time values on modal choice behavior). For either approach to forecasting, analysts need to question assumptions and data sources. Data for the second, more formal approach are typically derived from surveys generating time-series or cross-sectional data points. Often, the potential funder of programs or projects—such as the FTA, EPA, Department of Energy, Department of Education, or Department of Housing and Urban Development—will provide the formulae, data measures, and requirements. So, for a large capital project like the Purple Line, the FTA needs to know estimated trips generated and the likely distribution of modal trip choices. If, using the standardized data and methods required, the MTA is unable to forecast the appropriate level of demand, then by FTA standards the project would be cost ineffective and not be funded. This method offers transparent comparability and evaluation. Competitors know that they will be fairly treated and typically have a good idea beforehand whether their project is cost effective.

For transportation forecasts, analysts need to calculate the probability of different modal choices. If it is evident that travelers would not prefer transit along a specific route, the project would likely fail to generate the number of trips needed for acceptance and funding. Thus, the question is how much utility one derives from each mode? In the case, the utility function is the sum of different utilities for in-vehicle time (IVT), out-of-vehicle time (OVT), and cost. In his effort to forecast commuter modal choice among four options for the original San Francisco Bay Area Rapid Transit (BART) system in 1978, Train argued that cost and time are related because: "By definition the value of time is the extra cost that a person would be willing to incur to save time" (2009, 73). How does one know the utilities for each option in our case? For transportation forecasts, primary survey research is used to develop coefficients, such as on-board surveys, measured travel volumes, and household surveys assessed against known travel-system performance (speeds, vehicle counts, travel times, fares, tolls for different roadway types, transit routes, frequencies, and capacities). For the exercise, the process of obtaining these coefficients and utilities is not known and therefore we are given the coefficients as constants. Like regression coefficients, the constants indicate the marginal increase in the associated independent variable (Ward 2009). The analyst is answering the question: Given values of time and cost for each modal option here (carpool, transit, solo driver), what is the likelihood that a person will select a particular option? The problem is similar to the Purple Line appraisal, which required forecasting of trips generated and estimation of time saved for the no-build, bus, and rail options.

For added precision in forecasting modal choice probabilities, analysts now employ *logit* models. Previous models over- or underpredicted demand. For this reason, current emphasis is on building accurate forecasting models that can be calibrated and validated by comparison with actual demand. These are simple threshold models that, in the case of a new transit line, assume that the only change going forward is that transit line. Such models predict the value of time on demand, or time elasticity of demand (Benz 2009). For development and use of logit models, analysts specify utility functions for each choice faced by a decision maker (Train 2009, 35). The dependent variable Y is thus a logged odds transformation of a choice. To try to improve the interpretation of logistic regressions of binary outcomes, policy analysts can transform the probabilities of linear relationships to odds ratios. Consistent with the formula, the odds of a particular choice are found by dividing the value of exponentiated utility by the sum of the exponentiated utilities associated with each choice (P = Eu/Sum Eu).

To forecast the number of trips and their distribution for the exercise, the time and cost data are given (7–45). First, the utilities for transit must be calculated as they were for the other four modes, by multiplying the constants or coefficients by the time and cost for each mode (independent variables).

Table 4.5   Utility Estimation

Transit Mode	Mode-Specific Constant	OVT (–0.050)	IVT (–0.0250)	COST (–0.0024)	TOTAL Ui
Variable	–0.30	7	33	160	–1.855
Utility		–0.35	–0.825	–0.38	

Table 4.6   Trip Estimation by Mode

Mode	Trips (Zone 5 to Zone 1)
Solo Driver	3,574 (24%)
2-Person Carpool	3,261
3-Person Carpool	3,186
4-Person Carpool	3,008
Transit	1,802 (12.2%)
TOTAL	14,891

Based on the data, it appears that transit would not be the preferred commuter option—providing the least utility of all five choices (–1.855 is much lower than any of the other four). The logit model is now applied to the utilities to estimate the logged odds of the utilities translating into choice. Using your calculator, the root of the natural log (Ex) for the solo driver option (–1.155) would be 0.31506, as given in the exercise. Following the formula, divide each modal logged utility by the total utility for all five modes (1.29094). With this data, the transit logged utility and choice probability would be 0.15645 and 0.121, respectively. Again, this is the lowest probability of the five options.

Trips generated and percentages can now be estimated with this data. Multiply the data probabilities by the total number of trips (14,891) to get the estimated trips for each mode.

As indicated, the expected trips for the transit line are the lowest and for solo driver the highest (12.2% and 24% of the total trips, respectively). Again, the logit model can be applied to any modal choice probability issue where data and measures are provided by industry sources.

In short, the Purple Line case provides the opportunity to view the strengths and weaknesses of policy-forecasting methods in action. First, most policies and programs, such as urban transit, depend on stable financing and stable demand. Funding sources are multiple and diversified. Planned appropriations and fiscal transfers need to arrive as planned in the budget. Demand, translated into fare revenues, must be as planned, or service and administrative cutbacks or fare increases will result. Generally, revenue forecasts are more reliable than expenditure forecasts. Revenues are based on predictable bases and rates, and, barring major events such as recessions, they are relatively stable. User-charge and fee revenues based on customer demand are also relatively stable and predictable from year to year. Revenue data are also typically available in longer and more consistent time series—usually on a cash basis. If the forecasts are wrong, the effect is often immediate: reduced income and property tax revenues, and reduced transit ridership as the economy contracts and jobs are lost. Fee and user-charge revenues may change dramatically in response to sudden economic events.

Nevertheless, expenditure forecasts are less predictable, because they filter through institutional layers and policy processes. They are subject to modification, transfers, and reprogramming during the year; funds may not be spent because of absorptive capacity weaknesses. In addition, expenditure data may be misinterpreted because of differences in cash and modified accrual accounting methods, and institutional changes that merge or disaggregate expenditures. These impede the validity and reliability of forecasts. More importantly, later calibration of models based on misunderstanding of internal rule systems should indicate that the models are either unreliable or invalid, or valid only by accident (via countervailing inaccurate predictions).

Chapter Four, Appendix A

Time-Series Data Analysis

A discussion of classical time-series analysis is the foundation for any examination of more complex policy forecasting techniques. Time-series data are affected by four components: secular trends, seasonal variations, cyclical fluctuations, and irregular movements. Secular trends include long-term growth or decline in a time series, such as reductions in arrests per 1,000 people. Seasonal variations consist of periodic variations in a time series recurring within a one-year period or less, such as patterns of sales around holidays. Cyclical fluctuations could periodically extend unpredictably over a number of years, such as the Ripper murders did. Irregular movements are irregular fluctuations in a time series, such as strikes and natural disasters (Dunn 1994, 205).

A simple example can serve to demonstrate the effects of these components on forecasting accuracy. Past data trends are important in establishing whether, for example, a drug-abuse policy problem exists. Weighing the costs and benefits of alternative policy responses to time-series data requires an estimate of future data behavior; in this case, cocaine use. Looking at figure A4.1, we see that cocaine use, the time-series variable on the Y-axis or vertical ordinate, had been leveling off for blacks, whites, and Hispanics from 1988 to 1995. These trends follow periods of increased rates of cocaine-related treatment episodes in 1990–91 and 1993–94. Do the data suggest a cycle of growing use that will recur? The question is whether we can validly forecast future trends in use and hospital visits on the X-axis or horizontal abscissas from these data.

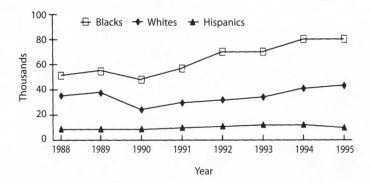

Figure A4.1   Trends in Cocaine-Related Emergency Department Episodes, 1988–95 (*Source:* National Institutes on Drug Abuse)

Similar time-series data could be plotted to determine whether public health policies should focus on control and elimination of cockroaches in inner cities. The results of a 1992–93 study published in the *New England Journal of Medicine* showed that youths allergic to cockroaches and exposed to the insects at home were three times more likely to be hospitalized than other asthmatic youths. The pattern is unique in the United States because inner-city young people were most afflicted by cockroach allergens. For those under eighteen years of age, asthma cases per 1,000 persons increased from 41 to 69% in the ten-year period from 1984 to 1994: 62% of the cases were in inner cities, where 78% of the 1,500 cases analyzed happened to be among black Americans (Suplee 1997). Although the study did not examine cost-effectiveness in detail, one implication of the time-series data is that a relatively small expenditure on cockroach control could result in substantial public health benefits. Reducing the population of cockroaches through control of food and water sources, regular cleaning, and routine use of insecticides (similar to dealing with the rat problem in New York City, cited in chapter 3) would lead to fewer school days missed and less hospitalization of inner-city children.

Simpler time-series techniques, such as the classical time series, visual estimation (also called the "black thread" technique), moving averages, exponential smoothing, and regression analysis, rely on the assumption that the ordinate and abscissa will move together. This is assumed whether causality is substantive or specious, such as in the notion that sunspots produce changes in stock market prices. How the two axes move together depends on the degree of impact by the four trend components listed above. Where the other three components reveal irregular variation over time, other variables need to be included in a causal model to develop forecasts in which we can have greater confidence.

For example, the cocaine-related episodes for the three groups in figure A4.1 seem to exhibit a secular trend, or "smooth long-term growth or decline in time-series" (Dunn 1994, 203). If so, one might have confidence in the results of averaging techniques to produce a forecast of future trends. There does not seem to be any seasonal variation (within a one-year period) or cyclical fluctuation (regular long-term changes that can change trends) that would upset assumptions of regularity and persistence of trends. To forecast cycles, one must know how the many determinants of drug abuse—including price, enforcement, and user susceptibility—will affect the pattern of ultimate use. This means utilization of a causal model.

But closer inspection of figure A4.1 indicates that for blacks and whites, cocaine use exhibits irregular movements. In 1996, 54% of cocaine-related episodes occurred among blacks, 29% among whites, and 8% among Hispanics.

Between 1994 and 1995, there was no change in cocaine-related episodes by gender or race/ethnicity except for Hispanics, among whom there was a decrease of 13% (from 13,400 to 11,600) (National Institute on Drug Abuse 1997, 1). The curious shifts in use (1989 drop, 1990 increase, 1993 increase) may have been due in part to measurement problems, enforcement practices, social mores, or family structures. Whatever their causes, forecasting cyclical fluctuations or describing trends is thus made much more difficult. This underscores our earlier assertion that good data are essential both for defining a policy problem and for analyzing policy options. Later shifts in trends that reveal irregular events actually to be part of regular cycles are important in redefining the problem, perhaps midway through the enforcement period. Such new data trends, turned up as part of a midterm policy forecast, are important in redefining policy and ultimately in improving policy results.

Despite the benefits of regular forecasts with new data during the problem-definition or policy-implementation phases, forecasters often assume that trends will continue for the short term. They also tend to assume that changes in underlying variables, such as migration and birth rates affecting population trends, will "not change dramatically or unexpectedly over short periods of time" (Liner 1983, 84). Given the relative freedom to engage in short-term trend forecasting, let us apply several simple techniques to the drug use data. Where application is made difficult by data limitations, we will employ alternative data for "whiskey excise taxes" in a small city in the United States.

PROPORTIONATE CHANGE OR AVERAGING TECHNIQUES

At the lowest level on any policy forecaster's scale of technical sophistication are averaging techniques. These are also called "moving average" (Toulmin and Wright 1983, 226) or "proportionate-change" methods (Rabin, Hildreth, and Miller 1983, 35). As we will see, simplicity and accuracy are not necessarily opposites. Averaging techniques are rudimentary time-series analysis methods widely used because of their simplicity and ease of calculation. Moving averages can be applied whenever it is necessary to make an estimate of a variable value for a short-term forecast of one to three time periods (e.g., months, years). "The concept of the moving average is based on the assumption that the past data observations reflect an underlying trend that can be determined, and that the averaging of these data will eliminate the randomness and seasonality in the data. The averaging of the data to develop a forecast value provides a 'smoothing' effect on the data" (Toulmin and Wright 1983, 226). Averaging depends on the assumptions that past patterns will continue and that "turning points" (irregular components) will not take place in the period to be forecast.

Suppose that we were asked to forecast cocaine use (table A4.1) for users age twenty-six and older for 1996. We know from chapter 2's discussion of the difficulty of defining the problem that past trends are affected by both cyclical and irregular components, so that linear or nonlinear forecasting techniques may boil down to nothing more than sophisticated guesswork. Nevertheless, we need some kind of reading, with the usual caveats of uncertainty that apply to all forecasting efforts. Applying the averaging technique to the data in table A4.1, we must find the percentage changes in use for preceding years, average them, and multiply the average percentage change by the last year to obtain the forecast for the next year.

How did we calculate the percentage changes? First, we found the differences in reported use between each year. The difference between 1991 and 1992 was a drop of –1.7%. To find the percentage change from 1991 to 1992, we divided 1.7 by the figure for the base year (7.8) and found it to be .217, or –22%. We then averaged the percentage changes by totaling the column (= –5.2) and dividing it by the number of changes (5). The average percentage change was found to be –1.04%. Since this will be our multiplier, we took the product of the last data year (7.1) and –1.04 and found the expected level of use in 1997 to be 7.4%, or a 0.3% increase over 1996. The total reported percentage use for 1997 should then be 7.4% = 7.1 × 1.04. Thus, by this method, change in projected cocaine use for 1997 will be 4.2% more than in 1996.

Table A4.1 Reported Trends in Cocaine Use by High School Seniors, 1991–96

Year	Reported Use (%)	Change (%)
1991	7.8	0
1992	6.1	–22.0
1993	6.1	0
1994	5.9	–3.2
1995	6.0	1.7
1996	7.1	18.3
1997	—	—

The same moving average technique is often used by municipal revenue forecasters for annual budgeting. The accuracy of the revenue forecast will affect budget management during the year as managers attempt to manage cash flow. It will also determine the size of any budget deficit that needs to be financed (through arrears, carry-overs, or short-term financing). The success of entire policies can depend upon this technique. For example, cities such as San Diego and Pittsburgh are basing their economic development strategies on new sports stadiums. Local bond repayments from the budget will depend largely upon earmarked revenue sources such as the hotel tax (*The Economist* 1999b, 39). Whether revenues from this tax will grow or decline needs to be included in the analysis of proposed economic development policies. Hotel tax receipts are often successfully forecast by using the moving average method. In the annual budget document, assumptions underlying the revenue forecast will determine whether the city attains its financial goals.

Proportionate-change trend analysis is an easy and reasonably accurate statistical technique for predicting future revenues from revenue base or collection data over the preceding five to six years. This method allows determination of the average rate of change from collections over a trend period of years and application to the last year. Suppose we want to estimate anticipated revenue from building permit receipts for FY 2011. The following five steps will provide an answer:

1. Monthly receipts data for the building-permits revenue source are needed. Add this up for a yearly total, for example, $1,000 for 2005.

2. To come up with the rate of change, calculate the difference in the amount collected between each fiscal year. This can be done with a simple hand calculator. For six years, there will be five rates of change:

$$\frac{\text{Target (Current Fiscal Year)} - \text{Base or FY1 (PY)}}{\text{Base Year FY1}} = \text{rate of change}$$

1. $\dfrac{\text{FY 2006} - \text{FY 2005}}{\text{FY 2005}} = \dfrac{1200 - 1000}{1000} = .2 \text{ or } 20\%$

2. $\dfrac{\text{FY 2007} - \text{FY 2006}}{\text{FY 2006}} = \dfrac{1300 - 1200}{1200} = .8 \text{ or } 80\%$

3. $\dfrac{\text{FY 2008} - \text{FY 2007}}{\text{FY 2007}} = \dfrac{1500 - 1300}{1300} = .15 \text{ or } 15\%$

4. $\dfrac{\text{FY 2009} - \text{FY 2008}}{\text{FY 2008}} = \dfrac{1900 - 1500}{1500} = .26 \text{ or } 26\%$

5. $\dfrac{\text{FY 2010} - \text{FY 2009}}{\text{FY 2009}} = \dfrac{2100 - 1900}{1900} = .10 \text{ or } 10\%$

3. Add all rates of change and compute average rate of change for the period FY 2005–FY 2010:

20%

8%

15%

26%

10%

79

79/5 = 16% average rate of change

4. Multiply average rate of change by the current year collections:

$2,100 \times .16 = 336$

5. Add 336 to current year collections of $2,100 to obtain the estimated revenue from building permits for FY 2011:

$2,100 + 336 = \$2,436$ estimated FY 2011 building permit revenue.

The accuracy of every revenue source estimate rests on the validity of the assumptions made, and local policymakers should make them explicit in the budget document. In this case, using the $2,436 figure requires two assumptions. First, there is no change in permit fees over the last year (or change in rates), and second, there is no local ordinance in the near future that would encourage or discourage people from building new structures or adding to existing ones. In addition, local tax offices should consider other factors affecting the accuracy of revenue estimates, such as inflation rates (price changes) and other regulatory ordinances.

It should be evident from the two examples that the strength of the averaging technique is also its telling weakness. It is based on a straight-line projection of average past changes that assumes that average differences between years will be a guide to next year. Specifically, as in regression analysis, which will be discussed next, the averaging technique gives each data point the same weight in the analysis "whereas, in actuality, the latest data may be of more importance because they may indicate the beginning of a new trend" (Toulmin and Wright 1983, 234). Note that after increasing from 60 to 100% between 1974 and 1977, the yearly percentage change in cocaine use dropped from 90 to 11% in the two most recent data years. Nevertheless, this method gives the 11% data point the same weight as the 100% for forecasting purposes. What this means is that a turning point may have occurred in 1985 and that the 65% figure may be too high for next year. In fact, as was indicated in chapter 2, there is evidence that use may have stabilized or even declined despite the increases in incarceration rates for drug offenders (with attendant jail overcrowding) that were caused mainly by rigid state three-strike laws.

CAUSAL OR REGRESSION ANALYSIS

Moving up the scale of time-series forecasting sophistication, better results should be obtainable through regression analysis. Even though many refer to linear regression as "causal analysis" (Toulmin and Wright 1983; Klay 1983), we use the latter term in reference to deductive theory–based, often econometric analyses that employ linear multiple regressions and correlational analyses (Dunn 1981, 150). All regression is linear in the sense that it is curve fitting, and a straight line is one form of a curve.

The results of multiple and correlational analysis do not prove causation. For example, suppose one finds that a linear regression line closely links changes in food consumption (Y) with changes in family income (X). The data on the scattergram fall into a linear pattern with a beta, "b," slope or "regression coefficient" that tells us how much the dependent variable will change in "a," or alpha, for changes along that line. It could be concluded that higher food consumption depends on higher income, that higher income depends on higher food consumption, or that they are both influenced by some other factor(s). Since both X and Y increase together at a specific magnitude, any of these theories of relationship could be supported (Schroeder, Sjoquist, and Stephan 1986, 22). Causal models will be discussed in the next section.

Here we illustrate how regression analysis can aid forecasting. While regression framework is not dependent upon least-squares optimization technique, the latter is: "The most accurate technique for extrapolating linear trend is least-squares trend estimation, a procedure that permits mathematically precise estimates of future social states on the basis of observed values in a time series. While least-squares regression is technically superior to the black-thread technique, it is based on the same assumptions of persistence, regularity and data reliability" (Dunn 2008, 144). Of course, the precision of least-square estimations depends on data quality.

The regression model also assumes that there are no measurement errors. Unless this assumption is challenged, forecasting results can be distorted. The ordinary least-squares (OLS) regression model assumes that (1) the error term associated with one observation is uncorrelated with the error term associated with all other observations, (2) error terms can be small or large but are not related to the independent variables used, and (3) error terms are not correlated with the independent variables. The most common problem associated with these errors for time-series data (successive time periods) is termed "autocorrelation" or "serial correlation." In such cases, the residual error terms from different observations are correlated. Autocorrelation can be caused by such factors as omission of important explanatory variables, or the tendency of effects to persist over time. Use of a test statistic called the Durbin-Watson coefficient can provide clues to the existence of autocorrelation. This coefficient can be used to test the null hypothesis that successive error terms are not autocorrelated. When serially correlated error terms are detected, such methods as the generalized least-squares regression technique can be used (Schroeder, Sjoquist, and Stephan 1986, 74–75).

Policy analysts first need to focus on the exploratory task of finding which variables are related to a given variable, such as population growth, per capita income, and consumer expenditure patterns, in relation to sales tax collections. This gives us the "correlation coefficient"—a "descriptive statistic that measures the degree of linear association between two variables," denoted "r" for each pair of variables (Schroeder, Sjoquist, and Stephan 1986, 25). The correlation coefficient only measures the degree of association. It says nothing about the reasons for the correlation, which may be cause and effect, mutual causation, both related to a third variable, or coincidence. However, the correlation coefficient (r, which ranges from −1.0 to +1.0 and indicates the direction of the relationship) and the coefficient of determination (R^2, which is an index of the amount of variation in the dependent variable that is explained by the independent variable) can supplement regression analysis and enable it to provide "much more information of direct relevance to policymakers than other forms of estimation" (Dunn 1981, 195).

Let us examine the regression technique more closely and indicate its strengths and weaknesses for forecasting. According to David Nachmias (1979, 113), "The objective of regression analysis is to formulate a function by which the researcher can predict or estimate the scores on a target variable from scores on independent variables." Looking at figure A4.2, we note that each pair of X and Y values is a coordinate, and where all coordinates fall on a straight line, the function relating X to Y is a linear function. The regression equation is $Y = \alpha + (\beta)(X)$. This suggests that Y is a linear function of X. The slope of the regression function (β) indicates how many units in Y are obtained for each unit change in X. The more rigorously we can estimate a regression line, the better chance of predictive accuracy for the future. The symbol (α) represents the point at which the regression line crosses the Y-axis (where X = 0), which is called the y-intercept (Finkler 2005, 119). Linear regression

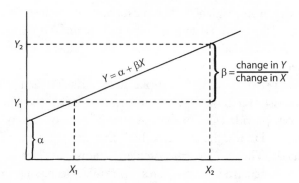

Figure A4.2   The Regression Equation

uses a set of paired x and y values to estimate the slope (β) and the intercept (α) (Finkler 2005, 120).

The regression equation hypothesizes that observed coordinates will fall along a straight line. A means of averaging the distances to obtain the best fitting line is needed. "Goodness of fit" tests, such as the coefficient of determination (R^2), discussed above, indicate the strength of the relationship between the dependent and independent variables. The most common form of regression analysis is least-squares regression, which focuses on the need to minimize errors (differences between observed and actual points due to randomness in behavior of other factors). By squaring errors, the possibility that distances above and below the line would cancel each other out is eliminated. By not squaring errors, that is, by not using least-squares regression, we could use several lines to minimize the sum of non-squared errors (Schroeder, Sjoquist, and Stephan 1986, 20). "Thus, if we draw vertical lines from each of the points to the least-squares line, and if we square these distances and add, the resulting sum will be less than a comparable sum of squares from any other possible straight line" (Blalock 1972, 371). According to Nachmias, "The least-squares method is a way for finding the one straight line that provides the best fit for an observed bivariate distribution" (Nachmias 1979, 112). Put more simply, the line will minimize the residual distance between the function line and any observed point on the scattergram (see figure A4.3). Simply averaging, as we did before, overlooks the possibility that several lines could fit if we ignore the need to minimize residual distances.

Let us now apply least-squares regression to extrapolate a trend from the data. Since the technique requires valid data, employing cocaine-use data, for example, might be problematic. Cocaine-use data are often based on a small sample to generalize to large populations. In one case, cocaine-use data based

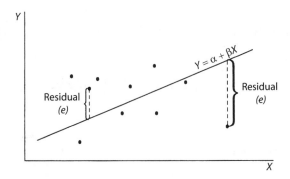

Figure A4.3 A Geometrical Interpretation of Residuals

on a sample of only four thousand to eight thousand users were used to project the behavior of about 12 million admitted users (Kerr 1986). Let us therefore use whiskey excise tax collected receipts from a small city for five years to project collections for the following fiscal year. This is more realistic and useful for our case exercise below, in that many commodity and excise tax projections must often be aggregated into one comprehensive sales tax revenue projection.

Based on the assumptions and formulas for least-squares regression, where a and b are calculated, it is possible to estimate the Y variable (here, revenues) in the observed time series, or in any projected time period. While we are demonstrating how this and other forecasting techniques can be performed with little more than hand calculators, in most cases policy analysts will use software that requires data entry according to the programs. The calculations to project whiskey tax collected receipts for FY 1997 are illustrated in table A4.2.

Table A4.2 Least-Squares Regression of Whiskey Tax Collected Receipts, 1992–96

(X) Fiscal year	(Y) Collections	Coded time value (X)	Cross-Products (Xy)	Squared (X2)
1992	$98,751	−2	−197.5	4
1993	95,075	−1	−95.0	1
1994	94,131	0	0	0
1995	97,794	+1	+97.7	1
1996	103,354	+2	+206.7	4
N = 5	$\Sigma Y = \$489,105$	$\Sigma x = 0$	$\Sigma (xY) = +11.9$	$\Sigma (x^2) = 10$

Calculating the trend values according to $Y = a + b(x)$, we now have enough data to calculate both a and b. The formula for a (termed "level in the central year" in table A4.3) =

$$\frac{\Sigma Y}{N} \text{ or } \frac{489.1}{5} = 97.8 \quad \text{and for } b = \frac{\Sigma(xY)}{\Sigma(x^2)} \text{ or } \frac{11.9}{10} = 1.19$$

With a and b, we can now compute the values for the trend line for each fiscal year in the past series and project the trend line for FY 1996 and 1997 (table A4.3).

We are now ready to graph the least-squares line (figure A4.4). This can be done by hand (!) or in Microsoft Excel. Instructions can be found on the Web page for *Essentials of Cost Accounting for Health Care Organizations* at: www.musc.edu/hap/costaccounting/exercise/chapter7/Information/ linearregression.htm (Finkler 2005, 120). Two questions arise on the utility of the least-squares method, now that we have our forecasts. First, how confident can we be in the forecast values? Second, how useful are linear methods such as least squares, when most ill-structured policy problems have data that are "often nonlinear, irregular, and discontinuous" (Dunn 1981, 160)? The first question we will attempt to answer by using a method known as "percentage calculation of trend." The second we will answer by changing the linear least-squares equation for secular trends to one suitable for nonlinear growth trends.

Table A4.3 Whiskey Tax Receipts Forecast for FY 1996 and FY 1997

	(a)	+	(x)		(b)	=	Y
Fiscal Year	Level in Central Year		Numbers from Central Year		Slope		Trend Line
1991	97.8	+	(−2	×	1.19)	=	95.4
1992	97.8		−1		1.19	=	96.6
1993	97.8		0		1.19	=	97.8
1994	97.8		+1		1.19	=	98.9
1995	97.8		+2		1.19	=	100.2
1996	97.8		+3		1.19	=	101.4
1997	97.8		+4		1.19	=	102.6

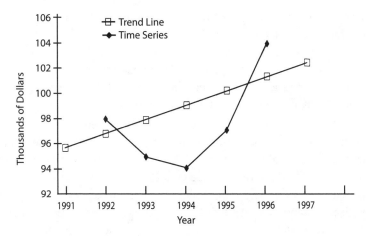

Figure A4.4   Plot of Least-Squares Line for Whiskey Tax Receipts

To measure our confidence in the forecasts just obtained, we need to see how far past receipts data varied from the trend line (table A4.4). According to Charles Liner (1983, 41): "Cyclical components will show up as high or low percentages of trend values during years of expansion and contraction. Major irregular components will show up as one-time deviations. . . . Confidence in the accuracy of the trend is gained if the percentages of trend values are close to 100%, and the assumption can be made that the variation in actual collections is due to the underlying trend. In contrast, if the percentage of trend values varies significantly above or below 100%, many other factors might account for the collections."

Table A4.4   Calculation of Percentage of Trend

Fiscal Year	Actual Collections	Calculated Trend Value	Percentage of Trend
1991	$98,751	95.4×100	103.5
1992	$95,075	96.6×100	98.5
1993	$94,131	97.8×100	96.2
1994	$97,794	98.9×100	98.9
1995	$103,354	100.2×100	103.1

The calculated percentages of trend values suggest that we should have a relatively high level of confidence in our forecasts, since the past has been largely unsullied by cycles or irregular (nonlinear) events. However, where past observations reveal a nonlinear pattern—"the amounts of change increase or decrease from one time period to the next" (Dunn 1981, 158)—other techniques must be used to forecast future time-series values.

It was noted that, in general, public expenditure trends are less irregular than revenues, but problems exist that make it difficult to fit a curve or line to revenue data. The small sample size and problems with internal accounting procedures were noted above. Revenue cycles may be nonlinear fluctuations— or, since segments of a cycle may be linear or curvilinear, revenue cycles may occur with persistence and regularity. Trends or cycles within time-series data can confuse cumulative receipts from year to year, and this can weaken forecasts. Growth or decline curves (S-shaped patterns) can occur between years, decades, or longer periods. If we use a linear regression equation for data that appears to be increasing (according to the scattergram), our forecast will be off. For example, if the data suggest a growth curve, such as the growing increases of $1,000 gaining compound annual interest, a linear equation would produce a forecast appropriate only for constant increases, such as putting in $100 each year on a $1,000 account.

CAUSAL FORECASTING

Policy analysts will typically have large portfolios of techniques that can be used for extrapolating linear and nonlinear trends from past data. Unfortunately, the techniques themselves can produce different results. For this reason, forecasting is part technical method and part judgment—an art and a science. Causal forecasting is one of the more complex and sophisticated techniques. A cautionary note on the word *cause*. Statistical techniques such as regressions do not prove causation; they merely associate variables from which inferences about causation can be made. A droll illustration of this is the link between mad cow disease and beef consumption. The former, through the latter, has led to human illness and death. Turning this around, Bolling (1997) notes that a single factor, human consumption of beef due to increased barbecuing, may be increasing the rate of cattle mortality.

Similarly, economic policymakers grapple with the causes of current account deficits in order to predict dangerous capital flight from a country. To predict changes in the current account (e.g., trade balance, flow of transfers, foreign income flows), the policymakers often refer to sophisticated economic models that tend to be both static and excessively hard to use. Many have found that such sophisticated models as the Mundell-Fleming framework, which includes multiple variables, are rarely used. In fact, economists find that good rules of thumb (e.g., don't worry about current account deficits under 5% of GDP) work just as well to predict when capital flight might occur (*The Economist* 1998).

Trend extrapolation has little to do with policy theory, other than in the exploratory phase of suggesting variables for possible correlation coefficients. Causal forecasting, by contrast, makes use of empirically testable laws or propositions that make predictions (Dunn 1981, 148). Causal modeling is useful for identifying determinants of public policies (Dunn 1994, 229). As opposed to subjective, inductive, or retroductive logic, this approach is deductive, reasoning from general statements and propositions to particular sets of data and claims. Deduction and induction are related logics in that deductive arguments are strengthened by empirical research, often turning the deductive statement into an inductive generalization. Deduction implies a model or systematic set of propositions that can be empirically affirmed or rejected.

Above we used the example of income and food purchases to illustrate regressions. On a more complex plane, the regression could serve as a test of economic pricing theory. Such a theory would postulate that the quantity of a good purchased by an individual depends on both their disposable income and the price of the product (Manning and Phelps 1979, cited in Schroeder, Sjoquist, and Stephan 1986, 29). An empirical test would verify or reject both the theoretical proposition and the statistical relationship. The purpose of using a model or theory is not simply elegance. According to William Klay (1983, 299), for example, "The advantage of building formal revenue-forecasting models is that it forces the participants to think clearly about the relationships and assumptions which underlie their forecasts." The inductive methods applied so far do not require thinking about underlying causal relationships—only whether the curve or line fits the data.

Here we will discuss two kinds of causal models for revenue forecasting:

- Single-equation regression models, which may have one or more explanatory variables.
- Multiple-equation models, which incorporate several regression equations (Klay 1983, 299). Multiple-equation models are useful for causal forecasting because "they more nearly approximate the real world situation in which several factors may influence and act on a dependent variable" (Toulmin and Wright 1983, 233).

Single-Equation Regression Models

An example of a single-equation multiple-regression model is that developed for forecasting sales tax receipts for the city of Mobile, Alabama (figure A4.5).

The regression equation on which this model is based ($Y = a + b_1X_1 + b_2X_2 + b_3X_3$) states that based on past relationships, the city's sales tax can be forecast by the sum of a constant ("a," or the y-intercept) and three products. Put another way, there are three multiple, independent causes of Y. The regression coefficients in multiple-regression models are interpreted as "partial slopes" (Nachmias 1979, 129). Partial slopes indicate how much change in Y is expected for each independent variable when all others are held statistically constant. Assuming no intercorrelation among independent variables, the regression coefficients will be the same as if the independent variables were regressed one at a time with Y. As in bivariate regression, the intercept and regression coefficients are estimated by the least-squares method (Nachmias 1979, 130). Since we are solving for three unknowns (a, b_1, and b_2), three equations must be solved by using the following least-squares formulas (which will also be used in the MARTA sales tax case for chapter 4):

$$b_1 = \frac{(\sum x_1 y)(\sum x_1^2) - (\sum x_1 x_2)}{(\sum x_1^2)(\sum x_2^2) - (\sum x_1)}$$

$$b_2 = \frac{(\sum x_1^2)(\sum x_2 y) - (\sum x_1 x_2)}{(\sum x_1^2)(\sum x_2^2) - (\sum x_1 x)}$$

$$a = \frac{\sum Y - b_1 \sum X_1 - b_2 \sum X_2}{N}$$

Once the regression values are obtained, various measures of goodness-of-fit should be calculated, as in the two-variable case. As noted, these measures enhance the utility of regression analysis by telling us the direction and strength of the relationships. More technically, goodness-of-fit tests indicate how closely the regression line minimizes the sum of the squared error term (Schroeder, Sjoquist, and Stephan 1986, 26). For example, the difference between the actual and estimated value is "the error, also called the residual," and "these are analyzed through computation of a statistic such as the 'standard error of the estimate' (or SEE) to develop judgment as to how well the model fits the past relationships" (Klay 1983, 300).

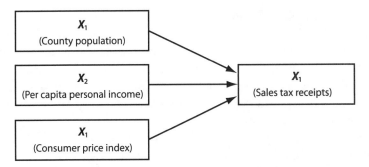

Figure A4.5 Single-Equation Multivariate Projection Model for Sales Tax Receipts

The SEE would be 0, for example, where the regression line fits actual observations and the residual sum of squares is minimized (Nachmias 1979, 116). The SEE must be first calculated to develop another measure of fit commonly used by policy analysts, called the "coefficient of determination," or R^2. This is a measure of the relative closeness of the fit between the regression line and the data points, which, as indicated by the R^2, is also the square of the correlation coefficient. In this case, R would be the multiple-correlation coefficient (Blalock 1972, 454). The R^2 measures variation in the dependent variable Y explicable by X_1, X_2, and X_3 as a percentage of total variation in Y (Nachmias 1979, 133).

It may be recalled that in the second edition of this book, we used a single-equation regression equation to forecast sales tax receipts (X_1—taxable sales, X_2—per capita income, and Y—sales tax receipts). The importance of the forecast was noted for policymaking: The Metropolitan Atlanta Rapid Transit Authority (MARTA) is required by its 1965 Act to cover 35% of its forecasted operating costs for the year. Since the 1% two-county sales tax is MARTA's major source of revenue (50–60%), if the forecast is inaccurate, it must act to cut service, cut staff, raise fares, or some combination of these options (Guess and Farnham 2000, 190).

Multiple-Equation Regression Models

Policy analysts can also forecast policy options by using causal models with several regression equations. Single-equation models assume that the value of each independent variable is determined independently of the dependent variable. So, for example, Mobile's sales tax receipts do not affect consumer personal income to the extent that they could contribute indirectly to the levels of receipts themselves. But in reality, "some of the independent variables might be causes of others" (Nachmias 1979, 145), meaning that we need to construct more complex multivariate models. Such models require equations for each dependent variable that include "disturbance terms" (E), allowing for the possibility that they are also independent variables (affected by exogenous forces, or variables not explicitly defined in the model). The equations are then solved together as simultaneous structural equations.

Structural equation models can be "recursive" or "nonrecursive." Recursive models assume that the direction of influence from any variable does not feed back to it, meaning that each variable is an independent cause but can be influenced by prior variables. "Path coefficients" are often used in recursive models to measure the magnitude of linkage between two or more variables (Nachmias 1979, 149). Path analysis is used in causal modeling "to identify those independent variables [e.g., income] that singly and in combination with other variables [e.g., political participation] determine changes in the dependent variable [e.g., welfare expenditures]" (Dunn 1994, 230). For example, Gary L. Tompkins (1975, cited in Nachmias 1979, 154–56) found that ethnicity exerts a strong direct effect on welfare expenditures, but that income level also has a strong indirect effect via ethnicity and party competition. To derive forecasts of the next year's welfare expenditures, it would be extremely useful to employ such a recursive model, assuming that it could be used post hoc to forecast past spending levels. However, in reality, variables often feed back into other variables. Welfare expenditures, for example, would also affect income, party competition, and even ethnicity (migration patterns). Nonrecursive models permit the use of both exogenous and endogenous variables via simultaneous equations (Nachmias 1979, 156).

The use of causal modeling may be more appropriate for advanced policy analysis, such as that conducted by the CBO or the Brookings Institution. Since few expenditure- or revenue-forecasting assignments at the state or local levels of government would ever require such time-consuming, expensive, and sophisticated techniques, we will end the discussion of these methods here and move on to a less complicated and more likely forecasting assignment.

Chapter 4, Appendix B
Annual Transit Passenger Trips, 1999–2013

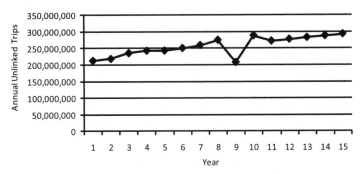

Year

* The authors wish to thank Erica Smith (MPP '09) for her excellent forecasting calculations, performed in Dr. Guess's Budget & Cost Analysis course at American University.

Year	Annual Unlinked Trips	% Change
1	212,620,976	
2	218,273,257	2.66
3	235,731,726	8.00
4	242,794,078	3.00
5	243,188,066	0.16
6	250,659,980	3.07
7	259,430,086	3.50
8	274,767,272	5.91
9	207,907,332	−24.33
10	288,039,725	38.54
11	271,966,748	−5.58
12	277,171,384	1.91
13	282,376,019	1.88
14	287,580,655	1.84
15	292,785,291	1.81

SUMMARY OUTPUT

Regression Statistics	
Multiple R	0.601154854
R-Square	0.361387159
Adjusted R-Square	0.281560553
Standard Error	22,217,991.92
Observations	10

ANOVA

	df	SS	MS	F	Significance F
Regression	1	2.23478E+15	2.23478E+15	4.527151792	0.066027909
Residual	8	3.94911E+15	4.93639E+14		
Total	9	6.18389E+15			

	Coefficients	Standard Error	t Stat	P-value	Lower 95%	Upper 95%	Lower 95.0%	Upper 95.0%
Intercept or b	214,715,752.00	15,177,777.95	14.15	0.00	179,715,733.30	249,715,770.70	179,715,733.30	249,715,770.70
X-Coefficient or slope	5,204,635.96	2,446,120.40	2.13	0.07	(436,127.80)	10,845,399.73	(436,127.80)	10,845,399.73

REFERENCES

Ammons, David N. 1991. *Administrative Analysis for Local Governments*. Athens: University of Georgia, Carl Vinson Institute of Government.

Axelrod, Donald. 1995. *Budgeting for Modern Government*. 2nd ed. New York: St. Martin's.

Benz, Greg. 2009. Phone interviews.

Bierce, Ambrose. 1911. *Devil's Dictionary*. New York: Doubleday.

Blalock, Hubert M. 1972. *Social Statistics*. New York: McGraw-Hill.

Bolling, Ruben. 1997. Tom and the Dancing Bug Presents: America's Consumption of Beef May Be Killing Cows. *Washington Post*, September 12.

Bradley, Katherine, Michael Harreld, and John Hill. 2009. The Pain and the Gain for D.C. Schools. *Washington Post*, October 18.

Brownlee, Shannon, and Jeanne Lenzer. 2009. Shots in the Dark. *The Atlantic Monthly*, November.

Chandler, Clay. 1997. Hitting the Jackpot on Capitol Hill. *Washington Post*, May 3.

Cleary, Paul. 1997. Red Face over $5 Billion Slip-Up in Deficit Figures. *Sydney Morning Herald*, February 27.

Committee for a Responsible Federal Budget (CRFB). 2009. *Red Ink Rising: A Call to Action to Stem Mounting Federal Debt*. Washington, DC: Pew-Peterson Foundation.

Congressional Budget Office (CBO). 1997. *An Analysis of the President's Budgetary Proposals for the Fiscal Year 1998*. Washington, DC: Congressional Budget Office.

Coplin, William D., and Michael K. O'Leary. 1976. Teaching Political Strategy Skills with 'The Prince.' *Policy Analysis* 2 (1): 144–60.

Daniels, Lee A. 1986. U.S. Oil Output Is Declining. *New York Times*, December 11.

Dunn, William N. 1981. *Public Policy Analysis: An Introduction*. Englewood Cliffs, NJ: Prentice Hall.

———. 1994. *Public Policy Analysis: An Introduction*. 2nd ed. Englewood Cliffs, NJ: Prentice Hall.

———. 2008. *Public Policy Analysis: An Introduction*. 4th ed. Englewood Cliffs, NJ: Pearson Prentice Hall.

The Economist. 1997a. Fujimori against El Niño. September 27.

———. 1997b. France's Budget: Circle Squared. September 27.

———. 1998. Figures to Fret About. July 11.

———. 1999a. Social Security Reform. March 13.

———. 1999b. Are Stadiums Good For You? March 13.

———. 2009a. A Good Man in Washington. June 20.

———. 2009b. Big Government Fights Back: Rescue Efforts. January 31.

———. 2009c. A Bubble in Beijing? October 10.

Finkler, Steven A. 2005. *Financial Management for Public, Health, and Not-for-Profit Organizations.* 2nd ed. Upper Saddle River, NJ: Pearson Prentice Hall.

———. 2009. *Financial Management for Public, Health, and Not-for-Profit Organizations.* 3rd ed. Upper Saddle River, NJ: Pearson Prentice Hall.

Fisher, Mark, 2008. As the Purple Line Creeps Closer, Hard Choices Loom. *Washington Post*, December 21.

Fisher, Ronald C. 2007. *State and Local Public Finance.* 3rd ed. Mason, OH: Thomson/South-Western.

Guess, George M., and Paul G. Farnham. 2000. *Cases in Public Policy Analysis.* 2nd ed. Washington, DC: Georgetown University Press.

Halsey, Ashley III. 2009. With Snow Removal, D.C. Area Gets What It Pays For. *Washington Post*, December 31.

Healey, Joseph F. 2005. *Statistics: A Tool for Social Research.* 7th ed. Belmont, CA: Thomson Wadsworth.

Hedderson, John. 1991. *SPSS/PC+ Made Simple.* Belmont, CA: Wadsworth.

Humbert, Thomas M. 1984. Understanding the Federal Deficit, Part 1: How Forecasters Get It Wrong. Backgrounder #328. Washington, DC: Heritage Foundation.

Kerr, Peter. 1986. Anatomy of an Issue: Drugs, the Evidence, the Reaction. *New York Times*, November 17.

Kiester, Edwin, Jr. 1997. Water Water Everywhere. *Smithsonian* 28 (5): 34–46.

Kilborn, Peter T. 1987. The Business Cycle Rolls Over and Plays Dead. *New York Times*, January 11.

Klay, William Earle. 1983. Revenue Forecasting: An Administrative Perspective. In *Handbook on Public Budgeting and Financial Management*, ed. Jack Rabin and Thomas D. Lynch, 287–317. New York: Marcel Dekker.

Lane, Earl. 1998. Crisis Forecasting Offers New Ways to Predict Natural or Human Events. *Washington Post*, January 2.

Liner, Charles D. 1983. Projecting Local Government Revenue. In *Budget Management: A Reader in Local Government Financial Management*, ed. Jack Rabin, W. Bartley Hildreth, and Gerald J. Miller, 83–92. Athens: University of Georgia Press.

Litman, Todd. 2004. Transit Price Elasticities and Cross Elasticities. *Journal of Public Transportation* 7 (2): 37–58.

Manning, Willard G., Jr., and Charles E. Phelps. 1979. The Demand for Dental Care. *Bell Journal of Economics* 10 (2): 503–25.

Maryland Transit Administration (MTA). 2008. *Purple Line: Public Outreach and Coordination Technical Report.* Baltimore: MTA.

———. 2009. Re-Connecting Washington's Streetcar Suburbs. PowerPoint Slides. Baltimore: MTA.

McMaster, James. 1991. *Urban Financial Management: A Training Manual.* Washington, DC: World Bank.

Michel, R. Gregory. 2001. *Decision Tools for Budgetary Analysis.* Chicago: Government Finance Officers Association.

Mikesell, John L. 2007. *Fiscal Administration: Analysis and Applications for the Public Sector.* Belmont, CA: Thomson/Wadsworth.

Montgomery, Lori. 2009. In Health Debate, Those Numbers Are Just Numbers. *Washington Post*, October 19.

Nachmias, David. 1979. *Public Policy Evaluation: Approaches and Methods.* New York: St. Martin's.

National Institute on Drug Abuse. 1997. *Annual Trends in Cocaine-Related Episodes.* Washington, DC: National Institute on Drug Abuse.

Nelson, Ray D., and Gary C. Cornia. 1997. Monitoring Single-Source Revenue Funds throughout the Budgeting Process. *Public Budgeting and Finance* 17 (2): 37–57.

New York Times. 1986. Two Syracuse Teachers Rank Political Climate in 85 Nations. December 7.

Niskanen, William A. 1971. *Bureaucracy and Representative Government.* Chicago: Aldine.

Rabin, Jack, W. Bartley Hildreth, and Gerald J. Miller. 1983. *Workbook and Data Sourcebook.* Athens: University of Georgia.

Roughton, Bert. 1987. MARTA Fare to Be $0.75 This Sunday. *Atlanta Constitution*, June 23.

Samuelson, Robert J. 1998. The Way the World Works. *Washington Post*, January 7.

———. 2009. Economists Out to Lunch. *Washington Post*, July 6.

Schroeder, Larry D. 1984. Multi-Year Forecasting in San Antonio. In *Casebook in Public Budgeting and Financial Management*, ed. Carol W. Lewis and A. Grayson Walker, 268–300. Englewood Cliffs, NJ: Prentice Hall.

Schroeder, Larry D., David L. Sjoquist, and Paula E. Stephan. 1986. Understanding Regression Analysis: An Introductory Guide. Sage Paper no. 57. Beverly Hills: Sage.

Silk, Leonard. 1986. A Season of Cassandras. *New York Times*, December 10.

Simon, Julian L. 1978. *Basic Research Methods in Social Sciences: The Art of Empirical Investigation.* 2nd ed. New York: Random House.

Stein, Rob. 2009. Top Officials Defend Flu Vaccination Campaign. *Washington Post*, October 29.

Stone, Deborah A. 1988. *Policy Paradox and Political Reason.* Boston: Scott, Foresman.

Suplee, Curt. 1997. Most Serious Youth Asthma Cases Linked to Roaches, Study Finds. *Washington Post*, May 8.

Taleb, Nassim Nicholas. 2007. *The Black Swan: The Impact of the Highly Improbable.* New York: Random House.

Tompkins, Gary L. 1975. A Causal Model of State Welfare Expenditures. *Journal of Politics* 37 (2): 392–416.

Toulmin, Llewellyn M., and Glendal E. Wright. 1983. Expenditure Forecasting. In *Handbook on Public Budgeting and Financial Management,* ed. Jack Rabin and Thomas Lynch, 208–87. New York: Marcel Dekker.

Train, Kenneth E. 2009. *Discrete Choice Methods with Simulation.* Cambridge: Cambridge University Press.

Turque, Bill. 2009. Rhee Has Asked How to Regain Teachers' Trust Principals Say. *Washington Post,* October 28.

Tyson, Ann Scott. 2010. Metro Board Expected to Cut Back Service. *Washington Post,* January 7.

Ward, Marvin E. 2009. Interviews at American University, Washington, DC.

Washington Post. 2009. School Friction. October 11.

Weir, Kytja. 2009. Metro Proposes Cuts to Service, Layoffs to Close $40m Budget Gap. *Washington Examiner,* December 18.

Wildavsky, Aaron. 1979. *Speaking Truth to Power: The Art and Craft of Policy Analysis.* Boston: Little, Brown.

———. 1984. *The Politics of the Budgetary Process.* 4th ed. Boston: Little, Brown.

Young, Eoin, and Lisa Quinn. 2002. *Writing Effective Policy Papers: A Guide for Policy Advisers in Central and Eastern Europe.* Budapest: Local Government and Public Service Reform Initiative of the Open Society Institute.

NOTE

The authors wish to thank Marvin Ward for his technical inputs on forecasting with logit models. As an engineer (BS, Carnegie-Mellon) and PhD student in public affairs at American University, he has been an invaluable resource.

Chapter 5

Pricing and Public Policy:
The Case of Cigarette Taxes

In this chapter we combine the issues of problem definition and structuring discussed in chapter 2 with the empirical techniques covered in chapter 4 in order to analyze the role of pricing as a public policy tool. The specific case is the use of cigarette taxes to influence cigarette prices and smoking behavior. We are thus moving from the diagnostic phase of public policy analysis to the analytic phase. Public decision makers and regulatory agencies are often concerned with issues of how prices are set in the private sector. In addition, changing these prices through public-sector subsidies and taxation programs is a key element of many public policies. The goal of many public-sector programs is to modify the prices established in the private sector for the purpose of influencing individual behavior. Because economics is the primary discipline that focuses on analyzing the role of prices in the economy, this chapter will draw much more substantially on economic analysis than the previous chapters.

The issues raised in this chapter will also serve as a background for the following two chapters, which discuss the economic program-evaluation tools of cost-effectiveness analysis and cost-benefit analysis. These are two major analytic tools that are used to help make resource-allocation decisions about funding different public-sector programs. The quantitative techniques used in all three of these chapters will draw on microeconomic analysis of markets and their impact on consumers and producers in the economy. However, the issues raised in the economic analysis are also related to the political environment, because both of these are crucial elements of overall public policy analysis.

Smoking is generally considered to be a major public policy problem in the United States. Since 1964, the surgeon general of the US Public Health Service has repeatedly listed cigarette smoking as one of the country's most significant sources of death and disease. An estimated 19.8% of US adults (43.4 million persons) were current smokers in 2007. Of these persons, 77.8% (33.8 million) smoked every day, while 22.2% (9.6 million) smoked some days.

The prevalence of smoking was highest among young and middle-aged adults (22.2% of persons aged 18–24 years old; 22.8% of persons aged 25–44 years old) and lowest among those 65 years and older (8.3%) (CDC 2008a). During the period 2000–2004, an estimated 443,000 persons in the United States (269,000 males and 174,000 females) died prematurely each year as a result of smoking or exposure to secondhand smoke. The three major causes of smoking-attributable deaths were lung cancer, ischemic heart disease, and chronic obstructive pulmonary disease. During this same period, smoking accounted for an annual estimated 3.1 million years of potential life lost for males and 2.0 million years for females. Average annual smoking-attributable productivity losses were $96.8 billion, while annual smoking-attributable health care expenditures were $96 billion (CDC 2008b).

A variety of public policies have been used to discourage smoking in the population, including moral suasion from the publicity surrounding the various surgeon generals' reports on smoking produced over the past twenty-five years; restrictions on cigarette advertising; policies limiting how cigarettes can be sold, such as restrictions on the use and location of vending machines; and cigarette taxation that changes the price, and therefore affects the consumption, of cigarettes. Public policy analysis focuses on which of these policies are most effective in reducing cigarette consumption, particularly in light of the costs of implementing the policies. All of these policies can be described in economic terms as being designed to affect either the demand for or the supply of cigarettes and, thus, the amount consumed. However, only taxation operates by changing the price of cigarettes. The other policies operate by changing individuals' attitudes toward smoking, their knowledge about cigarettes, or the availability of the product. Thus, a comparison of the policies involves evaluating the role of price compared to other influences on human behavior. Economic analysis provides particular insights into the role of pricing and human behavior.

This chapter explores how the prices of goods and services affect individual behavior and how they can be useful tools for public policy. The case study focuses on cigarette taxes as a public policy to reduce the rate of smoking and to raise revenues for other public-sector programs. These goals are intertwined and may sometimes be in conflict. In the United States, these policies have been impacted by the 1998 Master Settlement Agreement (MSA) between state governments and the major tobacco companies (Schroeder 2004).

In this chapter we analyze the reasons why cigarette taxes may be such a potent weapon for reducing cigarette consumption and for preventing individuals from becoming smokers. We first explore the basic role of prices in a market economy and how they influence behavior through the forces of supply and demand, and then describe the price elasticity of demand, the means by which economists quantify the effect of prices on consumer behavior. Drawing on the statistical issues presented in chapter 4, we will discuss the empirical methods for estimating price elasticities and for separating the influence of price from that of all other factors on cigarette consumption. We then present the case and summarize the issues that relate to these theoretical concepts. We discuss the results of the major empirical studies that have estimated the response of teenagers and adults to changes in cigarette prices and taxes, and we present recent studies that measure other responses to increased cigarette taxation, which may partially offset the effect of reduced consumption. The chapter ends with a discussion of how the technical information from economic analyses influences the policy process.

PRICES AND MARKETS: THE ROLE OF DEMAND AND SUPPLY

Pricing is the key element in an economic system based on the marketplace. Prices help determine the answers to the fundamental resource-allocation questions that all economies face: What goods and services should be produced from the vast range of available inputs? How should these goods and services be produced, if more than one method of production is feasible? How should the output of the economy be distributed among the individuals in the society? In a market economy, those goods and services that are the most profitable, or for which there is the largest difference between their price and the costs of production, tend to be produced. Yet when profits are earned in particular industries, other firms are attracted to produce the same or similar goods, thus causing prices to decrease. If more than one method of production is feasible for a particular good or service, firms in a market economy have an incentive to find the least costly means of production. This strategy involves using larger quantities of inputs, for which prices are lower. The prices received by the owners of the factors of production (e.g., labor, land, capital equipment) help determine the distribution of income among the individuals in a society and thus influence the ability of these persons to purchase market-produced goods and services. This is the essence of the pricing system in a market economy.

Public policies often attempt to influence either the process by which market prices are established or the final prices themselves. For example, policy-makers may consider some prices, such as those for agricultural products or the wages paid for low-skill jobs, too low. Thus, legislators have enacted both farm price support and minimum wage programs. When prices are thought to be too high, various forms of price controls have been implemented, including the rent controls passed by various city councils and the general controls temporarily enacted under the Nixon administration's Economic Stabilization Program in the early 1970s. Sometimes particular goods and services are subsidized through the use of food stamps, housing vouchers, or the federal Medicare program. This government intervention into the pricing system is undertaken for reasons related to income distribution or equity issues. The policy concern is whether certain groups of people have the necessary resources to purchase particular goods and services.

Public policy can also influence prices through the regulation of business activity. Some of this regulation occurs because of concern over the acquisition of market or monopoly power by firms, which allows companies to charge prices that are substantially higher than the costs of production. The Antitrust Division of the US Department of Justice analyzes the behavior of different firms and industries to determine whether the general public is being harmed by the firms' pricing policies and other strategies. In the case of regulated electric or gas utilities, a government commission or agency explicitly determines how prices are set in relation to costs. Some of this regulation relates to problems of income distribution. Other utility-price-setting policies focus on the efficient use of gas or electricity when there is a peak-load problem. In these cases, the demand for and the cost of producing gas or electricity varies substantially by time of day or season of the year. Efficient use of these resources requires setting higher prices during the peak-load periods. Problems with the utility regulatory process, however, have led to a much greater use of competitive markets in the past decade (Viscusi, Harrington, and Vernon 2005).

Other regulation arises because businesses do not always consider the full costs of production when determining prices. Pollution occurs when companies use the air or water for waste disposal without recognizing that they may be imposing costs on other groups of individuals. The prices of these companies' products may not reflect these environmental costs. Environmental policy is concerned with correcting this problem through either taxation, regulation, or, more recently, the use of markets for trading allowances or the rights to pollute (Keohane 2009).

Finally, governments provide certain services (i.e., public goods such as national defense) through a political process because they will not be provided in the marketplace. Markets fail to provide these goods because people cannot be excluded from consuming them once they are provided; therefore, a market price cannot be charged for these goods. In these cases, the government must explicitly decide what the services are worth to the citizens of the country and what tax price should be imposed to cover the costs of production. Any form of taxation will cause a further burden on consumers and influence the prices of goods and services established in the private marketplace (Rosen and Gayer 2010).

In a competitive marketplace with many buyers and sellers, prices are established through the forces of demand and supply. We will briefly review these basic economic concepts, and then focus in more detail on demand, which is the most relevant concept for analyzing the public policy issues in this case. Demand is a product of the variables affecting the behavior of the consumers of a good or service, while supply reflects producer behavior. Analysis of both of these concepts uses the fundamental economic approach of examining the relationship between two variables while holding everything else constant.

Although *demand* and *supply* are used in everyday language, these terms have very precise meanings in economics. Demand is a functional relationship between the price of a good and the quantity desired of the good, all else held constant. (The Latin phrase *ceteris paribus* is often used in place of "all else held constant.") A demand function shows, either symbolically or mathematically, all the variables that influence the demand for a particular product. It can be represented as follows:

$$Q_{XD} = f(P_X, T, I, P_Y, P_Z, \ldots) \qquad \text{(Eq.5-1)}$$

where

Q_{XD} = quantity demanded of good X,

P_X = price of good X,

T = variables representing an individual's tastes and preferences,

I = income,

P_Y, P_Z = prices of goods Y and Z, which are related in consumption to good X.

Equation 5-1 indicates that the quantity demanded of good X is a function of the variables inside the parentheses. An ellipsis is placed after the last variable to signify that many other variables may also influence the demand for a specific product. These may include variables under the producer's control, such as the size of the advertising budget, or variables not under anyone's control, such as the weather. Every consumer has a demand function for a particular product. We can also create a market demand function for a good that shows the quantity demanded by all consumers in the market at any given price.

Equation 5-1 shows the typical variables included in a demand function. Socioeconomic variables such as age, sex, race, and level of education are often used to represent an individual's tastes and preferences for a particular good. An individual's income also affects demand—the concept of demand incorporates both an individual's willingness and ability to pay for the good. If the demand for a good varies directly with income, that good is called a normal good. If the demand varies inversely with income, the good is termed an inferior good. There are two major categories of other goods whose prices influence the demand for the given good: substitute and complementary goods. If the price of a substitute good increases, the demand for the given good will increase. If the price of a complementary good increases, the demand for the given good will decrease.

Demand is a functional relationship between alternative prices and the quantities demanded at those prices. This is most easily seen when drawing a demand curve for a particular product, as in figure 5.1.

Demand curves are generally downward sloping, showing an inverse relationship between the price of a good and the quantity demanded at that price, ceteris paribus. Thus, when the price falls from P_1 to P_2, the quantity demanded is expected to increase from Q_1 to Q_2, if nothing else changes. Likewise, an increase in the price of the good results in a decrease in quantity demanded. The movement between points A and B along the given demand curve in figure 5.1 is called a change in quantity demanded. It results from a change in the price of the good, all else held constant. It is also possible for the entire demand curve to shift, which results when the values of one or more of the other variables held constant in defining a given demand curve changes. For example, if consumers' incomes increase, the demand curve for the good generally shifts outward or to the right, assuming that individuals purchase more of the good if their incomes increase. This shifting of the entire demand curve represents a change in demand.

The demand curve in figure 5.1 has been drawn as a straight line, representing a linear demand function. This is used both for simplification and because it is often believed that this form of a demand function best represents individuals' behavior. Not all demand functions are linear. The implications of the particular form of demand function will be discussed in greater detail below, in the context of our presentation of the price elasticity of demand, an important concept for analyzing the issues in this chapter's case study.

A supply function for a product is defined in a similar manner. Supply is the relationship between the price of a good and the quantity supplied, all else held constant. A supply function is shown as follows:

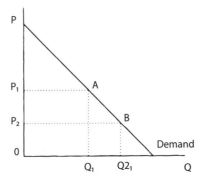

Figure 5.1 The Demand Curve for a Product

$$Q_{XS} = f(P_X, TX, P_1, P_A, P_B, \ldots),\qquad\qquad\text{(Eq.5-2)}$$

where

Q_{XS} = quantity supplied of good X,

P_X = price of good X,

TX = technology,

P_1 = prices of the inputs of production,

P_A, P_B = prices of goods A and B, which are related in production to good X.

As with the demand function, we can distinguish between the supply function for an individual producer and the supply function for all producers in a given market.

Equation 5-2 shows the variables typically included in a supply function. The state of technology is included because it determines how the good is actually produced and affects the costs of production. Input prices are the prices of all of the factors of production—labor, capital, land, and raw materials—used to produce the given product. These input prices will affect the costs of production and, therefore, the prices at which producers are willing to supply different amounts of output. The prices of other goods related in production are also included in a supply function. Supply curves generally slope upward, showing a positive relationship between the price of the product and the quantity producers are willing to supply. A higher price typically gives producers an incentive to increase the quantity supplied.

In a competitive market, it is the interaction of demand and supply that determines the equilibrium price, the price that will actually exist in the market

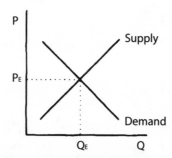

Figure 5.2 Demand, Supply and Equilibrium

or toward which the market moves. Figure 5.2 shows the equilibrium price for good X.

The equilibrium price is the price at which the quantity demanded of good X by consumers just equals the quantity producers are willing to supply. At any other price, there will be an imbalance between quantity demanded and supplied. Forces will be set in motion to push the price back toward equilibrium.

Reactions of both consumers and producers to changes in prices, as well as changes in the other variables in the demand and supply functions, cause changes in the equilibrium quantities of different goods. Thus, the quantity and price of cigarettes can be influenced by shifts on either the demand or the supply side of the market.

If the public policy goal is to reduce cigarette smoking among adults and teenagers, the relevant policy questions include: Will supply- or demand-side variables have the greatest impact on cigarette consumption? What is the role of cigarette price compared to the other variables in the demand and supply functions in influencing cigarette consumption? Will increased cigarette prices cause other behavioral changes that influence the overall public policy goals? To answer these questions, we need to develop a quantitative measure, elasticity, to assess the responsiveness of cigarette consumption to changes in prices and the other variables, and we need to determine how to disentangle the effects of all the variables influencing the consumption of cigarettes.

DEMAND ELASTICITIES

An elasticity is a quantitative measure of the responsiveness of the quantity demanded of a particular product to a change in one of the variables included in the demand function for that product. Thus, elasticity can be calculated with regard to product price, consumer income, the prices of other goods and services, advertising budgets, education levels, or changes in the weather, depending on which of these variables are in the demand function. The important point is that elasticity measures this responsiveness in terms of percentage changes in both variables. Thus, elasticity is a ratio of two percentage changes: the percentage change in quantity demanded relative to the percentage change in the other variable. Percentage changes are used so that comparisons can be made among elasticities for different variables and products.

The elasticity that is most analyzed in economics and that is most important for this case is the price elasticity of demand. The price elasticity is defined as the percentage change in the quantity demanded of a given good, X, relative to a percentage change in its price. It is shown as follows:

$$e_p = (\%\Delta Q_x) / (\%\Delta P_x), \qquad (Eq.5\text{-}3)$$
$$e_p = (\Delta Q_x / Q_x) / (\Delta P_x / P_x) = (\Delta Q_x / \Delta P_x)(P_x / Q_x),$$

where

e_p = price elasticity of demand,

Δ = the absolute change in the variable: $(Q_2 - Q_1)$ or $(P_2 - P_1)$,

Q_x = the quantity demanded of good X,

P_x = the price of good X.

A percentage change in a variable is the ratio of the absolute change to a base value of the variable. The price elasticity of demand is illustrated as the movement from point A to point B in figure 5.1.

Economists and policy analysts are interested in the size of various price elasticities to determine how responsive the quantity demanded is to a change in the price of a product, such as cigarettes. Since the calculated value of all price elasticities for downward-sloping demand curves will be negative (given the inverse relationship between price and quantity demanded), it is customary to drop the negative sign and examine the absolute value ($|e_p|$) of the number. This leads to the definitions shown in table 5.1.

As shown in table 5.1, demand is elastic if the number is greater than 1 in absolute value and inelastic if the number is less than 1. Elastic demand implies a larger consumer responsiveness to changes in prices than does inelastic demand. The fourth column of table 5.1 shows the relationship between price elasticity, changes in prices, and total revenue (which is defined as price times quantity). Total revenue to a producer also equals the total expenditure on the good by consumers. If demand is elastic, higher prices result in lower total revenue, while lower prices result in higher total revenue. This results from the

Table 5.1   Values of Price Elasticity of Demand

Value of Elasticity	Elasticity Definition	Relationship among Variables	Impact on Total Revenue
$\|e_p\| > 1$	Elastic demand	$\%\Delta Q_x > \%\Delta P_x$	Price increase results in lower total revenue. Price decrease results in higher total revenue.
$\|e_p\| < 1$	Inelastic demand	$\%\Delta Q_x < \%\Delta P_x$	Price increase results in higher total revenue. Price decrease results in lower total revenue.
$\|e_p\| = 1$	Unit-elastic demand, or unitary elasticity	$\%\Delta Q_x = \%\Delta P_x$	Price increase or decrease has no impact on total revenue.

fact that the percentage change in quantity is greater than the percentage change in price. If the price increases, the decrease in units sold at the higher price is enough so that total revenue actually decreases. The opposite holds for inelastic demand: In this case, if the price increases, the total revenue increases also because the percentage change in quantity is less than the percentage change in price. If the price increases, enough units are still sold at the higher price to cause total revenue to increase. If demand is unit-elastic, changes in price have no impact on total revenue because the percentage change in price is exactly equal to the percentage change in quantity.

The price elasticity of demand is an extremely important concept for producers, since it tells producers what will happen to revenues if the price of the product is changed. It can also help firms develop a pricing strategy that will maximize their profits. For example, the price elasticity of demand for airline travel for pleasure travelers is around −1.9, while that for business travelers is around −0.8 (Morrison 1998). The airlines typically charge business travelers much higher fares because they know that these travelers are not very price sensitive. The number of trips that business travelers take will not decrease substantially if fares increase. Price elasticity of demand is important in the public sector, such as when a transit agency needs to know the impact of a fare increase on its revenues. Price elasticity is also a key concept for this chapter's case: Estimates of the price elasticity of demand for cigarettes will tell a policy analyst how sensitive individuals are to changes in cigarette prices and whether elasticities differ between teenagers and adults. Price elasticity estimates can also be used to calculate the tax revenue flowing to the government from increased cigarette taxes.

Although price elasticities are of great importance, economists also want to know the size of the other elasticities in the demand function for a given product. Two other commonly used elasticities are the income elasticity and the cross elasticity of demand. These are shown in table 5.2.

The income elasticity of demand shows how consumers change the quantity demanded of a particular product in response to changes in income, all else held constant. If an increase in income results in an increase in the quantity demanded or vice versa (a positive income elasticity of demand), the good is called a normal good. If an increase in income results in a decrease in quantity demanded or vice versa (a negative income elasticity), the good is termed an inferior good. Thus, the sign of the income elasticity of demand is important, as well as the size of the elasticity, which measures the responsiveness of the demand to income changes.

Table 5.2   Other Demand Functions

Elasticity Name	Elasticity Definition	Elasticity Value	Impact on Demand
Income elasticity: e_1	$(\%\Delta Q_x) / (\%\Delta I)$	$E_1 > 0$ Normal good	Increase in income results in increase in quantity demanded, and vice versa.
		$E_1 < 0$ Inferior good	Increase in income results in decrease in quantity demanded, and vice versa.
Cross elasticity: e_C	$(\%\Delta Q_x) / (\%\Delta P_Y)$	$e_C > 0$ Substitute good	Increase in the price of good Y results in increase in the quantity demanded of good X.
		$e_C < 0$ Complementary good	Increase in the price of good Y results in decrease in the quantity demanded of good X.

The cross elasticity of demand measures how the demand for one good, X, varies with changes in the price of another good, Y. Two goods with a positive cross elasticity of demand are said to be substitute goods. An increase in the price of good Y will cause consumers to demand more of good X, because they are substituting good X for good Y. If two goods have a negative cross elasticity of demand, they are called complementary goods. An increase in the price of good Y will result in a decrease in the quantity demanded of good X if the two goods are used together or are complements.

All the discussion in this section of the chapter is conceptual. The important thing for policy analysis is to know how to determine the actual signs and sizes of the relevant elasticities for different variables in a demand function. This is necessary for analyzing the usefulness of cigarettes taxes compared with other policies for reducing cigarette consumption. Before discussing the case, we will briefly explain how economists and policy analysts empirically estimate demand functions and the various elasticities of demand for different products. This will help us to evaluate the empirical studies of the factors influencing cigarette consumption by teenagers and adults.

ESTIMATING DEMAND FUNCTIONS

In chapter 4 we examined various statistical and econometric techniques that can be used to forecast the future values of policy variables. Many of these same techniques are appropriate for examining the factors that affect cigarette consumption and determining whether these factors differ between teenagers and adults. The analysis here falls under the heading of causal forecasting in chapter 4 because the empirical analysis is based on a deductive model of behavior (i.e., the economic theory of demand). This analysis differs from the use of correlation and regression analysis simply to explore relationships among variables, which was also discussed in chapter 4. The goal of this analysis is to estimate the magnitude of the effect (the elasticity) of each policy-relevant variable on cigarette consumption, while holding constant the effects of all other relevant variables. In the physical sciences, many of these types of relationships can be tested experimentally in the laboratory. However, an experimental approach is not possible for most of the policy questions addressed in this book. Experiments in the social and policy sciences can be very expensive, time consuming, and complex to perform. Although the use of experimental approaches has been increasing, most research relies on econometric techniques, such as multiple-regression analysis, to examine the relationship between two variables while statistically holding constant the effect of all other variables.

Equation 5-1 above gave a generalized form of a demand function for a particular good. To obtain information useful for the policy question of cigarette taxes, we must estimate a specific demand function for cigarettes. This requires specifying the form of the demand function to be estimated, the variables to be included in the estimation process, and the data to be used in the analysis.

Economists typically estimate two major forms of demand functions: the linear function and the log-linear function. These functions are used because they are believed to appropriately model individuals' behavior and because they permit a relatively easy calculation of the relevant elasticities.

A simple linear demand function is shown in equation 5-4:

$$Q_X = a + bP_X + cI + dP_R + , \qquad (Eq.5-4)$$

where

Q_X = quantity demanded of good X,

P_X = price of good X,

I = consumer income,

P_R = price of a related good (substitute or complement),

a = constant term,

b, c, d = estimated coefficients,

, = an error term.

The economist or policy analyst collects data on the variables to be included in the demand function. In this simple case, the economist or analyst would need data on the price of good X, the quantity of good X demanded, consumer income, and the price of a good related in consumption to good X. These data could represent either the behavior of individuals across time (time-series data) or the differences among individuals at a point in time (cross-section data). More recent studies also use panel data sets, which are based on the same cross-section data observed at several points in time. There needs to be a large enough sample of observations and sufficient variation among the observations to permit estimation of the desired relationships. The economist then uses a multiple-regression analysis program in one of the standard statistical software packages to estimate the coefficients (b, c, and d) that best fit the sample data. Details of this estimation process were given in chapter 4.

In the linear model, these coefficients represent the change in the quantity demanded of good X resulting from a one-unit change in the independent variable (price of good X, consumer income, or price of the related good), ceteris paribus. Multiple-regression analysis coefficients show the effect of each independent variable while statistically holding constant the effects of the other variables that are hypothesized to affect the quantity demanded of good X. Thus, in equation 5-4, the estimated coefficient, b, is equal to $(\Delta Q_x / \Delta P_X)$, holding constant the effects of consumer income and the price of good R. Referring back to equation 5-3, this term is part of what is needed to calculate the price elasticity of demand. The coefficient, b, can then be multiplied by a specific value of $(P?_x / Q?_x)$ to determine the price elasticity at a specific point on the demand curve. The other estimated coefficients, c and d, can be used to calculate the income and cross elasticity of demand in a similar manner.

The linear demand function (equation 5-4) implies both that there is some maximum price that drives the quantity of the product demanded by consumers back to zero, and that there is some maximum quantity of the product that people demand at a zero price. The price elasticity of demand also changes at different prices along a linear demand curve, since $(Q_x /)P_x)$ is constant, but (P_x / Q_x) varies along the curve. These outcomes may not always adequately represent the behavior of different groups of individuals.

It is often hypothesized that a nonlinear demand function of the following form better represents individuals' behavior:

$$Q_x = (a) \, (P?_x{}^b) \, (I^c) \, (P_R{}^d)€,\qquad\qquad (Eq.5\text{-}5)$$

where the variables are defined as above. This function is often called a log-linear demand function because it can be transformed into a linear function by taking the logarithms of all the variables in the equation. This function is also called a constant-elasticity demand function. It can be shown that the elasticities are constant for all values of the input variables and the elasticities are represented by the exponents b, c, and d, in equation 5-5. Thus, the price, income, and cross elasticities can be directly read from the statistical results if this type of function is used in the estimation process. No further calculation is needed to determine the elasticities.

Demand functions for actual products are obviously much more complex than the simple examples presented in equations 5-4 and 5-5, and are estimated with advanced econometric techniques. However, the estimation process and the choice of functional form are similar to what has been presented here. The policy analyst must decide which variables to include in the analysis. Various types of statistical problems can arise if relevant variables are excluded from the analysis or if irrelevant variables are included. The choice of variables is derived from economic theory, real-world experience, the policy problem under consideration, and common sense. Variable choice can also be influenced by data availability; in many cases, analysts would like to include certain variables, but a consistent set of observations for all individuals included in the analysis may not be available. Analysts may also have to use other variables as proxies for the variables of greatest interest.

Every multiple-regression analysis study is also influenced by the sample of data—time-series, cross-sectional, or panel—that is used. The policy analyst wants to estimate behavioral relationships that can be generalized beyond the sample of observations included in the analysis. Yet large-scale data collection can be very expensive and time consuming. Thus, the analyst has to be concerned that the estimated relationships may only hold for the sample of data analyzed, and not the larger population. The analyst tests hypotheses to determine how much confidence can be placed in the results of a particular analysis and whether these results can be generalized to a larger population. An analyst usually focuses on whether an estimated coefficient from the regression analysis is statistically significant, that is, whether it is statistically different from zero. If it is, then the independent variable actually has an influence on the dependent variable in the larger population. The statistical results are then believed to be not simply a function of the data used in the given analysis. Standard tests for statistical significance can be found in any econometrics textbook (Greene 2008). These issues were also discussed in chapter 4.

Data for demand estimation are often drawn from large-scale surveys undertaken by the US federal government, universities, or nonprofit groups. Not every relevant variable for a given analysis may be included in a single data source, so the results of various surveys may need to be combined. Some data sources may have better information on economic variables, while others may have more data on personal characteristics of the individuals included in the analysis.

Although the details of demand estimation are very technical and can be found in standard sources, the policy analyst is often more concerned with interpreting the results of these analyses than with performing them. Variations in the functional form of the estimating equations, the variables included, and the data sets employed can all influence and cause differences in the results of various statistical analyses of the same problem. Thus, researchers, policy-makers, and advocates can criticize and debate the results of any empirical study.

The policy issues of cigarette taxation are discussed in the chapter 5 case study of cigarette demand and the estimates of the impact of taxes on that demand. The study is taken from a *Wall Street Journal* article by Betsy McKay (2009).

Chapter 5 Case Study

Cigarette Tax Clouds Boosts among States

By Betsy McKay, *Wall Street Journal*

The hefty increase in the federal cigarette tax to help fund a children's health-insurance program has buoyed tobacco foes, who say it will breathe new life into efforts to curb smoking. But last week's move by Washington could also complicate efforts around the US to boost state cigarette taxes.

Officials in at least 16 states are weighing proposals for significant cigarette-tax increases to fill gaping budget holes or fund programs, calling in some cases for levies more than four times as high as current amounts. The sharply increased federal levy could alter their calculus, because higher cigarette prices are likely to decrease sales, eroding the projected tax revenue.

Politicians frequently turn to so-called sin taxes—targeting liquor, tobacco, and gambling—in tough economic times, and states are facing budget gaps totaling $47.4 billion for the 2009 fiscal year, according to the National Conference of State Legislatures. While some states are also weighing increases on alcohol taxes, tobacco taxes are particularly popular thanks to growing concern about ballooning health-care costs. . . .

The federal tax will rise in April to $1.01 a pack from 39 cents today. The average state tax, meanwhile, is $1.19 a pack, and the average price of a pack of cigarettes is $4.32, excluding local taxes and the new federal tax, according to the national Campaign for Tobacco-Free Kids.

Jacking up cigarette prices is one of the best means of curbing smoking, particularly among price-sensitive teens, according to public-health experts. . . .

A 10% increase in the price of a pack reduces consumption by about 4%, said Frank J. Chaloupka, an economist and tobacco-tax expert at the University of Illinois at Chicago. Although higher prices reduce the number of cigarettes smoked, tobacco-tax revenue has still risen in nearly every state that imposed significant tax increases, he said. The new federal tax could motivate states to raise their own taxes to help offset the expected drop in cigarette sales, Mr. Chaloupka said.

But back-to-back federal and state tax increases could significantly drive down revenue from sales, as well as foster counterfeit trade, warns David Sutton, a spokesman for Altria Group Inc., the country's largest cigarette maker.

After years of opposing an increase in Mississippi's tax of 18 cents a pack, Gov. Haley Barbour late last year proposed raising it 24 cents a pack on cigarettes sold by companies that settled a lawsuit with the state in 1997, and 43 cents a pack on brands whose makers haven't been making payments to the state for health-care programs. . . .

But the federal tax, signed into law last week, "throws the state's proposals up in the air" because tax-revenue projections need to be recalculated, said Dan Turner, a spokesman for Mr. Barbour.

South Carolina Gov. Mark Sanford proposed raising his state's tax of seven cents a pack—the nation's lowest—to 37 cents, to help offset tax relief he proposes to offer through an optional flat income tax. . . . In neighboring Georgia, which faces about a $2.2 billion budget gap, a new bill calls for raising the cigarette tax by $1 to $1.37 a pack. In Kentucky, which has the nation's highest rate of smoking-related deaths, Gov. Steve Beshear has called for raising the tax to $1 a pack, up from 30 cents a pack.

The National Association of Tobacco Outlets estimates that the federal tax increase, which applies to several forms of tobacco, will lead to the loss of 117,000 of the industry's 1.2 million jobs. . . .

The organization is faxing letters to state legislators arguing that the federal tax diminishes prospects for raising state revenue through tobacco taxes.

The new federal and proposed state taxes are still likely in most cases to fall below those of other developed nations, where taxes make up about two-thirds of a cigarette pack's price, said Michael Eriksen, a former director of CDC's Office on Smoking and Health who is now director of Georgia State University's Institute of Public Health.

Note

Betsy McKay, "Cigarette Tax Clouds Boosts among States," *Wall Street Journal*, February 9, 2009, A5. Article slightly abridged from its original form.

THE CASE: CIGARETTE TAXATION AS A POLICY TOOL

The case in this chapter focuses on the use of cigarette taxes to reduce smoking in the United States, to raise revenue for the federal and state governments, and to fund other public programs such as children's health insurance. Public health experts call the policy of increasing cigarette prices through taxation "one of the best means of curbing smoking, particularly among price-sensitive teens" (McKay 2009). Tobacco-tax expert Frank Chaloupka directly addresses the question of price elasticity when he states that a 10% increase in the price of a pack reduces consumption by about 4%. Based on the discussion in the first part of the chapter, this indicates that the price elasticity of demand for cigarettes is –4% / 10%, or –0.4. In absolute value, this elasticity coefficient is less than one, indicating inelastic demand.

Inelastic demand leads to the use of cigarette taxation as a desirable method for the federal and state governments to raise revenue. As noted previously, an increase in price results in an increase in total revenue when demand is inelastic, because the percentage decrease in quantity demanded is less than the percentage increase in price. However, all levels of government are aware of this fact and want to use cigarette taxes to raise revenues, particularly when facing budget deficits. Officials in sixteen states had been considering substantial increases in cigarette taxes at the same time that the federal excise tax was increasing from $0.39 per pack in February 2009 to $1.01 per pack in April 2009. Thus, the impact of all of these tax increases on cigarette consumption and the resulting tax revenues becomes a more difficult question. A spokesman for the cigarette industry noted that large tax increases could result in greater counterfeit trade. There may also be other consequences of cigarette taxation that require additional analysis, such as the effects of differential state taxation rates and cross-border purchases, the switch to different types of cigarettes or differential smoking behavior in response to higher taxes, and variation in the types of taxation of different tobacco products.

The case notes that the use of cigarette and other sin taxes may be less controversial than other forms of taxation, particularly when tax revenues are used to support politically popular programs such as children's health insurance. In addition, cigarette tax revenues are often earmarked to support antismoking and tobacco control programs. Public health advocates often argue for the use of a comprehensive package of tobacco control strategies as the best means of reducing smoking behavior and preventing individuals from starting to smoke.

Thus, the facts of this case illustrate several important public policy issues:

- How do prices influence individual behavior?
- What is the quantitative effect of a given price increase on the consumption of cigarettes (i.e., price elasticity of demand)?

- How does price elasticity differ among subgroups in the population (i.e., teenagers versus adults)?
- How important is price versus other factors in influencing cigarette consumption?
- What are the implications of the role of price for the design and implementation of different public policies to reduce cigarette smoking?
- What is the strength of the scientific evidence that supports various tobacco control policies?

We will now discuss the empirical studies that help provide answers to these public policy questions.

ESTIMATING CIGARETTE DEMAND FUNCTIONS

Table 5.3 summarizes the results of the major empirical studies of the demand for cigarettes in the 1980s and 1990s.

Other studies of cigarette demand functions have been summarized in the reports *Reducing Health Consequences of Smoking: 25 Years of Smoking* (US Department of Health and Human Services 1989), *Preventing Tobacco Use Among Young People: A Report of the Surgeon General* (US Department of Health and Human Services 1994), and by Viscusi (1992), Grossman and Chaloupka (1997), and Chaloupka and Warner (2000).

All of these studies show that cigarette smoking by both teenagers and adults is sensitive to the price; that is, the price elasticity of demand is greater than zero in absolute value. Most of the studies conclude that young people are more sensitive to changes in price than are adults. The estimates by Frank Chaloupka and Michael Grossman (1996) suggest that the impact of a price increase on teenagers is about three times that on adults. Approximately half of the smoking reduction results from a decrease in the probability of a youth smoking, while half results from a reduction in average daily cigarette consumption.

This larger price sensitivity among young people would be expected for several reasons (Grossman and Chaloupka 1997). Teenagers are likely to spend a greater proportion of their disposable income on cigarettes than are adults. There are also substantial peer-pressure effects operating on young people. Any change in cigarette taxes, and therefore prices, has both a direct negative effect on consumption, as measured by the empirical studies, and a peer-pressure effect (i.e., fewer peers whom a teenager might emulate are smoking). It is often argued that teenagers tend to discount the future by underestimating future health hazards and the likelihood of addiction. Given the nature of addiction, small reductions in cigarette consumption by young people due to price increases could have much greater future effects. Reducing teenage smoking appears to be an effective policy overall because few individuals begin smoking after the age of twenty.

It can be seen from the results in table 5.3 that there is variation in the estimates of the price elasticity of demand for cigarettes. This variation relates to the issues discussed earlier in this chapter: the nature of the estimating equations, the data sets employed, and the other variables included in the estimations.

Cigarette demand studies have been based both on aggregate data, typically at the state level or across a sample of states, and on microlevel individual data drawn from surveys of different groups in the population. The price elasticity estimates from the aggregate data studies typically fall in the range from –0.14 to –1.23, with the majority varying from –0.20 to –0.50 (US Department of Health and Human Services 1994). Studies using cross sections of state-level data must control for smuggling or border-crossing problems. If cigarette taxes or prices differ significantly among adjoining states, state cigarette-consumption data may be inaccurate if there are substantial sales from the low-price (tax) state to residents of the higher-price (tax) states. At the aggregate level, researchers must also consider the interaction between supply and demand in determining cigarette prices. Ignoring this simultaneity could lead to faulty estimates of cigarette price elasticities (US Department of Health and Human Services 1994). This is an example of the distinction between single- and multiequation models that was discussed in chapter 4.

Using microlevel individual data avoids some of the above-cited empirical problems. Since no individual smoker consumes enough cigarettes to affect the overall price, the simultaneity problem in the aggregate data studies is not an issue here. Individual data also allow researchers to model cigarette demand as the outcome of two separate, but interrelated, decisions: (1) the decision to begin smoking (estimating the probability of smoking or the participation rate); and (2) the number of cigarettes consumed, once a decision to begin smoking has been made. It is possible and quite likely that cigarette prices and other variables, including other antismoking policies, have different effects on these two decisions. Aggregate data studies can focus only on average cigarette consumption for some large geographic unit. Individual data allow researchers to examine the factors influencing smoking in various age or socioeconomic groups in the population, and the decisions to both begin and quit smoking.

Examples of both aggregate and individual data studies are given in table 5.3. Gary Becker, Michael Grossman, and Kevin Murphy (1994) used a time series of state cross sections of per capita cigarette consumption from 1955 to 1985. They assumed that the data reflected the behavior of a representative consumer. Theodore Keeler et al. (1993) used monthly time-series data on per capita adult cigarette consumption in California from 1980 to 1990. The event influencing smoking behavior in this study was the cigarette tax increase from $0.10 to $0.35 per pack in 1989. Individual-data studies by Jeffrey Wasserman et al. (1991), Eugene Lewit and Douglas Coate (1982), and Lewit, Coate, and Michael Grossman (1981) use data drawn from the major ongoing health interview surveys sponsored by the federal government, the National Health Interview Survey and the Health Examination Survey, while other researchers have located university-based surveys. Frank Chaloupka and Henry Wechsler (1997) use the 1993 Harvard College Alcohol Study of nearly 17,000 students at 140 US colleges and universities, while Chaloupka and Grossman (1996) use surveys of eighth, tenth, and twelfth grade students drawn from the Monitoring the Future Project at the University of Michigan's Institute of Social Research. As shown in table 5.3, the sample sizes of the data sets in these studies vary substantially, also contributing to differences in the statistical reliability of the results.

The individual-data studies show different impacts of cigarette price and other antismoking variables on the decision to smoke versus the quantity of cigarettes consumed. Chaloupka and Wechsler (1997) and Chaloupka and Grossman (1996) estimate that half of the reduced cigarette consumption from increased prices in their samples of college and high school students results from a reduced probability of smoking, and half results from a decrease in the quantity of cigarettes consumed. This contrasts with the results of Wasserman et al. (1991), who found a very small price effect in their teenage sample: Their actual estimated price coefficient was positive, the opposite of what is predicted by economic theory. However, they could not reject the hypothesis that the teenage price elasticity was significantly different from the adult sample estimate of −0.23. Wasserman et al. (1991) also found that for adults, price changes have the greatest effect on the decision to become a smoker rather than on the number of cigarettes smoked.

The effect of prices on cigarette demand may be intertwined with the effect of other antismoking policies. Disentangling these effects may be a substantial empirical challenge. Wasserman et al. (1991) argue that their low estimates of cigarette price elasticity resulted from the inclusion of an index of antismoking regulations in their estimating equations. They conclude that price elasticity estimates in other studies may have been biased upward because they were capturing some of the effect of antismoking regulations and public sentiment against smoking. Although this conclusion has been debated by

(Text continues on p. 264)

Table 5.3 Empirical Estimation of Cigarette Demand Functions: Selected Recent and Often-Cited Studies

Study	Data Set	Price Elasticity Estimates	Results — Effect of Other Smoking Variables	Results — Effect of Other Variable
Chaloupka and Wechsler (1997)	1993 Harvard College Alcohol Study; N = 16,570 students at 140 US four-year colleges and universities.	−0.906 to −1.309. Half of the decreased consumption was from reduced participation in smoking; the other half was from a reduction in the number of cigarettes consumed by smokers.	Relatively strong restrictions on smoking in public places, particularly restaurants and schools, discourage college students from smoking.	Age, gender, race, marital status, religion, parental education, on-campus living, fraternity/sorority membership, employment, college characteristics, regional indicators included. Results not reported. Sample also adjusted for students crossing borders to localities with lower taxes/prices.
Chaloupka and Grossman (1996)	1992, 1993, 1994 surveys of eighth, tenth, twelfth grade students from Monitoring the Future Project, Institute for Social Research, University of Michigan. N = 110,717 youths.	−0.846 to −1.450 for full sample. −1.254 to −1.702 for sample adjusted for border-crossing problem. −1.313 is average estimate. Half of smoking reductions were from decrease in probability of a youth smoking; half were from reduction in average daily cigarette consumption.	Relatively strong restrictions on smoking in public places, such as workplaces, restaurants, or retail stores, reduce the probability of smoking, but have little impact on average daily cigarette consumption. Restrictions on smoking in schools are significant for this sample.	Variables decreasing likelihood of smoking: race; religious attachment; rural location; families with both parents present; greater parental education. Variables increasing likelihood of smoking: age; higher incomes (e_I = +0.294); employed; working mothers.

Table 5.3 (Continued)

Chaloupka and Grossman (1996) (continued)			Limits on availability of tobacco products, such as minimum legal purchase age and restrictions on vending machine sales, have little effect. These laws may not be well enforced. Educational antismoking activities appear to reduce youths' smoking.
Becker, Grossman, and Murphy (1994)	Time-series of state cross-sections of per capita cigarette consumption from 1955 to 1985. Assume the data reflect the behavior of a representative consumer. N = 1,517.	−0.75 for long-run response to permanent change in price. −0.40 for short-run response to permanent change in price. −0.30 for temporary change in price.	Control for income and differences in state taxes, which influence smuggling incentives among states.
Keeler et al. (1993)	Monthly time-series data in California from 1980 to 1990. Per capita adult consumption (ages 15 years and older). Cigarette tax increase from $0.10 to $0.35 per pack occurred on January 1, 1989.	−0.30 to −0.50 in the short run. −0.50 to −0.60 in the long run.	Antismoking ordinances have a significant negative effect on cigarette consumption, but they do not overshadow the effects of price. Effects of income are weak, insignificant, and negative. Negative income elasticity may be due to superior education of higher-income groups (earlier data revealed a positive elasticity). Cigarette consumption increases around holiday periods and before a tax increase. Bootlegging due to state tax differentials can be an important determinant of demand.

Table 5.3 Empirical Estimation of Cigarette Demand Functions: Selected Recent and Often-Cited Studies (Continued)

Study	Data Set	Price Elasticity Estimates	Effect of Other Smoking Variables	Effect of Other Variable
			Results	
Wasserman et al. (1991)	Study uses *National Health Interview Survey* data from 1970 and 1985. N = 207,647. Assume all consumption is underreported by one-third. Also used *National Health and Nutrition Examination Survey II* for teenage smoking between 1976 and 1980. N = 1,960. Discuss use of individual versus state data in other studies.	−0.017 in 1974 to −0.226 in 1985 for adult sample. +0.859 for teenagers. Yet one cannot reject hypothesis that teenage elasticity is significantly different from adult estimate of −0.23 in 1985. Teenage estimate much lower than in other studies. For adults, price changes have greatest effect on decision to become a smoker rather than on number of cigarettes smoked.	Adult sample: Antismoking regulations would decrease consumption but did not affect decision to smoke. Teenage sample: Antismoking regulations have strong negative and statistically significant effect on consumption. Major effect was on the probability of being a smoker. Price elasticity results affected by inclusion of regulatory variables. Public sentiment against smoking may be related to the regulation variables.	Adult sample: Price and income elasticities are changing over time. Income elasticities change from positive to negative. Cigarette consumption declines as education increases. Cohort effects (especially for males) are important. Whites smoke more than nonwhites. Married people smoke less than nonmarried. Teenage sample: Cigarette consumption negatively related to family income and parental education. Study shows distributional consequences of taxing cigarettes.

Table 5.3 (Continued)

Lewit and Coate (1982)	1976 *Health Interview Survey.* N = 19,266 individuals age 20 to 74 years.	−0.42 overall, −0.26 for participation rate, and −0.10 for quantity demanded. −0.89 for 20–25 years age group, twice as large as estimate for other age groups. −0.74 for participation rate in this age group.	Control for family income, education, age, sex, marital status, race, and health status. Results not reported.
Lewit, Coate, and Grossman (1981)	Cycle III of the *U.S. Health Examination Survey.* National sample of 6,768 noninstitutionalized youths age 12 to 17, conducted from 1966 to 1970.	−1.2 for the decision to smoke; −1.4 for the quantity-smoked equations.	Substantial negative effect of antismoking messages on participation rates. Border-crossing problem likely to be smaller for teenagers than adults because quantity of cigarettes smoked is smaller and teenagers are less likely to be able to drive. Control for real family income, number of children in family, parents' schooling, whether mother works, age, race, sex, student status, working status, region. Results not reported.

other researchers, who also included both price and antismoking variables in their equations and found little effect on estimated price elasticities, the debate shows the influence of empirical estimation issues on policy conclusions. More recent studies are likely to include variables measuring the effect of other anti-smoking policies, given the current interest in the full range of policies to reduce smoking. Chaloupka and Wechsler (1997) and Chaloupka and Grossman (1996) found that relatively strong restrictions on smoking in public areas such as work places, restaurants, and schools were effective in discouraging young people from smoking. There was a greater estimated effect on the probability of smoking than on the quantity of cigarettes consumed. Limits on the availability of tobacco products, such as a minimum legal purchase age and restrictions on vending machine sales, appeared to have little effect, perhaps because these laws are not well enforced. Wasserman et al. (1991) found a difference in the effects of antismoking regulations on teenagers and on adults. For teenagers, the major impact was on the probability of being a smoker, whereas for adults, the regulations appeared to decrease consumption but did not affect the decision to smoke.

Given the range of results and data sets used in the above studies, policy-makers can use assistance in evaluating the policy literature in any field. The independent, nonfederal Task Force on Community Preventive Services, which developed the "Guide to Community Preventive Services" (available at www.thecommunityguide.org/index.html), has undertaken reviews of the literature for health care prevention interventions. Development of the guide was supported by the US Department of Health and Human Services (DHHS), in collaboration with public and private partners and with support staff provided by the Centers for Disease Control and Prevention (CDC). The Task Force created a systematic approach to selecting interventions to evaluate, searching for and retrieving evidence, assessing the quality of the information reviewed, translating evidence of effectiveness into recommendations, and identifying and summarizing research gaps.

In 2001 the Task Force published a review of strategies to reduce tobacco-use initiation and to increase tobacco-use cessation (Hopkins et al. 2001). In both of these categories, the Task Force reviewed studies of interventions to increase the unit price of tobacco products through excise taxation. Selected studies that met the review criteria were considered to be of moderate or good study design and fair or good quality of execution. The studies of interventions to reduce tobacco-use initiation focused on children, adolescents, and young adults. Price elasticity of demand estimates included both participation (tobacco-use prevalence) and consumption (cigarettes per day).

Regarding prevalence, the estimates ranged from no statistically significant effect to –1.19, with a median of –0.37. For consumption, the estimates ranged from 0 to –0.68, with a median of –0.23. The review of price elasticity estimates in the smoking-cessation interventions ranged from –0.27 to –0.76, with a median of –0.41, for aggregate studies based on cigarette sales data and from +0.5 to –0.84, with a median of –0.42, for studies based on individual behavior. The Task Force found consistent evidence of the effect of cigarette prices on consumption, regardless of the type of measurements reported or calculated, the setting or period of time for the analysis, or differences in the controls for potential confounders. The Task Force concluded that there was strong scientific evidence that increasing the price of tobacco products is an effective way to reduce smoking initiation and increase smoking cessation.

Quantitative reviews of the literature have also used meta-analysis, a statistical technique that makes formal comparisons among studies of varying research designs and approaches. Gallet and List (2003) performed a meta-analysis on eighty-six studies that reported estimates of price, income, and advertising elasticities for cigarettes. Across the studies, they found a mean price elasticity of –0.48, a mean income elasticity of 0.42, and a mean advertising elasticity of 0.10. Although these elasticity estimates were fairly robust, the researchers found that they were impacted by the specification of the demand functions, the data used in the studies, and the estimation methodology.

Although there is a reasonable consensus on the influence of price on cigarette consumption, there may be other changes in the behavior of smokers arising from increased cigarette taxation that partially offset the goal of the taxation policy. Grossman and Chaloupka (1997) noted that in response to higher cigarette prices, smokers may switch to brands with higher tar and nicotine contents, inhale more deeply, reduce idle burn time, or switch to the use of smokeless tobacco. It has also been argued that extremely high cigarette taxes will lead to an increase in black market activity and smuggling. None of these effects were addressed in the above empirical studies, and most had not been well researched at that time.

More recent research has begun to analyze these questions. In response to higher prices, smokers may attempt to get more tar and nicotine out of the cigarettes they smoke by altering their smoking behavior or switching to cigarettes that are higher in tar and nicotine content. Using cross-section data from the 1979 and 1987 National Health Interview Survey, Evans and Farrelly (1998) found that smokers did switch to cigarettes with higher tar and nicotine contents in response to tax and price increases. Farrelly et al. (2004) reexamined the issue using longitudinal data from the Community Intervention Trial of the National Cancer Institute, in which individual behavior over time could be observed, thus providing a stronger test of the relationships. As with other studies, these researchers found that cigarette consumption was responsive to price and that this responsiveness decreased with age of the smoker. Farrelly et al. also found that smokers switched to cigarettes with higher nicotine per cigarette. For smokers age 25–34, they estimated an elasticity for nicotine of +0.31, which means that a 10% increase in cigarette price results in a 3.1% increase in nicotine in the cigarettes usually smoked. They estimated a similar elasticity of +0.25 for smokers aged 45 and older. Thus, smokers appear to compensate for the decrease in cigarettes consumed from higher prices by increasing the tar and nicotine consumed, reducing the health benefits of policies that use taxes to increase cigarette prices. Farrelly et al. argued that a better public policy would be to tax cigarettes on the basis of their tar content to minimize this compensating or substitution behavior.

Adda and Cornaglia (2006) explored the effects of taxes on other compensating behaviors: increasing the intensity of smoking by varying the number of puffs, the degree and length of inhalation, or by blocking the ventilation holes on the filter. These researchers used data from the National Health and Nutrition Examination Surveys (NHANES III and NHANES 1999–2000), which contained information on smoking behavior and on the cotinine concentration, a marker of nicotine intake, in the saliva of smokers. Cotinine concentrations are influenced by both the size and type of cigarette smoked and by the manner in which the cigarette is smoked. The NHANES behavioral data were merged with cigarette excise tax data that varied across states and over time, from 1988–94.

Adda and Cornaglia (2006) found that increases in cigarette taxes in the 1990s led to an increase in the intensity of smoking, with a 1% increase in taxes increasing smoking intensity by about 0.4% (an intensity elasticity of +0.4). Their study also showed that smoking intensity differed according to socioeconomic characteristics. Individuals with higher education extracted less nicotine per cigarette, while African Americans had the highest smoking intensity. This study also illustrated that the positive public health benefits of cigarette taxation could be partially offset by changes in individual behavior.

The effects of cigarette taxation policies may also be mitigated by cigarette smuggling (purchasing cigarettes in low-tax states and selling them in high-tax states, or exporting abroad and re-importing without paying appropriate taxes) or by cross-border purchases (individuals in high-tax states purchasing cigarettes from low-tax states or Indian reservations). Stehr (2005) investigated these issues by comparing tax-paid cigarette sales data from the Tobacco Institute with cigarette consumption data from the Behavioral Risk Factor Surveillance System (BRFSS) from 1985 to 2001. He argued that large changes in sales relative to consumption at the time of large tax increases were consistent with tax avoidance. Stehr's analysis showed that the response of tax-paid sales was significantly larger than the response of consumption to tax changes, and that the price elasticity was much larger in states and years when taxes were high than in other states. He concluded that up to 85% of the tax-paid sales response was from tax avoidance, and that 9.6% of cigarettes consumed from 1985 to 2001 were purchased without payment of state cigarette taxes. Stehr argued that these smuggling and border-crossing problems meant that states with high cigarette taxes needed effective policies to curb smuggling and other forms of tax avoidance, or that they should employ other policies to curb smoking, such as counter-advertising and smoking restrictions.

The cigarette companies have also responded to differential taxation by marketing little cigars that have been packaged as a substitute for cigarettes (Delnevo and Hrywna 2007). Sales of little cigars quadrupled between 1971 and 1973, partially because the Public Health Cigarette Smoking Act did not restrict their advertising on television, as it did cigarette ads, and partially because cigars did not require warning labels. Little cigars also had a low excise tax that made them considerably less expensive than cigarettes. RJ Reynolds launched its Winchester brand in 1972 and was particularly successful in states where the cigarette tax was high. Although the television ban loophole was closed in 1973, the tax and price disparities between little cigars and cigarettes were an important part of the product's success. These same issues have continued in more recent times. Little cigar sales reached an all-time high in 2006, given a continued disparity between little cigar and cigarette taxes. In states with high cigarette taxes, little cigars cost less than half as much as a pack of cigarettes. Little cigars were also free from the costs and restrictions imposed on cigarettes by the Master Settlement Agreement (MSA), discussed below.

IMPLICATIONS FOR PUBLIC POLICY

The preceding discussion may leave students and policy analysts wondering what they can conclude from these differences in theoretical issues and empirical results for this one policy area. Although there are various estimates of the precise magnitude of the response to cigarette price increases, there is substantial consensus in the research literature that prices do reduce cigarette consumption, in terms of both the decision to smoke and the quantity of cigarettes consumed. These results have led two prominent cigarette-demand researchers, Michael Grossman and Frank Chaloupka, to argue that a "substantial real tax hike to curb youth smoking should move to the forefront of the antismoking campaign" (Grossman and Chaloupka 1997, 297). Public health advocates also argue that combinations of policies are needed for an effective tobacco control intervention. All of these interventions have been influenced by the 1998 Master Settlement Agreement between the states and the tobacco companies.

In 1994 the attorneys general of Mississippi and Minnesota sued the large tobacco companies to recover the costs to their state Medicaid programs of treating tobacco-related illnesses (Schroeder 2004). All other states followed this action. Four states settled with the tobacco companies in 1997, while the remaining forty-six states reached the Master Settlement Agreement (MSA) with the four large tobacco companies in 1998 to recover their Medicaid expenses and penalize the companies for deceptive practices. The tobacco companies awarded the states $206 billion, to be paid over twenty-five years, in return for the states abandoning their suits. The states were to have discretion over how the funds were used. The MSA also created the American Legacy Foundation for public education and other tobacco control activities, to be supported for at least five years at a cost of approximately $1.7 billion. Finally, the settlement required the dissolution of the Tobacco Institute and other organizations that promoted the industry; prohibited advertising directed to young people; and permitted wide dissemination of previously secret industry documents.

The MSA funds have become a source of income for states to help control budget deficits and avert new taxes (Schroeder 2004). In many states, tobacco-control activities have been dismantled to deal with other fiscal problems. Some states are mortgaging future MSA payments through bond issues. New York and California sold tobacco bonds that were backed by state revenues, creating a financial incentive for the states to keep the tobacco industry healthy, because the financial obligations would revert to the states if the companies forfeit their MSA payments. However, the tobacco companies' price increase of $0.45 per pack to pay for the antitobacco programs required by the MSA may be one of the most important outcomes of the program. Cutler et al. (2002) estimated modest benefits from the MSA in terms of reduced Medicaid spending from lower smoking, but much larger gains in the longevity benefits of reduced smoking. Their best estimate was $65.0 billion through 2025 for Massachusetts, with gains for the nation being thirty to forty times this amount.

Public policy is often impacted by simultaneous measures aimed at the same goal. In November 1998, California voters passed Proposition 10, the California Children and Families First Act, which increased the state excise tax on cigarettes from $0.37 to $0.87 per pack in 1999 (Sung et al. 2005). Revenues were earmarked for early childhood development programs. The signing of the MSA, which caused the tobacco companies to raise the price of cigarettes by $0.45 per pack, coincided with this state tax increase. Sung et al. (2005) investigated the combined effects of Proposition 10 and the MSA on California cigarette consumption from 1984 to 2002. Their time-series analysis indicated that from 1999 to 2002, cigarette consumption was reduced by 2.4 packs per capita per quarter, or 1.3 million packs in total, and state excise tax revenues increased by $2.1 billion. This was a strong disincentive for smokers in a state with the lowest smoking-prevalence rates in the United States. The authors estimated an elasticity (defined as the percentage reduction in cigarette sales associated with a 1% tax increase relative to price) of –0.44 for Proposition 10 and the MSA combined. This contrasted with an estimate of –0.60 for Proposition 99, a ballot initiative that increased the cigarette tax by $0.25 per pack in 1989 over the rate of $0.10 per pack that had been maintained since 1967. The authors argued that this smaller elasticity may have resulted from more aggressive advertising and promotion by the tobacco companies after the MSA, combined with decreased funding for the California Tobacco Control Program in the subsequent years. Given the restrictions of the MSA, the tobacco companies shifted their resources from media advertising to other forms of marketing, particularly promotions targeted at retail outlets. Keeler et al. (2004) found that tobacco industry advertising from 1996 to 2000 partially offset the effects of the higher cigarette prices induced by the MSA, by 33–57%.

New York City began a comprehensive, five-component tobacco-control strategy in 2002 (Frieden et al. 2005). The city's cigarette tax increased from $0.08 to $1.50 per pack in July 2002, following an increase of New York State's cigarette tax from $1.11 to $1.50 per pack in April 2002. These combined tax increases raised the price of a pack of cigarettes approximately 32%, to $6.85. The city also implemented the Smoke-Free Air Act of 2002, which made virtually all indoor workplaces, including restaurants and bars, smoke free. Nicotine-dependence treatment guidelines were sent to all physicians, and a nicotine-patch distribution program was implemented. The city expanded education efforts, such as publications and advertisements in broadcast and print media, and began a systematic evaluation of all program components.

The evaluation of the program used smoking-prevalence data from 1993 through 2001, drawn from the New York State Behavioral Risk Factor Surveillance System, as well as data on health care and smoking behaviors drawn from community health surveys undertaken in 2002 and 2003. The 2002 survey was considered to be the pre-intervention sample, while the 2003 surveys were treated as the post-intervention sample. Frieden et al. (2005) found that after a decade of smoking prevalence remaining almost constant, the prevalence decreased from 21.6%to 19.2% from 2002 to 2003. The decline corresponded to almost 140,000 fewer adult smokers. This decline was attributed to the tobacco control strategy, given the policy change during this period. Also, among eight metropolitan areas that did not intensify tobacco-control programs in 2002–3, six showed increases of 4–18% in smoking prevalence, one showed no change, and one showed a slight, nonsignificant decrease in smoking prevalence. The researchers estimated that 33–54% of the decline in smoking prevalence was due to increased taxation, 13–21% to the smoke-free workplace legislation, and 8% to the nicotine-patch program. Public education and changing social norms may have accounted for the remaining decline in prevalence.

Frieden et al. (2005) acknowledged that the cross-sectional nature of the research may have made the causal associations uncertain. However, the surveys were large and representative of New York City. The researchers also noted that proportion of cigarettes purchased outside New York City increased from 17.4% in 2002 to 32.9% in 2003. They estimated that 29.0% of these sales occurred in New York State outside New York City, 21.7% in a different state, 18.1% over the internet, 12.4% from another person, and 7.8% from an Indian reservation. This is evidence of the dilution of the public health benefit from cigarette taxation that we discussed above.

Research, particularly the econometric literature discussed in this chapter, can never definitively prove a hypothesis about the relationship between two variables. It can, however, suggest that the weight of the evidence supports a given relationship. The policy analyst needs to review surveys of the literature that distill and analyze the results of numerous studies, to determine whether there is a consensus about the impact of different policy variables. This is a relatively easy task in the area of smoking behavior, given the policy interest in the question since the first surgeon general's report on smoking in the 1960s. Major reports by the federal government (US Department of Health and Human Services 1989, 1994), key summary articles (Warner et al. 1995; Grossman and Chaloupka 1997; Chaloupka and Warner 2000), systematic reviews by the Task Force on Community Preventive Services (Hopkins et al. 2001), and meta-analyses (Gallet and List 2003) can help the policy analyst organize and summarize the existing literature and determine what empirical and policy questions still need to be addressed. For other policy areas, the literature may be very sparse or of poor quality. However, analysts can access a wide range of literature in a relatively short time using the variety of electronic databases in most libraries and sources currently available on the internet.

The great body of the smoking literature supports the hypothesis that raising cigarette prices through taxation will reduce smoking, particularly among teenagers—thus, pricing has a significant impact on human behavior in this case and can be used as a policy tool. The justification for and desirability of doing so will depend upon the values of different policy advocates as well as the perspectives of different academic disciplines. For example, different policy recommendations can follow from the economic and the public health perspectives. Participants in a 1995 meeting of economics-based smoking researchers concluded that "economic analysis can inform but never resolve the debate on how much society should tax cigarettes," and that "neither the discipline of economics nor any other could determine what is socially 'right' or 'wrong'"(Warner et al. 1995, 384).

It is likely that to influence smoking behavior, particularly among teenagers, policies based on pricing will need to be combined with other approaches to behavior change. We previously discussed comprehensive strategies for the case of New York City (Frieden et al. 2005). There is also a growing literature analyzing the cost-effectiveness of antismoking programs (Elixhauser 1990; Hopkins et al. 2001). Studies in this literature directly analyze specific interventions and alternative theories of behavior change to determine their effectiveness, both under idealized experimental conditions and in actual operation among different populations. This is a quite different approach than simply measuring the effects of these programs by determining the statistical significance of a variable in an econometric estimation equation, as in much of the literature discussed in this chapter. The use of program-evaluation techniques, such as cost-effectiveness and cost-benefit analysis, will be discussed in the following chapters, with applications to other policy areas.

Policy analysts may have to synthesize literature across a variety of academic disciplines to try to form a complete picture of the impact of pricing compared to other variables in influencing human behavior. Analysts must be aware that the difficult task is to untangle the effects of multiple influences on human behavior. This can be accomplished through a variety of research approaches, each of which has its own strengths and weaknesses. It is clear from the issues discussed in this chapter that pricing policies do have an impact on smoking behavior and cigarette demand. Thus, pricing and taxation should be considered as tools in this policy arena.

REFERENCES

Adda, Jerome, and Francesca Cornaglia. 2006. Taxes, Cigarette Consumption, and Smoking Intensity. *American Economic Review* 96 (4): 1013–28.

Becker, Gary S., Michael Grossman, and Kevin M. Murphy. 1994. An Empirical Analysis of Cigarette Addiction. *American Economic Review* 84 (3): 396–418.

Centers for Disease Control and Prevention (CDC). 2008a. Cigarette Smoking Among Adults—United States, 2007. *Morbidity and Mortality Weekly Report* 57 (45): 1221–26.

———. 2008b. Smoking-Attributable Mortality, Years of Potential Life Lost, and Productivity Losses—United States, 2000–2004. *Morbidity and Mortality Weekly Report* 57 (45): 1226–28.

Chaloupka, Frank J., and Michael Grossman. 1996. Price, Tobacco Control, and Youth Smoking. NBER Working Paper Series, Working Paper 5740. Cambridge, MA: National Bureau of Economic Research.

Chaloupka, Frank J., and Kenneth Warner. 2000. The Economics of Smoking. In *The Handbook of Health Economics*, ed. Joseph Newhouse and Andrew Culyer, 1541–1647. Amsterdam: North Holland.

Chaloupka, Frank J., and Henry Wechsler. 1997. Price, Tobacco Control Policies and Smoking among Young Adults. *Journal of Health Economics* 16 (3): 359–73.

Cutler, David M., Jonathan Gruber, Raymond S. Hartman, Mary Beth Landrum, Joseph P. Newhouse, and Meredith B. Rosenthal. 2002. The Economic Impacts of the Tobacco Settlement. *Journal of Policy Analysis and Management* 21 (1): 1–19.

Delnevo, Christine D., and Mary Hrywna. 2007. A Whole 'Nother Smoke or a Cigarette in Disguise: How RJ Reynolds Reframed the Image of Little Cigars. *American Journal of Public Health* 97 (8): 1368–75.

Elixhauser, Anne. 1990. The Costs of Smoking and the Cost-Effectiveness of Smoking Cessation Programs. *Journal of Public Health Policy* 11 (Summer): 218–37.

Evans, William N., and Matthew C. Farrelly. 1998. The Compensating Behavior of Smokers: Taxes, Tar, and Nicotine. *The RAND Journal of Economics* 29 (3): 578–95.

Farrelly, Matthew C., Christina T. Nimsch, Andrew Hyland, and K. Michael Cummings. 2004. The Effects of Higher Cigarette Prices on Tar and Nicotine Consumption in a Cohort of Adult Smokers. *Health Economics* 13 (1): 49–58.

Frieden, Thomas R., Farzad Mostashari, Bonnie D. Kerker, Nancy Miller, Anjum Hajat, and Martin Frankel. 2005. Adult Tobacco Use after Intensive Tobacco Control Measures: New York City, 2002–2003. *American Journal of Public Health* 95 (6): 1016–23.

Gallet, Craig A., and John A. List. 2003. Cigarette Demand: A Meta-Analysis of Elasticities. *Health Economics* 12 (10): 821–35.

Greene, William H. 2008. *Econometric Analysis.* 6th ed. Upper Saddle River, NJ: Prentice Hall.

Grossman, Michael, and Frank J. Chaloupka. 1997. Cigarette Taxes: The Straw to Break the Camel's Back. *Public Health Reports* 112 (July/August): 291–97.

Hopkins, David P., Peter A. Briss, Connie J. Ricard, Corinne G. Husten, Vilma G. Carande-Kulis, Jonathan E. Fielding, Mary O. Alao, et al. 2001. Reviews of Evidence Regarding Interventions to Reduce Tobacco Use and Exposure to Environmental Tobacco Smoke. *American Journal of Preventive Medicine* 20 (2): 16–66. Suppl. no. 1.

Keeler, Theodore E., Teh-wei Hu, Paul G. Barnett, and Willard G. Manning. 1993. Taxation, Regulation, and Addiction: A Demand Function for Cigarettes Based on Time-Series Evidence. *Journal of Health Economics* 12 (1): 1–18.

Keeler, Theodore E., Teh-wei Hu, Michael Ong, and Hai-Yen Sung. 2004. The U.S. National Tobacco Settlement: The Effects of Advertising and Price Changes on Cigarette Consumption. *Applied Economics* 36 (15): 1623–29.

Keohane, Nathaniel O. 2009. Symposium: Alternative U.S. Climate Policy Instruments: Cap and Trade, Rehabilitated: Using Tradable Permits to Control U.S. Greenhouse Gases. *Review of Environmental Economics and Policy* 3 (1): 42–62.

Lewit, Eugene M., and Douglas Coate. 1982. The Potential for Using Excise Taxes to Reduce Smoking. *Journal of Health Economics* 1:121–45.

Lewit, Eugene M., Douglas Coate, and Michael Grossman. 1981. The Effects of Government Regulation on Teenage Smoking. *Journal of Law and Economics* 24 (3): 545–69.

McKay, Betsy. 2009. Cigarette Tax Clouds Boosts among States. *Wall Street Journal*, February 8.

Morrison, Steven A. 1998. Airline Service: The Evolution of Competition Since Deregulation. In *Industry Studies*, ed. Larry L. Duetsch, 147–75. 2nd ed. Armonk, NY: M. E. Sharpe.

Rosen, Harvey, and Ted Gayer. 2010. *Public Finance*. 9th ed. New York: McGraw-Hill.

Schroeder, Steven A. 2004. Tobacco Control in the Wake of the 1998 Master Settlement Agreement. *New England Journal of Medicine* 350 (3): 293–301.

Stehr, Mark. 2005. "Cigarette Tax Avoidance and Evasion," *Journal of Health Economics* 24 (2): 277–97.

Sung, Hai-Yen, Teh-wei Hu, Michael Ong, Theodore E. Keeler, and Mei-ling Sheu. 2005. A Major State Tobacco Tax Increase, the Master Settlement Agreement, and Cigarette Consumption: The California Experience. *American Journal of Public Health* 95 (6): 1030–35.

US Department of Health and Human Services. 1989. *Reducing the Health Consequences of Smoking. 25 Years of Progress. A Report of the Surgeon General.* Atlanta: US Department of Health and Human Services, Public Health Service, Centers for Disease Control, Center for Chronic Disease Prevention and Health Promotion, Office on Smoking and Health.

————. 1994. *Preventing Tobacco Use Among Young People: A Report of the Surgeon General.* Atlanta: US Department of Health and Human Services, Public Health Service, Centers for Disease Control and Prevention, National Center for Chronic Disease Prevention and Health Promotion, Office on Smoking and Health. Reprinted with corrections, July 1994.

————. 1999. *Targeting Tobacco Use: The Nation's Leading Cause of Death, At-a-Glance.* Atlanta: US Department of Health and Human Services, Centers for Disease Control and Prevention.

Viscusi, W. Kip. 1992. *Smoking: Making the Risky Decision.* New York: Oxford University Press.

Viscusi, W. Kip, Joseph E. Harrington Jr., and John M. Vernon. 2005. *Economics of Regulation and Antitrust.* 4th ed. Cambridge, MA: Massachusetts Institute of Technology Press.

Warner, Kenneth E., Frank J. Chaloupka, Philip J. Cook, Willard G. Manning, Joseph P. Newhouse, Thomas E. Novotny, Thomas C. Schelling, and Joy Townsend. 1995. Criteria for Determining an Optimal Cigarette Tax: The Economist's Perspective. *Tobacco Control* 4:380–86.

Wasserman, Jeffrey, Willard G. Manning, Joseph P. Newhouse, and John D. Winkler. 1991. The Effects of Excise Taxes and Regulations on Cigarette Smoking. *Journal of Health Economics* 10 (1): 43–64.

Chapter 6

Cost-Effectiveness Analysis:
The Case of HIV Prevention Programs

This chapter discusses the use of cost-effectiveness analysis to evaluate alternative public policies. The specific case chosen for the chapter is the cost-effectiveness of screening programs for human immunodeficiency virus (HIV). A health care example was chosen because of the vast increase in the number of cost-effectiveness studies in the health care area and the development and standardization of economic evaluation techniques that have occurred over the past decade. Preventing transmission of HIV is a major health policy concern both in the United States and around the world. Although the chapter focuses on HIV, the cost-effectiveness techniques discussed here are used for a wide variety of health issues and other policy areas. These techniques have been used, for example, to analyze the alternative antismoking strategies that were discussed in the previous chapter.

We begin by defining cost-effectiveness analysis and discussing how it compares with other program evaluation tools, such as cost-benefit analysis. The latter is the subject of chapter 7 in this book. Although chapters 6 and 7 focus on different policy areas and evaluation techniques, there are many similar elements in and connections between the two chapters. We will then discuss the features and problems that are common to all cost-effectiveness analyses, drawing on the major publications that summarize the issues regarding the application of cost-effectiveness analysis in health policy decisions (Gold et al. 1996; Haddix et al. 1996, 2003; Drummond et al. 2005).

WHAT IS COST-EFFECTIVENESS ANALYSIS?

Cost-effectiveness analysis is one of a series of techniques that can be used to provide a systematic economic evaluation of alternative public policies. These economic evaluation techniques all focus on relating some measure of the output, outcomes, or consequences of a program to the costs of the inputs used to provide those outcomes. The techniques provide a decision maker with a useful way to clearly identify alternatives to a given policy and to focus on the consequences of using scarce resources for one program instead of another. Like all forms of economic analysis, these techniques derive from the facts that the resources available to fund any program are limited and that choices must be made among alternatives.

Economic evaluation differs from other forms of program evaluation that concentrate on describing the process by which the program is implemented (Rossi and Freeman 1993). These evaluations may define their outputs simply as the number of clients served or the number of counseling sessions offered. Although these measures may be useful for describing and monitoring the operation of a particular program, they do not show the impact of the program on the population. Economic evaluation focuses on measuring the production process or "production function" inherent in the program—the relationship between the flow of program inputs and the resulting outcome that has an impact on the final consumers or clients.

Because economic evaluation focuses on the program's final impact on the population, it often uses modeling techniques. Modeling is particularly useful when some of the alternatives being considered have not actually been implemented or when there is great uncertainty about the actual effectiveness of the intervention. For example, decision makers in HIV prevention might be interested in the costs and consequences of needle-exchange programs in the United States, or of a policy of mandatory HIV testing of pregnant women to prevent transmission of HIV to their infants. However, there has been only limited use of needle-exchange programs in the United States, and there is no mandatory HIV counseling and testing of pregnant women, given the political, ethical, and legal issues surrounding these strategies. Therefore, little or no direct evidence exists about the costs and consequences of such programs. Researchers need to develop models of how these programs would work, using the best data available from comparable programs or making educated guesses about certain parameters.

Although modeling may seem like an academic exercise, models "can be very helpful in making assumptions explicit and in forcing examination of the logic, coherence and evidence for each step in the process" (Haddix et al. 2003, 6). Sometimes, simply the process of logically going through the steps inherent in a public policy will highlight issues that might otherwise have been overlooked, even if the model is never fully estimated. Modeling forces a decision maker to explicitly confront alternatives and to develop the logic of what might happen under each alternative. "Modeling may help in identifying the important issues for which data are needed and thereby help to formulate a research agenda. . . . The use of models makes the decision process explicit and can help to clarify the criteria upon which decisions are based" (Haddix et al. 2003, 5). This role for modeling relates to the problem-definition issues discussed in chapter 2 of this book. We noted there that many public policy problems are only moderately or ill structured, and that one of the main tasks of policy analysis is the resolution of ill-structured problems.

Alternative Economic Evaluation Techniques

The various economic evaluation techniques differ in how they measure, value, and compare costs and consequences (Gold et al. 1996; Haddix et al. 1996, 2003; Drummond et al. 2005). In cost-effectiveness analysis (CEA), the program outcomes or consequences are measured in terms of the most appropriate natural effects or physical units. In the health care area, the number of infections prevented or the number of life-years saved by a medical or prevention intervention are typical outcome measures. These are basic measures that can simply be counted to determine the effectiveness of the intervention. No valuation is placed on the outcome measures. Thus, cost-effectiveness analysis is most appropriately used where there is already general agreement on the nature of the program outcomes and where the outcomes of the alternatives being compared are the same or very similar. The decision maker wants to choose the alternative that has the lowest additional cost for achieving the additional outcomes. For example, one might compare the cost-effectiveness of two alternative strategies for preventing HIV infection. In this case, estimating the number of infections prevented under each strategy might be a sufficiently precise measure of program output, given the common goal of the alternatives.

Cost-effectiveness analysis becomes a less useful tool even in the health care arena when comparisons are made across broader program areas. Suppose that the question facing the decision maker is how to allocate resources between programs aimed at preventing HIV and heart disease, respectively. The question then is how to rank a case of HIV infection prevented in relation to a case of heart disease prevented.

One could answer this question by analyzing the cost per life-year saved in each case. However, this measure focuses solely on the mortality outcome of the intervention, the extension in the number of years of life, and ignores major issues about the quality of the life-years saved and the values individuals attach to them. An individual with HIV could live with the disease for twenty to thirty years with the use of antiretroviral therapies. The stigma that has been attached to HIV, as well as the inconvenience and side effects associated with following current drug regimens, means that the quality of life for a person living with HIV is quite different from that of a noninfected individual. These differences are not considered in the analysis if only the number of life-years saved by an HIV-prevention program is measured. In evaluating cholesterol screening to prevent heart disease, the reduction in mortality is an important outcome. "But simply counting deaths, or even life-years gained, may leave out other important health outcomes, such as the morbidity repercussions of angina and heart attacks, as well as the psychological concerns that accompany a diagnosis of hypercholesterolemia" (Gold et al. 1996, 84). Thus, the usefulness of cost-effectiveness analysis is limited when the decision maker is trying to compare programs across broad policy areas, when there are multiple outcomes of interest in each program, and when some outcomes are valued more highly than others.

In health care policy, cost-utility analysis (CUA) has been developed as a modification of cost-effectiveness analysis to focus on these quality-of-life issues. In cost-utility analysis, the outcome measure is typically a quality-adjusted life-year (QALY), in which the number of life-years gained by an intervention has been adjusted for factors relating to the quality of those life-years. "In the QALY approach, the quality adjustment is based on a set of values or weights called utilities, one for each possible health state, that reflect the desirability of the health state" (Drummond et al. 2005, 138). Cost-utility analysis would be the economic evaluation technique to use when: (1) health-related quality of life is the most important outcome, such as in the treatment of arthritis, which has no expected impact on mortality; (2) health-related quality of life is an important outcome (e.g., evaluating neonatal intensive care for low-birthweight infants); (3) interventions, such as many cancer treatments, affect both morbidity and mortality, and the decision maker wants a single measure incorporating both effects; (4) the programs being compared have a wide range of outputs, and a common unit for comparison is needed; or (5) a decision maker wants to compare a new program with one that has already been evaluated in terms of cost-utility analysis (140).

Although cost-utility analysis helps in making comparisons across alternative health-related prevention and treatment programs, decision makers may be asked to make even broader comparisons across more disparate activities. Legislators and other policymakers must make decisions regarding resource allocation to health care, national defense, education, job training, and a variety of other programs, all of which provide benefits to society and yet have outcome measures that are not directly comparable. In these cases, cost-benefit analysis may be the most appropriate economic evaluation technique. Cost-benefit analysis (CBA) attempts to put a monetary valuation on the consequences of the intervention. This monetary measure is understood to reflect the amount of money society is willing to pay for the output of the program. Dollars then become the common metric for making comparisons between the outcomes of policies in a variety of programmatic areas and for measuring these outcomes against the costs of the programs. Policymakers can assess the benefit-cost ratios or the net benefits (benefits minus costs) of alternative programs to devise a rank ordering of priorities. However, as will be discussed in much greater detail in chapter 7, there are numerous conceptual and empirical problems in developing these willingness-to-pay estimates, including the task of placing a value on the lives saved by a particular program (Fisher, Chestnut, and Violette 1989; O'Brien and Gafni 1996; Mrozek and Taylor 2002). Health researchers have often been averse to making these valuations, so that cost-effectiveness analysis and cost-utility analysis are used much more widely in the health care arena. However, recent methodological developments incorporate the concept of willingness to pay for a QALY, and also summarize variation in this willingness to pay with threshold analyses and cost-effectiveness acceptability curves, thus making closer links among CEA, CUA, and CBA (Pauly 1995; Willan and Briggs 2006; Briggs, Claxton, and Sculpher 2006).

Use of Cost-Effectiveness Analysis

The cost-effectiveness approach was used in the early years (1965–68) of the planning, programming, and budgeting era in the US Department of Health, Education, and Welfare (now the Department of Health and Human Services). This federal agency undertook a number of studies of various disease-control programs to determine which programs had the highest payoff in terms of number of lives saved and disabilities prevented per dollar of cost (Grosse 1970). For the cancer-control program from 1968 to 1972, it was found that the cost per death averted ranged from a low of $2,217 for uterine-cervical cancer, to $6,046 for breast cancer, $43,729 for cancers of the head and neck, and $46,181 for cancers of the colon and rectum. These figures were used to compare the return on investments in these programs with other programs designed to save lives, such as seatbelt education and the prevention of drunk driving (Grosse 1970, 532–36).

Applications of cost-effectiveness analysis in health care began to expand during the 1970s (Weinstein and Stason 1977; Shepard and Thompson 1979). Much of this literature was clinical in nature, and some of it was controversial. For example, Duncan Neuhauser and Ann Lewicki (1975) studied a recommended protocol for screening cancer of the colon. The procedure consisted of six sequential stool tests for occult blood: If any of the tests were positive, a barium enema would be administered. Sherman Folland, Allen Goodman, and Miron Stano (1997, 579) summarize the marginal and average cost per case of colon cancer detected drawn from the study. The marginal cost per case detected is calculated by dividing the incremental or additional screening cost of the next test by the additional number of cancer cases detected, while the average cost per case is calculated by dividing the total screening costs by the total number of cases detected. Neuhauser and Lewicki (1975) showed that the average cost per case detected was small and increased relatively slowly to $2,451 after six tests. However, the marginal cost rose much more rapidly and exceeded $47 million for the sixth test. Although criticisms have been raised about the Neuhauser and Lewicki study (Brown and Burrows 1990; Gastonis 1990), the example shows how cost-effectiveness analysis can help alert health policymakers to issues regarding program costs and outcomes that might otherwise have remained obscure.

The federal government began to use cost-effectiveness analysis to examine public health policies much more extensively in the late 1970s and 1980s. This trend led to the publication in the 1990s of two federally supported guides to the use of cost-effectiveness analysis. *Prevention Effectiveness: A Guide to Decision Analysis and Economic Evaluation* was originally written "to introduce Centers for Disease Control and Prevention staff to the concepts of decision and economic analysis, to provide guidance on methods to maximize comparability of studies, and to provide access to frequently used reference information. It has been adapted to meet the need of scientists and managers in state and local health departments and managed care organizations as well as students in public health" and other disciplines (Haddix et al. 1996, ix).

Similarly, the Panel on Cost-Effectiveness in Health and Medicine, a group of experts appointed by the US Public Health Service, was charged with "assessing the state of the science in cost-effectiveness analysis; with identifying methodologic inconsistencies and fragilities in the technique; with fostering consensus, where possible, with respect to standardizing the conduct of studies; and with proposing steps that can be taken to address remaining issues and uncertainties in the methodology" (Gold et al. 1996, vii). The outcome of this panel was the book *Cost-Effectiveness in Health and Medicine*. Much of the material in this chapter is drawn from these two works, from the second edition of *Prevention Effectiveness* (Haddix et al. 2003), and from the work of Michael Drummond et al. (2005). Briggs, Claxton, and Sculpher (2006) have recently summarized the statistical issues in the use of cost-effectiveness analysis.

The economic analysis of disease-prevention programs, as compared with programs focusing on the treatment and cure of disease, was stimulated in part by Louise Russell's work (1986). Prevention is often argued to be the better policy, given the advantages of avoiding disease rather than repairing the damage it causes. Pain and suffering can be avoided and possible death may be averted. Furthermore, it is often argued that prevention costs less than treatment, given the savings in medical treatment costs from the cases of disease prevented. In a 1979 surgeon general's report, President Jimmy Carter wrote that prevention "can substantially reduce the suffering of our people and the burden on our expensive system of medical care" (US Department of Health, Education, and Welfare 1979).

Louise Russell notes that it is unclear whether the cost-savings argument is valid in all cases, or whether it is even the appropriate criterion for evaluating disease-prevention programs. The costs of a disease-prevention program relate to the size of the population at risk, while the benefits are received by the much smaller group of people who would have contracted the disease in the absence of prevention. The costs and benefits of a treatment program are focused only on those who have actually become ill. Thus, the costs per person of acute care may be much higher than those for prevention, while still producing the same or lower cost per life saved or case avoided. There are also risks with the preventive treatment, such as side effects of vaccines or possible misdiagnoses. Whether these potential side effects are worth the possible gain in length of life is a question of individual values. Furthermore, the time span between preventive measures and their associated health benefits may be considerable, whereas there is a much more direct association between incurring costs and receiving the benefits in the treatment of disease (Russell 1986, 7–9; 1993, 1994). Investment in prevention can be worthwhile, even if costs are not saved by the particular intervention. What matters is the comparison between the additional health impact and the added costs of the intervention. If these comparisons are similar to investments in other policy areas, then investment in prevention activities is a sound economic decision. These issues will be discussed in more detail in the following sections of this chapter and in the case study to be analyzed.

THE COMPONENTS OF A COST-EFFECTIVENESS ANALYSIS

The following are the major steps to be undertaken in any cost-effectiveness analysis (Haddix et al. 2003):

1. Frame the problem and identify the options to be considered.
2. Identify the appropriate outcome measures for the problem.

3. Identify intervention and outcome costs.

4. Use the most appropriate model to analyze the alternatives under consideration.

5. Identify the probabilities and other data needed to construct the analytic model.

6. Specify the discount rate for any future costs or outcomes in the model.

7. Identify the sources of uncertainty and plan sensitivity analyses.

8. Define the feasibility of analyzing any distributional effects of alternative strategies.

Framing the Problem

The first step, framing the problem, might seem to be basic and obvious. However, the policy analyst often has to give considerable thought to this stage of the analysis. As we noted with the examples given in chapter 2, most policy problems are not well structured. In the news media a particular public program or strategy is often said to be cost effective. The real question, however, is whether the program or strategy is cost effective compared with an alternative. Cost-effectiveness analysis always involves a comparison of the outcomes and costs of one or more alternatives. For example, Farnham et al. (2008) compared the cost effectiveness of alternative HIV-screening strategies in different health care settings. In some cases, one alternative may be the status quo, or no policy.

In other health policy areas, researchers have compared the costs and effects of screening women for cervical cancer to a policy of no screening, but have also compared screening every five years to screening every three or two years or even annually. This is known as extending screening on the intensive margin (Phelps 2010). Other alternatives could be compared, such as extending cervical cancer screening to groups of women who are currently not being screened, particularly the elderly and women of Hispanic origin (Russell 1994). For mammography screening for breast cancer, protocols typically focus on women over fifty years old, in whom the incidence of the disease is the greatest. The issue of how often women in their forties should be screened became a flashpoint in fall 2009, when the US Preventive Services Task Force recommended that these women be tested every other year rather than every year. Many professional and advocacy groups argued that this policy would deprive women of a life-saving test (Kolata 2009). Applying a screening procedure to specific groups would be extending the screening on the extensive margin (Phelps 2010).

In extending a screening policy on either the intensive or extensive margin, it would be expected that the additional benefits of the extension, such as the number of additional cases of breast or cervical cancer detected, would decline as the intervention was being extended to populations in which the prevalence of the disease was lower. Since the additional costs of these extensions would probably increase, a policy that might be cost effective in one population could easily become less so when extended elsewhere.

In all of these studies, analysts need to consider what may happen under the different policy alternatives regarding such issues as the behavior of participants, the quality of the screening procedures used, and the prevalence of the health condition in various populations. Each of these factors will influence the costs and outcomes of the various alternatives. The question is always what would happen with the given policy in place, compared to what would happen without the policy or with a specific alternative. Thus, cost-effectiveness analysis involves a "with and without" comparison, not a "before and after" comparison.

Because there are often no empirical data on what might have happened if the policy had not been in place, or what could happen under some hypothetical alternative, the policy analyst must often use a modeling technique, such as decision-analysis or state-transition modeling, to compare alternative policy options. The logic of a decision-analysis model forces the analyst to clearly think through the steps by which a policy option could be implemented and how these steps differ among policies under consideration. In health care policy, the counterfactual, or what would have happened under another scenario, may be difficult to determine, given the uncertainties associated with many health care events (Rice 2003). However, the uncertainty associated with many individual decisions about health care may be reduced in the study of populations, since describing in probability terms the prevalence of disease among different populations is the task of epidemiologists.

Perspective of the Analysis

Choosing a perspective for the analysis is an integral part of framing the problem and selecting the alternatives. The perspective recommended by both Haddix et al. (1996, 2003) and the Panel on Cost-Effectiveness in Health and Medicine (Gold et al. 1996) is the societal perspective. Using the societal perspective means that all costs and effects of the programs must be included, regardless of who pays the costs and who receives the benefits. This approach is the most comprehensive and the most relevant for making policy decisions that will determine the allocation of society's resources among competing activities. Using the societal perspective may have a particular impact on the definition and measurement of program costs. Program costs are often listed in an agency's budget or in the financial statements of a private-sector firm; these costs could simply be added together and compared with the program's output. However, from the societal perspective in economic program evaluation, monetary costs in these types of documents may not adequately reflect the true economic costs of the program, or measure all the costs to society related to the provision of the program's output.

In examining both the private and public sectors of the economy, economists usually employ the societal perspective that measures the opportunity costs of producing various types of output. These costs must be included when using the societal perspective for either cost-effectiveness or cost-benefit analysis, and so this discussion is relevant for both this chapter and the one that follows. Opportunity costs measure the cost of using society's resources in one activity in terms of the opportunities foregone or the activities not undertaken. In some cases these costs are equal to the monetary costs found in an agency's budget. However, in other cases budgetary costs reflect an accounting definition rather than an economic definition of costs.

Furthermore, some opportunity costs are not found in a given agency's budget and may not easily be evaluated in monetary terms. Certain external costs, such as those resulting from pollution, are imposed on other individuals from the production of a given output and are not recognized by the producer. Opportunity costs also include resources not available to society due to an illness or injury. The loss of a person's contribution to the work force is often considered in a cost-effectiveness analysis since it is an opportunity cost, as would be the value assigned to a person's healthy time that has been lost (Haddix et al. 1996, 2003). Issues in measuring opportunity costs from the societal perspective will be discussed in more detail below.

Although the societal perspective is recommended as the standard for cost-effectiveness analysis, decision makers may also want to adopt other perspectives for various studies. These include the perspectives of:

1. federal, state, and local governments (the impact on the budgets of specific agencies undertaking a prevention program or on programs such as Medicaid and Medicare, which fund the purchase of health services);

2. health-care providers (the costs imposed on various types of hospitals, health maintenance organizations [HMOs], or other providers because of the adoption of particular prevention programs;

3. business (the impact of illnesses or prevention activities on health-related employee benefits); and

4. individuals (the costs of undertaking a current prevention activity with uncertain future benefits or the costs of illness paid out-of-pocket) (Haddix et al. 1996, 16).

For example, to answer questions from the business community about the impact of HIV in the workplace and to engage the business community in HIV prevention, the CDC requested a study of the costs to business of an HIV-infected worker (Farnham and Gorsky 1994). This study focused on the impact of HIV on employee health and life insurance, company retraining costs, and employee pension plans, factors typically not considered when estimating the costs of illness from the societal perspective.

Identifying Outcome Measures

The second step in a cost-effectiveness analysis is to identify the outcome measures appropriate for the analysis. Outcome measures must be relevant to the interventions analyzed and must be the same for all interventions. Ideally, a cost-effectiveness analysis should focus on the final outcomes resulting from an intervention, such as life-years gained, rather than any intermediate outcomes, such as the number of cases identified or the number of persons treated under a given intervention. Intermediate outcomes may be used if data on final outcomes are not available, or if it is difficult to make a link between the intermediate and final outcomes. For example, the outcome of a clinical intervention to treat hypertension could be measured by the amount of blood pressure reduction achieved, while the treatment of high cholesterol could be measured by the percentage of serum cholesterol reduction. Outcomes of HIV-screening programs could be measured by the number of infections identified. Although these intermediate outcomes may have value in their own right, such as confirming the correct diagnosis of cases of HIV infection, the objects of interest for policy analysts are typically the final outcome and the links between intermediate and final outcomes. The relevant questions are (1) how reduced blood pressure or serum cholesterol affects the length and quality of an individual's life, and (2) how many cases of HIV infection are prevented, or how many life-years are saved, by a prevention strategy. Links between intermediate and final outcomes may be derived directly from the results of clinical trials or by extrapolation of clinical trial data. "For example, Oster and Epstein (1987) used an epidemiological model, based on the risk equations in the Framingham Heart Study, to link reduction in total serum cholesterol with coronary heart disease risk and survival" (Drummond et al. 2005, 108). This is a good example of how analysts confront the issue of problem complexity discussed in chapter 2.

In some cases, there may not be a well-established link between the intermediate and final outcome. For example, in evaluating an intervention designed to reduce the blood-lead level in children, the number of children with blood-lead levels less than a certain amount may be selected as the outcome measure. The final outcome measure of interest would more likely relate to the gains in IQ points from lowering blood-lead levels. But because the relationship between blood-lead levels and IQ has not been definitively established, the intermediate outcome may be more appropriate in this case (Haddix et al. 1996). Thus, in using intermediate outcome measures, the policy analyst should either "(1) make a case for the intermediate endpoint having value or clinical relevance in its own right; (2) be confident that the link between intermediate and final outcomes has been adequately established by previous research; or (3) ensure that any uncertainty surrounding the link is adequately characterized in the economic study" (Drummond et al. 2005, 109).

The choice of outcome measures can also influence the results of the analysis. For example, the use of survival statistics can bias evaluation results in favor of a screening intervention. The results of a prostate cancer screening intervention may be reported in terms of the length of time the patient survived after diagnosis resulting from a screening exam or blood test. Yet this screening exam may simply serve to identify the cancer early, while having little or no impact on life expectancy. This is called "lead-time bias," and it can be an important factor in evaluating prostate cancer screening; many prostate cancers may be slow growing and never result in the patient's death, and treatment for the disease is uncertain in effectiveness and has many unpleasant side effects (Russell 1994).

Serious side effects of an intervention should be included in the cost-effectiveness analysis if they exist. For example, it has been proposed to fortify cereal grains with folic acid to increase the intake of women of childbearing age to try to prevent neural tube defects. Since the increased intake of folic acid by older persons may complicate the diagnosis of vitamin B-12 deficiency and ultimately result in permanent neurological complications and death, these side effects should be included in an economic evaluation of alternative strategies for preventing neural tube defects (Haddix et al. 1996).

Similarly, analysts performing economic evaluations of counseling and testing programs often diverge in their definition of program outcomes. Some studies simply measure the number of persons screened or the number of infections identified by a screening process. Others make assumptions about the number of HIV infections that will be prevented by a particular screening process. Substantial variation exists in these economic evaluations of HIV counseling and testing programs in different settings (Farnham 1998).

Defining and Measuring Costs

Defining and measuring the relevant costs for a cost-effectiveness analysis is also an ambiguous exercise. The net cost of a disease-prevention intervention is typically defined as the cost of the intervention minus the cost of illnesses averted minus the productivity losses averted. Thus the net cost measures the cost of the intervention, including the cost of side effects and the costs to participants, while subtracting out the costs of diagnosis and treatment associated with cases of the health problem averted and the productivity losses averted as a result of the intervention (Haddix et al. 1996). "An ideal cost-effectiveness analysis begins by identifying all of the consequences of adopting one intervention or another, including use of resources (medical services use, public health program costs, informal caregiving, and patient time costs . . .) and the effects of the intervention on health status. . . . The amount or magnitude of each change is measured. Finally, these changes are valued: Changes in resource use are converted into a summary cost using dollar values for each input" (Gold et al. 1996, 178).

We discussed the importance of cost-accounting systems for public policy implementation in chapter 3. Many of the issues discussed there, such as the focus on costs per unit of production, on marginal changes in cost per result, and on accounting for the full pattern of costs over time, are relevant for cost-effectiveness analysis. However, some costs necessary for the economic evaluation of public programs are different from those used for management and control. Ideally, economic evaluation of a program is incorporated as the program is developed and implemented, so that relevant cost information can be obtained from the program's accounting system. In reality, economic evaluation is often added on later, and analysts must contend with the fact that few or no data have been collected on the relevant costs.

Some of the costs that economic evaluation needs to assess (explicit) are easily measured, since they result from market transactions, while other types of costs (implicit) may have to be imputed for the analysis. This is particularly important if the analysis is performed from the societal perspective, as discussed above. Intervention costs typically include the costs of tests, drugs, supplies, health care personnel, and medical facilities. Other nonmedical costs that may be relevant include child care costs for a parent attending a smoking cessation program, the increased costs of a special diet, the costs of transportation to and from a clinic, and the implicit costs of the time spent by family members or volunteers in providing home health care (Gold et al. 1996). Peter Arno (1986) has argued that the implicit costs of volunteer time were very important in the early years of the AIDS epidemic. Since the use of volunteers was much more widespread in the San Francisco area than in other parts of the country, these implicit costs could have accounted for geographic differences in the estimated monetary costs of treating HIV/AIDS.

The value of the patient or client's time is another potentially important implicit cost that is often not measured. Failure to include these implicit costs could bias the results of economic evaluations against interventions that required more use of market-purchased inputs and less use of patient time, since the measured money cost of these interventions would be higher than for those that required a greater portion of patient time. This could be important in evaluating the cost effectiveness of street outreach HIV-prevention programs, compared to those located at a particular site (Wright-DeAguero, Gorsky, and Seeman 1996). A crucial difference between these programs would be the use of professionals' time versus patients' time. More than half of the studies surveyed in an analysis of HIV counseling and testing programs in various settings used only aggregate cost figures, with no breakdown among the categories of counseling and testing costs. Outreach costs that may be incurred to find HIV-infected and high-risk persons who do not appear for counseling and testing in established settings have typically not been analyzed. Only two of the forty-three studies surveyed included any valuation of patient or client time (Farnham 1998).

When measuring costs from the societal perspective, opportunity costs must truly reflect the value of using the resource in a particular activity. This value must be included in a cost-effectiveness analysis even if the agency conducting the analysis does not have to pay this cost. For example, a city might be considering two alternative sites for a proposed park. In one case the city already owns the vacant plot of land, while it has to purchase the land in the other case. It might be tempting to argue that the cost of the first alternative is lower than that of the second. Although it is true that the monetary cost to the city is lower in the first case, the opportunity cost of using the first plot of land is not necessarily lower. The city needs to determine the value of the first plot of land in its next best alternative use, or what price it would command in the marketplace. This opportunity cost must be included in a cost-effectiveness analysis, because the city could lease or sell that plot of land. The cost of using that land to provide park and recreation services is not zero, unless there is no alternative use for the land. Of course, the city might not want to include this implicit opportunity cost if, for political or other reasons, decision makers were already in favor of the one park option. The decision makers might also argue that the implicit cost is neither understandable by nor relevant to their constituents, since this is not an out-of-pocket cost.

A similar example from the private sector would be the treatment of time spent by the owner of a company in the production of a good or service. In a family-operated business, the owner may not explicitly be paid a salary, so that the costs of his or her time may not be included as a cost of production. This practice will result in an overstatement of the firm's profits. If the owner could earn $40,000 per year by working in some other activity, that figure represents the opportunity cost of the individual's time in the family business, but this cost may not be reflected in any existing financial statement.

In a competitive market economy in which resources are fully employed, the market price that an agency must pay for its inputs typically reflects their opportunity costs. For example, if the wages of construction workers are determined by the forces of supply and demand (as discussed in the previous chapter), and if all workers who want to work are able to do so, then the monetary cost of hiring those workers for a public-sector program, which is reflected in the agency's budget, should equal the opportunity cost of employing the workers. The only way to draw workers into the public sector is to pay them what they could earn in the private sector. However, if certain types of workers face the prospect of continuing unemployment, the opportunity cost of employing them for a public-sector project may be less than the monetary cost in the agency's budget.

In a detailed study of construction projects, Robert Haveman (1983) estimated the proportion of labor and capital that was drawn from unemployed resources by comparing the pattern of resource demands with the occupational and regional pattern of labor unemployment and the industrial pattern of excess plant capacity. He argued that the opportunity cost of the expenditures for these projects in 1960 varied between 70% and 90% of the monetary costs. The validity of adjusting monetary costs to reflect problems of unemployment depends upon whether the opportunity cost of using unemployed labor is zero or extremely low. The value of that nonworking time may not be zero if it is used, for instance, for family activities or going to school. Furthermore, macroeconomic conditions also influence the rates of unemployment. Edward Gramlich (1981, 67) argues that the opportunity cost of unemployed labor is less than its monetary cost only if: "(1) The reduction in unemployment can be sustained. Inflationary pressures will not be set up which require other cutbacks in spending demand, generating corresponding increases in unemployment somewhere else in the economy. (2) The project is responsible for reducing unemployment. Tax reductions, monetary policy, or price flexibility would not have done so anyway. (3) It can be persuasively argued that the supply curve or some other notion of social externality makes the opportunity cost below the market wage."

Since valuing labor costs below their monetary costs makes a public-sector project look more favorable, advocates of a project will often be tempted to follow this procedure. Gramlich argues that this approach must be resisted if the above three conditions are not met. Otherwise, public-sector projects either do not really create jobs, or they are not the only way to do so, or they create jobs that do not have much social value (Gramlich 1981, 1990).

A good health care example of the problems of adjusting budgetary costs and of measuring all costs associated with a program is given by Burton Weisbrod (1983) in his comparison of hospital- with community-based treatment of the mentally ill. He argues that the cost figures that the State of Wisconsin provided for inpatient care at the Mendota Mental Health Institute (MMHI) differ from the true social or opportunity costs in three respects: "(1) The opportunity cost of the land on which the hospital is located had been disregarded; (2) the depreciation of the hospital buildings was based on historical cost rather than replacement cost; and (3) research carried out at MMHI was included in the per diem cost figure for the hospital" (Weisbrod 1983, 237). The land-valuation problem was discussed above. Depreciation presents a problem because accounting procedures typically use historical costs. Yet it is the current cost of replacing the asset that best reflects the opportunity cost of using the asset to provide output. Research costs were included in the per diem figure for accounting purposes, but these costs were not directly related to the treatment of patients. Thus, the per diem cost estimated by the state "was adjusted upward to allow for an opportunity cost of 8% on the estimated value of the land and the depreciated replacement cost of the physical plant, and it was adjusted slightly downward to account for research services" (237).

Other costs that Weisbrod attempted to measure included secondary treatment costs by other agencies, institutions, and professions; law enforcement costs associated with the different modes of treatment; external costs caused by the patients' illnesses; and patient maintenance costs. Secondary costs included those of other hospitals and psychiatric institutions, halfway houses, visiting nurses, and counseling services. Law enforcement costs were obtained from patient interviews about the number of police and court contacts, the number of nights spent in jail, and the number of contacts with probation and parole officers. External costs related to members of the patients' immediate families or other individuals who suffered from the illegal or disruptive behavior of the patients. It was impossible to place monetary values on these costs. However, family members were asked whether they had experienced work or school absences, disruption of domestic or social routines, trouble with neighbors, or stress-related physical ailments as a result of the patient's illness. They were also questioned about expenses incurred that were related to the patient. These responses were used to categorize each family as suffering a "severe," "moderate," "mild," or "no" burden from the patient's illness. Although the attempt was made to count only the incremental patient maintenance costs associated with the inpatient program, data limitations meant that all maintenance costs were actually included in the analysis (Weisbrod 1983, 239–41). Thus, implementation problems may prevent analysts from calculating all costs as theoretically desired, or from valuing all costs in monetary terms. These problems should be noted and their implications discussed, so that decision makers have full information about the limits of the analysis.

Another cost measurement issue that may be important in evaluating health care policies is the difference between the costs of and the charges for medical and health care services. There may be substantial differences between the fees that hospitals and other institutions charge for their services and the actual economic costs of providing the services (Finkler 1982; Drummond et al. 2005). Hospitals engage in cost shifting both to maximize their revenues from various public and private third-party payers and to provide services for those patients without insurance who are unable to pay. Different individuals or groups may, therefore, be charged fees that are more or less than the actual cost of providing the service to them.

Many studies do not provide a clear distinction between these two terms. For example, in estimating the lifetime cost of HIV and AIDS, Fred Hellinger (1993, 474) uses the term *cost*, but defines this as "total charges for services." Data on provider charges are generally much more readily available than data on the actual opportunity cost of providing the services. However, cost-to-charge ratios are often used to make the adjustment between these two sets of concepts. The analyst can use one hospital-level ratio to make the adjustment, or take a more detailed approach: "(1) The patient's detailed bill is reconfigured into a set of exhaustive charges, or billing, categories; (2) each charge category is assigned to a specific hospital cost center; (3) the cost-to-charge ratio for each center is used to convert these assigned charges to their corresponding cost estimates; and (4) the latter are summed to yield the cost of admission"

(Gold et al. 1996, 205). Gold and co-authors provide further details on how this approach has been implemented for different health care services.

Timing of Costs

A final issue in measuring the costs of an intervention involves the timing of the costs, if they extend a number of years into the future. Since this discussion also relates to the stream of future health outcomes or benefits of a program, measured in monetary terms, it is also relevant to cost-benefit analysis, presented in the following chapter. As noted above, these issues may be particularly relevant for evaluating disease-prevention interventions with either cost-effectiveness or cost-benefit analyses, since the outcomes or benefits of these interventions may occur many years in the future, while many of the costs may arise in the present. The question is how to compare costs and benefits that arise during different periods.

We discussed the issue of multiyear costs from the budgeting perspective in chapter 3. There we argued that decision makers must consider the difference between capital costs and current operating costs to fully account for all the costs of a program and to plan the correct methods of financing multiyear projects. The issues here are similar but are now being discussed from the perspective of program evaluation.

The timing problem arises because individuals weigh benefits and costs that occur now or in the near future more heavily than those that occur in the distant future. A dollar that I receive next year is worth more than a dollar that I receive ten years from now, because I can invest next year's dollar so that it will be worth more than $1 in ten years. This argument relates to the productivity of capital and investments, and has nothing to do with the inflation rate. It would still be relevant in a world of zero inflation. Thus, it is necessary to calculate the present value of both costs and benefits in real terms, in order to make them comparable in terms of the time dimension. This present-value calculation involves the choice of a discount rate. What discount rate to choose is an extremely controversial question; the choice of rate can have a major impact on the results of a cost-effectiveness or a cost-benefit analysis.

The calculation of the present value of a flow of costs or benefits is the reverse of the compound-interest problem. Compound interest attempts to determine what a given amount of money will be worth a given number of years in the future at a given interest rate for compounding. Thus, $100 will be worth $110 one year from now, if the interest rate is 10%. If this amount is left to compound for another year, it will grow to $121. Conversely, the present value of $110 received one year from now is $100, using a discount rate of 10%. This result can be calculated from the following formula: Present value = $110 / (1 + 0.10) = $100. The present value of $121 received two years from now is also $100; this can be calculated as $121 / (1 + 0.10)^2$. Thus, the present value of an annual stream of costs or benefits flowing n years in the future can be derived as follows:

$$\text{Present value} = R_1 / (1 + i) + R_2 / (1 + i)^2 + \ldots + R_n / (1 + i)^n,$$

where R_n is the dollar amount of the cost or benefit in the nth year and i is the discount rate.

The choice of a discount rate can have a significant impact on the resulting present-value calculations. Suppose that benefits from Project A equal $100 in year one and $0 thereafter, whereas benefits of Project B are $0 in the first nineteen years and $100 in year twenty. This is an extreme example of a short-term versus a long-term project with equal monetary benefits. Using the above formulas and a discount rate of 5%, the present value of benefits for Project A is $95.23, while for Project B it is $37.89. Thus, benefits received one year from now are weighted much more heavily than benefits received twenty years from now. If a discount rate of 20% is used, the present value of the benefits of Project A is $83.33, while the present value for Project B is only $2.61. The present value of benefits for both projects decreases with the higher rate, but there is a much larger drop for Project B. Thus, raising the discount rate favors the short-term investment project. Low rates favor long-term investments.

The following more realistic example shows how changing the discount rate can significantly affect the relationship between a project's benefits and costs. Suppose that the project life is twenty-five years and that the initial capital cost is $5 million. Operating costs are $100,000 per year for twenty-five years, and benefits are $600,000 per year. Table 6.1 shows the benefits, costs, benefit-cost ratio, and net benefits (benefits minus costs) calculated for four different discount rates, ranging from 0% (no discounting) to 10%.

It can be seen in table 6.1 that the undiscounted benefits of $7.5 million drop to $3.7 million when a discount rate of only 3% is used in the example. The net benefits keep decreasing with a higher discount rate and become negative when a 10% rate is used. Thus, raising the discount rate alone can change the net benefits of a project from positive to negative. These issues are of particular importance to many health care interventions, for which benefits and costs may extend over a significant period of time.

Given the importance of the discount rate, the question becomes: What rate should be used in cost-effectiveness and cost-benefits studies? In cost-effectiveness analysis, there is also the question of whether health outcomes,

Table 6.1 The Effects of Discount Rates on Project Evaluation

	Discount Rates (%)			
	0.00	3.00	5.00	10.00
Benefits (B)	$15,000,000	$10,448,000	$8,456,000	$5,442,000
Costs (C)	$7,500,000	$6,741,000	$6,409,000	$5,906,000
B / C	2.00	1.55	1.32	0.92
B – C	$7,500,000	$3,707,000	$2,047,000	–$464,000

B = benefits; C = costs; B / C = benefit-cost ratio; B – C = net benefits.

which are not measured in dollar terms, should be discounted. These questions are controversial both in theory and in actual practice.

It is often argued that the opportunity cost, or the rate of return that resources could earn in the private sector, is the appropriate choice for a discount rate (Baumol 1970; Gramlich 1981, 1990; Drummond et al. 2005). If resources are drawn from the private sector of the economy into the public sector, they should provide a rate of return in the public sector at least as great as what could have been earned in the private sector. However, the question still remains of what rate measures this opportunity cost, since interest rates vary with the source from which the project's resources are drawn. A variety of interest rates in the private sector reflect differences in risk, the impact of distortionary taxes, and imperfections in the marketplace. Government monetary and fiscal policies in pursuit of various macroeconomic goals also influence interest rates. A weighted average of different rates may be most appropriate, although the choice of rates is unclear.

There is another viewpoint that argues that a social discount rate derived through the political process should be used instead of any market-related rates (Baumol 1970; Gramlich 1981, 1990; Gold et al. 1996; Krahn and Gafni 1993; Drummond et al. 2005). Arguments for the use of a social discount rate lower than market rates reflect concern about whether society overvalues present consumption relative to future consumption, and whether individuals have preferences for social outcomes that differ from their preferences for private market outcomes. Even if these arguments are accepted, there is still the question of determining the optimal social discount rate.

There has also been considerable debate about whether nonmonetary health outcomes should be discounted; that is, should a year of life gained ten years from now be valued differently than a year of life gained one year from now? Marthe Gold et al. (1996) and Anne Haddix et al. (1996) present comprehensive summaries of the literature on this debate. A consensus seems to have developed that future health outcomes should be discounted at the same rate as monetary costs and benefits: "Future health outcomes are also discounted, not because health outcomes realized today are more valuable than health outcomes realized tomorrow, but because in prevention-effectiveness studies, if health outcomes are not discounted but costs are discounted, the cost per health outcome prevented will decrease over time. Thus discounting health outcomes at the same rate as monetary outcomes creates an 'exchange rate' for dollars and health outcomes that is time invariant" (Haddix et al. 1996, 79).

The actual range of discount rates used in cost-effectiveness and cost-benefit analyses reflects the uncertainties in the theoretical discussions. Robert Lind (1982, 82) recommended a rate of 1% for "safe investments" and 2% for "safe long-term assets." J. A. Lesser and R. O. Zerbe (1994) argued for a real discount rate between 2.5 and 5.0% for public projects. The British National Health Service uses a real discount rate of 6% (Parsonage and Neuburger 1992), while the World Bank (1993) has settled on a 3% rate. The US Office of Management and Budget has suggested rates between 2 and 3% for cost-effectiveness studies that focus on the least-cost means for the government to achieve some predetermined objective, and a 7% real rate for cost-benefit analyses in which all outcomes and costs are measured in monetary terms (Gold et al. 1996). The two major guidelines for health care economic evaluations have reached a reasonable consensus on this issue. Haddix et al. (1996) recommended either a 3% or 5% real rate, with sensitivity analysis undertaken with rates ranging from 0% (no discounting) to 8%. Gold et al. (1996) suggested 3%, with sensitivity analysis ranging from 0% to 7%. Haddix et al. (2003) argued for a 3% real rate, which had become standard in health policy analysis by this time.

Use of Decision Analysis and Other Analytic Methods

Decision analysis is a key quantitative tool used to derive the relationships between costs and outcome measures in a cost-effectiveness analysis. "Decision analysis is an explicit, quantitative, and systematic approach to decision making under conditions of uncertainty" (Haddix et al. 2003, 103). It is a tool that can be used to calculate the expected utility, cost, or benefit of different policies or alternative courses of action. For use in cost-effectiveness analysis, most decision-analysis programs can be run so as to simultaneously calculate both the expected cost and the expected outcome of each policy being analyzed. The costs and outcomes are "expected" in that they are influenced by the probability of certain events occurring that are not under the control of the decision maker. An expected outcome is calculated by multiplying the value associated with that outcome and the probability of that outcome occurring. This may be done repeatedly, depending upon the chain of events associated with each policy option.

As outlined by Haddix et al. (2003), the basic steps in a decision analysis are the following:

1. Specify the decision problem and objectives.
2. Develop a model to structure the decision problem.
3. Estimate the relevant probabilities.
4. Value the outcomes or consequences.
5. Analyze the base case.
6. Interpret the results in light of the inherent uncertainty.

A decision node is the first point of choice in a decision tree, which shows the alternative options or policies being evaluated. Chance nodes are then built into the tree, reflecting events whose outcomes are not under the control of the decision maker. Probabilities, based on literature searches, the results of scientific studies, estimates made by a panel of experts, or educated guesses, are assigned to each chance node. Outcome measures are assigned to each terminal node or endpoint of the sequence of events. To obtain measures of expected costs and consequences, decision trees are averaged out or folded back. This means that the value of the outcome for each branch is multiplied by its respective probability. At each chance node, the products of this multiplication process for each of the branches emanating from that node are summed. This process, which is repeated until the analyst has arrived at the decision node, then gives a measure of the expected costs and outcomes associated with each decision option or policy.

Because the decision tree underlying any cost-effectiveness analysis usually contains numerous input variables (probabilities, cost, and outcome measures), and because the values of many of these variables may not be known with great certainty, sensitivity analysis is used to determine how much the expected costs and outcomes of the model are affected by changes in the input variables. Sensitivity analysis can be used to show how much an expected cost or outcome changes if the numerical value of a probability or outcome measure is changed, or how much an estimated input value would have to change to produce a different result for the entire analysis. It can also show what value a variable would need to have for two policy options to have equal expected value (threshold analysis), or what happens to the results of the model if best-case or worst-case scenario estimates are used (Haddix et al. 2003).

Constructing a decision tree is such a useful tool for cost-effectiveness analysis because it forces the policy analyst to explicitly outline the various policy options and identify the costs and consequences associated with each option. The decision tree can provide a much more comprehensive analysis than simply using intuition; it compiles more information and can consider many more options. Decision analysis can help an analyst understand and convey information about policy options more clearly; it lends structure, organization, and reason to what are often very difficult decision-making processes (Haddix et al. 2003).

Recent analyses have started to make greater use of state-transition models, which focus on transitions between different health states. Health states are related to factors such as disease stage and treatment status. Transition probabilities govern how individuals in the models move among the states. One special type of state-transition model is the Markov model, in which the transition probabilities depend only on the current state and not on previous states. These state-transition models are evaluated either by running cohorts of the population through the model, or with Monte Carlo simulations in which patients are randomly selected from a cohort and run through the model one at a time. Details on these methods are provided by Haddix et al. (2003) and Briggs, Claxton, and Sculpher (2006).

Use of Quality-Adjusted Outcome Measures in HIV Prevention

The Panel on Cost-Effectiveness in Health and Medicine recommended the use of QALYs as the preferred outcome measure in health care cost-effectiveness studies (Gold et al. 1996). Research on the use of QALYs for HIV-prevention interventions has been summarized by Holtgrave and Qualls 1995; Holtgrave, Qualls, and Graham 1996; Holtgrave and Pinkerton 1997; Tengs and Lin 2002; and Drummond et al. 2005. Given the development of new drug therapies and rapidly changing approaches to treating HIV infection, estimates of these quality-adjusted outcomes have changed considerably over time.

David Holtgrave and Steven Pinkerton (1997) framed their analysis in terms of a simplified cost-utility ratio for comparing a new HIV counseling and testing program with a do-nothing option (i.e., leaving the program unfunded). Thus, the cost-utility ratio would be $[C - (A)(T)] / [(A)(Q)]$, where C is the cost of the intervention relative to no program, A is the number of HIV infections averted by the program, T is the present value of the medical costs saved by preventing an HIV infection, and Q is the number of QALYs saved by preventing an infection. Although their study focuses on updating estimates of both T and Q, the discussion here will only be on the outcome measure.

Measuring QALYs involves both developing a framework for the stages of disease and attaching weights for the quality of life associated with each stage. In an earlier study, David Holtgrave and Noreen Qualls (1995) adapted a disease-progression framework from an earlier work (Guinan, Farnham, and Holtgrave 1994), with an additional assumption that the average age at the time of HIV infection was twenty-six years. Holtgrave and Qualls then reviewed the available literature on the quality of life for HIV-infected persons to develop the following weights for different disease stages: (1) full health, or a value of 1.0, for persons unaware of their HIV infection; (2) 0.90 of full health for persons aware of their HIV infection but with a moderate disease stage; (3) 0.65 for persons with symptoms and in a more advanced disease stage; and (4) 0.40 of full health for persons with AIDS (acquired immune deficiency syndrome) as defined by clinical conditions, the most advanced disease stage. Assuming that individuals who are not infected with HIV enjoy full health, Holtgrave and Qualls (1995) calculated the average number of QALYs saved (before age 65) by preventing an HIV infection as 28.85. This result represents the difference between the number of years between age 26 and age 65 in perfect health, valued at 1.00 per year, and the number of years in each disease stage, valued with the above weights. Since it was argued above that health outcomes should be discounted to make them comparable to monetary costs, the undiscounted number of 28.85 QALYs is reduced to 9.26 QALYs when a discount rate of 5% is used (Holtgrave and Pinkerton 1997). These calculations are shown in table 6.2.

Given the development of new combination drug therapies in the mid-1990s, which have had an impact on both treatment costs and length and quality of life, David Holtgrave and Steven Pinkerton (1997) updated the estimates presented above. They developed a new model of the progression of the disease that incorporated increased monitoring of HIV in the body and the use of both two- and three-drug therapies. These researchers also surveyed literature on quality of life for persons with HIV: Most of this literature was based on quality-of-life estimates by persons living with HIV. This literature did not fully meet the recommendations of the Panel on Cost-Effectiveness in Health and Medicine that quality adjustments be made on the basis of community-wide surveys of persons not necessarily living with the particular disease in question (Gold et al. 1996). However, those types of data were not

Table 6.2   Calculating the Number of Quality-Adjusted Life Years
(QALYs) for Preventing a Case of HIV Infection

Disease State	No. of Years	Utility Weight	QALYs
Perfect health (age 26–65)	39	1.00	39.00
HIV/AIDS			
Infected, unaware	6	1.00	6.00
Aware, asymptomatic	3	0.90	2.70
Aware, symptomatic	1	0.65	0.65
AIDS-affected	2	0.40	0.80
Sum for HIV/AIDS			10.15

QALYs saved by preventing one infection (undiscounted) = 39 – 10.15 = 28.85

QALYs saved by preventing one infection (discounted at 5%) = 9.26

available for HIV infection. Holtgrave and Pinkerton found fewer differences in the quality-of-life estimates for advanced stages of HIV infection and AIDS, compared with earlier disease stages, than had existed in previous literature. They argued that this might have resulted from "patients learning to cope with HIV disease and using these coping strategies to improve or maintain their quality of life even as health problems mount" (Holtgrave and Pinkerton 1997, 57). These authors noted that community-wide surveys of both infected and noninfected individuals might result in quite different quality weights for advanced disease stages than those derived only from HIV-infected individuals. Holtgrave and Pinkerton also had to make several arbitrary estimates for the weights pertaining to the less severe disease stages, given the lack of empirical estimates for these variables.

Holtgrave and Pinkerton (1997) estimated the number of QALYs saved by preventing an HIV infection to be 11.23, when discounting at the rate of 3% recommended by the Panel on Cost-Effectiveness in Health and Medicine. This estimate is higher than the 9.26 estimate from the Holtgrave and Qualls study (1995), largely due to the use of a 3% rather than a 5% discount rate employed in the earlier study. This increase occurred even though several factors would have lowered the more recent estimate: "First, the new quality of life estimates employed in our calculations of Q are higher than previous estimates of quality of life weights; this tends to decrease Q. Second, our assumption of increased survival from new treatments also tends to decrease the parameter Q. Both of these downward tendencies, however, are more than off-set by the change in the discount rate" (Holtgrave and Pinkerton 1997, 60).

These changes in QALYs saved can have an impact on the economic evaluation of HIV-prevention programs. Since Holtgrave and Pinkerton estimated a larger value for both the costs of treating an HIV infection and the QALYs saved by preventing an infection, their results make HIV-prevention programs appear more cost effective. Some HIV-prevention programs that might not have appeared cost effective using the earlier estimates may be considered cost effective with the new estimates. This example shows how the empirical data drawn from many studies and the assumptions made to incorporate this data in economic evaluations can have an impact on policy judgments about different prevention interventions. It also illustrates how a technical factor, the choice of a discount rate to calculate the present value of costs and outcomes, can have a substantial influence on the results of the evaluation.

Tengs and Lin (2002) noted the variation in the published utility weights for various stages of HIV infection. These weights ranged from 0.69 to 0.88 for asymptomatic HIV infection, 0.48 to 0.82 for symptomatic HIV infection, and 0.24 to 0.79 for AIDS. The variation in these weights was likely due to differences in the methods used for eliciting utility weights, differences in the respondents, or variation in the ways researchers defined the lower and upper bounds of utility scales. The three major methods for eliciting preferences for health states are the standard-gamble, time–trade-off, and rating methods (Patrick and Erickson 1993; Gold et al. 1996; Haddix et al. 2003; Drummond et al. 2005). The standard-gamble method often yields higher utility estimates than the time–trade-off method, while the latter results in higher weights than the rating method. People who have experienced the health condition in question generally report higher weights than those who have not experienced the condition. The zero and one end-points of the utility scale have also been defined differently in various studies.

Tengs and Lin (2002) undertook a meta-analysis of HIV/AIDS utility estimates based on twenty-five published articles reporting seventy-four utilities elicited from 1,956 respondents, in order to pool the results from multiple studies and obtain a combined estimate. They estimated the following values, using patients as respondents: 0.94 for asymptomatic infection; 0.82 for symptomatic infection; and 0.70 for AIDS. The corresponding values for non-patients were: 0.68 for asymptomatic HIV infection; 0.56 for symptomatic infection; and 0.44 for AIDS.

One further question in cost-utility analysis is what the benchmark standard for the cost per QALY gained should be for a program to be considered cost effective. If a program saves costs, it is definitely cost effective. However, a program can also be cost effective if it has a positive cost-effectiveness ratio as long as that ratio is comparable to those for other programs. The standard of $50,000 per QALY, which has long been used in the literature, goes back to 1982, when it was the approximate cost-effectiveness ratio for the use of dialysis for patients with renal failure. Because the Medicare program covered dialysis, it was argued that this cost-effectiveness ratio should be the standard for other programs (Ubel et al. 2003). However, this figure was never even adjusted for inflation over time. Current research indicates that a threshold between $100,000 and $200,000 may be a more realistic benchmark for health policy analyses (Ubel et al. 2003; Braithwaite, Meltzer, et al. 2008; Weinstein 2008). Briggs, Claxton, and Sculpher (2006) outline the procedures for developing cost-effectiveness acceptability curves, which show the proportion of interventions that are cost effective at varying thresholds of dollars spent per QALY gained.

Chapter 6 Case Study

Fighting HIV, a Community at a Time

By Susan Okie, *New York Times*

Washington—Federal health officials are preparing a plan to study a bold new strategy to stop the spread of the AIDS virus: routinely testing virtually every adult in a community, and promptly treating those found to be infected. The strategy is called "test and treat," and officials say the two sites for the three-year study will be the District of Columbia and the Bronx—locales with some of the nation's highest rates of infection with human immunodeficiency virus.

The officials emphasize that this is just a first step. The goal is not to measure whether "test and treat" actually works to slow an epidemic, but whether such a strategy can even be carried out, given the many barriers to being tested and getting medical care. On the path from infection to treatment, "we lose people at every single step," said Dr. Shannon L. Hader, director of the HIV/AIDS administration at this city's Department of Health.

As many as 5 percent of the adults in the District of Columbia are infected—a rate Dr. Hader says is comparable with those in West Africa—and one-third to one-half do not even know they harbor the virus. . . . And even when infection is diagnosed, "getting people from the field to the doctor is the hardest component," said Angela Fulwood Wood, deputy director of Family and Medical Counseling Service, an agency that operates a mobile HIV testing clinic here. Often, she added, someone who has just tested positive "can walk off that day and decide, 'I'm going to pretend that never happened.'"

In 2006, only about half of Washington residents who had a new diagnosis of HIV saw a doctor about the problem within six months. The C.D.C. recommends routine, voluntary HIV testing for everyone ages 13 to 64 as part of regular medical care. But experts say the recommendation is not being followed in many hospitals, clinics and medical practices. Even when doctors do offer the test to patients, "a significant number refuse," said Dr. Anthony S. Fauci, director of the National Institute of Allergy and Infectious Diseases, which is to pay for the test and treat feasibility study.

Researchers planning the study have been meeting with hospital and health officials in Washington and the Bronx to discuss making HIV testing a routine part of visits to doctors, clinics and emergency rooms. Dr. Fauci said testing might also be widely offered in nonmedical settings. "When you have a campaign like this, you've got to pull out all the stops," he said. "How are we going to get everybody? Should we have testing in Wal-Mart? Should we have testing at Nathan's hot dog places?"

The test and treat approach is part of a broader shift toward using medicines for HIV to prevent infection. When an infected person starts taking one of the standard three-drug regimens, the level of the virus in blood and other body fluids drops rapidly, often to undetectable levels. Current treatment guidelines do not call for antiretroviral drugs until there is evidence of progressive damage to the immune system—generally, until the number of CD4 cells, the white blood cells attacked by the virus, drops to 350 per cubic millimeter or lower. (A normal count is at least 1,000.)

The guidelines are intended to balance the treatment benefits with the side effects from the drugs and the possibility of fostering drug resistance in the virus. But there is mounting evidence that early treatment keeps infected people healthy longer. And that could have much wider benefits, researchers say. Last January, Dr. Reuben Granich and colleagues at the World Health Organization published a provocative study using mathematical models to predict the effects of universal testing and immediate treatment on a severe HIV epidemic among heterosexuals. They reported that such a policy, if combined with prevention efforts like promotion of condoms and male circumcision, could virtually eliminate transmission of the virus within 10 years. So far, despite some ambitious efforts, no city or country has come close to achieving universal testing for H.I.V. and treatment for all those infected. But researchers and public health officials are eager to test the potential of such a strategy for stemming the epidemic.

Among specialists, there is already a move toward starting treatment earlier. But in low-income neighborhoods in Washington, some people are reluctant to start treatment, said Ms. Wood, whose HIV testing program and clinic are based in Anacostia, a community in Southeast Washington that has long had high rates of drug abuse and HIV infection, as well as a shortage of health services. Early HIV drugs had multiple side effects, including fat deposits on the upper back that created an unsightly hump. "People saw that when others started taking the medicine, they seemed to get worse," Ms. Wood recalled.

Although the latest drugs have far fewer side effects, many patients still fear that "going on medicines means I'm starting to get sick," she added. A critical component of test and treat will be conveying the message: "Don't wait until you're sick. Do it early."

In the District of Columbia in 2006, only 50 percent of those with new diagnoses of HIV saw a doctor for the problem within six months. Community outreach workers who perform testing are now being retrained to focus on getting their clients into treatment. Positive results obtained with the kits are reported to the health department but are considered preliminary and must be confirmed by a different test that requires a blood sample. "There are so many people who test 'preliminary reactive [positive]' who never return," said Torena White, who was leading the outreach team that afternoon. Often, testers following up on such results must repeatedly call clients or send them letters. If someone with a positive test still does not respond, a health department worker is dispatched to try to track the person down.

Community testing programs are likely to attract people who suspect that they might have contracted HIV. But Ms. Wood said the key to test and treat would be capturing those who did not volunteer for testing because they did not believe they could be infected—"people who are promiscuous at college, the partygoers, the young professionals who go to the club," as she put it.

"Routine testing at either emergency rooms or physicians' offices," she continued. "I think that's our biggest chance of really catching people earlier."

Note

1. Susan Okie, "Fighting HIV, a Community at a Time," *New York Times*, October 27, 2009. This article has been abridged from its original form.

COST-EFFECTIVENESS OF HIV SCREENING AND TREATMENT WITH ANTIRETROVIRAL THERAPY

The case study for this chapter focuses on the "test and treat" strategy proposed in fall 2009 as a new method for preventing HIV infection. The proposed strategy of routinely testing virtually every adult in a community and immediately treating the infected with antiretroviral therapy (ART) builds on the 2006 recommendations by the Centers for Disease Control and Prevention (CDC), which advocated voluntary HIV screening for all patients aged 13 to 64 years as a normal part of medical practice in health care settings including hospitals, acute-care clinics, and sexually transmitted disease (STD) clinics, unless the prevalence of undiagnosed HIV has been documented to be less than 0.1% (CDC 2006). The 2006 policy contrasted with previous recommendations for routine counseling and testing for people at high risk for HIV and for those in acute-care settings in which HIV prevalence was greater than 1% (CDC 1993, 2001).

The case raises the issues of the effectiveness and cost-effectiveness of alternative strategies for addressing the HIV epidemic, including counseling, testing, providing individuals with their test results, and linking HIV-infected persons to care. Strategies differ in terms of the populations targeted for screening, the types of HIV tests used, the level of success in providing confirmed results to those tested, and the benefits of linking infected individuals to care and immediately starting them on antiretroviral therapy. The benefits of ART must be weighed against the side effects from the drugs and the possibility of developing drug-resistant forms of the virus. The issues focus on the costs of these alternative strategies and the impacts of the strategies on the final desired outcomes of increasing the length and quality of life for persons infected with HIV.

Economic evaluation techniques have been widely applied to HIV-prevention strategies, given the significant health and monetary impacts of the disease. The CDC estimates that more than 1.1 million people in the United States are currently living with HIV, while approximately 232,700 persons are undiagnosed and unaware of their infection (CDC 2008). Approximately 56,300 persons were newly infected with HIV in 2006, an increase from previous estimates of 40,000 infections per year (Hall et al. 2008). By the end of 2007, 583,298 persons had died of AIDS, the end stage of HIV infection (CDC 2009a), although the mortality rate has decreased substantially since the mid-1990s, given the advent of antiretroviral therapy.

HIV disease stage is measured in part by an individual's CD4 cell count, which declines as the disease progresses. Low CD4 counts may make individuals with HIV more susceptible to various opportunistic infections. CD4 count is an important measure of the status of an individual's immune system, with a count below 200 cells/μL indicating serious immune damage or AIDS (AIDS InfoNet 2009a).

Current guidelines call for patients to be treated with ART when their CD4 count falls below 350 cells/μL. Treatment regimens are a function of both the CD4 count and a patient's viral load, or the amount of HIV in the blood. The goals of therapy are to reduce the viral load as much as possible for as long as possible, restore or preserve the immune system, improve the patient's quality of life, and reduce the sickness and death caused by HIV (AIDS InfoNet 2009b). The issue of whether antiretroviral therapy should be started at CD4 counts higher than 350 cells/μL is the focus of the case in this chapter.

HIV prevalence is defined as the number of existing cases of disease, while incidence is defined as the number of new cases within a given timeframe. In the United States, the highest prevalence and incidence of HIV are observed among men who have sex with men (MSM) and members of racial minority groups. Of the estimated 56,300 annual new infections in 2006, 45% were among blacks, 53% were among MSM, and 27% were among women. HIV incidence for blacks was seven times that of whites and almost three times that of Hispanic persons (Hall et al. 2008; Buchacz et al. 2009).

Between 1996 and 2005, 38.3% of those diagnosed with HIV received a diagnosis of AIDS within the subsequent twelve months, indicating a late diagnosis; an additional 6.7% received an AIDS diagnosis from one to three years after their HIV diagnosis (CDC 2009b). Individuals who are unaware of their HIV infection are more likely to engage in high-risk sexual behavior that results in further transmission than those who have learned their status and have had the opportunity to modify these behaviors (Marks, Crepaz, and Janssen 2006).

There were no FDA-approved drugs to treat HIV infection before March 1987. Between March 1987 and October 1991, only one drug (zidovudine, or AZT) was approved, while dual drug therapy was common between 1992 and 1996. In December 1995 the first protease inhibitor (saquinavir) was approved, while two more protease inhibitors (ritonavir and indinavir) and one non-nucleoside reverse transcriptase inhibitor (nevirapine) were approved in 1996 (Hellinger 2006). Since that time, three- and four-drug combinations have become standard ART therapy. These drug regimens have increased treatment costs for HIV patients but have also increased the length and quality of their lives.

When it was first licensed in 1985, the primary function of the enzyme-linked immunosorbent assay (ELISA) to detect HIV antibodies was to screen the blood supply so that HIV-infected units of blood could be discarded or set aside for research purposes. However, the ELISA test became part of a nation-wide HIV counseling and testing program whose objectives were twofold: to help uninfected persons initiate and sustain behavior changes to prevent them from becoming infected, and to help keep infected persons from transmitting the infection to others. A further shift in the goal of HIV counseling and test-ing programs occurred in 1989 with the introduction of drugs such as ZDV, and then again in 1996 with the introduction of ART, when greater emphasis was placed on early detection so that infected persons could be referred for medical monitoring. These twin goals of behavior change and early detection have been intertwined in both the operation and evaluation of HIV counseling and testing strategies (Farnham 1998).

The goals of the 2006 CDC recommendations were to increase the num-ber of people aware of their infection through routine testing and to link them with appropriate care and treatment (CDC 2006). Testing based on risk assessment often fails to identify many infected people (Lyss et al. 2007). Also, people aware of their infection are likely to change their behaviors and reduce the risk of infecting others (Marks, Crepaz, and Janssen 2006). Because extensive pretest prevention counseling and written informed consent specifically for an HIV test sometimes posed barriers to testing, a streamlined screening strategy was recommended. With this approach, patients are informed that an HIV test will be performed unless they decline, and information about HIV infection is often provided in writing. Consent for HIV testing is now included in the general informed consent for medical care.

Concurrently, HIV screening has increasingly used rapid tests that provide test results during the same health care visit (Greenwald et al. 2006; Delaney et al. 2006). Compared to conventional testing with an enzyme immunoassay (EIA), rapid tests increase (by a factor of 1.5 to 2.2) the likelihood that both HIV-infected and uninfected patients receive their test results, because the results are delivered during the initial visit (Hutchinson et al. 2006). However, rapid tests typically cost more to perform than conventional tests.

Numerous cost-effectiveness studies have been performed related to the 2006 CDC recommendations. Two studies that used independently developed state-transition disease progression models were published in the *New England Journal of Medicine* in 2005 (Paltiel et al. 2005; Sanders et al. 2005). Sanders et al. (2005) reported a cost-effectiveness ratio of $41,000 per QALY gained with routine testing in a population with a prevalence of undiagnosed HIV infection of 1%. When the benefits of reduced transmission of HIV were included in the analysis, the ratio decreased to $15,000 per QALY gained. Paltiel et al. (2005) reported a ratio of $36,000 per QALY gained in a population with a 3% prevalence of undiagnosed HIV infection; $38,000 per QALY with a 1% prevalence; and $113,000 per QALY for a 0.1% prevalence. These studies provided strong support for the 2006 CDC guidelines (Walensky et al. 2007).

Farnham et al. (2008) updated the costs of both the conventional (EIA) and rapid tests and estimated the cost per HIV-infected person correctly notified of his or her test results in three different settings. This approach, based on a decision-analysis model of HIV testing in STD clinics and emergency department settings, adjusted the initial test costs for the likelihood of patients participating in the process and returning for and receiving correct test results. These researchers found that the complete rapid testing procedure was more expensive than conventional testing, due to higher test kit costs and increased counseling for HIV-infected patients during both their first and second clinic visits. However, when accounting for test acceptance and return rates in the different settings, the expected cost of correctly notifying an HIV-infected patient of his or her results was consistently lower with the rapid test procedure than with conventional testing. The return rate to receive results under conventional testing, a crucial variable in this analysis, was discussed through-out this chapter's case. The study by Farnham et al. (2008) also made a strong argument for the use of rapid testing and the expansion of HIV screening in health care settings.

The analysis by Granich et al. (2009) discussed in the case was based on a sophisticated mathematical model using data from South Africa as a test case for a generalized HIV epidemic and assuming that all transmission was het-erosexual. The results showed that universal voluntary testing of all people older than 15 years combined with immediate ART following diagnosis could reduce HIV transmission to the point that the generalized epidemic might feasibly be eliminated by 2020. The authors themselves recognized the chal-lenges of such an approach in terms of cost, drug resistance, or adverse events related to the medication. Testing on such a widespread scale would also mean that the occurrence of false-positive tests could become a significant issue. The study generated much criticism and comment focusing on the large-scale implementation issues, questions of individual rights versus benefits to larger populations, and the quality of the data used in the analysis.

Although, as the case notes, preliminary implementation studies of the test-and-treat approach are just beginning, there are some economic evaluation studies in the literature that focus on the policy of starting HIV-infected patients on ART at a CD4 count of 500 cells/µL, as compared to the current policy of starting at 350 cells/µL. For example, Braithwaite, Roberts, Chang, et al. (2008) analyzed the differences between starting ART at CD4 counts of 200, 350, and 500 cells/µL. These authors found that initiating ART at a CD4 count of 500 cells/µL may increase the life expectancy and quality-adjusted life expectancy of younger patients, particularly if they have high viral loads. This study weighed the harmful effect of ART on non-HIV-related mortality against its beneficial effect on HIV-related mortality. A subsequent study (Braithwaite, Roberts, Goetz, et al. 2009) suggested that early initiation of ART could be beneficial even if patients did not fully adhere to the drug regimens. In a model-based analysis that stratified patients by level of ART adherence, the benefits of preventing CD4 count decreases outweighed the concerns of drug resistance.

SUMMARY

In this chapter we discussed both the general issues in undertaking a cost-effectiveness analysis and the specific issues related to HIV screening and treatment with ART. We first described the conceptual problems involved with estimating both the costs and outcomes of various public policies. We noted that cost and outcome measurement may differ when the perspective is economic evaluation rather than program implementation and control, topics which were presented in earlier chapters of this book. We also showed how the time pattern of costs and outcomes and the discount rate selected to calculate the present value of these variables can impact the results of the analysis.

We then demonstrated how these economic evaluation principles can be used to evaluate alternative HIV screening and treatment programs, including the proposed test-and-treat program in the case. Most of these studies began with a decision-analysis or state-transition model to frame the question. Researchers then had to find the appropriate data on input variables and probabilities to conduct the study. However, even if the studies provided favorable effectiveness and cost-effectiveness results, as the case in this chapter illustrates, there are often many implementation questions that need to be answered if the results are to influence HIV-prevention policies.

Many of the issues discussed in this chapter will arise in the application of cost-benefit analysis to environmental problems, which is described in the following chapter. Readers should integrate the concepts from each chapter, since these chapters summarize the major components of economic evaluation for public policy analysis.

REFERENCES

AIDS InfoNet. 2009a. CD4 cell tests. Fact Sheet No. 124. http://www.aidsinfonet.org/.

———. 2009b. U.S. antiretroviral therapy guidelines. Fact Sheet No. 404. www.aidsinfonet.org/.

Arno, Peter S. 1986. The Nonprofit Sector's Response to the AIDS Epidemic: Community-Based Services in San Francisco. *American Journal of Public Health* 76 (11): 1325–30.

Baumol, William J. 1970. On the Discount Rate for Public Projects. In *Public Expenditures and Policy Analysis*, ed. Robert H. Haveman and Julius Margolis, 273–90. Chicago: Markham.

Braithwaite, R. Scott, Mark S. Roberts, Matthew Bidwell Goetz, Cynthia L. Gibert, Maria C. Rodriguez-Barradas, Kimberly Nucifora, and Amy C. Justice. 2009. Do Benefits of Earlier Antiretroviral Treatment Initiation Outweigh Harms for Individuals at Risk for Poor Adherence? *Clinical Infectious Diseases* 48 (6): 822–26.

Braithwaite, R. Scott, David O. Meltzer, Joseph T. King Jr., Douglas Leslie, and Mark S. Roberts. 2008. What Does the Value of Modern Medicine Say About the $50,000 per Quality-Adjusted Life-Year Decision Rule? *Medical Care* 46 (4): 349–56.

Braithwaite, R. Scott, Mark S. Roberts, Chung Chou H. Chang, Matthew Bidwell Goetz, Cynthia L. Gibert, Maria C. Rodriguez-Barradas, Steven Shechter, et al. 2008. Influence of Alternative Thresholds for Initiating HIV Treatment on Quality-Adjusted Life Expectancy: A Decision Model. *Annals of Internal Medicine* 148 (3): 178–85.

Briggs, Andrew, Karl Claxton, and Mark Sculpher. 2006. *Decision Modeling for Health Economic Evaluation.* New York: Oxford University Press.

Brown, Kaye, and Collin Burrows. 1990. The Sixth Stool Guaiac Test: $47 Million That Never Was. *Journal of Health Economics* 9 (4): 429–45.

Buchacz, K., M. Rangel, R. Blacher, and J. T. Brooks. 2009. Changes in the Clinical Epidemiology of HIV Infection in the United States: Implications for the Clinician. *Current Infectious Disease Reports* 11 (1): 75–83.

CDC. 1993. Recommendations for HIV Testing Services for Inpatients and Outpatients in Acute-Care Hospital Settings. *Morbidity and Mortality Weekly Report* 42 (RR-2): 1–6.

———. 2001. Revised Guidelines for HIV Counseling, Testing, and Referral. *Morbidity and Mortality Weekly Report* 50 (RR-19): 1–57.

———. 2006. Revised Recommendations for HIV Testing of Adults, Adolescents, and Pregnant Women in Health-Care Settings. *Morbidity and Mortality Weekly Report* 55 (RR-14): 1–17.

———. 2008. HIV Prevalence Estimates—United States, 2006. *Morbidity and Mortality Weekly Report* 57 (39): 1073–76.

———. 2009a. HIV/AIDS Surveillance Report, 2007. Vol. 19. Atlanta: US Department of Health and Human Services, Centers for Disease Control and Prevention. http://www.cdc.gov/hiv/topics/surveillance/resources/reports/.

———. 2009b. Late HIV testing—34 states, 1996–2005. *Morbidity and Mortality Weekly Report.* 58 (24): 661–65.

Delaney, K. P., B. M. Branson, A. Uniyal, P. R. Kerndt, P. A. Keenan, K. Jafa, A. D. Gardner, D. J. Jamieson, and M. Bulterys. 2006. Performance of an Oral Fluid Rapid HIV–1/2 Test: Experience from Four CDC Studies. *AIDS* 20 (12): 1655–60.

Drummond, Michael F., Bernie O'Brien, Greg L. Stoddart, and George W. Torrance. 2005. *Methods for the Economic Evaluation of Health Care Programmes.* 3rd ed. New York: Oxford University Press.

Farnham, Paul G. 1998. Economic Evaluation of HIV Counseling and Testing Programs: The Influence of Program Goals on Evaluation. In *Handbook of Economic Evaluation of HIV Prevention Programs*, ed. David R. Holtgrave, 63–79. New York: Plenum Press.

Farnham, Paul G., and Robin D. Gorsky. 1994. Cost to Business for an HIV-Infected Worker. *Inquiry* 31 (Spring): 76–88.

Farnham, Paul G., Angela B. Hutchinson, Stephanie L. Sansom, and Bernard M. Branson. 2008. Comparing the Costs of HIV Screening Strategies and Technologies in Health-care Settings. *Public Health Reports* 123:51–62. Suppl. no. 3.

Finkler, S. A. 1982. The Distinction between Costs and Charges. *Annals of Internal Medicine* 96 (1): 102–9.

Fisher, Ann, Lauraine G. Chestnut, and Daniel M. Violette. 1989. The Value of Reducing the Risks of Death: A Note on New Evidence. *Journal of Policy Analysis and Management* 8 (1): 88–100.

Folland, Sherman, Allen C. Goodman, and Miron Stano. 1997. *The Economics of Health and Health Care*. 2nd ed. Englewood Cliffs, NJ: Prentice Hall.

Gastonis, Constantine. 1990. The Long Debate on the Sixth Guaiac Test: Time to Move on to New Grounds. *Journal of Health Economics* 9 (4): 495–97.

Gold, Marthe R., Joanna E. Siegel, Louise B. Russell, and Milton C. Weinstein, eds. 1996. *Cost-Effectiveness in Health and Medicine*. New York: Oxford University Press.

Gramlich, Edward M. 1981. *Benefit-Cost Analysis of Government Programs*. Englewood Cliffs, NJ: Prentice Hall.

———.1990. *A Guide to Benefit-Cost Analysis*. 2nd ed. Englewood Cliffs, NJ: Prentice Hall.

Granich, Reuben M., Charles F. Gilks, Christopher Dye, Kevin DeCock, and Brian G. Williams. 2009. Universal Voluntary HIV Testing with Immediate Antiretroviral Therapy as a Strategy for Elimination of HIV Transmission: A Mathematical Model. *Lancet* 373: 48–57.

Greenwald, J. L., G. R. Burstein, J. Pincus, and B. Branson. 2006. A Rapid Review of Rapid HIV Antibody Tests. *Current Infectious Disease Reports* 8:125–31.

Grosse, Robert N. 1970. Problems of Resource Allocation in Health. In *Public Expenditure and Policy Analysis*, ed. Robert H. Haveman and Julius Margolis, 518–48. Chicago: Markham.

Guinan, Mary E., Paul G. Farnham, and David R. Holtgrave. 1994. Estimating the Value of Preventing a Human Immunodeficiency Virus Infection. *American Journal of Preventive Medicine* 10 (1): 1–4.

Haddix, Anne C., Steven M. Teutsch, Phaedra A. Shaffer, and Diane O. Dunet. 1996. *Prevention Effectiveness: A Guide to Decision Analysis and Economic Evaluation*. New York: Oxford University Press.

————. 2003. *Prevention Effectiveness: A Guide to Decision Analysis and Economic Evaluation*. 2nd ed. New York: Oxford University Press.

Hall, H. I., R. Song, P. Rhodes, J. Prejean, Q. An, L. Lee, J. Karon, et al. 2008. Estimation of HIV Incidence in the United States. *Journal of the American Medical Association* 300 (5): 520–29.

Haveman, Robert H. 1983. Evaluating Public Expenditure under Conditions of Unemployment. In *Public Expenditure and Policy Analysis*, ed. Robert H. Haveman and Julius Margolis, 167–82. 3rd ed. Boston: Houghton Mifflin.

Hellinger, Fred J. 1993. The Lifetime Cost of Treating a Person with HIV. *Journal of the American Medical Association* 270 (4): 474–78.

————. 2006. Economic Models of Antiretroviral Therapy: Searching for the Optimal Strategy. *Pharmacoeconomics* 24 (7): 631–42.

Holtgrave, David R., and Steven D. Pinkerton. 1997. Updates of Cost of Illness and Quality of Life Estimates for Use in Economic Evaluations of HIV Prevention Programs. *Journal of Acquired Immune Deficiency Syndromes and Human Retrovirology* 16 (1): 54–62.

Holtgrave, David R., and Noreen L. Qualls. 1995. Threshold Analysis and Programs for Prevention of HIV Infection. *Medical Decision Making* 15 (4): 311–17.

Holtgrave, David R., Noreen L. Qualls, and John D. Graham. 1996. Economic Evaluation of HIV Prevention Programs. *Annual Review of Public Health* 17:467–88.

Hutchinson, A. B., B. M. Branson, A. Kim, and P. G. Farnham. 2006. A Meta-Analysis of the Effectiveness of Alternative HIV Counseling and Testing Methods to Increase Knowledge of HIV Status. *AIDS* 20 (12): 1597–1604.

Kolata, Gina. 2009. Behind Cancer Guidelines, Quest for Data. *New York Times*, November 23.

Krahn, M., and A. Gafni. 1993. Discounting in the Economic Evaluation of Health Care Interventions. *Medical Care* 31 (5): 403–18.

Lesser, J. A., and R. O. Zerbe. 1994. Discounting Procedures for Environmental (and Other) Projects: A Comment on Kolbe and Scheraga. *Journal of Policy Analysis and Management* 13 (1): 140–56.

Lind, Robert C. 1982. A Primer on the Major Issues Relating to the Discount Rate for Evaluating National Energy Options. In *Discounting for Time and Risk in Energy Policy*, ed. Robert C. Lind, K. J. Arrow, G. R. Corey, et al., 21–94. Baltimore: Johns Hopkins University Press.

Lyss, S. B., B. M. Branson, K. A. Kroc, E. F. Couture, D. R. Newman, and R. A. Weinstein. 2007. Detecting Unsuspected HIV Infection with a Rapid Whole-Blood HIV Test in an Urban Emergency Department. *Journal of Acquired Immune Deficiency Syndromes* 44 (4): 435–42.

Marks, G., N. Crepaz, and R. S. Janssen. 2006. Estimating Sexual Transmission of HIV from Persons Aware and Unaware That They Are Infected with the Virus in the USA. *AIDS* 20 (10): 1447–50.

Mrozek, Janusz R., and Laura O. Taylor. 2002. What Determines the Value of Life? A Meta-Analysis. *Journal of Policy Analysis and Management* 21 (2): 253–70.

Neuhauser, Duncan, and Ann M. Lewicki. 1975. What Do We Gain from the Sixth Stool Guaiac? *New England Journal of Medicine* 293:226–28.

O'Brien, Bernie, and Amiram Gafni. 1996. When Do the "Dollars" Make Sense? Toward a Conceptual Framework for Contingent Valuation Studies in Health Care. *Medical Decision Making* 16 (3): 288–99.

Oster, G., and A. M. Epstein. 1987. Cost-Effectiveness of Antihyperlipidemic Therapy in the Prevention of Coronary Heart Disease: The Case of Cholestyramine. *Journal of the American Medical Association* 258:2381–87.

Paltiel, A. David, Milton C. Weinstein, April D. Kimmel, George R. Seage III, Elena Losina, Hong Zhang, Kenneth A. Freedberg, and Rochelle P. Walensky. 2005. Expanded Screening for HIV in the United States—An Analysis of Cost-Effectiveness. *New England Journal of Medicine*, 352 (6): 586–95.

Parsonage, M., and H. Neuburger. 1992. Discounting and Health Benefits. *Health Economics* 1 (1): 71–76.

Patrick, Donald L., and P. Erickson. 1993. *Health Status and Health Policy: Allocating Resources to Health Care*. New York: Oxford University Press.

Pauly, M. V. 1995. Valuing Health Care Benefits in Money Terms. In *Valuing Health Care: Costs, Benefits, and Effectiveness of Pharmaceuticals and Other Medical Technologies*, ed. F.A. Sloan, 99–124. New York: Cambridge University Press.

Phelps, Charles E. 2010. *Health Economics*. 4th ed. New York: Addison Wesley.

Rice, Thomas. 2003. *The Economics of Health Reconsidered*. 2nd ed. Chicago: Health Administration Press.

Rossi, Peter H., and Howard E. Freeman. 1993. *Evaluation: A Systematic Approach*. 5th ed. Newbury Park, CA: Sage Publications.

Russell, Louise B. 1986. *Is Prevention Better Than Cure?* Washington, DC: The Brookings Institution.

———. 1993. The Role of Prevention in Health Reform. *New England Journal of Medicine* 329 (5): 352–54.

———. 1994. *Educated Guesses: Making Policy About Medical Screening Tests*. Berkeley: University of California Press.

Sanders, Gillian D., Ahmed M. Bayoumi, Vandana Sundaram, S. Pinar Bilir, Christopher P. Neukermans, Chara E. Rydzak, Lena R. Douglass, Laura C. Lazzeroni, Mark Holodniy, and Douglas K. Owens. 2005. Cost-Effectiveness of Screening for HIV in the Era of Highly Active Antiretroviral Therapy. *New England Journal of Medicine* 352 (6): 570–85.

Shepard, D. S., and M. S. Thompson. 1979. First Principles of Cost-Effectiveness Analysis in Health. *Public Health Reports* 94 (6): 535–43.

Tengs, T. O., and T. H. Lin. 2002. A Meta-Analysis of Utility Estimates for HIV/AIDS. *Medical Decision Making* 22 (6): 475–81.

Ubel, Peter A., Richard A. Hirth, Michael E. Chernew, and A. Mark Fendrick. 2003. What Is the Price of Life and Why Doesn't It Increase at the Rate of Inflation?" *Archives of Internal Medicine* 163 (14): 1637–41.

US Department of Health, Education, and Welfare. 1979. *Healthy People: The Surgeon General's Report on Health Promotion and Disease Prevention* Washington, DC: US Government Printing Office.

Walensky, Rochelle P., Kenneth A. Freedberg, Milton C. Weinstein, and A. David Paltiel. 2007. Cost-Effectiveness of HIV Testing and Treatment in the United States. *Clinical Infectious Diseases* 45:S248–54. Suppl. no. 4.

Weinstein, Milton C. 2008. How Much Are Americans Willing to Pay for a Quality-Adjusted Life Year? *Medical Care* 46 (4): 343–45.

Weinstein, M. C., and W. B. Stason. 1977. Foundations of Cost-Effectiveness Analysis for Health and Medical Practices. *New England Journal of Medicine* 296:716–21.

Weisbrod, Burton A. 1983. Benefit-Cost Analysis of a Controlled Experiment: Treating the Mentally Ill. In *Public Expenditure and Policy Analysis*, ed. Robert H. Haveman and Julius Margolis, 230–59. 3d ed. Boston: Houghton Mifflin.

Willan, A. R., and A. H. Briggs. 2006. *Statistical Analysis of Cost-Effectiveness Data*. West Sussex, UK: John Wiley & Sons, Ltd.

World Bank. 1993. *World Health Development Report*. Washington, DC: World Bank.

Wright-DeAguero, Linda, Robin D. Gorsky, and G. M. Seeman. 1996. Cost of Outreach for HIV Prevention among Drug Users and Youth at Risk. *Drugs and Society* 9(1/2): 185–97.

Chapter 7

✳✳✳

Cost-Benefit Analysis:
The Case of Environmental
Air Quality Standards

Cost-benefit analysis is a policy evaluation tool closely related to cost-effectiveness analysis. All of the problems in measuring the costs of public programs discussed in chapter 6 apply to this evaluation technique also. The major differences between cost-effectiveness and cost-benefit analysis relate to how program outcomes are measured. We noted in chapter 6 that in cost-effectiveness analysis, program outcomes or consequences are measured in terms of the most appropriate natural effects or physical units. These basic measures can simply be counted to determine the effectiveness of the intervention and then compared with its costs. Thus, cost-effectiveness results are expressed in terms such as cost per HIV infection prevented, or cost per life-year saved from a cholesterol reduction program.

Cost-benefit analysis attempts to place a dollar value on the outcomes of a program or intervention. It tries to answer the question: How much is society willing to pay for the output of this program, or what are the benefits to society of having this output? The dollar valuation of this output (the benefits) is then compared with the costs of producing it. If the benefits exceed the costs, the program is considered to be an efficient use of society's resources. With cost-benefit analysis, the policy analyst must confront questions like what it is worth to society to prevent an HIV infection, or what is the value to society of a life saved by a cholesterol reduction program. In this chapter we will focus on the approaches used to answer these difficult questions.

The case for chapter 7 involves the updated air quality standards for particulate matter (smog and soot) issued by the US Environmental Protection Agency (EPA) on October 17, 2006, and partially remanded by the US Court of Appeals for the District of Columbia Circuit on February 24, 2009. This case study discusses the policy debate over the increased air quality standards, the role of various stakeholders in the regulatory process, and the use of cost-benefit analysis in a decision-making process.

We will begin this chapter by describing the components of cost-benefit analysis and the problems involved in measuring the benefits of a program or set of regulations. We will pay particular attention to the question of how to place a monetary value on any lives saved by environmental regulation. Cost-measurement issues will be given less attention because they were discussed in the previous chapter. The role of cost-benefit analysis in decision making and the limitations often placed on this role will also be discussed. We will then describe the policy issues in the debate over the tougher environmental air quality standards announced in October 2006 and relate these issues to the discussion of cost-benefit analysis methodology. We will consider specific benefit-measurement issues in air pollution cases and what role the uncertainty surrounding these issues has had in the policy debate.

AN OVERVIEW OF COST-BENEFIT ANALYSIS

Cost-benefit analysis has long been used by various government agencies to evaluate different public programs. The US Army Corps of Engineers was one of the earliest users of the tool, employing cost-benefit analysis to evaluate such physical investment projects as the dredging of harbors, construction of canals and waterways, and flood control. Indeed, the US Flood Control Act of 1939 specified the standard that "the benefits to whomever they accrue [be] in excess of the estimated costs" (Gramlich 1981, 7). In the 1960s cost-benefit analysis began to be applied to a much wider range of projects involving investment in human beings (human capital), as well as physical investment programs. This was due in part to President Lyndon Johnsons Great Society efforts to get the federal government actively involved in fighting poverty, creating jobs, and providing education and training. As the government moved into these new areas of activity, concerns arose about which type of programs provided the greatest return for the dollars invested. The use of cost-benefit analysis was also related to the formal installation of the planning, programming, and budgeting system (PPBS) in federal government agencies during the 1960s. Although the PPBS system was no longer being used formally by the mid-1970s, such evaluation techniques as cost-benefit and cost-effectiveness analysis survived. Indeed, in the areas of health care and environmental policy, there has been a greater emphasis on these techniques, given the concern over rising health care expenditures and the impact of environmental regulations (Warner and Luce 1982; Tolley, Kenkel, and Fabian 1994; Drummond et al. 2005).

The terms *benefit* and *cost* both have very specific meanings derived from economic theory. They are related to the basic economic concept of efficiency in resource allocation—making the best use of society's limited resources by comparing the value people place on different outputs with the cost of producing them. A program is said to be efficient if its benefits, that is, the total amount of money people are willing to pay for the output of the program, are greater than its program costs (i.e., the real opportunity costs reflecting what is sacrificed to produce the output). Cost-benefit analysis makes these comparisons explicit and relies on consumer evaluation of willingness to pay, whereas cost-effectiveness and cost-utility analyses involve implicit comparisons when a cost-effectiveness threshold (the maximum amount of dollars per outcome that society is willing to pay) is chosen by the decision maker (Bayoumi 2004).

This definition of efficiency is not without controversy, because it focuses on measuring program costs and willingness to pay without regard to who benefits and who pays the costs. The underlying theory is derived from welfare economics, the branch of economics that attempts to make value judgments about different policies, allocations of resources, and states of the world (Gramlich 1990; O'Brien and Gafni 1996; Drummond et al. 2005). According to this theory, based on the work of the Italian social scientist Vilfredo Pareto, a policy improves the welfare of society if it makes at least one person better off without making anyone worse off. A state of the world is considered to be Pareto-efficient if it is not possible to make someone better off without making someone else worse off. Since most policies and policy changes result in both gainers and losers, this strict Pareto rule is not very useful for evaluating real-world policy changes. British economists Nicholas Kaldor and John Hicks have modified the rule to state that a policy improves welfare if the gainers from the policy could compensate the losers from the policy and still be better off, or at least no worse off. This rule has become known as a potential compensation policy, because it does not require that the compensation from the gainers to the losers actually be paid (Gramlich 1990; Drummond et al. 2005). Cost-benefit analysis is an application of this compensation rule: It holds that a policy is efficient if society's benefits or willingness to pay for the program output (the gainers' gains) are greater than the costs of providing the output (the losers' losses).

This efficiency concept behind cost-benefit analysis has been criticized, particularly regarding policies having an impact on health and human life, in the context of important controversies over differential access to health care resulting from inequalities in the distribution of income. An economic or Pareto-efficient allocation of resources can be consistent with any distribution of income or resources among the citizens in a given society (O'Brien and Gafni 1996). This has led health economists Uwe Reinhardt (1992) and Thomas Rice (2003) to argue that economic efficiency may not be a very relevant criterion for evaluating alternative health care policies. Reinhardt (1992, 312–13) is particularly critical of the potential compensation concept:

Suppose, for example, that I feel very aggressive today and therefore would like to punch you in the nose. An honest referee (an economist) asks me what I would be willing to pay for that privilege. Suppose the maximum I'd be willing to pay were $1,000. Next, the honest referee asks you how much you would have to be paid to receive that punch in the nose without hitting me back. Because you are strapped for cash, you might accept the punch for $600. The referee (our economist) is ecstatic, for (s)he perceives here the opportunity to enhance social welfare. Consequently, the deal is struck, you kindly present your precious nose, I punch, you bleed and hold out your hand in anticipation of my payment of $1,000. Alas, I walk happily away, along with my $1,000, which I refuse to surrender. Not to worry. The honest referee (our economist) will soothe you with the expert assurance that, according to Nicholas Kaldor, and in principle, we have just witnessed a major enhancement in social welfare, to the tune of $400, even though the expected $1,000 bribe is not actually paid.

These issues should be kept in mind when examining the use of cost-benefit analysis as a tool for policy evaluation. Economists often briefly mention that the use of these tools for public policy analysis assumes either that the underlying distribution of income is satisfactory or that problems with the distribution of income can be handled with a separate set of policies (resource allocation is separated from income distribution problems). Neither of these situations is likely to exist. The vast number of government policies designed to influence individuals' ability to purchase food, shelter, and medical services clearly demonstrate society's concern with the existing distribution of income. Many of these policies change the prices people pay for various goods and services, thus having efficiency effects. Equity and efficiency issues are intertwined in most policy situations, and these problems will affect the use of cost-benefit analysis, as noted throughout this chapter. Cost-benefit analysis is a tool to assist a public policy decision-making process, in which all of society's values—legal, ethical, moral, and distributional—must be considered (Haddix, Teutsch, and Corso 2003; Freeman 1993). Cost-benefit analysis is not a decision in itself, and should not be considered a simple, mechanistic, quantitative tool for reaching a decision.

Since an economic evaluation adds up benefits and costs in relation to all the individuals receiving and paying them, there can be a decision-making problem if some of these benefits and/or costs pertain to individuals other than those undertaking the analysis. Dale Whittington and Duncan MacRae (1986) call this the problem of "standing" in cost-benefit analysis: Whose preferences count when summing benefits and costs? Richard Zerbe (1998) has discussed these issues more recently. A given agency may want to count only the benefits to itself or its constituency. This may result in an underestimation of the total benefits of the project. For example, individuals across an entire metropolitan region may receive the benefits of a project designed to control water pollution. However, the agency financing the project may be concerned only with the benefits accruing to its taxpayers. Not counting the benefits or costs to other parties may significantly bias the resulting cost-benefit calculation. Whittington and MacRae (1986) raise questions about whether benefits should include those flowing to illegal aliens or criminals. They also cite a case in which the US Nuclear Regulatory Commission (NRC) concluded that approximately one-third of the benefits of controlling radon gas emissions would accrue to individuals outside the United States. In its analysis, the NRC included the effects on Canadians and Mexicans but ignored the benefits to the rest of the world. Subsequently, EPA assigned a zero weight to everyone outside the borders of the country (Whittington and MacRae 1986, 675).

The benefits of a project may bear no particular relationship to the flow of revenues or tax receipts to the agency undertaking the project. For many government projects, there are no direct revenues to the agency. However, this does not mean that there are zero benefits from the project. The financing issues focus on the distribution of the benefits and costs, namely, who receives the benefits and who pays the costs. These issues may be very important from a decision-making point of view—indeed, they may determine whether a project is funded or not. In the 1970s, during the controversy over Westway, the proposed West Side Highway in New York City, construction options with less favorable cost-benefit ratios were favored over more efficient projects, because the federal government was willing to finance a larger share of the total costs of the former. Therefore, the costs to New York City taxpayers were lower for the less efficient options (Herzlinger 1979).

Distributional issues are typically not incorporated into the formal estimation of benefits and costs. Sometimes separate data are presented on how the benefits or costs are distributed by income group or region of the country, so that decision makers can see how different groups of people will be affected by the project. It has also been argued that distributional weights might be applied when the total benefits are being summed (Gramlich 1981, 1990).

This approach directly incorporates distributional or equity concerns into the efficiency calculations. However, it is not clear what weights should be applied. Should benefits to low-income groups be weighted twice, five times, or one-half as heavily as benefits to high-income groups? This approach also makes the estimation of program costs directly dependent on the method of financing the project. Many have argued that these issues should remain separate. In a review of seventy-one health care studies, Olsen and Smith (2001) found that only sixteen explicitly recognized the equity aspects of the willingness-to-pay criterion and most of these were the earliest studies reviewed. Of the twelve studies published since 1990 that recognized distributional issues, five were by the same author and two were by one other. Olsen and Smith (2001, 46) commented that "had it not been for them, explicit equity considerations would seem to have vanished completely in these studies."

As with cost-effectiveness analysis, discussed in the previous chapter, cost-benefit analysis involves a "with and without" comparison, as opposed to a "before and after" comparison (Haveman and Weisbrod 1983). Analysts attempt to calculate the benefits and costs of having the program, and then to compare these with what would happen without the program (the counterfactual). Thus, if a program provides job skills and training to teenagers, the increased wages these individuals will earn over their lifetime in contrast to what they would have earned otherwise may be considered some of the benefits of the program. This calculation is more complex than simply examining wages before and after the program. This example also illustrates the fact that the benefits and costs of a program may extend many years into the future. A teenager's working life may be forty years or more, while the life of a physical investment project may exceed one hundred years. Thus, cost-benefit analysis and cost-effectiveness analysis involve not only the technical details of benefit and cost estimation, but also the projection and comparison of dollar values over time. In the previous chapter, we discussed the use of a discount rate to calculate the present value of a future stream of benefits or costs.

An advantage of cost-benefit analysis compared to cost-effectiveness and cost-utility analyses is that cost-benefit analysis allows for comparison among a broader range of alternatives, because both outcomes and costs are measured in dollar terms. Cost-benefit analysis attempts to measure the value of all program outcomes. In cost-effectiveness and cost-utility analyses, costs are compared with one outcome at a time (i.e., the cost per infection prevented or the cost per quality-adjusted life year gained). This theoretical advantage may not actually be observed in practice. Olsen and Smith (2001) reviewed seventy-one empirical studies in health care to evaluate the types of benefits being estimated. They found that only seventeen studies described health outcomes using more than one health dimension. In addition to assigning a value to the use of health care services, studies could evaluate the option value, which places a value on the service being available for those who might possibly need it in the future, or the caring externality, in which individuals value other persons' health care use. Olsen and Smith (2001) concluded that these nonuse values were rarely considered in the programs they reviewed.

It may be extremely difficult if not impossible to place dollar values on some of the benefits and costs of particular projects. The alternative methods for evaluating a program that reduces the risk of death (discussed below) will differ in the comprehensiveness of the benefits estimated. Some benefit-cost analyses include unmeasured or intangible benefits and costs along with those measured in dollar terms. Burton Weisbrod's (1983) study of inpatient versus outpatient treatment of the mentally ill, discussed in the previous chapter, used this procedure. External costs caused by patients' illnesses were measured by the number of families reporting physical illness and the percentage of family members experiencing emotional strain due to patient behavior. Improved consumer decision making by patients was measured by the amount of insurance expenditures and by the percentage of the groups having savings accounts (Weisbrod 1983). These intangible costs and benefits were included because they were considered to be important, but they were not measured in dollar terms.

METHODS FOR ESTIMATING BENEFITS

As noted above, the benefits of a project are defined as the total amount of money individuals are willing to pay for the output of the project. Benefit analysis attempts to use an approach similar to that used in the marketplace to value private goods and services. We noted in chapter 5 that prices perform an allocating and rationing function in a market economy. If an individual is willing to buy a particular good at a certain price, that action gives us an estimate of how the person values the good. The goal of benefit analysis is to use that same approach in the valuation of public-sector, health-related, or environmental goods and services that may not be sold in the market or have any prices directly associated with them.

Figure 7.1 shows a demand curve for a particular good. Suppose that P_1 is the price of the good and Q_1 is the quantity demanded at that price. The amount of money spent on the good is price times quantity, or the area of the rectangle. However, this area does not represent the total amount that consumers would be willing to pay for the good, rather than go without it. That

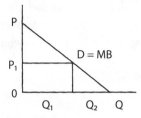

Figure 7.1   The Demand Curve for a Particular Good

total willingness to pay (WTP) is represented by the area underneath the demand curve up to quantity Q_1. This results from the fact that the prices measured along a demand curve represent consumers' marginal benefit or valuation, the dollar value they attach to each additional unit of the product.

Table 7.1 shows a hypothetical demand schedule for oranges. If I observe you buying four oranges when the price of oranges is $0.25, I can infer that you did not buy the fifth orange because it was worth less than $0.25 to you. If the price of oranges is $0.50 per orange and you buy only three oranges, I can infer that the third orange is worth $0.50, but the fourth orange is worth only $0.25. Likewise, the second orange is worth $0.75, and the first orange is worth $1.00. Thus, a market price reflects a consumer's marginal valuation or benefit, the amount of money he or she is willing to pay for the last, or "marginal," unit consumed.

If we add up all the valuations for each of the units, we obtain the total valuation or the amount consumers are willing to pay for all the units. This dollar amount, represented by the total area underneath the demand curve up to quantity Q_1 in figure 7.1, is the total willingness to pay, or the total benefit to consumers of that amount of output. If we look only at the actual consumer expenditure (the area of the rectangle in figure 7.1), we would typically underestimate the total willingness to pay, or the benefits to society of producing that output. In the numerical example of table 7.1, the total willingness to pay for four oranges rather than do without is the marginal benefit of the first orange ($1.00) plus the marginal benefit of the second ($0.75) plus that of the third ($0.50) and fourth ($0.25), for a total of $2.50. If the price of oranges were $0.25, the amount actually spent on oranges would be only $1.00. Furthermore, if the government had decided to provide the good free of charge, such as in the case of vaccinations by a public health clinic, there would be no consumer expenditure to measure. In this case, the quantity demanded in figure 7.1 would be Q_2 at the zero price, and the total willingness to pay would be the monetary value of the entire area underneath the demand curve up to quantity Q_2.

Table 7.1   Individual Demand for Oranges (Hypothetical)

Price	Quantity Demanded
$0.25	4
$0.50	3
$0.75	2
$1.00	1

This equating of price and marginal benefit, and the resulting efficiency arguments, have been questioned in the area of health care policy. Thomas Rice (1992, 1997, 2003) argues that the demand curve for health care goods and services may not reflect consumers' marginal benefits, given the lack of information and the inability of consumers to analyze and understand relevant data regarding the purchase of these goods and services. This is still a controversial argument (Pauly 1997; Gaynor and Vogt 1997), but it does raise questions about the use of the demand and efficiency criteria for health care policy.

Although willingness to pay is the term used in the cost-benefit literature, it must also be remembered, as noted in chapter 5, that income is one of the factors influencing the position of a demand curve. Oranges were chosen in the above example to illustrate the marginal benefit concept since for most people, income is not a constraining factor influencing their demand for oranges. It can be safely argued that the reason the consumer did not purchase the fifth orange when oranges were priced at $0.25 per orange is that the consumer did not value the fifth orange at $0.25, not that the individual did not have the income to purchase the fifth orange. For many other goods and services, both private and public, income does play a major role in influencing demand. Indeed, demand is often defined as the willingness and ability to purchase a good or service. Thus, a demand curve for a city recreation project could be further from the origin, and the total benefits larger, for a high-income neighborhood than for a low-income neighborhood, simply because the high-income residents have a greater ability to pay for the recreation output. This is an example of the income distribution problem discussed above. Government programs such as Medicare and Medicaid, which are designed to improve access to health care, demonstrate society's concern about income distribution problems in this policy area. Thus, even though cost-benefit analysis primarily focuses on efficiency issues, the distributional questions are never far removed. Olsen and Smith (2001) note that, unlike the use of quality-adjusted life years (QALYs) in cost-utility analysis, willingness to pay is not an income-neutral preference scale, because the premise is one dollar, one vote. Different groups in society have varying amounts of dollars or income that affect their willingness to pay.

This discussion shows that benefit estimation is directly connected to the economic concept of demand. The goal of benefit measurement is to estimate the demand and, thus, the willingness to pay for the output of the project. Therefore, all the empirical demand-estimation issues discussed in chapter 5 are relevant here. These include the problems of incorporating all relevant variables influencing demand and holding their effects constant while examining the relationship between price and quantity demanded.

Willingness-to-pay issues become more complicated in cost-benefit analysis, however, because many of the project outcomes being evaluated, such as good health or a clean environment, are not bought and sold in markets. Furthermore, prices may not be charged for many government-provided goods and services either because it is impossible to do so (the public goods problem) or because society has made a conscious decision not to do so (the income distribution or equity problem). Therefore, willingness to pay in these cases must be estimated, either through observation of behavior in hypothetical or contingent markets, or through inference from indirect methods on behavior in markets related to the project outcome in question. Thus, the choice is between methodologies that focus on how individuals answer questions about how they would behave in certain situations, and methodologies that infer willingness to pay from observing the behavior of individuals in markets affected by the relevant project outcome. These methods will be summarized and catalogued under several broad headings below. More detailed descriptions of all of these methods, particularly in relation to the health and environmental areas of interest in this chapter, can be found in Cummings, Brookshire, and Schulze (1986); Gramlich (1981; 1990); Freeman (1993); Tolley, Kenkel, and Fabian (1994); Portney (1994); Hanemann (1994); Diamond and Hausman (1994); Bjornstad and Kahn (1996); O'Brien and Gafni (1996); Smith (2003); Haddix, Teutsch, and Corso (2003); Bayoumi (2004); and Drummond et al. (2005).

Estimation of willingness to pay from surveys and other hypothetical situations is known as the contingent valuation method. This is the method most closely related to the direct estimation of a market demand curve, except that the market is hypothetical. Contingent valuation methods ask individuals to reveal their personal valuations of increases or decreases in unpriced goods, either through surveys or in experimental situations. Individuals are given information about the good in question, the institutional structure under which it will be provided, the method of payment, and the decision rule for determining the level of the provision of the good. Contingent markets are highly structured with scenarios designed to elicit contingent valuation: If this happens, what would you be willing to pay? This is a different process from determining peoples' attitudes or opinions about a subject (Cummings, Brookshire, and Schulze 1986; Bjornstad and Kahn 1996; Smith 2003; Haddix et al. 2003; Drummond et al. 2005).

Economists have traditionally preferred to rely on direct observation of individuals' behavior rather than on their responses to hypothetical questions about that behavior. However, the contingent valuation method has been widely used in the environmental area, particularly to evaluate willingness to pay for nonuse or existence values of environmental goods (Cummings, Brookshire, and Schulze 1986; Mitchell and Carson 1989; Carson 1991; Portney 1994; Hanemann 1994). Environmental economists argue that people may value the preservation of natural assets such as the Grand Canyon even if they never plan to visit or directly use it (Freeman 1993). This is called an existence value.

Contingent valuation methods have been subject to much professional debate about their accuracy, validity, and reliability (Cummings, Brookshire, and Schulze 1986; Diamond and Hausman 1994; Bjornstad and Kahn 1996; Smith 2003; Drummond et al. 2005). Although a conference of experts evaluating contingent valuation methods considered them to be "generally positive" (Cummings, Brookshire, and Schulze 1986), the controversy over the use of these methods continues. Much research has focused on validating contingent value estimates (i.e., comparing stated willingness to pay with actual willingness to pay). David Bjornstad and James Kahn (1996, 273) noted that current contingent valuation methodologies "are not universally accepted as valid, reliable, and unbiased," and that ongoing issues in environmental policy "provide an immediate and pressing need to develop stronger estimates of the value of changes in the quantity and quality of environmental resources, particularly those associated with passive use values." Smith (2003) argued that contingent valuation studies in health care generally performed poorly in the construction, specification, and presentation of the contingent market and that there had been little improvement in the previous fifteen years, especially compared with environmental studies. These authors noted that environmental studies often had vast, nonreversible financial and nonfinancial impacts.

O'Brien and Gafni (1996) and Drummond et al. (2005) noted the differences between the ex ante and ex post approaches to evaluating willingness to pay. In the ex post approach (based on the perspective of the user), the respondent is assumed to be at the point of consuming some amount of the program being evaluated and is asked about the willingness to pay for that amount. With the ex ante approach (based on the perspective of the insurance provider) in health care, the individual is assumed to be a person at risk for a disease who needs the treatment program. The individual is then asked about his or her willingness to pay for an insurance premium to have the program available. Drummond et al. (2005) discuss an example of an in vitro fertilization program in which individuals are asked about their willingness to pay in an ex post scenario (assuming infertility, what would you pay out-of-pocket?) or an ex ante scenario (what would you be willing to pay for insurance coverage for in vitro fertilization, assuming a 10% chance of being infertile?). The implied willingness to pay per statistical baby was much higher ($1.8 million) under the ex ante approach than the ex post approach ($0.17 million), because the insurance-based approach incorporated attitudes toward risk in valuing access to the program.

Contingent valuation methods have been used to evaluate the willingness to pay to reduce the risk of severe acute respiratory syndrome (SARS) in Taiwan in 2003 (Liu et al. 2005). Information was elicited on respondents' perception of the SARS risk, precautions taken, and the WTP for a hypothetical SARS vaccine. One survey was a telephone interview of 1,028 randomly selected Taiwan residents age 20–65 years old, conducted during the peak of the epidemic. A small, general health and food-safety survey of women in Taipei City and County that included SARS questions was also conducted with questionnaires and telephone interviews of 488 persons. The researchers measured public conceptions of risk. Respondents were also asked if they would be willing to purchase a vaccine (if it existed) that would eliminate the chance of becoming infected with SARS. The baseline risk of SARS, the conditional mortality risk, and the duration of protection were varied among the respondents.

SARS risk was generally perceived as fatal, moderately controllable, and not unknown. As expected, the fraction of respondents who indicated they would purchase a vaccine declined significantly with increases in the price. Willingness to pay increased with the size of the risk reduction. There was a positive effect of income on WTP, with an income elasticity of 0.3 to 0.5 (Liu et al. 2005).

The discounted future earnings approach, also called the "capital values" (Gramlich 1990) or "hedonic price" approach (Freeman 1993), is an indirect approach to benefit estimation. It focuses on the increased stream of future earnings from either individuals or land as a result of a public-sector investment project. Thus, a health, education, or job training program may make an individual more productive and increase his or her wages above what they would have been in the absence of the project. Land values may increase as a result of urban development, or recreation, transportation, or environmental improvements. This increased earning stream is a proxy for the valuation of the increased output to society by the more productive individuals. Thus, in his study of alternative means of treating the mentally ill, Weisbrod (1983) measured the increased earnings of inpatients compared with outpatients. A similar approach was taken by Peter Kemper, David Long, and Craig Thornton (1983) in their study of the Supported Work Experiment, a program providing work experience for individuals with severe employment problems, such as former drug addicts, ex-offenders released from prison, young school dropouts, and long-term recipients of Aid to Families with Dependent Children. Discounted future earnings are also related to the valuation-of-life problems to be discussed in the next section of this chapter.

Another indirect approach to benefit estimation focuses on the costs to society that are saved as a result of public-sector investment projects. This approach has been used in evaluating transportation, pollution control, and disease control projects. The costs to society that would have been incurred in the absence of a project are considered to be the benefits of the investment project. For transportation projects the emphasis is on time cost savings: the goal of a transportation project (e.g., bus, rapid rail system) is to move people from one point to another. Since the final good or output is having passengers arrive at their desired destination, the transportation investment lowers the "price" of this final output. Thus, cost savings are related to the basic willingness-to-pay concept of cost-benefit analysis. Transportation improvements would provide cost-saving benefits to those individuals who are currently using the system, who would then attract additional users to the system. Both of these gains must be measured, and they involve questions of the valuation of time saved.

The associated cost approach, which has been widely used in the evaluation of the benefits of wilderness recreation areas, is another method of benefit estimation. Early studies were done by Marion Clawson (1959) and Marion Clawson and Jack Knetsch (1966), while more recent research has been summarized by Myrick Freeman (1993). Many state and national parks either do not charge direct prices or charge prices that are not high enough to influence consumer decision making. Therefore, it is not possible to directly estimate demand curves for these projects; however, individuals do incur significant costs associated with reaching these recreation areas, including the money and time costs of traveling to these areas. These costs may be used as proxies for differences in "prices" faced by different groups of consumers. It would be expected that consumers facing higher associated costs would demand smaller quantities or make fewer visits to these recreation sites, and thus, differences in these associated costs could be used to derive an indirect measure of willingness to pay. Use of this method involves defining the areas from which visitors attend the facility and then collecting data on visits, distance, time costs of travel, size of the population, income, and other variables affecting the number of visits. The demand function is then estimated under the assumption that people would react to increases in the entrance fee as they react to increases in travel costs. The relevant area underneath the demand curve is thus the estimate of recreation benefits.

Many studies use a combination of these methods to try to capture different types of benefits. For example, in addition to measuring the increased wages of the mentally ill in the experimental and control programs, Weisbrod (1983) also attempted to measure increased work stability and improved consumer decision making. Data on absenteeism and on the number of "beneficial" and "detrimental" job changes were incorporated in the analysis. The subjects' expenditures on insurance and the percentage of the groups having savings accounts were included as a measure of forward thinking.

In a cost-benefit analysis of a program to vaccinate first-year college students living in dormitories against meningococcal disease, Scott et al. (2002) used treatment-cost savings (hospital expenses associated with acute treatment) and measures of the benefits of averting a premature death, including both estimates of lifetime productivity losses and the value of a statistical life, to assess the benefits of averting disease through vaccination. Cost-savings of averting disease-related sequelae were also included. This analysis indicated that the social costs of the vaccination program outweighed the benefits gained in all program cost scenarios considered, given the low incidence of disease and the high cost of a vaccination program.

ESTIMATING BENEFITS RELATED TO HEALTH AND THE VALUE OF LIFE

Environmental, health, disease control, and safety programs can all result in reductions in mortality (death) or morbidity (illness) in comparison with the rates that would have existed without the interventions. Placing a value on these reductions is a major problem in benefit estimation for these programs. We will discuss the conceptual problems involved with the different approaches to these questions and examine some of the numerical results of these analyses.

In an early discussion of the issues, Thomas Schelling (1968) pointed out that the question is not the worth of human life, but the value of life saving or preventing death. The question is not really about the value of human life, but about what society is willing to pay (WTP) to reduce the probability of death by a certain amount. The concern in this policy area is not with a particular death but with a statistical death. When a situation arises involving particular individuals (e.g., the collapse of a building, a liver transplant for a sick child), hundreds of thousands of dollars may be donated in response to media attention. However, there may be quite different responses when the issues involve a bill in Congress to increase construction safety standards or to devote more resources to medical research. Thus, the issue is the valuation of unidentified, statistical lives (VSL) in public programs. "For example, if each of 100,000 persons is willing to pay $20 for a reduction in risk from 3 deaths per 100,000 people to 1 death per 100,000 people, the total WTP is $2 million and the value per statistical life is $1 million (with 2 lives saved)" (Fisher, Chestnut, and Violette 1989, 89).

The key issue regarding the VSL is that it relates to very small reductions in the risk of death; the valuation is linked to an individual's willingness to pay to reduce that risk. It does not mean that an individual would be willing to pay $1 million to avoid certain death or that the person would be willing to accept $1 million to face certain death. The values do not generalize to these larger risk situations. The VSL is also not a measure of compensation for wrongful death. The latter, which attempts to address financial losses of an individual's survivors, is a form of insurance compensation, rather than a trade-off between money and reducing the risk of death (Viscusi 2009).

There have been two major approaches in the cost-benefit analysis literature to the problem of valuing reductions in the risk of death. The first is the discounted future earnings or human capital approach (Gramlich 1981, 1990; Freeman 1993; Tolley, Kenkel, and Fabian 1994; Haddix, Teutsch, and Corso 2003; Drummond et al. 2005). Using this method, researchers take the average age at which premature death occurs and then compute the expected future income individuals would have received if they had lived a normal term. This calculation rests on assumptions about labor force participation rates and average earning streams. Since much of this income would have been received at some point in the future, the flow of income is discounted, using the procedures discussed in the previous chapter.

This approach is based on the idea of maximizing society's present and future consumption. The value of preventing an individual's death is reflected in his or her contribution to the gross national product. Labor earnings are usually evaluated before taxes, reflecting society's viewpoint, instead of after taxes, which would be most relevant to the individual. Nonlabor income is generally excluded because capital holdings are not affected by an individual's continued existence (Gramlich 1990).

This approach appears to place a market value on lives saved. However, as Edward Gramlich (1990) notes, it is the wrong market: The labor market focuses only on the individual's productive activities and cannot value how much the individual actually enjoys life. The approach also implies that a low valuation should be placed on those individuals who have low market wages. This means that there will be different valuations for children versus adults, the working versus the retired, men versus women, those with high education and training versus others, and so on. Any differences in wages resulting from labor market discrimination and other institutional factors will be transmitted into the valuation of lives saved under this approach. Nonmarket activities are typically not included. If the discounted future earnings represent the decedent's utility loss from death, there are also losses to the individual's spouse, family, and friends. Some estimate of these losses would need to be made. This approach also ignores all costs of the fear of the risk of death and of nonmonetary suffering (Freeman 1993; Tolley, Kenkel, and Fabian 1994).

The choice of a discount rate for computing the present value of these income streams can have a major impact on the analysis, given that life expectancies of up to seventy-five years may be involved. Haddix, Teutsch, and Corso (2003, 251–56, table I.2) provide data for those earning wages in the labor force, and those not in the labor force keeping house, with the assumption of a 1% annual growth in productivity. The table shows the present value of expected future lifetime earnings for those in the workforce, and the present value of housekeeping services provided by those who are not, according to age and sex and calculated with discount rates ranging from 0% (no discounting) to 10%. Despite the conceptual difficulties of this method and the sensitivity to the choice of a discount rate, this approach has been widely used, given the relative ease of gathering the data necessary for the calculations, most of which are available from standard government sources.

The second technique focuses on estimating society's willingness to pay to reduce the probability of a statistical death. This approach follows directly from the methodology discussed earlier in this chapter. The problem is how to apply the willingness-to-pay concept to these valuation questions. Three major approaches have been used in the literature: required compensation or wage-risk studies, consumer market studies, and contingent valuation studies (Fisher, Chestnut, and Violette 1989; Viscusi 1992, 1993; Freeman 1993; Tolley, Kenkel, and Fabian 1994; Haddix, Teutsch, and Corso 2003; Drummond et al. 2005; Robinson 2007, 2009; Viscusi 2009). The first two approaches examine the choices that individuals make in labor or product markets in order to infer values of reducing the risk of death, while the third method attempts to estimate these values directly, using survey instruments.

Suppose there are two jobs that are alike in every respect except that there is no risk of death in one job but there is a positive risk in the other job. In a competitive labor market with a large number of available jobs and full information about the risks associated with each job, the only way companies with risky jobs could attract workers would be to pay them higher wages. These compensating wage differentials could be used as a measure of an individual's willingness to pay to reduce the risk of death. These differentials would have to be measured after controlling for education, race, experience, unionization, region, and all other factors that also contribute to differences in wage rates. The problems with this approach are obvious. Workers may not have freedom of choice among jobs, or they may be forced to take a particular job regardless of the risks involved if the only alternative is unemployment. Furthermore, workers may not have accurate information on the magnitude of the risks involved. Moreover, as in the case of certain chemicals, it may be that no one in society has adequate knowledge of the risks to human life in working with these products. Workers may also have different attitudes or preferences toward risk: those in risky jobs, for instance, may exhibit less risk aversion than the population as a whole. Even with good data, estimates based on wage differentials would typically omit the willingness to pay of most white-collar workers and of all nonworkers. Society's willingness to pay for a program to reduce the probability of a statistical death may also depend upon how painful the predeath stages of a disease are, whether the program is preventive or curative, and whether risks are "involuntary," such as those from nuclear power accidents or air pollution exposure (Fisher, Chestnut, and Violette 1989; Viscusi 1992, 1993; Tolley, Kenkel, and Fabian 1994).

Consumer market studies focus on the choices people make between risks and benefits in their consumption decisions, such as the purchase of smoke detectors, the use of automobile seat belts, speeding behavior by drivers, and the use of information about the risks of smoking. These studies are similar to the labor market studies since they analyze individuals' observed behavior, but this literature is much less extensive than the literature on wage-risk trade-offs. Since many of these consumption decisions are discrete decisions (e.g., the purchase of a smoke detector), these studies will not provide information about the consumer's total willingness to pay for safety, "because with such discrete decisions consumers are not pushed to the point where the marginal cost of greater safety equals its marginal valuation" (Viscusi 1993, 1996).

As discussed previously, contingent valuation studies are surveys of individuals conducted in the context of a hypothetical market situation in which the participants are asked about their willingness to pay for alternative levels of safety. These studies are based on what people say they would do, not on their actual behavior. It is unclear whether individuals can understand and give consistent answers to these types of questions, particularly when very small risks are involved. The literature in both psychology and economics shows that individuals tend to overestimate the likelihood of very low-probability events, particularly those called to one's attention (Viscusi 1993). An individual's answer may also depend on the wording of the question.

Variations in estimates of the VSL and the use of these estimates by the EPA and other government agencies will be discussed after the details of the case study are presented.

The Debate over Ambient Air Quality Standards for Fine Particulate Matter

To regulate air pollution in the environment, the US Environmental Protection Agency (EPA) sets National Ambient Air Quality Standards (NAAQS) for pollutants deemed likely to harm public health and welfare. The NAAQS regulate six common pollutants: ground-level ozone (smog), carbon monoxide, lead, nitrogen dioxide, sulfur dioxide, and particulate matter. The EPA sets primary standards to protect public health and secondary standards "to protect the public welfare from harm to crops, vegetation, wildlife, buildings and national monuments, and visibility" (US EPA 2006a; Nadadur et al. 2007). The agency is mandated to review the standards every five years through an assessment of the science regarding the effects of a specific pollutant on public health and welfare.

Particulate matter (PM) is a mixture of microscopic solids and liquid droplets suspended in the air. Particulate matter includes acids (i.e., nitrates and sulfates), organic chemicals, soil and dust particles, and allergens (i.e., fragments of pollen or mold spores). These particles can be inhaled deeply into the lungs and therefore can cause significant health problems. They can also impair visibility in cities and national parks (US EPA 2006a, 2006b).

The NAAQS regulate two categories of particulate matter: fine particles, PM-2.5, which are 2.5 micrometers in diameter and smaller, and inhalable coarse particles, PM-10, which are smaller than 10 micrometers. A micrometer is one one-thousandth of a millimeter, and there are 25,400 micrometers in an inch. To put this in perspective, fine particles (PM-2.5) are less than one-thirtieth the diameter of a human hair (US EPA 2006a, 2006b). Some particles can be seen directly, while others can only be observed with an electron microscope. Fine particles can aggravate heart and lung diseases and have been linked to heart attacks, asthma attacks, and bronchitis, resulting in increased hospital admissions and emergency department visits, absences from school and work, and restricted activity days. People with heart or lung disease, older adults, and children are particularly sensitive to the effects of exposure to fine particles (US EPA 2006b).

Fine particle pollution can arise from emissions of power plants, industrial facilities, automobiles, and other combustion sources. Coarse particles result from crushing or grinding operations and from dust from paved or unpaved roads. Other particles may be formed in the air when gases from burning fuels react with sunlight and water vapor. The composition of the particles in the air depends on location, the time of year, and the weather (US EPA 2006b, 2006c).

In September 2006, the EPA strengthened the 24-hour PM-2.5 standard from the 1997 level of 65 micrograms per cubic meter ($\mu g/m^3$) to 35 $\mu g/m^3$ and kept the existing annual PM-2.5 standard at 15 $\mu g/m^3$. The EPA also maintained the existing national 24-hour PM-10 standard of 150 $\mu g/m^3$. The agency revoked the annual PM-10 standard, arguing that the available evidence did not suggest a link between long-term exposure to current levels of coarse particles and health problems (US EPA 2006a).

The NAAQS apply to the concentrations of the pollutants in outdoor air that are monitored across the country. Geographic areas that meet the standards are designated as attainment areas. States without attainment areas must draft a state implementation plan (SIP) that outlines the measures the state will take to improve air quality (US EPA 2006c).

In October 2006, the EPA completed its Regulatory Impact Analysis (RIA) of the 2006 NAAQS for PM-2.5. This analysis examined the benefits and costs of reducing pollution to meet the revised standards, and illustrated emission control strategies that states might adopt to meet the standards efficiently. The agency did not use this benefit-cost analysis in setting the standards, because it was prohibited from doing so by the Clean Air Act. However, Executive Order 12866 of the US Office of Management and Budget requires the EPA to analyze the benefits and costs of any major rule (US EPA 2006d).

When the EPA first issued the PM-2.5 standards in 1997, several industry organizations and state governments challenged the rules in the US Court of Appeals for the District of Columbia (the DC Circuit Court). Litigation over several years resulted in a US Supreme Court decision in 2002 ruling that the EPA's approach to setting the NAAQS did not result in an unconstitutional delegation of authority, and that the Clean Air Act required the EPA to set standards at levels necessary to protect human health and welfare without consideration of the economic costs of implementing the standards (US EPA 2006c).

The revised 2006 standards faced a similar challenge over two years later when the DC Circuit Court remanded the annual NAAQS for PM-2.5 in February 2009. The court also remanded the secondary PM-2.5 NAAQS to the EPA, because it found that "the agency had unreasonably concluded that the secondary standards were adequate to protect the public welfare from adverse effects on visibility" (*Air Pollution Consultant* 2009). However, the court denied petitions challenging the 24-hour standard for PM-10, and it upheld the agency's decision to revoke the annual NAAQS for PM-10.

The 2006 NAAQS faced challenges by three types of organizations. Environmental and health advocacy petitioners including the American Lung Association, the Environmental Defense Fund, and the National Parks Conservation Association challenged the primary and secondary standards for fine particulates and the elimination of the annual standard for coarse particulates. State petitioners, which included several states and state agencies, challenged the primary annual standard for fine particulate matter. Industry petitioners including the American Farm Bureau Federation, the National Pork Producers Council, the National Cattlemen's Beef Association, and the Agricultural Retailers Association challenged EPA's retention of PM-10 as the indicator for coarse particulate matter (*Air Pollution Consultant* 2009).

The petitioners' challenges focused on the fact that the EPA had relied exclusively on studies of long-term exposure to PM-2.5, primarily research by Harvard University and the American Cancer Society, to justify its decisions. The state and environmental petitioners argued that the EPA did not adequately explain why studies of short-term exposure were not relevant. The agency had argued that studies of long-term exposure should be used to set the annual standard because the human body responds differently to exposure in the long term than in the short term. It also noted that long-term studies evaluated periods of exposure more relevant to the time frame of the annual standards (*Air Pollution Consultant* 2009).

References for the Case Study

Air Pollution Consultant. 2009. Ambient Air Quality Standards for Fine Particulate Matter Partially Remanded. 19 (3): 3.1–3.4.

Nadadur, Srikanth S., C. Andrew Miller, Philip K. Hopke, Terry Gordon, Sverre Vedal, John J. Vandenberg, and Daniel L. Costa. 2007. The Complexities of Air Pollution Regulation; The Need for an Integrated Research and Regulatory Perspective. *Toxicological Sciences* 100 (2): 318–27.

US Environmental Protection Agency. 2006a. *Fact Sheet: Final Revisions to the National Ambient Air Quality Standards for Particulate Pollution (Particulate Matter)*. www.epa.gov/particles/actions.html.

———. 2006b. *Fine Particle (PM$_{2.5}$) Designations: Basic Information*. www.epa.gov/pmdesignations/basicinfo.htm.

———. 2006c. *Fine Particle (PM$_{2.5}$) Designations: Frequent Questions*. www.epa.gov/pmdesignations/faq.htm.

———. 2006d. *Regulatory Impact Analysis of EPA's Final Revisions to the National Ambient Air Quality Standards for Particulate Pollution (Particulate Matter) Fact Sheet*. www.epa.gov/air/particlepollution.html.

TIGHTENING AIR QUALITY STANDARDS: THE POLICY DEBATE

In July 1997 EPA issued updated air quality standards for ozone and particulate matter, commonly known as smog and soot. The new ozone standards limited concentrations in the air to 80 parts per billion over an eight-hour period, compared with the existing standard of 120 parts per billion over a one-hour period. EPA proposed the change to control lower, but persistent and still damaging, levels of ozone, rather than concentrate on sharp increases lasting only a short period of time. Small particles had never been controlled previously under the Clean Air Act. The 1997 standards focused on fine particles of 2.5 microns in diameter, and limited daily averages to 65 micrograms per cubic meter of air and annual averages to 15 micrograms per cubic meter. EPA did provide more flexibility for compliance by the states in loosening its earlier proposed daily standard of 50 micrograms per cubic meter. The agency also allowed states five years to construct monitors to detect the fine particles and several more years before they actually had to control emissions.

Carol Browner, EPA director at that time, noted that the Clean Air Act of 1970 did not allow EPA to consider costs at the standard-setting stage of the process. Pollution limits must be based solely "on health, risk, exposure, and damage to the environment, as determined by the best available science" (Browner 1997, 367). She also argued that the costs of the regulations were always raised by opponents of any regulations and that these costs were often overstated. "Why? Because industry ultimately rises to the challenge, finding cheaper, more innovative ways of meeting the standards and lowering pollution" (Browner 1997, 367). Browner stated that compliance costs could be considered at the implementation stage of the process and that the administration would be flexible in enforcing the regulations.

Legislation governing air quality originated with the Air Pollution Control Act of 1955. This law was amended in 1970 by the Clean Air Act, which also created the Environmental Protection Agency. More than three hundred pages of amendments were added to the Clean Air Act in 1990, including amendments giving EPA authority to control particulate matter precursors. As noted in the case study, EPA has set National Ambient Air Quality Standards (NAAQS) for six key pollutants: lead, sulfur dioxide, nitrous oxide, particulates (soot), carbon monoxide, and ozone (smog), all of which are byproducts of industrialization and have a negative impact on public health and the economy (Hoffnagle 1997; Romani 1998). Title I of the 1990 amendments established a detailed and graduated program for attaining and maintaining the NAAQS. Title II regulated mobile sources of air pollution, while Title III established a list of hazardous pollutants to be regulated. Title IV established control programs for reducing acid rain precursors, Title V required a new permitting system for primary sources of air pollution, and Title VI limited emissions of chemicals that depleted stratospheric ozone (Ostro and Chestnut 1998; US EPA 1999; Chestnut, Mills, and Cohan 2006; Nadadur et al. 2007).

The case notes that these rules were updated and tightened in October 2006. The EPA reduced the 24-hour primary and secondary NAAQS for PM-2.5, while retaining the annual primary and secondary PM-2.5 NAAQS at their current levels. Regarding coarse particulate matter, the agency retained the 24-hour PM-10 standard and revoked the annual PM-10 standard. However, in February 2009 the DC Circuit Court remanded the annual PM-2.5 NAAQS to the EPA for failing to adequately explain why the standard was sufficient to protect public health while providing an adequate margin of safety. The secondary PM-2.5 standards were also remanded because the court claimed the EPA unreasonably concluded that the standards were adequate to protect the public welfare from adverse effects on visibility.

Environmental standards are an ongoing public policy debate among the various stakeholders. The case notes that organizations such as the American Lung Association, the Environmental Defense Fund, and the American Farm Bureau Federation filed petitions challenging the October 2006 rulings. In March 2008, when the EPA set a new air quality standard for smog-forming ozone, it was criticized by EPA's Clean Air Science Advisory Committee (CASAC) and by environmental groups for not being rigorous enough and by industry representatives, who called it unnecessary. The EPA administrator, Stephen Johnson, also asked Congress at this time to amend the Clean Air Act to allow the agency to consider economic factors in making decisions on air quality. He stated that the "Clean Air Act is not a relic to be displayed in the Smithsonian, but a living document that must be modernized to continue realizing results" (Bryner 2008). The executive director of the National Association of Clean Air Agencies, an association of state regulators, argued that a consideration of costs would mean that the standards were no longer health-based. California Senator Barbara Boxer stated that "it is outrageous that the Bush Administration would call for changes that would gut the Clean Air Act, which has saved countless lives and protected the health of millions of Americans for more than 35 years. . . . The Bush Administration would have us replace clean air standards driven by science with standards based on the interests of polluters" (Bryner 2008).

BENEFITS AND COSTS OF TIGHTENED AIR QUALITY STANDARDS

Air pollution consists of particulate matter (PM) of various sizes and composition, inorganic gases, and many volatile organic compounds (VOCs), combined with other biological materials. These pollutants arise from personal activities and the combustion of fossil fuels. Tailpipe emissions contribute to carbon monoxide (CO) and nitrogen oxides (NO_x). Power plants emit sulfur dioxide (SO_2), significant quantities of NO_x, and a variety of types of PM (Nadadur et al. 2007). Although much PM can be directly controlled, there are also efforts under way to control SO_2, NO_x, and organic compounds, which are major precursors to PM. Many pollutants have been analyzed in isolation, while interaction may alter their toxicity or impact. PM is a mixture rather than a single chemical compound. Regulators must understand how PM characteristics vary across space and time. Following the 1997 revisions to the NAAQS, the EPA developed several monitoring networks to determine the concentration of PM-2.5, the average composition of which varies across cities and regions. There are more carbonaceous materials in the northwestern United States, while California has high nitrate concentrations. Sulfate particles are the largest contributors to PM-2.5 in the southeast, and there is a mixture of sulfate and carbon in the northeastern United States (Nadadur et al. 2007).

Primary PM-2.5 consists of soot and accompanying organics, and is emitted from cars, trucks, heavy equipment, forest fires and burning waste, as well as from coke ovens and combustion and industrial processes. Secondary PM-2.5 forms in the atmosphere from precursor gases from power plants and other industries; from diesel and other mobile sources; and from solvents, fires, and agricultural operations. Fine particles can be transported hundreds or thousands of miles from their emission sources. Concentrations in a given area may result from regional transport as well as local sources (US EPA 2006, b-c).

Operating conditions, engine design parameters, and sampling methods can contribute to the variation of PM-2.5 in emission streams. Once emitted, these particles interact with water vapor, solar radiation, and other pollutants emitted from the same and other sources, all in ever-changing weather conditions. These changes can cause variation in the health effects of PM. For example, ultra-fine emissions from the burning of coal can contain much higher levels of iron and water-soluble metals than fine and coarse particles generated at the same time. Different coals produce particles with varying chemical composition (Nadadur et al. 2007).

Exposure to PM results in many different cardiopulmonary health effects. Research on these effects has been based on both population-based epidemiologic studies and animal toxicology studies, in which animals, typically rodents, are exposed to individual air pollutants or to different concentrations of pollutants (Nadadur et al. 2007).

All economic evaluations of pollution abatement programs require the following steps (Ostro and Chestnut 1998):

1. Estimate the quantitative relationship between ambient concentrations and the health response—the "concentration-response functions."

2. Estimate the size and composition of susceptible populations.

3. Estimate the change in air pollution concentrations under consideration.

4. Estimate the economic value of the reduction in health effects.

Ostro and Chestnut (1998) undertook a study to quantify the potential nationwide reductions in ambient PM-10. They drew on concentration-response functions in the epidemiologic literature estimating the change in the number of cases of each health effect that would be expected from changes in ambient PM-10 concentrations. A key assumption from these studies is that the relationship between air pollution and health effects is causal. Observational epidemiologic studies cannot prove that a relationship is causal. However, for particulate matter, numerous studies have found a similar magnitude of effect for mortality and for a variety of adverse health outcomes. There are always concerns about whether there are thresholds below which the particulate matter does not have adverse effects. PM thresholds have been difficult to identify, so that increased morbidity and mortality may be occurring in locations that currently meet federal standards.

To determine PM concentration levels, the authors used data on PM-10 because the existing PM-2.5 database was limited. They assumed a ratio between the average concentrations of the two sizes of particles. This ratio was 0.5 for California and 0.6 for the rest of the country. Average concentrations were derived from the EPA air quality–monitoring database, involving 865 monitoring locations in 502 counties and representing 57% of the US population.

When valuing the health effects, Ostro and Chestnut (1998) used estimates of both willingness to pay and cost of illness. There were studies in the WTP literature addressing small changes in the risk of death and changes in the risks of developing chronic bronchitis, the two most serious health effects associated with PM exposure. When WTP estimates were not available, cost-of-illness information was used, although these estimates were adjusted upward by a factor of 2, given that WTP is typically greater than cost of illness for a given health effect. The health effects included in the analysis were premature mortality, chronic bronchitis, hospital admissions, emergency room visits, restricted activity days for adults, lower-respiratory illness in children, asthma symptoms, and acute respiratory symptoms.

The largest health effects in this study were reduced days with acute respiratory symptoms and reduced days of restricted activity. However the monetary valuation was dominated by premature mortality (82% of the total monetary value) and chronic bronchitis (12%) (Ostro and Chestnut 1998).

Section 812 of the 1990 Clean Air Act Amendments (CAAA) mandates that the EPA develop periodic reports to Congress on the benefits and costs of the CAAA. The first report was published in 1997 and focused on the period 1970–90. The second report, published in 1999, focused on the period 1990–2010 and analyzed the marginal benefits and costs of the 1990 CAAA (US EPA 1999). This report did not include the benefits and costs of the 1997 revisions to the NAAQS. The report compared pre-CAAA and post-CAAA scenarios: The former froze federal, state, and local air pollution controls at the levels of stringency and effectiveness that prevailed in 1990, while the latter assumed that all federal, state, and local rules developed in support of the 1990 CAAA were implemented. The report also assumed that the geographic distributions of population and economic activity remained the same between the two scenarios. The pre-CAAA scenario assumed that states and localities would not have invested further in air pollution controls in the absence of the federal CAAA.

The analysis consisted of six steps: (1) emissions modeling, (2) direct cost estimation, (3) air quality modeling, (4) health and environmental effects estimation, (5) economic valuation, and (6) results aggregation and uncertainty characterization (US EPA 1999). Emissions estimates were generated by constructing an inventory for the base year (1990), projecting emissions for the pre-CAAA case for the years 2000 and 2010, and constructing post-CAAA estimates for the same two target years using a regulatory framework consistent with the 1990 CAAA implementation plan. The emissions inventories were translated into estimates of air quality conditions under each scenario. Air quality was then translated into physical outcomes (mortality, emergency room visits, or crop yield losses) through the use of concentration-response functions. Next the economic value of the reduction in the incidence of these adverse effects was estimated and compared with the costs of implementing the regulations. The report summarized the major sources of uncertainty for each of the analytic steps and considered each source of uncertainty as either major or minor, depending on whether it had an effect of more than 5% on the total net benefits.

This chapter's case noted two broad categories of benefits corresponding to the primary and secondary effects of the NAAQS: human health effects of morbidity and mortality, and welfare effects including agricultural and ecological benefits, visibility, and worker productivity. The benefit of reductions in premature mortality risk dominated the overall net benefit estimate because of the high monetary value assigned to the avoidance of premature mortality relative to the unit value of other health endpoints. The report used estimates of mean WTP where available, and the cost of treating or mitigating the effect as an alternative estimate. Mortality risk was influenced by age (children and the elderly were at particularly high risk) and health status prior to exposure. The study estimated specific health effects for chronic bronchitis, chronic asthma, respiratory-related ailments, minor restricted-activity days, and hospital admissions for cardiovascular and respiratory conditions (US EPA 1999).

The report attributed total annual human health benefits of $68 billion in 2000 and $110 billion in 2010 to Titles I through V of the CAAA. It assumed that 50% of the estimated cases of avoided mortality occurred within the first two years and the remaining 50% were distributed over the next three years. The report addressed uncertainty in many parameters by expressing values as statistical distributions around an estimate rather than simply point estimates (US EPA 1999).

The EPA's second prospective analysis focuses on the period 1990–2020 and will compare costs and benefits for each major emitting source category as well as for CAAA overall. In some cases, comparisons of costs and benefits may be based on nonmonetary evaluations of the benefits of the provisions. Updated epidemiologic analysis will be included. Health effects from PM have been based on the Harvard Six Cities Study and the American Cancer Society study, which found consistent relationships between fine-particle indicators and premature mortality across multiple locations in the United States (Industrial Economics 2003).

Although economic factors cannot be considered in the establishment of air quality standards, costs and benefits can guide implementation by the states in terms of timelines, strategies, and policies. The EPA developed a Regulatory Impact Analysis (RIA) for the 2006 changes in the standards. The RIA included the incremental benefits and costs of the selected regulatory approach compared with one less stringent and one more stringent option. It also included an assessment of the nature and sources of PM-2.5, estimates of current and future emissions that contribute to the problem, development of control strategies to attain the alternative standards in future years, analysis of incremental costs and benefits, and an examination of uncertainties and limitations in the analyses (US EPA 2006e).

The RIA forecasts emissions and air quality in 2015 and 2020 under a regulatory base case incorporating national, regional, state, and local regulations already in place or adopted. Analysis showed that although PM-2.5 air quality would be significantly better in 2020 than today under current requirements, several eastern and western states would have to develop and adopt additional controls to attain the revised standards. Greater reductions would be needed in western areas, particularly California (US EPA 2006e).

Benefits in the RIA include the monetized value of reductions in mortality and morbidity. The study also estimated monetary benefits associated with improvements in visibility in selected national parks and wilderness areas in 2020. Estimates of the impact of reductions in premature death were drawn from published epidemiologic literature and from an expert elicitation study conducted by the EPA in 2006. Estimates based on the American Cancer Society's study of health effects showed that the benefits of meeting the revised 24-hour PM-2.5 standard would be $17 billion per year in 2020. Incremental annualized costs of the revised standards were between $5.0 and $5.1 billion, using 3% and 7% discount rates. Cost estimates were uncertain because the report extrapolated the costs of full attainment in California and Salt Lake City. Total social costs, including the impacts on GDP, were slightly higher— $5.4 billion in 2020 for the revised standards and $7.9 billion for the alternative standards (US EPA 2006e).

The air pollution model in this study performed well in predicting monthly and seasonal concentrations, although there was less certainty in the 24-hour predictions. There was also uncertainty about the relative contribution of mobile source emissions to overall PM levels; the impact of economic growth and increased technological efficiencies; and the effectiveness of future control programs. The analysis might not have accounted for emerging control devices and learning by doing and was based on the assumption that controls are well maintained throughout their equipment life. The report assumed that inhalation of fine particles at levels experienced by most Americans on a daily basis is causally associated with premature death. The weight of the available epidemiologic, toxicological, and experimental evidence supported an assumption of causality. The analysis also assumed that all fine particles, regardless of their chemical composition, are equally potent in causing premature mortality, and the report noted the inherent uncertainties in projecting emissions and air quality out to 2020 (US EPA 2006e).

MEASURING THE HEALTH EFFECTS OF AIR POLLUTION REGULATIONS

There are numerous uncertainties in measuring the effects of air pollution, which is typically measured for outdoor air at a few points in a city or metropolitan area. Since most people only spend a small amount of time outdoors (and not in vehicles), these measurements may not truly reflect the quality of the air that people breathe most of the time. Some data are derived from clinical studies of a sample of volunteers: These studies are usually done under very controlled conditions, and they do not allow for the fact that people in real-world situations will probably take actions to avert or at least mitigate the air pollution (Cifuentes and Lave 1993).

The EPA has noted that two types of data are used to monitor air quality: ambient concentrations and emissions estimates. Ambient concentrations are "measurements of pollutant concentrations in the ambient air from monitoring sites across the country," while emissions estimates "are based largely on engineering calculations of the amounts and kinds of pollutants emitted by automobiles, factories, and other sources over a given period" (US EPA 1998, 8). Changes in ambient concentrations do not always match changes in emissions estimates for several reasons. Air quality monitors are usually in urban areas, so they measure urban emissions from mobile sources more accurately than they do rural emissions from large stationary sources. The amount of pollution measured at the monitoring stations is also influenced by any chemical reactions in the atmosphere and other meteorological conditions (US EPA 1998).

In trying to measure premature deaths due to air pollution, researchers must try to distinguish between deaths that are actually caused by the air pollution and deaths that would have occurred in any case. It is often said that air pollution is simply "harvesting" deaths that would likely have occurred within a few days even without the pollution. This is another example of the problem of the counterfactual that was first discussed in the previous chapter. Studies done in the past may not reflect the changes in outcomes that have occurred over time as other environmental regulations were put into effect. Clinical studies of the morbidity effects of air pollution may use either very precise measures of pulmonary functions and other symptoms, such as eye or throat irritation or shortness of breath, or more comprehensive measures such as restricted activity days, which include days spent in bed, days missed from work, and other days when normal activities are restricted due to illness (Cifuentes and Lave 1993).

Associations between mortality and long-term exposure to fine-particulate air pollution have been observed in population-based and cohort studies since the 1970s. Epidemiologic studies published between 1989 and 1996 reported health effects at lower than expected concentrations of air pollution. The 1997 NAAQS were based on the Harvard Six Cities Study and the American Cancer Society study (Dockery et al. 1993; Pope, Thun, et al. 1995). Pope, Burnett et al. (2002) reanalyzed the American Cancer Society data, including in their study longer follow-up times, expanded exposure-data collected subsequent to the 1997 NAAQS, improved controls for occupational exposures to pollution and for dietary variables, and recent advances in statistical modeling. All of their indices of fine-particulate air pollution were associated with cardiopulmonary and lung cancer mortality, but not mortality from all other causes combined. Controlling for smoking, education, marital status, and other factors had little effect on these associations.

Pope, Ezzati, and Dockery (2009) assessed these associations for fifty-one US metropolitan areas, comparing data for the period from the late 1970s to the early 1980s with matched data from the late 1990s to the early 2000s. New monitoring networks were established after the implementation of the NAAQS standards for PM-2.5 in 1997. Improvements in life expectancy during the 1980s and 1990s were associated with reduction in fine-particulate pollution even after adjustment for various socioeconomic, demographic, and proxy variables for prevalence of smoking. From 1980 to 2000, the average increase in life expectancy was 2.72 years for the counties in this analysis. The increase in life expectancy due to reduced levels of air pollution was 0.4 year. The study used both cross-sectional and temporal analysis. Income per capita was a proxy variable for access to medical care, higher-quality diets, and healthier lifestyles. Death rates from lung cancer and chronic obstructive pulmonary disease (COPD) were used as proxies for smoking. The authors concluded that although "multiple factors affect life expectancy, our findings provide evidence that improvements in air quality have contributed to measurable improvements in human health and life expectancy in the United States" (Pope, Ezzati, and Dockery 2009, 385).

VALUATION OF LIVES SAVED DUE TO AIR QUALITY STANDARDS

The valuation placed on the lives saved from the stricter air quality standards has also been debated. Federal agencies must select appropriate estimates of the value of a statistical life (VSL) from the available literature, adapt study estimates to the particular regulatory context, and derive a point estimate, range of values, or probability distribution for use in their analyses and rule-making processes. Variation in the types of risks addressed by different agencies is a key issue. Wage-risk compensation studies are usually based on the risk of accidental deaths by workers in their mid- to late-thirties, while individuals affected by air pollution regulations are likely to be much older, face health risks unrelated to pollution, and confront air pollution risks that are less voluntary and controllable than the choice of a job (Robinson 2007).

Agencies may use estimates of both VSL and the value per statistical life-year (VSLY), which is an adjustment of the VSL to incorporate differences in remaining life expectancy. The VSLY is calculated by dividing the VSL by the discounted expected number of life-years remaining for the average individual studied. The VSLY is applied to the expected number of discounted life years saved by a regulation. Robinson (2007, 285) gives the following example from an EPA assessment of the Clean Air Act:

> *Assuming that the VSL is $4.8 million (in 1990 dollars), the remaining life expectancy averages thirty-five years for the population studied, and the VSL estimate reflects a 5-percent discount rate, the EPA obtained a VSLY of $293,000. If the average individual whose life is extended by the program would survive for an additional fourteen years (as a result of reduced exposure to pollutants), the present value of the risk reductions would be $2.9 million (i.e., the discounted value of fourteen years × $293,000 per year). In other words, under this approach, the total value of the mortality risk reduction would be $4.8 million for a younger individual who would survive for thirty-five additional years, and $2.9 million for an older individual who would survive for only fourteen more years.*

This example highlights the fact that this approach places a higher value on the life of a younger person than on that of an older individual. The calculation also assumes that the VSL is proportional to the discounted remaining life expectancy (Robinson 2007).

The US Office of Management and Budget (OMB) directs the regulatory process across federal agencies. Its role is framed by Executive Order 12866, Regulatory Planning and Review, which directs agencies to evaluate alternative strategies for all economically significant regulations, including those with an impact of $100 million or more on the economy. The order requires an analysis of benefits and costs, along with distributive impacts, equity, and other non-quantifiable effects. Guidance is provided in OMB's Circular A-4, Regulatory Analysis. The circular suggests that agencies present both VSL and VSLY estimates, and reports that the range of VSL estimates in the literature is generally between $1 and $10 million (Robinson 2007).

The EPA relied on research conducted in the early 1990s to support its analyses of the Clean Air Act in 1997 and 1999. The mean VSL estimated in these studies ranged from $0.6 to $13.5 million, with an overall mean of $4.8 million (1990 dollars). These estimates were derived from twenty-six VSL estimates: twenty-one from wage-risk studies and five from contingent valuation studies. Estimates from the contingent valuation studies tended to cluster at the lower end of the range of estimates. The wage-risk studies were based on workers in their mid- to late-thirties. More recently the EPA has used results from meta-analyses of the literature (Mrozek and Taylor 2002; Kochi et al. 2006; Viscusi and Aldy 2003), each of which used a somewhat different methodology and reported different ranges of best estimates. Mrozek and Taylor found a mean VSL estimate of $2.6 million (1998 dollars), while Kochi et al. reported a mean of $5.4 million (2000 dollars), and Viscusi and Aldy found means ranging from $5.5 to $7.6 million (2000 dollars) (Robinson 2007).

Viscusi (2009) describes the controversy that erupted in 2003 when the EPA presented an analysis of air pollution regulations in which the reduced risks to lives of persons over age 65 received a lower VSL than that placed on younger persons. The EPA abandoned this practice after a political firestorm erupted over the "devaluation of life" for older persons. Elderly citizens groups such as AARP protested over what came to be known as the "senior discount" or the "senior death discount." The impact of this age adjustment was not inconsequential. In one policy analysis, it lowered the estimated benefits of reduction to long-term exposure to air pollution by $13 billion annually.

There was further controversy in 2008 when the EPA Office of Air Quality Planning and Standards lowered the VSL figure used in regulatory analyses of air pollution regulations. As a result, Senator Barbara Boxer of California proposed legislation—the "Restoring the Value of Every American in Environmental Decisions Act"—that would ban procedures that reduced the value of life over time or decreased the VSL based on demographic factors, including age.

Viscusi (2009) argued that much of the reaction to the lowering of VSL estimates likely stemmed from several cognitive effects. There might be an anchoring bias, in which people tend to judge current VSL levels as correct; therefore lower values appear to be inappropriate because they are a decrease from the established value. People also exhibit loss aversion, in which individuals place a much larger value on losses in income or wealth than on the equivalent gains. These are both examples of status quo biases; people focus on the status quo (income, insurance, level of government benefits) and may have an irrational bias against departures from the status quo.

Viscusi (2009) noted that the VSL estimates used in regulatory analysis are not standardized across agencies or at any point in time. The figures, all converted to 2008 dollars in his table 1 (p. 108), range from $1.2 to $6.8 million. The estimates are quite different for the Department of Transportation, the Food and Drug Administration, and different divisions of the Department of Agriculture. The "devaluation estimates" of the EPA are higher than many estimates used by other federal agencies that did not cause public debate. It appeared to be the change in VSL levels rather than the absolute level that caused the controversy.

Viscusi (2009) also argued that it is not entirely unreasonable that the VSL declines with age. Research has indicated that VSL may display an inverted U-shaped pattern over an individual's lifetime. However, the upward trend when people are young is much steeper than the downward trend after age 60. There is evidence that the VSL for people in their 20s is less than that for people age 60. Individual willingness to pay for risk reduction is related to wealth, and older persons are likely to have more funds to purchase risk reductions. However, the issue continues to be controversial. The use of uniform values for VSL places a higher value per expected life-year saved for the old than for the young. Willingness to pay is thus related to income effects and the equity issues discussed previously.

As noted above, the EPA was criticized in 2008 for lowering the VSL used in assessing air pollution regulations. The EPA Office of Air Quality Planning and Standards began using a VSL in 2008 dollars of $7.0 million, compared with previous values of $7.7 to $7.8 million. Some criticized this move as politically motivated by the Bush administration. Viscusi (2009) noted that VSL estimates have generally increased over time due to increases in societal income levels. The income elasticity of the VSL has been estimated at 0.5–0.6, so that a 10% increase in income levels should increase the VSL by 5–6%. This reduction by the EPA was not made across the agency. Some of these changes resulted from the use of new meta-analyses by Mrozek and Taylor (2002), Kochi, Hubbell, and Kramer (2006), and Viscusi and Aldy (2003), which had different methodological assumptions. Much of the controversy arose because the EPA Office of Air Quality Planning and Standards did not present the VSL amounts in current dollars but reported the values in nominal dollars of a previous year. Several EPA analyses used a VSL of $5.5 million in 1999 dollars, which actually equaled $7.0 million in 2008 dollars, a value well within the range of VSLs used by other federal agencies.

Viscusi (2009) criticized the legislative response to the controversy, specifically the "Restoring the Value of Every American in Environmental Decisions Act" proposed by Senator Barbara Boxer. He argued that this legislation would politicize the selection of the VSL and threaten the integrity of economic policymaking. The legislation proposed that the VSL used by the EPA could never be reduced below the highest value used before the legislation, must be increased at least once a year to reflect changes in average income, and could never be decreased "based on age, income, race, illness, disability, date of death, or any other personal attribute or relativistic analysis of the value of life" (Viscusi 2009, 119). Viscusi claimed that the legislation would give Congress control of a key economic parameter and that the wording of the bill implied that the current VSL methodology was not an appropriate approach to the issue.

Robinson (2009) noted the challenges of communicating to the general public any policies involving risk. Changes made for technical reasons may appear to be politically motivated. The lower VSL for older people included in the sensitivity analyses for existing legislation in the 1990s under the Clinton administration did not attract the same attention as those under the Bush administration in 2002 and 2003. The media also characterized the issue as having to do with the value that the EPA places on life, as opposed to a methodology involving preferences for small changes in risk. Technical details of sensitivity analyses are generally not discussed in the media. The issue of the VSL age adjustment also raised the question of how equity effects should be incorporated into benefit-cost analysis, as noted earlier in the chapter.

SUMMARY

The issues discussed here reveal the problems in undertaking any cost-benefit analysis and illustrate how that analysis is used in a decision-making process. There is a significant degree of uncertainty involved in determining the impact of many programs and regulations and in assessing the valuation of these impacts. The case in this chapter showed that these uncertainties arise in assessing air pollution, in estimating the effects of pollution on human health and the environment, and in valuing the benefits and costs of regulations to improve air quality. Some of this uncertainty can be dealt with through sensitivity analysis and the development of alternative scenarios. The existence of multiple studies also supports the effectiveness of a program, even if all the studies have some methodological problems. As noted in the discussion of VSL estimates, meta-analyses have increasingly been used to quantitatively integrate findings from numerous studies.

There is a need for economic evaluation studies using the tools of cost-effectiveness, cost-utility, and cost-benefit analysis, even given their weaknesses. "Unless mechanisms exist for placing bounds on our risk reduction efforts, we can end up pursuing policies of diminishing marginal impact and diverting resources from more productive uses" (Viscusi 1996, 120). However, there is also a need for more comprehensive and uniform analyses of government regulations and investment programs. This decision-making problem is the greatest challenge in the future for the economic evaluation of public sector programs, regulations, and interventions. Moreover, it must be remembered that economic evaluations are the decision-making tools, not the decision; that the uncertainties in the analyses should be recognized; and that policy decisions are always influenced by the various stakeholders in the process.

REFERENCES

Bayoumi, Ahmed M. 2004. The Measurement of Contingent Valuation for Health Economics. *Pharmacoeconomics* 22 (11): 691–700.

Bjornstad, David J., and James R. Kahn, eds. 1996. *The Contingent Valuation of Environmental Resources.* Cheltenham, UK: Edward Elgar.

Browner, Carol M. 1997. Smog and Soot: Updating Air Quality Standards. *Public Health Reports* 112 (5): 366–67.

Bryner, Michelle. 2008. EPA Tightens Ozone Standard; Seeks Clean Air Act Revisions. *Chemical Week* 170 (9): 16.

Carson, Richard T. 1991. Constructed Markets. In *Measuring the Demand for Environmental Quality*, ed. John Braden and Charles Kolstad, 267–305. Amsterdam: Elsevier.

Chestnut, Lauraine G., David M. Mills, and Daniel S. Cohan. 2006. Cost-Benefit Analysis in the Selection of Efficient Multipollutant Strategies. *Journal of the Air and Waste Management Association* 56 (4): 530–36.

Cifuentes, Luis A., and Lester B. Lave. 1993. Economic Valuation of Air Pollution Abatement: Benefits From Health Effects. *Annual Review of Energy and the Environment* 18:319–42.

Clawson, Marion. 1959. *Methods for Measuring the Demand for and the Value of Outdoor Recreation.* Washington, DC: Resources for the Future.

Clawson, Marion, and Jack L. Knetsch. 1966. *Economics of Outdoor Recreation.* Baltimore: Johns Hopkins University Press.

Cummings, Ronald G., David S. Brookshire, and William D. Schulze. 1986. *Valuing Environmental Goods: An Assessment of the Contingent Valuation Method.* Savage, MD: Rowman & Littlefield.

Diamond, Peter A., and Jerry A. Hausman. 1994. Contingent Valuation: Is Some Number Better Than No Number? *Journal of Economic Perspectives* 8 (4): 45–64.

Dockery, Douglas W., C. Arden Pope, Xiping Xu, John D. Spengler, James H. Ware, Martha E. Fay, Benjamin G. Ferris Jr., and Frank E. Speizer. 1993. An Association between Air Pollution and Mortality in Six US Cities. *New England Journal of Medicine* 329:1753–59.

Drummond, Michael F., Mark J. Sculpher, George W. Torrance, Bernie J. O'Brien, and Greg L. Stoddart. 2005. *Methods for the Economic Evaluation of Health Care Programmes*. 3rd ed. Oxford: Oxford University Press.

Fisher, Ann, Lauraine G. Chestnut, and Daniel M. Violette. 1989. The Value of Reducing the Risks of Death: A Note on New Evidence. *Journal of Policy Analysis and Management* 8 (1): 88–100.

Freeman, A. Myrick, III. 1993. *The Measurement of Environmental and Resource Values: Theory and Methods*. Washington, DC: Resources for the Future.

Gaynor, Martin, and William B. Vogt. 1997. What Does Economics Have to Say about Health Policy Anyway? A Comment and Correction on Evans and Rice. *Journal of Health Politics, Policy and Law* 22 (2): 476–96.

Gramlich, Edward M. 1981. *Benefit-Cost Analysis of Government Programs*. Englewood Cliffs, NJ: Prentice Hall.

———. 1990. *A Guide to Benefit-Cost Analysis*. 2nd ed. Englewood Cliffs, NJ: Prentice Hall.

Haddix, Anne C., Steven M. Teutsch, and Phaedra S. Corso. 2003. *Prevention Effectiveness: A Guide to Decision Analysis and Economic Evaluation*. 2nd ed. New York: Oxford University Press.

Hanemann, W. Michael. 1994. Valuing the Environment through Contingent Valuation. *Journal of Economic Perspectives* 8 (4): 19–43.

Haveman, Robert H., and Burton A. Weisbrod. 1983. Defining Benefits of Public Programs: Some Guidance for Policy Analysts. In *Public Expenditure and Policy Analysis*, 3rd ed. ed. Robert H. Haveman and Julius Margolis, 80–104. Boston: Houghton Mifflin.

Herzlinger, Regina. 1979. Costs, Benefits, and the West Side Highway. *The Public Interest* 55 (Spring): 77–98.

Hoffnagle, Gale F. 1997. New NAAQS Demand Reductions. *Power Engineering* 101 (13): 41–45.

Industrial Economics, Incorporated. 2003. Benefits and Costs of the Clean Air Act 1990–2020: Revised Analytical Plan For EPA's Second Prospective Analysis. Report prepared for the US Environmental Protection Agency, May 12.

Kemper, Peter, David A. Long, and Craig Thornton. 1983. A Benefit-Cost Analysis of the Supported Work Experiment. In *Public Expenditure and Policy Analysis*, 3rd ed. ed. Robert H. Haveman and Julius Margolis, 260–300. Boston: Houghton Mifflin.

Kochi, Ikuho, Bryan Hubbell, and Randall Kramer. 2006. An Empirical Bayes Approach to Combining and Comparing Estimates of the Value of a Statistical Life for Environmental Policy Analysis. *Environmental & Resource Economics* 34 (3): 385–406.

Liu, Jin-Tan, James K. Hammit, Jung-Der Wang, and Meng-Wen Tsou. 2005. Valuation of the Risk of SARS in Taiwan. *Health Economics* 14 (1): 83–91.

Mitchell, Robert C., and Richard T. Carson. 1989. *Using Surveys to Value Public Goods: The Contingent Valuation Method.* Washington, DC: Resources for the Future.

Mrozek, Janusz R., and Laura O. Taylor. 2002. What Determines the Value of Life? A Meta-Analysis. *Journal of Policy Analysis and Management* 21 (2): 253–70.

Nadadur, Srikanth S., C. Andrew Miller, Philip K. Hopke, Terry Gordon, Sverre Vedal, John J. Vandenberg, and Daniel L. Costa. 2007. The Complexities of Air Pollution Regulation; The Need for an Integrated Research and Regulatory Perspective. *Toxicological Sciences* 100 (2): 318–27.

O'Brien, Bernie, and Amiram Gafni. 1996. When Do the "Dollars" Make Sense? Toward a Conceptual Framework for Contingent Valuation Studies in Health Care. *Medical Decision Making* 16 (3): 288–99.

Olsen, Jan Abel, and Richard D. Smith. 2001. Theory Versus Practice: A Review of "Willingness to Pay" in Health and Health Care. *Health Economics* 10 (1): 39–52.

Ostro, Bart, and Lauraine Chestnut. 1998. Assessing the Health Benefits of Reducing Particulate Matter Air Pollution in the United States. *Environmental Research* 76 (2): 94–106.

Pauly, Mark V. 1997. Who Was That Straw Man Anyway? A Comment on Evans and Rice. *Journal of Health Politics, Policy and Law* 22 (2): 467–73.

Pope, C. Arden, Richard T. Burnett, Michael J. Thun, Eugenia E. Calle, Daniel Krewski, Kazuhiko Ito, and George D. Thurston. 2002. Lung Cancer, Cardiopulmonary Mortality, and Long-Term Exposure to Fine Particulate Air Pollution. *Journal of the American Medical Association* 287 (9): 1132–41.

Pope, C. Arden, Majid Ezzati, and Douglas W. Dockery. 2009. Fine-Particulate Air Pollution and Life Expectancy in the United States. *New England Journal of Medicine* 360 (4): 376–86.

Pope, C. Arden, Michael J. Thun, M. M. Namboodiri, D. W. Dockery, J. S. Evans, F. E. Speizer, and C. W. Heath Jr. 1995. Particulate Air Pollution as a Predictor of Mortality in a Prospective Study of US Adults. *American Journal of Respiratory Critical Care Medicine* 151 (3): 669–74.

Portney, Paul R. 1994. The Contingent Valuation Debate: Why Economists Should Care. *Journal of Economic Perspectives* 8 (4): 3–17.

Reinhardt, Uwe E. 1992. Reflections on the Meaning of Efficiency: Can Efficiency Be Separated from Equity? *Yale Law & Policy Review* 10:302–15.

Rice, Thomas. 1992. An Alternative Framework for Evaluating Welfare Losses in the Health Care Market. *Journal of Health Economics* 11 (1): 88–92.

———. 1997. Can Markets Give Us the Health System We Want? *Journal of Health Politics, Policy and Law* 22 (2): 383–426.

———. 2003. *The Economics of Health Reconsidered*. 2nd ed. Chicago: Health Administration Press.

Robinson, Lisa A. 2007. "How US Government Agencies Value Mortality Risk Reductions. *Review of Environmental Economics and Policy* 1 (2): 283–99.

———. 2009. Valuing Lives, Valuing Risks, and Respecting Preferences in Regulatory Analysis. *Regulation & Governance* 3 (3): 298–305.

Romani, Paul N. 1998. Environmentally Responsible Business. *Supervision* 59 (2): 6–9.

Schelling, Thomas C. 1968. The Life You Save May Be Your Own. In *Problems in Public Expenditure Analysis*, ed. Samuel B. Chase, 127–76. Washington, DC: The Brookings Institution.

Scott, R. Douglas, Martin I. Meltzer, Lonny J. Erickson, Philippe De Wals, and Nancy E. Rosenstein. 2002. Vaccinating First-Year College Students Living in Dormitories for Meningococcal Disease: An Economic Analysis. *American Journal of Preventive Medicine* 23 (2): 98–105.

Smith, Richard D. 2003. Construction of the Contingent Valuation Market in Health Care: A Critical Assessment. *Health Economics* 12 (8): 609–28.

Tolley, George, Donald Kenkel, and Robert Fabian. 1994. *Valuing Health for Policy*. Chicago: The University of Chicago Press.

US Environmental Protection Agency. 1998. *National Air Quality and Emissions Trend Report*, 1997. Research Triangle Park, NC: US Environmental Protection Agency.

———. 1999. *The Benefits and Costs of the Clean Air Act 1990 to 2010*. Washington, DC: Office of Air and Radiation, Office of Policy.

———. 2006a. *Fact Sheet: Final Revisions to the National Ambient Air Quality Standards for Particulate Pollution (Particulate Matter)*. www.epa.gov/particles/actions.html.

———. 2006b. *Fine Particle (PM$_{2.5}$) Designations: Basic Information*. www.epa.gov/pmdesignations/basicinfo.htm.

———. 2006c. *Fine Particle (PM$_{2.5}$) Designations: Frequent Questions*. www.epa.gov/pmdesignations/faq.htm.

———. 2006d. *Regulatory Impact Analysis of EPA's Final Revisions to the National Ambient Air Quality Standards for Particulate Pollution (Particulate Matter) Fact Sheet*. www.epa.gov/air/particlepollution.html.

———. 2006e. *Regulatory Impact Analysis: 2006 National Ambient Air Quality Standards for Particulate Pollution, Executive Summary*. www.epa.gov/ttn/ecas/ria.html.

Viscusi, W. Kip. 1992. *Fatal Tradeoffs: Public & Private Responsibilities for Risk*. New York: Oxford University Press.

———. 1993. The Value of Risks to Life and Health. *Journal of Economic Literature* 31 (4): 1912–46.

———. 1996. Economic Foundations of the Current Regulatory Reform Efforts. *Journal of Economic Perspectives* 10 (3): 119–34.

———. 2009. The Devaluation of Life. *Regulation & Governance* 3 (2): 103–27.

Viscusi, W. Kip, and Joseph E. Aldy. 2003. The Value of a Statistical Life: A Critical Review of Market Estimates throughout the World. *Journal of Risk and Uncertainty* 27 (1): 5–76.

Warner, Kenneth E., and Bryan R. Luce. 1982. *Cost-Benefit and Cost-Effectiveness Analysis in Health Care*. Ann Arbor, MI: Health Administration Press.

Weisbrod, Burton A. 1983. Benefit-Cost Analysis of a Controlled Experiment: Treating the Mentally Ill. In *Public Expenditure and Policy Analysis*, 3rd ed. ed. Robert H. Haveman and Julius Margolis, 230–59. Boston: Houghton Mifflin.

Whittington, Dale, and Duncan MacRae Jr. 1986. The Issue of Standing in Cost-Benefit Analysis. *Journal of Policy Analysis and Management* 5 (4): 665–82.

Zerbe, Richard O., Jr. (1998). Is Cost-Benefit Analysis Legal? Three Rules. *Journal of Policy Analysis and Management* 17 (3): 419–56.

Chapter 8

Summary and Conclusions

In this chapter we summarize the issues developed earlier in this book and discuss practical lessons from the case applications. The aim in the previous chapters was to present generic analytic tools and indicate how adaptable they are to particular cases. In that sense, there is no one tool for problem definition or forecasting policy options, but rather, many variants. The professional policy analyst will have the judgment to select and adapt tools and methods and integrate appropriate values into his or her analyses. As we have emphasized, policy analysis is part art and part science.

Our approach has been critical. The supply side is often weak. What passes for analysis in many cases is superficial and shoddy and violates even the most basic rules for data use. Decision makers therefore need to know how to spot incomplete analyses before deciding on options and recommendations. On the demand side, when policymakers are familiar with the range of analytical tools, they can more effectively assess a given analysis, thus increasing the likelihood that if a decision is made on the basis of that analysis, it will be sound. This was in part the rationale for the creation of such in-house policy analysis bodies as the Congressional Research Service (CRS), which aids individual House and Senate members in their policy choices; the Congressional Budget Office (CBO); and the Government Accountability Office (GAO), which assists the members in economic policymaking. The information produced independently by these bodies is considered more trustworthy than that produced by the executive branch of government. Other regular sources of trustworthy analysis include NGOs (e.g., the Government Finance Officers Association and the International City/County Management Association) and think tanks (e.g., the Brookings Institution and the Heritage Foundation).

ANALYTIC FRAMEWORKS
AND DECISION VALUES REVISITED

As discussed in chapter 1, the issue of values is inherent in policy analysis. Many analysts would prefer to eliminate values problems with more helpings of quantitative data and methods. But that is neither possible nor desirable, since values must be recognized and weighed in even the most technical engineering analyses of, for example, roads and other infrastructure choices. Analytic tools can narrow the range of the values problem, but cannot eliminate it, because values are built into many of the tools themselves. For example, with cost-benefit analysis, decision makers attempt to compare the value of policy A (an education program) with that of policy B (an irrigation program). Yet, as discussed in chapter 7, the criterion of economic efficiency that underlies the cost-benefit analysis tool is based on value judgments about what improves social welfare (the potential compensation policy). There are also conflicts between equity and efficiency issues in the application of cost-benefit analysis, and the conflicts are not resolved simply by adding more data and using more quantitative tools.

We noted in chapter 1 that the emphasis of the book would be on the third of four phases of policy analysis (figure 1.1). The focus has been on tools and methods to optimize decisions in order to maximize net resource benefits. Given the linkage of values, analytic tools, and frameworks, we conclude here with a word on decision making. Analysts should be skeptical of one-size-fits-all methods when deciding on policies, given the underlying subjectivity of broader frameworks. Proponents of the planning, programming, and budgeting system (PPBS) "program structure" approach of the 1960s claimed that it was a new tool that would facilitate analysis of proposed public policies by comparing means and ends and integrating institutional and budgetary questions (Axelrod 1995). Rather than facilitate analysis, the new framework posed many unanswerable questions and generated quantities of data that did not contribute to better policy analysis or decisions. Much of the information generated was useless for decisions by existing organizations and institutions, especially elected officials in all three levels of government. By bringing in multiple actors and analysts with their own political agendas, program structures actually deepened the level of conflict. Paradoxically, the new policy analysis framework often impeded analysis.

The major problem with such overarching frameworks is that they are too general to serve as a guide. They cannot point to the right questions or provide criteria to evaluate the answers. For example, "program structures" could not point to the core issues or criteria for institutional analysis. Although some observers such as Carlson believed them absolutely essential to program analysis, others such as Wildavsky identified them correctly as vehicles to pile up meaningless data (cited in Axelrod 1995). A significant drawback is that the program-structures approach ignored the political costs of the structural changes to institutions that were often needed to rationalize budget allocations (e.g., consolidation and elimination of departments and bureaus).

In addition, policy analysis frameworks can lead the analyst to believe that institutional life is simple. They often presume that one decision maker or institution is doing the deciding. That is, tools may focus on comparing single programs or policies that deal with only one institution. In fact, most real-world problems—such as planning wars in Iraq and cutting health care costs while increasing coverage—deal with trade-offs between multiple policies in an environment of multiple institutional responsibilities, often for the same program. For example, the Departments of Defense, State, Commerce, and Treasury, as well as the United States Agency for International Development, are all involved in the foreign aid program.

The dilemma is how to decide which policies to fund and implement using decision tools that simplify reality—but not too much! This is the hard part of providing analysis to optimize decisions, which takes place in the third phase of policy analysis, as described in chapter 1 (see figure 1.1). As we have seen through review of the cases, policymakers need tools, methods, models, and systems to narrow the range of disagreement over technical issues. Many of these tools were discussed in chapters 4, 6, and 7. However, technical disagreements often turn on fundamental value differences. As one might expect, there is disagreement over both which tools are appropriate and which criteria should be used to assess policies and programs. One remedy for this problem is the weighted score table or weighting-and-scoring model described in chapter 4 and illustrated by table 4.2. Weighting-and-scoring models serve the overt purpose of structuring choices in cases where stakeholders have multiple values and argue about multiple criteria (Lehan 1984). Such models or tables are useful because criteria in most decisions are not of equal importance, which makes it difficult if not impossible to evaluate alternatives (Michel 2001, 14).

These decision models are derived from methods used to select capital projects, but they can feasibly be applied to current programs and policies. Moreover, investment programs include not only physical assets such as buildings, but human capital (health and education), as well as research and development. For example, health care requires medical personnel, testing and operating equipment, as well as hospital and clinic facilities. This makes it difficult to distinguish relative rates of return for subcomponents of particular policies. Beyond the methodological problem, most policymakers do not have access to quantitative economic studies on relative rates of return before allocating funds to programs (Posner, Lewis, and Laufe 1998, 17). For this practical reason, providing more criteria for decision making can increase the chances that a program will be transparent, acceptable, and ultimately effective. As noted, the weighting-and-scoring model uses multiple criteria that allow the ranking and trading of policy options based on stakeholder values. It can serve as a summary framework to structure choices once problems have been defined and analytic tools utilized to isolate potentially beneficial programs and policies.

Whatever method of policy selection is used, it should incorporate some assessment of intangible values (e.g., social benefits, health risk if deferred, availability of central transfers) as well as quantitative cost-benefit criteria. There are many possibilities here, and analysts should develop a system that utilizes the values from assessments (e.g., health clinic facility conditions) to produce a separate and overall summary score for decision making. The goal of such systems should not be to replace judgment or exclude political considerations. Rather, a ranking system is needed to make issues and trade-offs explicit.

For example, as indicated in table 8.1, using a combination of existing and recommended criteria, health project planners could assign scores of 0, 1, or 2 for each category (e.g., assessments of cost-sharing possibilities, benefits, and needs). The weighting-and-scoring model then produces rankings based on these combined scores (see table 8.1). To determine timing of implementation, the scores can be added and projects classified according to six categories of urgency (e.g., a total score of 14–16 = urgent). For example, the World Bank uses an ascending scale (1–3) of project rehabilitation to schedule needed renovations: (1) minimal level, (2) increased level of services, and (3) higher level of services. These criteria, which are the basis of overall projected weighted scores and later rankings, are in the "Needs" column. Since the interest is to bring health and education facilities up to minimal levels of service standards, for instance, a 2 might be assigned for "minimal" existing levels of service, a 1 for "increased levels," and a 0 for "higher levels" of service. The table 8.1 matrix could be used for ranking health or education projects.

Based on the total score in the last column from use of the weighting-and-scoring model, policymakers could classify programs or projects according to such values as: (1) urgent (cannot be postponed for safety reasons), (2) essential, (3) necessary, (4) desirable, (5) acceptable (meaning adequately planned but deferrable), or (6) deferrable (policies that are not only deferrable but also do not meet cost-benefit or timing criteria).

Table 8.1 Sample Weighting-and-Scoring Matrix for Health Investment Projects

Capital Repair Project	Cost Sharing (Or Alternative Funding): 2-High 1-Some 0-Low	Benefits (Or Forecast Demand): 2-High 1-Some 0-Low	Condition: 2-Bad 1-Fair 0-Good	Needs: 2-Minimal 1-Increased Level 0-Higher Level of Service	Location: 2-Rural 1-Semirural 0-Urban	Investment: 2-Repair 1-Replace 0-Complete Construction	Cost: 2-Less Than $850,000 1-$850,000– $1 Million 0-Greater than $1 Million	Occupancy: 2-75–100% 1-50–74% 0-Less Than 50%	Score
A									
B									
C									

In short, useful policy tools should provide guidance in ranking and trading off proposed programs, policies, and projects. These total weighted scores provide decision makers with a rank-order of candidates for financing. How ranked policies are to be financed (e.g., tax and fee-charge rates, contribution of private capital, means of leveraging public assets through leases and concessions) is typically a separate review phase (involving financial analysis to supplement economic analysis, on which we have focused in this book) (see Mikesell 2007; Fisher 2007). To the extent that problems have been properly defined, options accurately forecasted, and cost-benefit or cost-effectiveness appraisals professionally conducted, the multiple criteria of the weighted score framework should allow policymakers to make appropriate choices. In this way, when cost-benefit, efficiency, and effectiveness data have been assembled, the weighting-and-scoring model can inform the decision-making process.

LESSONS FROM THE CASE STUDY ANALYSES

We hope that our survey of policy analysis stages, from problem identification to decision-optimizing methods, will provide students and practitioners with useful tools and insights into their application to real-world policy problems.

Structuring Policy Problems

In chapter 2 we learned that policy problems represent unrealized values that produce dissatisfaction over issues (Dunn 2008). To be actionable later, problems should have an empirical basis, meaning that data should exist on the scope and intensity of the proposed problem. We learned that some policy problems are well structured, involving few decision makers and a small number of options; examples might include sanitation services, rat control, or scheduling of facilities maintenance. Moderately well-structured problems involve more decision makers and a wider array of options. Such problems often contain both well- and ill-structured components, such as current demographic changes and social insurance liabilities for future generations. Ill-structured or messy problems are the most common type of policy problem. They have multiple, overlapping decision makers and many options; one example would be the regulation of tobacco use and its widely varying implications for numerous stakeholders in the economy.

We indicated that there are many methods of structuring problems, including brainstorming, as well as boundary, classification, causal, and assumptional analyses. Some or all of these methods should be applied when decision makers are faced with an obviously messy problem, such as the case of jail overcrowding. The following lessons can be useful in applying such methods to a particular case:

- Do not define the problem so narrowly as to exclude related problems. To do so invites major unintended consequences at the implementation stage of policymaking. Jail overcrowding is related to drug use and apprehension of offenders.

- Include all relevant stakeholders to avoid a narrow mechanical definition of the problem. Failure to include all relevant stakeholders may allow the problem to be defined by powerful industry interest groups, such as prison construction and engineering firms.

- To avoid being overwhelmed with conflicting data and studies, isolate and study the major explanatory arguments and data trends. Current studies on the effects of racial preference systems in university student selection, for example, are largely contradictory and need to be sorted out before the problem-structuring process can begin.

- Examine remote causes as well as immediate, actionable ones. Problems must be defined in actionable terms. A college dean in Pristina, Kosovo, for example, would be unable to contain a conflict caused by long-term, deep-seated ethnic and religious tensions. Defining a local autonomy problem with ethnic and nationalistic roots as a problem of inadequate classroom space would be both reductionist and oblivious to the more remote causes.

- Isolate controlling variables. Three-strikes legislation and similar types of punitive statutes are major determinants of jail overcrowding.

- Brainstorm for alternatives to develop counterintuitive causal links and problem definitions. For example, it might be stated that the problem of jail overcrowding results from the lack of sufficient judicial discretion to define crimes as misdemeanors. This perspective suggests that the problem is of a single dimension. Defining a multidimensional problem leads to more innovative solutions, such as hybrid policies that legalize certain drugs, provide treatment, and strengthen enforcement and regulation.

Forecasting Problems: Institutional Effects

To structure and define actionable policy problems, we learned that institutions are very much part of the problem, as well as the solution. As noted in chapter 2, the US Department of Justice has its own preferences on the allocation of funds for enforcement instead of treatment of drug abuse, and this powerfully contributes to the persistence of the jail overcrowding problem. Whether this is as important a cause as existing legislation is a matter for further analysis. Institutions clearly matter to problem definition and policy design. Policies are not simply rules consisting of language that can be modified by legislatures or administrative agencies. Policies operate in institutional contexts that must be analyzed. The question is where to start and what tool to use. How can we narrow the analysis to make such work feasible within the context of calendar deadlines?

Chapter 3 proposed two dimensions of analysis: organizational structure and institutional functions, particularly financial management. There is no "one best way" to perform this analysis, and jurisdictions must improvise and develop their own methods that are then transferred and adopted elsewhere. Textbooks typically offer little help here except to report existing innovative practices by the public sector.

Thus, analysis of policy options should include available data on the performance of existing organizational structures. Specifically, the analyst should review data on the following:

- Are there too many layers of management (using such data as management-to-staff ratios)?
- Is the span of control appropriate to existing tasks and staff technical capacities (is the task appropriate to levels of capability and are reporting requirements consistent with task performance)?
- Is the method of service delivery appropriate (using comparative staffing ratios for similar services in other jurisdictions and analyzing the relationship between service and outcome, such as fire services focusing on prevention versus cure and resultant number of accidents or deaths)?
- Are costs of service delivery by a public department comparable with full costs of contractor use?

With these data, the analyst can make a reasonable assessment of the contribution of structural problems to policy problems.

The second level of analysis focuses on institutional functions, particularly administrative and financial management. The analyst should probe repetitive processes, such as licensing, contracting, and permit issuing, which are major tasks of many government agencies. The efficiency and effectiveness of these processes will have an important effect on how legislated policies actually perform. Thus, the analyst can apply workflow-processing techniques to inventory the number of required steps and the clearances and time required for each. Elimination of unnecessary licensing and permit-granting steps can streamline government and increase the productivity of private investments in a particular jurisdiction.

The analyst should also examine how well financial management functions are performed and how they relate to each other. Are budgeting and accounting performed separately? Is procurement or payroll linked to budgeting and cash management? If not, how does this affect the results of particular public policies? Analysts can examine obvious spending categories that are unlinked to budget codes and accounting systems. For example, purchasing commitments or obligations (i.e., purchase orders) are often not recorded; this then affects the ability of the finance department to manage cash effectively. Cash shortfalls will profoundly affect policy implementation in many cases. Thus, the agency's capacity to perform each function and the enforcement of procedures to ensure that information flows between functions in an integrated system are critical for detecting potential issues in policy implementation.

In chapter 3 we used the case of Washington, DC, school reform as an example of how empirically demonstrated textbook reforms can face deep-seated and powerful institutional constraints. In order for a reform administration to design and implement new policies, officials need to tackle the problems incrementally but forcefully. Beginning in 2007, the administration of Chancellor Michelle Rhee applied many of the techniques and tools suggested here to improve schools, teaching, and student performance. Some lessons can be drawn from that case:

- Focus on the legal and regulatory variable (see table 3.2) by mobilizing civil society organizations to prevent political and legal intrusion into the educational reform process. Failure to mobilize this support can be fatal to implementation later.

- At the structural level, ensure that productivity and performance reporting systems are in place to generate data for progress reviews, accountability, and communicating with the media and political classes. To the extent possible, strengthen value-for-money audit institutions that can monitor and act upon financial and programmatic problems.

- At the functional operations level, conduct a functional review of institutional systems to identify constraints to management efficiency and effectiveness. On the basis of this review and comparative information on educational reform performance elsewhere, recommend new policies—or substantiate claims that existing reform policies are working.

- At the financial management systems level, focus on components such as procurement, payroll, and accounting to determine if the financial management system is fragmented. If so, perform a transaction analysis of the most common public-sector processes, such as paying teachers and administrators, as well as equipment and service vendors. As noted, there are often islands of information that are unlinked, usually not because of carelessness or lack of technical capacity, but often precisely the opposite: Officials perceive opportunities to short-circuit reporting for personal gain. Payroll systems may not be linked to accounting and budgeting, permitting "ghost workers" to be hired and paid without appearing on the personnel rosters.

Forecasting Policy Options for a Cost-Effective Transit Line

Policy analysts also need to know how to forecast future trends of policy problems. Using available trend data, analysts will apply a combination of statistical and common sense techniques to develop reasonable forecasts for their clients. The purposes of forecasting are not always the same. The analyst may need to project the impact of several "high"-policy options in the energy sector. Or the assignment may be to forecast the effects of new spending programs on an existing base, assuming no changes in policies. Finally, the analyst may have to forecast the exogenous effects of new policies on stakeholders, such as country political risks for new investors.

In chapter 4 we reviewed several approaches to forecasting and indicated the problems with each method. Judgmental forecasting examines hard data trends and uses judgments to assess future patterns. Problems here include the identification of turning points at which trends shift directions and the possibility of within-year data variations. Time-series or trend extrapolation is a common technique based on the assumption that past observed patterns will continue into the future. Analysts often have to assume that this will be the case, at least for the short term. The proportionate-change method of analyzing time-series data is frequently used to project tax receipts and ridership. In the second edition of this book, we determined through analysis of MARTA forecasts of sales tax receipts that in some cases, the less elegant method may be the most accurate. Analysis of WMATA ridership through trend techniques produced a plausible estimate that was ultimately vitiated by the economic recession of 2007–09. Causal or regression analysis is the most sophisticated method and can employ single- or multi-equation techniques. Regressions and correlations alone cannot prove causation. Hence the analyst must revert to judgment to fashion a comprehensive framework of problem causation. Only with a clear picture of causation can forecasts be accurate over time. One can get lucky for a year or two, perhaps with countervailing errors canceling each other out. But over time, the analyst must understand the causation of each variable that affects the problem at hand. Beyond regression techniques, we also described simulation-assisted estimation techniques such as the logit model. This is a newer technique used in transit-demand forecasting where survey data and structured methodology and performance criteria are known in advance. Such is normally the case in capital assistance proposals for public transit.

As indicated in chapter 4, in the case of the Purple Line, policymakers needed to demonstrate a preferred option that would minimize cost and maximize ridership. The benefit was commuter time saved that would translate into more trips by that mode. The Maryland MTA analyzed eight options and substantiated the preferred option of the medium-cost light-rail system. This option will be forwarded to the Federal Transit Administration and now faces national competition for funding against other urban system proposals based on the same data systems, "New Starts" criteria for cost effectiveness, and a scoring system that makes it clear whether or not the proposed system is likely to receive funds.

The Role of Pricing

In chapter 5 we combined the issues of problem definition, institutional performance, and quantitative techniques, which were discussed in the earlier chapters, to analyze the use of pricing as a tool to achieve public policy objectives. Changing prices through taxation, subsidization, and regulation is a key element of many public policies. Both consumers and producers respond to changes in the prices of goods and services purchased or the inputs or factors of production sold. Influencing prices though public policy is, therefore, an effective means of changing behavior. We illustrated the role of prices in several different policy contexts and then examined the specific case of using cigarette taxes to reduce smoking, particularly among teenagers. The efficacy of this tool has been noted by both the tobacco industry and antismoking advocates.

Since economics is the primary discipline that focuses on the role of pricing, this chapter drew more heavily on basic economic analysis than did the previous chapters. We reviewed the elements of demand, supply, and price determination. We then discussed the important concept of price elasticity, which is used to measure consumer responsiveness to changes in prices. This was followed by a description of the statistical tools, many of which had already been presented in chapter 4, that are used to provide empirical estimates of different elasticities. Although many readers of this book may not ever undertake such empirical studies, the readers need to be able to interpret the results of such studies and assess their strengths and limitations. In the case of cigarette taxes, as with most policy issues, the key task is to separate the influence of one variable, price, from that of all other variables that affect cigarette consumption. Multiple-regression analysis is the major empirical tool used to perform this task. The empirical studies using these techniques also illustrated other changes in behavior that might arise from higher cigarette taxes, including switching to brands with higher tar and nicotine content, inhaling more deeply, and switching to smokeless tobacco. High cigarette taxes may also lead to smuggling and black market activity. All of these outcomes may partially offset the goals of the taxation policy.

We also noted in chapter 5 that public policy analysis often draws on different disciplines and methodologies. To analyze the role of taxes and pricing on cigarette consumption, analysts rely heavily on the economic theory of consumer behavior and the statistical technique of multiple-regression analysis to estimate cigarette demand functions. Since pricing policies will likely be combined with other approaches to prevent smoking, analysts must also draw on studies from psychology, public health, and other behavioral sciences that attempt to directly measure the impact of these interventions. The evaluation of these programs often raises questions regarding their impacts on the population and the costs of achieving these outcomes. These are issues in the economic evaluation of public policies, topics in chapters 6 and 7 of this casebook.

Cost-Effectiveness Analysis

In chapter 6 we illustrated an important technique for the economic evaluation of public policies: cost-effectiveness analysis. This is one of several tools, including cost-utility analysis and cost-benefit analysis, that are used to compare the outcomes or impacts of public programs and regulations with the costs of achieving these outcomes. We illustrated the use of cost-effectiveness analysis primarily in the health care sector, given recent developments in the use of economic evaluation techniques in this area and the rapid increase in the number of health care cost-effectiveness studies. The specific case for this chapter was the analysis of a strategy proposed in fall 2009 to routinely test virtually every adult in a community for human immunodeficiency virus (HIV) infection and to immediately begin treating the infected with antiretroviral therapy.

We first outlined the major steps that must be undertaken in any cost-effectiveness analysis:

1. Frame the problem and identify the options to be analyzed.

2. Identify the appropriate outcome measures.

3. Measure intervention and outcome costs.

4. Use the most appropriate model to analyze the alternatives under consideration.

5. Identify the probabilities and other data needed to construct the analytic model.

6. Specify the discount rate for any future costs or outcomes in the model.

7. Identify the sources of uncertainty and plan sensitivity analyses.

8. Define the feasibility of analyzing any distributional effects of alternative strategies.

We noted how steps 1, 2, and 4 relate directly back to the problem-structuring issues that were discussed in chapter 2 of this book. We also described how the timing of program benefits and costs is an important issue in both cost-effectiveness and cost-benefit analysis. The budgetary and implementation aspects of multiyear costs and revenues were discussed previously in chapter 3. There are both similarities and differences between viewing costs from the perspective of accounting and control and viewing costs from the perspective of economic evaluation.

We also discussed the role of cost-utility analysis in chapter 5. This is an economic evaluation technique that lies between cost-effectiveness and cost-benefit analysis. Cost-utility analysis attempts to weight program outcomes, although that weight is not measured in monetary terms, as it is in cost-benefit analysis. Thus, cost-effectiveness analysis would measure a program outcome as the number of life-years saved by a health care intervention, while cost-utility analysis would use the number of quality-adjusted life-years.

Cost-benefit analysis would try to place a monetary valuation on the number of lives or life-years saved by an intervention.

Cost-Benefit Analysis

In chapter 7 we focused on the key aspect of cost-benefit analysis that distinguishes it from other tools for economic evaluation of public policies. This distinguishing feature is that cost-benefit analysis attempts to value all outcomes of the policy in monetary terms and to estimate society's willingness to pay for those outcomes. The case for this chapter was the updated air quality standards for particulate matter (smog and soot) issued by the US Environmental Protection Agency in 2006 and partially remanded by the US Court of Appeals for the District of Columbia Circuit in 2009.

In this chapter we discussed the alternative approaches for deriving estimates of society's willingness to pay for program outcomes. We paid particular attention to the "value of life" questions, or what society is willing to pay to reduce the probability of death by a certain amount. We illustrated the strengths and weaknesses of different approaches to this issue. In analyzing the policy debate over the increased air quality standards, we saw that most of the arguments centered on different estimates of program costs and benefits. These estimates could be influenced by stakeholder positions in the debate, but also by scientific disagreement or uncertainty about program effects and how they should be valued.

Decision Making

We concluded that economic evaluation is an important dimension of public policy analysis because it forces decision makers to logically consider program outcomes and costs and the alternative uses of resources. However, none of the techniques discussed in chapters 5, 6, and 7 are a substitute for the decision-making process itself. There are always values and criteria, presented in the earlier chapters, that must be considered in that process and that cannot be adequately incorporated in any quantitative tool.

In this book we demonstrated that policy analysis is a sequence of logical steps in which messy data and conflicting information are used to structure alternatives to complex problems. We restricted our discussion to problem identification and definition methods in the diagnostic phase, and institutional capacity, pricing, and economic evaluation tools in the forecasting phase. It is our view that the analyst who masters many of the techniques used in these case applications will be capable of monitoring policy performance problems and resolving them during the actual implementation and evaluation phases.

REFERENCES

Axelrod, Donald. 1995. *Budgeting for Modern Government*. 2nd ed. New York: St. Martin's.

Dunn, William N. 2008. *Public Policy Analysis: An Introduction*. 4th ed. Englewood Cliffs, NJ: Pearson Prentice Hall.

Fisher, Ronald C. 2007. *State and Local Public Finance*. 3rd ed. Mason, OH: Thomson/South-Western.

Lehan, Edward. 1984. *Budgetmaking: A Workbook of Public Budgeting Theory and Practice*. New York: St. Martin's.

Michel, R. Gregory. 2001. *Decision Tools for Budgetary Analysis*. Chicago: Government Finance Officers Association.

Mikesell, John L. 2007. *Fiscal Administration: Analysis and Applications for the Public Sector*. Belmont, CA: Thomson/Wadsworth.

Posner, Paul, Trina Lewis, and Hannah Laufe. 1998. Budgeting for Capital. *Public Budgeting and Finance* 18 (13): 11–24.

Glossary

Accrual Accounting System: Captures the cost of programs in resources consumed and obligations to pay. To prevent overestimation of revenues, governments often use "modified accrual" systems that combine cash-based revenues with accrued expenditures.

Associated Cost Approach: An indirect method of estimating the benefits of a program or public policy that focuses on the costs associated with the outcomes of the program. For example, differences in travel costs could be used to value the benefits of a wilderness recreation area.

Audit: A systematic examination of resource use to determine the legality and accuracy of financial transactions and whether financial statements represent the actual financial position and operations of the government entity.

Budget Classification: Breakdown of a budget into mutually exclusive categories for such purposes as control (e.g., objects of expense like salaries and supplies); organizational responsibility (e.g., departments); sectoral planning and allocations (e.g., agriculture, education); activity measurement (e.g., workload in passenger miles of bus service); efficiency measurement (e.g., unit costs per passenger mile of bus service); and effectiveness (i.e., attainment of policy objectives, such as the percentage of the population with adequate health care coverage or access).

Budgetary Obligations: Commitments made by government through such recorded transactions as orders placed, contracts awarded, or services rendered.

Budget Outlays: Actual payments of budgetary obligations through checks issued or interest accrued on public debt.

Capital Budgeting: Planning and allocation for durable assets that provide longer-term benefits (e.g., health care and educational facilities, highways).

Cash-Accounting System: Captures flow of funds into and out of budgetary accounts based on actual receipts and outlays.

Cash Management System: System to prevent running out of cash during the fiscal year, failure to collect bills and deposit receipts, and failure to invest idle funds. Cash management systems rely on timely reporting by the accounting system of expenditures, revenues, and cash flow (e.g., daily cash reports, operating balances). Such data enable finance departments to manage cash effectively in order to fund programs and implement policies.

Ceteris Paribus: Latin phrase for "all else held constant"; used when defining the concepts of demand and supply in economic analysis.

Change in Demand: A shift in a demand curve that results from a change in one or more of the factors held constant when defining the demand curve (e.g., income, tastes, and preferences).

Change in Quantity Demanded: A movement along a demand curve for a good or service, resulting from a change in the price of that good or service.

Complementary Good: A good that is consumed together with another good. Complementary goods have a negative cross elasticity of demand.

Contingent Valuation Method: A method for evaluating benefits or willingness to pay that asks individuals to reveal their personal valuations of increases or decreases in unpriced goods through surveys or in experimental situations.

Cost-Accounting System: Based on the fact that budgets do not usually reflect the full costs of programs and policies, cost-accounting systems attempt to measure not just agency expenditures but actual resources consumed. Among the missing costs are allocated portions of agency overhead, fringe benefits, depreciation of equipment, allocation of personnel time to specific programs and activities, and operating costs of capital assets.

Cost-Benefit Analysis: An economic evaluation tool that places a monetary valuation on the outcomes of a program, representing society's benefits or willingness to pay for those outcomes. Benefits are then compared with the costs of the program.

Cost Centers: Categories for classifying an organization's costs for purposes of cost analysis. They are any unit or department in an organization for which a manager is assigned responsibility for costs. Often, an organization's departments serve as cost centers (e.g., a hospital department of radiology). Cost centers can also be functions, programs, or even objects of expense.

Cost-Effectiveness Analysis: An economic evaluation tool that compares the costs of a program with its primary benefits, measured in the most appropriate natural effects or physical units (e.g., the number of infections prevented or the number of life-years saved).

Cost-Savings Approach: An approach to estimating the benefits of a program that measures the costs saved as a result of the program. Often used in evaluating transportation, pollution control, and disease control programs.

Cost-to-Charge Ratio: A tool for making adjustments between the economic costs of providing health care services and the amount of money charged for those services.

Cost-Utility Analysis: An economic evaluation tool that compares a quality-adjusted measure of a program's outcome (such as a quality-adjusted life year) with the program's costs.

Counterfactual: What would have happened if a given event had not occurred; used as a comparison case in economic evaluation.

Cross Elasticity of Demand: A number that measures the percentage change in the quantity of one good relative to the percentage change in the price of another good; used to distinguish between substitute and complementary goods.

Demand: An economic concept defined as the relationship between the price of a good and the quantity demanded of that good, all else held constant (ceteris paribus).

Discount Rate: An interest rate chosen to calculate the present value of a flow of costs or benefits; used to make comparable a flow of expenditures at different points in time.

Discounted Future Earnings Approach: A method of estimating the benefits of a program that measures the increased stream of future earnings from individuals or land resulting from a public-sector investment project. The flow of earnings is discounted to account for the time pattern of the earnings.

Economic Evaluation: A set of techniques that focus on relating some measure of the output, outcomes, or consequences of a program to the costs of the inputs used to provide those outcomes.

Encumbrance/Obligation Accounting System: Captures cash flow together with government commitments in the form of salaries, other bills, and purchase orders. This form of accounting prevents overexpenditure and ensures coverage of future commitments.

Equilibrium Price: The price that exists in a competitive market that is determined by the forces of supply and demand.

Ex Parte Contacts: During the notice-and-comment period of administrative rulemaking, contacts between agency commissioners and interested participants are prohibited apart from the record. If contacts occur, they must be made part of the rulemaking record so that interested parties may comment on them. Failure to place such contacts on record (ex parte contacts) contaminates the process, and the rule may therefore be challenged as arbitrary and capricious.

Explicit Cost: A cost that is actually paid out to another party and that usually is recorded in an accounting or budgetary system.

Extensive Margin: Applying a screening procedure to a different group of people, such as extending recommendations for mammography screening from women over 50 years old to women between 40 and 50 or between 30 and 40 years old.

Fixed Cost: A cost that does not increase or decrease with corresponding changes in the amount of service provided (e.g., rent).

Forecast: A single projection chosen from a series of possible projections.

Implicit Cost: A cost that may have to be imputed for economic evaluation since it is not actually paid out to someone. The value of a volunteer's or a patient's time would be an implicit cost.

Income Elasticity of Demand: A measure of the percentage change in quantity demanded of a good relative to the percentage change in consumers' income; used to distinguish between normal and inferior goods. It is the sensitivity of demand to changes in income.

Inferior Good: A good for which the quantity demanded decreases as income increases. Inferior goods have a negative income elasticity of demand.

Informal Rulemaking: Development of administrative rules by a process akin to legislative lawmaking until the end of a formal notice-and-comment period.

Integrated Financial Management Systems (IFMS): A single database providing financial data from different points of view (e.g., budget reports, budget execution analysis, revenue collections, and cash management). The core IFMS typically consists of budgeting and accounting functions. The more advanced or noncore system includes purchasing, payroll, and capital budgeting.

Intensive Margin: Applying a screening procedure to a given group of individuals at different time intervals. For example, screening for cervical cancer could be done every five years, every three years, or even annually.

Internal Controls: Review of financial sufficiency and legal authority for expenditures, primarily by agency auditors and accountants. Reviews by agencies have broadened to include analysis of resource utilization (value-for-money or performance audits). Internal control systems also subdivide official duties so that no single employee handles a financial transaction from beginning to end.

Iron Triangles: Continuing coalitions of congressional representatives and staff members, executive officials, and interest groups that influence the shape and content of public policies (e.g., agriculture). Iron triangles are considered closed policymaking subsystems.

Issue Networks: Shared-knowledge groups with mutual interests in maximizing influence over particular aspects of public policies (e.g., health policy through US Public Health Service officials, insurance companies, and medical professional organizations). These are temporary groups that contribute to policymaking fragmentation in the United States.

Marginal Benefit: The valuation a consumer places on an additional unit of a good or service. The price of a good measures this marginal benefit.

Meta-Analysis: A systematic review of a body of literature on a given subject to determine what conclusions can be drawn from that literature; often used to evaluate different medical or health care interventions.

Normal Good: A good whose quantity demanded increases as income increases. Normal goods have a positive income elasticity of demand.

Notice-and-Comment Period: A formal period established for administrative rulemaking, during which notice of the proposed rule is published and formal written and oral comments on the proposed rule are invited (e.g., seatbelt rules by the National Highway Traffic Safety Administration).

Opportunity Cost: The cost of using society's resources in one activity in terms of the opportunities foregone or the activities not undertaken; includes both explicit and implicit costs.

Pareto Efficiency: A concept for evaluating alternative policies or states of the world. A state of the world is Pareto-efficient if it is not possible to make someone better off without making someone else worse off.

Performance Audit: A type of value-for-money audit that consists of three elements: (1) a program results review—whether the entity is doing the right thing, (2) an economy and efficiency review—whether the entity is doing things right, and (3) a compliance review—whether in doing the right thing in the right way, the entity observes rules imposed on it in the form of laws, regulations, and policies.

Performance Budget: A budget that bases expenditures primarily on measurable performance of activities and workloads.

Planning, Programming, and Budgeting System (PPBS): A budgeting system instituted in the federal government in the 1960s that attempted to identify and examine goals and objectives in each area of government activity, analyze program output in terms of its objectives, measure program costs over several years, and analyze alternatives to find the most effective means of reaching program objectives at the least cost.

Policies: Common rules, standards, or norms guiding or directing government activities that are promulgated by such rulemaking bodies as parliaments and administrative regulatory agencies.

Potential Compensation Policy: A rule that modifies the Pareto efficiency concept for evaluating alternative states of the world. A policy improves social welfare if the gainers from the policy could compensate the losers and still be better off or at least no worse off. This rule forms the basis for cost-benefit analysis.

Price Elasticity of Demand: A measure of the percentage change in the quantity demanded of a good relative to the percentage change in the price of that good.

Pricing: The use of prices to allocate and ration goods and services; often used as a tool of public policy.

Program: A group of related activities performed by one or more organizational units for the purpose of accomplishing measurable goals and objectives. The measurable goals and activities are often part of a function for which government is responsible.

Program Budget: A budget that allocates money to the functions or activities of a government rather than to specific objects of expenditure or departments.

Project: A set of microactivities that implement all or part of a program. For example, training and technical assistance projects implement financial management programs.

Projection: A range of forecasts based on extrapolation of data.

Quality-Adjusted Life Year (QALY): An outcome measurement in cost-utility analysis in which the number of life-years gained by an intervention has been adjusted for factors relating to the quality of those life-years.

Randomized Controlled Trials: A method for evaluating medical procedures in which subjects are randomly assigned to an experimental and a control group to test the efficacy of the procedure. These are usually "double-blind," so that neither the participants nor the evaluators know who is in which group.

Reprogramming of Funds: Shifting funds within appropriations accounts (e.g., supplies to maintenance). Reprogramming agreements between appropriations committees and an agency typically establish thresholds below which the agency can reprogram funds without congressional approval.

Step-Function Cost: A cost that is added in lumps as volume of service increases (e.g., staff salaries, additional faculty members added to cover increased student enrollments).

Substitute Good: A good that can be used instead of another. Substitute goods have a positive cross elasticity of demand.

Supplemental Appropriations: Additional budget authority provided during the fiscal year by Congress to cover urgent needs for programs and activities.

Supply: An economic concept defined as the relation between the price of a good and the quantity producers are willing to supply at that price, all else held constant (ceteris paribus).

Transfer of Funds: Shifting funds between appropriations accounts requiring congressional approval. In the classic example, President Nixon transferred foreign assistance account funds to the US Department of Defense to bomb Cambodia.

Variable Cost: A cost that increases or decreases with increases or decreases in the amount of service provided (e.g., supplies).

Willingness to Pay: The amount of money society will pay for a good or service; used as a measure of the benefits of a program in a cost-benefit analysis.

Zero-Based Budgeting: An alternative budgeting system that encourages analysis of the incremental inputs and outputs at marginally different levels of expenditure. This was first used in the public sector by the State of Georgia in the early 1970s and later applied to the federal government in 1977.

Index

About the Authors

✳ ✳ ✳

George M. Guess is currently a senior fellow at the Center for Public Finance Research and a scholar in residence in public administration and policy at American University, Washington, DC. From 2004 to 2007 he was director of research at the Open Society Institute's Local Government and Public Services Reform Initiative in Budapest, where he was acting director of the Master of Public Policy Program at Central European University. From 1993 to 2004, Dr. Guess was a senior public administration specialist at Development Alternatives, Inc. (DAI). He has worked for more than twenty years providing technical assistance and training to strengthen and reform central and local government fiscal management and policymaking systems. Dr. Guess served for two years in the fiscal affairs department of the International Monetary Fund (IMF), providing assistance on budget execution and control in the former Soviet Union and Eastern Europe. In addition to providing overseas technical assistance and training, he was a professor of public administration at Georgia State University in Atlanta. He was an OAS Fellow to Costa Rica and a Fulbright Scholar twice—once to Uruguay and later, in the Central American Research Program, to Honduras, Belize, and Costa Rica. He has published in such journals as *Policy Sciences*, *Public Budgeting and Finance*, and *Public Administration Review*. He is coauthor with Lance T. Le Loup of *Comparative Public Budgeting: Global Perspectives on Taxing and Spending* (Albany: State University of New York Press, 2010) and editor of *Managing and Financing Urban Public Transport Systems: An International Perspective* (Budapest: Local Government and Public Service Reform Initiative of the Open Society Institute, 2008). Guess received his BA from the University of California, Berkeley; his MPA from the University of Southern California; and his PhD in political science from the University of California, Riverside.

Paul G. Farnham is associate professor emeritus of economics at Georgia State University, Atlanta. His areas of specialization are health care economics, the economics of HIV/AIDS, public sector economics, and public policy. He has been a visiting health economist at the Centers for Disease Control and Prevention, where he analyzed the economic costs of HIV/AIDS to business and worked on the economic analysis of HIV prevention programs. His research has been published in journals such as *Public Health Reports*, the *American Journal of Preventive Medicine*, and *Inquiry*. His earlier research on local government debt and expenditure decisions has been published in the *Southern Economic Journal*, *Public Choice*, *Public Finance Quarterly*, *Urban Affairs Quarterly*, and *Social Science Quarterly*, among other journals. He has also published the first and second editions of *Economics for Managers* (Prentice Hall, 2005, 2010). Farnham received his BA in economics from Union College, Schenectady, New York, and his MA and PhD in economics from the University of California, Berkeley.